W. H. AUDEN IN CONTEXT

W. H. Auden is a giant of twentieth-century English poetry whose writings demonstrate a sustained engagement with the times in which he lived. But how did the century's shifting cultural terrain affect him and his work? Written by distinguished poets and scholars, these brief but authoritative essays offer a varied set of coordinates by which to chart Auden's continuously evolving career, examining key aspects of his environmental, cultural, political, and creative contexts. Reaching beyond mere biography, these essays present Auden as the product of ongoing negotiations between himself, his time, and posterity, exploring the enduring power of his poetry to unsettle and provoke. The collection will prove valuable for scholars, researchers, and students of English literature, cultural studies, and creative writing.

TONY SHARPE is Senior Lecturer in English and Creative Writing at Lancaster University. He is the author of critically acclaimed books on W. H. Auden, T. S. Eliot, Vladimir Nabokov, and Wallace Stevens. His essays on modernist writing and poetry have appeared in journals such as *Critical Survey* and *Literature and Theology*, as well as in various edited collections.

W. H. AUDEN IN CONTEXT

EDITED BY

TONY SHARPE

Lancaster University

CAMBRIDGE UNIVERSITY PRESS
Cambridge, New York, Melbourne, Madrid, Cape Town,
Singapore, São Paulo, Delhi, Mexico City

Cambridge University Press
32 Avenue of the Americas, New York, NY 10013-2473, USA

www.cambridge.org
Information on this title: www.cambridge.org/9780521196574

First published 2013

Printed in the United States of America

A catalog record for this publication is available from the British Library.

Library of Congress Cataloging in Publication data
W. H. Auden in context / [edited by] Tony Sharpe,
Lancaster University, England
pages   cm
Includes bibliographical references and index.
ISBN 978-0-521-19657-4 (hardback)
1. Auden, W. H. (Wystan Hugh), 1907–1973 – Criticism and interpretation.
I. Sharpe, Tony, 1952– editor of compilation.
PR6001.U4Z8914   2012
811'.52–dc23   2012021040

ISBN 978-0-521-19657-4 Hardback

In Memory of My Father
L. W. Sharpe (1920–2010)

Contents

List of Contributors   *page* xi
Acknowledgements   xvii
A Note on Editions and Abbreviations   xix

Introduction   1
Tony Sharpe

PART I   CONTEXTS OF PLACE

1. Auden's Northerliness   13
    Tony Sharpe

2. Two Cities: Berlin and New York   24
    Patrick Deer

3. Ideas about England   35
    Stan Smith

4. Ideas of America   47
    Aidan Wasley

5. At Home in Italy and Austria, 1948–1973   56
    Justin Quinn

PART II   SOCIAL AND CULTURAL CONTEXTS

6. Auden and the Class System   69
    Adrian Caesar

7. The Church of England: Auden's Anglicanism   79
    Tony Sharpe

8. British Homosexuality, 1920–1939   89
    Gregory Woods

9. American Homosexuality, 1939–1972 99
Richard R. Bozorth

10. Auden among Women 107
Janet Montefiore

11. Auden and the American Literary World 118
Aidan Wasley

12. Atlantic Auden 128
Michael Wood

PART III   POLITICAL, HISTORICAL, AND
THEORETICAL CONTEXTS

13. Communism and Fascism in 1920s and 1930s Britain 141
Matthew Worley

14. Auden and Wars 150
Patrick Deer

15. Auden and Freud: The Psychoanalytic Text 160
John R. Boly

16. Auden's Theology 170
Alan Jacobs

17. Auden in History 181
Susannah Young-ah Gottlieb

PART IV   (I)   CREATIVE CONTEXTS

18. The Body 195
Edward Mendelson

19. The Cinema 205
Keith Williams

20. 1930s British Drama 217
Steve Nicholson

21. The Documentary Moment 228
David Collard

22. Travel Writing 237
Tim Youngs

23. Auden and Post-war Opera   246
    Michael Symmons Roberts

PART IV (II) PRECURSORS AND CONTEMPORARIES

24. Earlier English Influences   257
    Chris Jones

25. Auden and Shakespeare   266
    Stephen Regan

26. Yeats   276
    Michael O'Neill

27. Eliot   286
    Hugh Haughton

28. Some Modernists in Early Auden   297
    Gareth Reeves

29. Auden in German   306
    Rainer Emig

30. Auden and Isherwood   316
    James J. Berg and Chris Freeman

PART V THE 'MOST PROFESSIONAL' POET

31. Auden in Prose   329
    Sean O'Brien

32. Auden and Little Magazines   337
    Andrew Thacker

33. Double Take: Auden in Collaboration   347
    Richard Badenhausen

34. Auden and Prosody   359
    Sean O'Brien

35. Auden's Forms   369
    Seamus Perry

Guide to Further Reading   381
Index   391

Contributors

RICHARD BADENHAUSEN is Professor and Kim T. Adamson Chair at Westminster College in Salt Lake City, where he also directs the Honours program. He teaches classes in the humanities, war literature, theories of place, and trauma studies and is the author of *T. S. Eliot and the Art of Collaboration* (Cambridge University Press, 2005).

JAMES J. BERG is Dean of Arts and Sciences at the College of the Desert in California. He is co-editor, with Chris Freeman, of three books: the Lambda Literary Award–winning collection *The Isherwood Century* (University of Wisconsin Press, 2000), *Conversations with Christopher Isherwood* (University Press of Mississippi, 2001), and *Love, West Hollywood* (Alyson Books, 2008). He also edited and introduced *Isherwood on Writing* (University of Minnesota Press, 2007).

JOHN R. BOLY teaches modern literature and theory at Marquette University. He is the author of *Reading Auden: The Returns of Caliban* (Cornell University Press, 1991).

RICHARD R. BOZORTH is Associate Professor of English at Southern Methodist University. He has written on modernism and LGBT literature, and is author of *Auden's Games of Knowledge: Poetry and the Meanings of Homosexuality* (Columbia University Press, 2001).

ADRIAN CAESAR was formerly Associate Professor of English at UNSW@ADFA, and is currently an Honorary Visiting Fellow at the Australian National University in Canberra. He is the author of three literary-critical studies, a prize-winning non-fiction novel, and four books of poetry. His latest book of poems is *High Wire* (Pandanus Press, ANU, 2006).

DAVID COLLARD is an independent scholar based in London. He is currently researching *Auden on Film,* a study of all the poet's writings for and about the cinema.

PATRICK DEER is Associate Professor of English at New York University, where he focuses on war literature and culture, modernism, and contemporary British literature. He is the author of *Culture in Camouflage: War, Empire and Modern British Literature* (Oxford University Press, 2009) and was Guest Editor of *The Ends of War*, a special issue of *Social Text* 91 (Summer 2007). He is currently writing *Deep England: Forging British Culture After Empire*.

RAINER EMIG is Chair of English Literature and Culture at Leibniz University in Hanover, Germany. His publications include *Modernism in Poetry* (Pearson, 1995), *W. H. Auden* (Macmillan, 1999), and essays on Auden in *Translation and Nation* (Multilingual Matters, 2001), *The Cambridge Companion to W. H. Auden* (2004), and *The Oxford Book of British and Irish War Poetry* (2006).

CHRIS FREEMAN is co-editor, with James J. Berg, of *The Isherwood Century* (University of Wisconsin Press, 2000); *Conversations with Christopher Isherwood* (University Press of Mississippi, 2001), and *Love, West Hollywood* (Alyson Books, 2008). He teaches English and Gender Studies at the University of Southern California.

SUSANNAH YOUNG-AH GOTTLIEB is Associate Professor of English and Comparative Literary Studies at Northwestern University, where she is associate chair of the English Department and director of the Poetry and Poetics Colloquium and Workshop. She is the author of *Regions of Sorrow: Anxiety and Messianism in Hannah Arendt and W. H. Auden* (Stanford University Press, 2003) and the editor of *Hannah Arendt: Reflections on Literature and Culture* (Stanford University Press, 2007). Her current book project is entitled *The Importance of Metaphysics: The Intellectual Heresies of W. H. Auden*.

HUGH HAUGHTON is Professor of English and Related Literature at the University of York. He is the editor (with Valerie Eliot) of *The Letters of T. S. Eliot*, volumes 1 and 2 (Faber, 2009). Other recent publications include *The Poetry of Derek Mahon* (Oxford University Press, 2007), an edition of Sigmund Freud, *The Uncanny* (Penguin, 2003), and *Second World War Poems* (Faber, 2004).

ALAN JACOBS is the Clyde S. Kilby Professor of English at Wheaton College in Illinois. He has published a critical edition of Auden's *The Age of Anxiety* (Princeton University Press, 2011) and is currently working on an edition of *For the Time Being*. His most recent book is *The Pleasures of Reading in an Age of Distraction* (Oxford University Press, 2011).

CHRIS JONES is the author of *Strange Likeness: The Use of Old English in Twentieth-Century Poetry* (Oxford University Press, 2006). He teaches English at the University of St Andrews.

EDWARD MENDELSON teaches English and Comparative Literature at Columbia University and is the literary executor of the Estate of W. H. Auden.

JANET MONTEFIORE is Professor of Twentieth Century English Literature at the University of Kent, where she has taught since 1978. Her books include *Feminism and Poetry* (Pandora, 1987, 1993, 2004), *Men and Women Writers of the 1930s* (Routledge, 1996), and *Rudyard Kipling* (British Council/Northcote House, 2007).

STEVE NICHOLSON is Professor of Twentieth Century Theatre and Performance and Director of Theatre in the School of English at the University of Sheffield. He has written extensively about aspects of theatre and politics in the inter-war period and also about contemporary playwrights. He is currently completing the fourth and final volume of a study of theatre censorship in Britain between 1900 and 1968, as well as a book about British theatre in the 1960s for Methuen's new *Modern British Playwriting* series.

SEAN O'BRIEN's latest book of poems, *November* (Picador, 2011), is a Poetry Book Society Choice; his previous collection, *The Drowned Book* (Picador, 2007), won the T. S. Eliot and Forward Prizes. His *Collected Poems* appeared in 2012. He is Professor of Creative Writing at Newcastle University.

MICHAEL O'NEILL is Professor of English at Durham University. His recent books include, as editor, *The Cambridge History of English Poetry* (2010) and a study of Romantic poetry's influence on poets since 1900 (including Auden), *The All-Sustaining Air* (Oxford University Press, 2007; paperback 2012). He is the co-author, with Michael D. Hurley, of *The Cambridge Introduction to Poetic Form* (2012) and the author of two collections of poetry, *The Stripped Bed* (Collins Harvill, 1990) and *Wheel* (Arc, 2008).

SEAMUS PERRY is a Fellow of Balliol College, where he is Tutor in English Literature, and a lecturer in the Faculty of English at the

University of Oxford. He has published on a range of nineteenth- and twentieth-century writers, and his 2008 Chatterton lecture to the British Academy was on Auden.

JUSTIN QUINN is Associate Professor at the University of Western Bohemia and Charles University, Prague. He has published two studies of twentieth-century American poetry and, most recently, *The Cambridge Introduction to Modern Irish Poetry, 1800–2000.* His fifth collection of poetry is *Close Quarters* (Gallery Press, 2011).

GARETH REEVES is part-time Reader in English at Durham University. He is the author of *T. S. Eliot: A Virgilian Poet* (Macmillan, 1989) and *T. S. Eliot's 'The Waste Land'* (Harvester, 1994) and, with Michael O'Neill, of *The Thirties Poetry: Auden, MacNeice, Spender* (Macmillan, 1992). As well as many essays on twentieth-century English, American, and Irish poetry, he has also published two volumes of poetry, *Real Stories* (Carcanet, 1984) and *Listening In* (Carcanet, 1993). *To Hell with Paradise: New and Selected Poems* was published by Carcanet in 2012.

STEPHEN REGAN is Professor of English at Durham University. His publications include books and essays on Philip Larkin and other modern poets, including W. B. Yeats, Robert Frost, Louis MacNeice, and Seamus Heaney. He is the editor of *Irish Writing: An Anthology of Irish Literature in English 1798–1939,* and he is currently preparing a new edition of George Moore's *Esther Waters,* both titles in the *Oxford World's Classics* series.

MICHAEL SYMMONS ROBERTS'S poetry has won the Whitbread Poetry Award (for *Corpus*) and been shortlisted for the Eliot Prize, the Forward Prize, and the Griffin International Prize. As a librettist, working primarily with composer James MacMillan, his work has been performed around the world; *The Sacrifice* received the Royal Philharmonic Society Award for Opera. He is Professor of Poetry at Manchester Metropolitan University.

TONY SHARPE was for several years Head of the Department of English and Creative Writing at Lancaster University, where he still teaches. He is the author of books on T. S. Eliot (Macmillan, 1991), Vladimir Nabokov (Edward Arnold, 1991), Wallace Stevens (Palgrave, 2000), and W. H. Auden (Routledge, 2007), as well as of various essays and chapters reflecting his interest in modern poetry generally and Auden's work in particular.

STAN SMITH, Professor Emeritus in English at Nottingham Trent University, has published widely on modern and contemporary literature. He has edited *The Cambridge Companion to W. H. Auden* (2004) and published two critical studies of the poet (Blackwell, 1985; British Council/Northcote House, 1997). Recent books include *Poetry and Displacement* (Liverpool University Press, 2007), *Patrick Kavanagh* (ed., Irish Academic Press, 2009), and, with Jennifer Birkett (eds), *Right/Left/Right: Revolving Commitments, France and Britain 1929–1950* (Cambridge Scholars, 2008). A sonnet sequence, *Family Fortunes* (Shoestring Press), appeared in 2008.

ANDREW THACKER is Professor of Twentieth Century Literature at De Montfort University, where he is also Director of the Centre for Textual Studies. He is the author or editor of several books on modernism including *The Imagist Poets* (2011) and *The Oxford Critical and Cultural History of Modernist Magazines, vol.1: Britain and Ireland* (2009). He is an editor of the journal *Literature & History* and is currently Chair of the British Association for Modernist Studies.

AIDAN WASLEY teaches British and American poetry at the University of Georgia and is the author of *The Age of Auden: Postwar Poetry and the American Scene* (Princeton University Press, 2011).

KEITH WILLIAMS is Senior Lecturer in the English and Film programme at the University of Dundee and chairs the Scottish Word and Image Group. He is the author of several books and articles on literature and inter-mediality in the early twentieth century, including *British Writers and the Media, 1930–45* (Palgrave Macmillan, 1996). His most recent monograph is *H. G. Wells, Modernity and the Movies* (Liverpool University Press, 2007), and he is currently completing a study of *James Joyce and Cinematicity: Before and After Film*.

MICHAEL WOOD teaches at Princeton University, where he is Charles Barnwell Straut Professor of English and Comparative Literature. His most recent book is *Yeats and Violence* (Oxford University Press, 2010).

GREGORY WOODS is Professor of Gay and Lesbian Studies at Nottingham Trent University. His main critical books are *Articulate Flesh: Male Homo-eroticism and Modern Poetry* (1987) and *A History of Gay Literature: The Male Tradition* (1998), both from Yale University Press. His poetry collections are *We Have the Melon* (1992), *May I Say*

Nothing (1998), *The District Commissioner's Dreams* (2002), *Quidnunc* (2007), and *An Ordinary Dog* (2011), all from Carcanet Press.

MATTHEW WORLEY is Reader in History at the University of Reading. He is the author of several books on British political history, including *Oswald Mosley and the New Party* (Palgrave, 2010).

TIM YOUNGS is Professor of English and Travel Studies at Nottingham Trent University. His books include *Travellers in Africa* (Manchester University Press, 1994), *The Cambridge Companion to Travel Writing* (ed. with Peter Hulme, 2002), and a forthcoming multi-volume anthology of travel writing criticism, edited with Charles Forsdick. He continues to edit *Studies in Travel Writing*, the journal he founded in 1997.

Acknowledgements

I am grateful, first of all, to contributors who believed in this project and whose work is represented here; some offered helpful behind-the-scenes advice, as did some Auden scholars who couldn't personally participate. Lancaster University assisted with a period of leave. Ray Ryan at Cambridge University Press suggested the volume and has had to draw on reserves of patience he may not have realized he possessed in awaiting its completion; my wife, Jane, has philosophically endured the travails of one whose partner has been long immersed in typescript. The dedication gratefully remembers another who merited Auden's tribute to his own, 'No gentler father ever lived'.

A Note on Editions and Abbreviations

Auden's revisions and expurgations of his own work have practical consequences for a book like this, as do other aspects of his complicated
publication history. Although when completed the *Collected Works* will
solve most problems of reference, having already covered dramatic and
operatic work and the majority of his prose, the poetry still poses problems, with different editions sometimes offering different versions of the
'same' poem. Nor can the problems be simply solved by citing individual volumes of poetry as first published, because of variations between
English and American versions: occasionally different pagination and in
two cases different titles for the same volume (*Look, Stranger!* and *On
This Island*; *The Double Man* and *New Year Letter*). These differences persisted into the collected volumes Auden oversaw in his lifetime, when the
Random House and Faber versions were similar but not identical. Under
Edward Mendelson's editorship, the *Collected Poems* issued in 1976 was
revised and reset in 1991 and, further revised, was reissued to coincide
with Auden's centenary in 2007. In addition to the poems, this handsome
volume contains a good deal of important material, including Auden's
earlier forewords to collected volumes and a description of the different
titles he used for poems at different periods. While valuable as a record
of Auden's judgment on what he wanted his canon to include, it is the
end product of processes of authorial revision not universally applauded;
poems included he sometimes radically altered (usually by shortening),
and poems excluded are some that readers deem indispensable: notably,
'September 1, 1939'. If it is truthful as a historical reflection of Auden's
literary taste applied to his own poetry late in his life, in another way it
falsifies the historical record by occluding the sequence and nature of his
poetic output and its interactions with current events: the omission of
'Spain' and its modified successor 'Spain, 1937' suppresses an important
aspect of his literary career. Although Auden's savagest editorialism pre-
dominantly affected the poetry written before or soon after his move to

America, what many consider to be his finest post-war poem, 'In Praise of Limestone', has some significant differences in its *Collected Poems* version from what had appeared in *Nones*.

The debate whether Auden's alterations improved or damaged his poems can be noted here, but not resolved. My own preference is for the earlier versions, but the highest priority of a volume such as this must be to assist its readers, not all of whom will have easy access to a research-standard university library with complete first editions of his work. For pre-1940 poetry, references are given to *The English Auden*, which contains reliable versions of the earliest book publication of that period's poems – excepting 'Spain', which was printed as a pamphlet and never collected: 'Spain' is most easily available in Mendelson's editions of the *Selected Poems*. For subsequent poetry I have not wished to impose an editorial preference on contributors who might disagree with it; whether they have chosen to use the *Collected Poems* (*CP*) or cite individual volumes I have left to them; but to help readers find quotations where individual volumes have been cited I have added page references to *Collected Poems* (2007). The warning must be given, however, that the *CP* version may not be identical: in instances where two such references are given, the first is always definitive of source. A less urgent duality occurs in relation to the prose, where Auden's own books of criticism, *The Enchafèd Flood* and *The Dyer's Hand*, have now appeared in the collected edition; here I have not followed a parallel procedure of doubled reference, as this seems unnecessary.

ABBREVIATIONS

AN	*The W. H. Auden Society Newsletter* (earlier issues available in archive, accessible via the W. H. Auden Society Web site; current issues available by subscription)
Ansen	Alan Ansen, *The Table Talk of W. H. Auden*, ed. Nicholas Jenkins (London: Faber and Faber, 1991)
AS I, AS II, AS III	*Auden Studies*, vols. I, II, III, ed. Katherine Bucknell and Nicholas Jenkins (Oxford: Clarendon Press, 1990, 1994, 1996)
AT	W. H. Auden, *Another Time* (London: Faber and Faber, 1940)
AtH	W. H. Auden, *About the House* (London: Faber and Faber, 1966)

Carpenter	Humphrey Carpenter, *W. H. Auden: A Biography* (London: Faber and Faber, 1981)
CCWHA	*The Cambridge Companion to W. H. Auden,* ed. Stan Smith (Cambridge University Press, 2004)
CP 2007	W. H. Auden, *Collected Poems*, ed. Edward Mendelson (London: Faber and Faber; New York: Random House, 2007). *This is a further revision of the reset 1991 edition that itself revised the 1976 edition.*
Cunningham 1988	Valentine Cunningham, *British Writers of the Thirties* (Oxford University Press, 1988)
CW	W. H. Auden, *A Certain World: A Commonplace Book* (London: Faber and Faber, 1970)
DH	W. H. Auden, *The Dyer's Hand and Other Essays* (London: Faber and Faber, 1963). *First published USA, 1962.*
DM	W. H. Auden, *The Double Man* (New York: Random House, 1941)
EA	*The English Auden: Poems, Essays and Dramatic Writings 1927–1939*, ed. Edward Mendelson (London: Faber and Faber, 1977)
Early Auden	Edward Mendelson, *Early Auden* (London: Faber and Faber, 1981)
F&A	W. H. Auden, *Forewords and Afterwords*, selected by Edward Mendelson (London: Faber and Faber, 1973)
Fuller 1998	John Fuller, *W. H. Auden: A Commentary* (London: Faber and Faber, 1998)
Haffenden	John Haffenden, ed., *W. H. Auden: The Critical Heritage* (London: Routledge and Kegan Paul, 1983)
HtC	W. H. Auden, *Homage to Clio* (London: Faber and Faber, 1960)
JtW	W. H. Auden and Christopher Isherwood, *Journey to a War* (London: Faber and Faber, 1939)
Juv	Katherine Bucknell, ed., *W. H. Auden Juvenilia: Poems 1922–1928*, 'expanded paperback edition' (Princeton University Press, 2003)

LA	Edward Mendelson, *Later Auden* (London: Faber and Faber, 1999)
LfI	W. H. Auden and Louis MacNeice, *Letters from Iceland* (London: Faber and Faber, 1937)
Lib	W. H. Auden and Chester Kallman, *Libretti and Other Dramatic Writings 1939–1973* (London: Faber and Faber; Princeton University Press, 1993)
MCP	J. A. Pike, *Modern Canterbury Pilgrims* (Oxford: A. R. Mowbray & Co., 1956)
N	W. H. Auden, *Nones* (London: Faber and Faber, 1952)
NYL	W. H. Auden, *New Year Letter* (London: Faber and Faber, 1941)
Plays	W. H. Auden and Christopher Isherwood, *Plays and Other Dramatic Writings 1928–1938*, ed. Edward Mendelson (London: Faber and Faber; Princeton University Press, 1989)
Prose I	W. H. Auden, *Prose and Travel Books in Prose and Verse, Vol. I: 1926–1938*, ed. Edward Mendelson (London: Faber and Faber; Princeton University Press, 1996)
Prose II	W. H. Auden, *Prose, Vol. II: 1939–1948*, ed. Edward Mendelson (London: Faber and Faber; Princeton University Press, 2002)
Prose III	W. H. Auden, *Prose, Vol. III: 1948–1955*, ed. Edward Mendelson (London: Faber and Faber; Princeton University Press, 2008)
RD-H 1995	Richard Davenport-Hines, *Auden* (London: Heinemann, 1995)
SP 1979	W. H. Auden, *Selected Poems*, ed. Edward Mendelson (London: Faber and Faber, 1979)
SP 2007	W. H. Auden, *Selected Poems,* ed. Edward Mendelson (London: Faber and Faber, 2007) 'expanded edition'
SW	W. H. Auden, *Secondary Worlds* (London: Faber and Faber, 1968)
Tribute	Stephen Spender, ed., *W. H. Auden: A Tribute* (London: Weidenfeld and Nicolson, 1975)

Introduction

Tony Sharpe

Conventionally, introducing a collection of essays such as this involves mentioning each contributor, in order to persuade prospective readers that the volume amounts to a coherently-argued whole. Where essayists are numerous and space limited, this is at best a rather perfunctory courtesy, and at worst risks turning the editor into a kind of major domo at some grand event, announcing the names of new arrivals as they hand across their 'invite with gilded edges'. In the present case, it would also be misleading, because a book offering current perceptions of Auden's work should quite properly reflect a range of views, that range itself reflective of the variety of responses which one who was not uncontroversial during his own lifetime continues to elicit. Any imposed coherence would additionally mislead, by misrepresenting the nature of Auden's career and ignoring the warning given by Barbara Everett, for whom he is 'the genius of the makeshift, the virtuoso of contingency': 'to perfect his achievement is to endanger his essential character'.[1] Auden, after all, was not always in agreement with himself, seen in his sometimes substantial later modifications of published poems and on occasions in their brusque ejection from his canon – 'thrown out', he genially if tersely explained, 'because they were dishonest, or bad-mannered, or boring' (*CP* 2007, p. xxix). That invite with gilded edges could, then, be summarily withdrawn from unsatisfactory poems, whose abrupt relegation to the category of uninvited guest formed part of the quarrel with himself out of which Auden's poetry characteristically emerged (rather more visibly than with Yeats, who coined the phrase).

Poetry, if the most important element of Auden's *oeuvre*, is nevertheless just one aspect of a career that also saw the production of a very substantial quantity of critical prose, a number of co-authored plays, travel books and libretti, participation in the making of documentary films and the compilation of various literary anthologies. Later, it included the functions of a public intellectual, called on to adjudicate literary prizes and asked to deliver lectures and graduation addresses – this last a reminder of Auden's practical as well as theoretical involvement in education, at both school and university levels.

Responding to this multiplicity, the essays which follow offer various perspectives in which Auden's career may be perceived and his work considered. He himself was very aware of the power of contexts to shape or distort thought and action and aware, too, of a certain ambiguity in their nature: there were contexts one could choose and others which claimed you for themselves. You could not choose the social class into which you happened to be born, yet much could follow from that initial fact – and interestingly, Auden continued to define himself with relation to the English class-system, long after it might be assumed to have lost relevance to his circumstances. Nor could you choose the nation into which you were born; yet that, it turned out, *could* be changed: one could decide, as he did, to stop being English and start being American. Gender was more complex; there seems to have been a period when Auden believed his homosexuality could be altered, which he attempted; later he regarded it more as a given of who he was. If nationality and the attitudes it encouraged serves as one example of a distorting context, another, about which he had professional sensitivity, was that of the expectations readers bring to the work of literature. Both in his own regard and that of others, he tried to ward off the potential harm this brought. When compiling the schools' poetry anthology *The Poet's Tongue* (1935) with John Garrett, they arranged the poems anonymously in alphabetical order of first line, in order to decontaminate a reader's 'bias' toward 'great names and literary influences' (*Prose I*, p. 109); Auden adopted a similar strategy for his first *Collected Poems*, published in America a decade later; again, this was a deliberately preventative measure, designed to thwart any reader keen to use that collection as a means to analyse the poet's development.

'Consider this and in our time', runs the opening line of one of his characteristically imperative early-period poems (*EA*, p. 46; written 1930), which goes on to enforce a sequence of insistent perspectives. While Auden had increasingly few illusions about what sense might emerge from what he much later styled 'History's criminal noise' ('The Common Life', *CP* 2007, p. 714), he could never have penned T. S. Eliot's notorious 1923 definition, 'the immense panorama of futility and anarchy which is contemporary history'.[2] To conceive poetry as a means of engagement with his current times – rather than an evasion or dismissal of them, for example by preference for some timeless realm of Art – was a position Auden consistently held. '*What should I write in Nineteen-Hundred-and-Seventy-One?*'

was a question of much greater import, he asserted, than '*What should I write at Sixty-Four?*' The notion of a poet's particular responsibility to be 'in [his] time' was illustrated by the 'Short' immediately following, when 'two poems' begging to be written each have to be refused: '*Sorry, no longer, my dear! Sorry, my precious, not yet!*' (*CP* 2007, p. 858, both). But, for all that, there is potentially a tension between 'our' collectively historical time and the essentially personal growth of a poet's mind in his privately demarcated lifetime. Were those two poems denied composition because of the date on the calendar or the stage reached in his own life? The question is made more relevant by the fact that one effect of Auden's continuing revisions of his canon was, by inference, to associate the work more closely with his life: he didn't amend or reject poems because it was 1971 but, surely, because, aged 64, he had lost sympathy with the earlier self who had written them.

The dialogue (or dispute) between private and public impulsions and responsibilities was a continuing provocation of his work. His decision at the end of the 1930s to relocate to America may have been driven by essentially personal and professional considerations, but took on a public significance because of when it occurred. Despite her wish to diminish the significance of that decision in any proper understanding of Auden's career, Everett acknowledges that '(f)or Auden to have left England at that time had a kind of terrible gracelessness, from which the poet's reputation has never really recovered' (Everett 1986, p. 218). This 'graceless-ness' may, in fact, have been more evident in his turning up in England at the end of the war in American uniform, keen to inform old friends in a self-consciously Americanized accent that, compared with the bombed-out German cities, they'd got off lightly during the London Blitz, which of course he hadn't himself endured. But even in such an episode, a different contextual understanding might see these details less in the light of his repudiation of England than in the light of essentially courteous acts of affiliation with his adopted country – and, with regard to his judgment of the relativities of destruction, in the light of an actual, if somewhat tactless, truth.

A significant proportion of Auden's writing of the 1930s had seemed to engage with what he so memorably termed 'the dangerous flood/ Of history' (*EA*, p. 157), understood to be the unignorable claim of 'our time', with its imbalanced tyrannies, injustices and inequalities, on the responsive individual. Even an iconic poem like 'Out on the lawn I lie in bed' (1933) is – especially in the earlier version (*EA*, pp. 136–38) – alert to the wilfulness inherent in its very evocation of social and spiritual harmony, when set in the context of the underprivileged outsiders excluded from such gratifying tranquillities. The personal as well as poetic culmination of the troubled decade's claims on Auden came with the Spanish Civil War, when he explained his intention to enlist in the International Brigade in terms of a sensed obligation: 'here', he wrote to E. R. Dodds (8 December 1936), 'is something I can do as a citizen and not as a writer', adding, later the same month, 'in a critical period such as ours, I do believe that the poet must have direct knowledge of the major political events ... I shall probably be a bloody bad soldier but how can I speak to/for them without becoming one?'[3] Contrasting with such anticipation, the weeks he spent there were unsettling and anticlimactic, even if 'Spain', the poem written and published on his return, showed little sign of this in its repeated insistence on 'to-day the struggle' (*SP* 1979, p. 51). But this poem marked the first of Auden's serious quarrels with himself; George Orwell fiercely criticized some aspects and although Auden thought his objections rather dense he made alterations and, later still, outdid Orwell in his own misunderstandings of what he had written, suppressing the poem altogether.

Auden would become increasingly aware of what might be termed the dangerous flood of language, the 'false emotions, inflated rhetoric, empty sonorities' that could drip from his pen at the prompting, he told Stephen Spender, of 'my own devil of unauthenticity' (*Early Auden*, quoted p. 206). 'Spain' was probably a case in point; for although, as Nicholas Jenkins has argued, 'the sense of great literary powers placed, decisively but without full conviction, in the service of a just cause, is essential to [its] effect', the actualities of the evolving conflict meant that 'the language and structure of "Spain" became increasingly compromised by their links to a Government which was more and more clearly the tool of a repressive Soviet foreign policy' ('Auden and Spain', *AS I*, p. 93). What happened to this particular poem highlights issues of authenticity in its relations to history, language, and readership that were of more general and enduring concern to Auden in coming to see, if not exactly the kind of writer he desired to be, then more certainly the kind he earnestly wished *not* to be. These issues are audible in the crucial transitional poem composed almost immediately on arrival in America, in which he addressed the newly completed life and career of the poet whose injurious influence on his own writing Auden would later summarize in those phrases quoted previously.

'In Memory of W. B. Yeats' (*EA*, pp. 241–43) uses the occasion of Yeats's transition to non-being as a covert parallel for Auden's own move toward a new state and a new state of mind. Although the poem performs some of the conventional work of an elegy, there is a governing austerity of tone (especially on its first American publication in March 1939, when it lacked the second section added in April for magazine publication in England) that nowhere indicates especial grief.[4] That the current of Yeats's feeling has 'failed' – in the poem's oddly-objectifying phraseology – is symptomatic of failures of feeling discernible not only amongst the 'living nations' but also in the poem itself, poised uneasily between the disfigurements of public pronouncement and the fugitive, ambivalent personal response. The exilic note in other 1939 poems such as 'Refugee Blues' and the elegy for Freud is also sounded here, as the 'peasant' forests of European legend give way to American 'ranches of isolation'; for Yeats, indeed, interment has comprised no return to significant soil, since he died in France and was temporarily buried there. The 'Irish vessel' remains literally empty (and would do so until the ceremonial repatriation of his body after the war – although Louis MacNeice claimed the wrong one had been brought back); Yeats's defining contexts are henceforward 'unfamiliar' or 'foreign'. The poem's other named writers, Kipling and Claudel, had also, like him, lived for significant periods outside their mother countries: as Auden himself would do.

The rhetoric of diminution – Yeats has merely 'disappeared', only 'A few thousand' are likely to take much notice of the loss of this major poet – reaches its logical climax in the assertion that 'poetry makes nothing happen': the elegy's most famous phrase. Yeats's disappearance as a contingent inhabitant of 'our time', anonymous now ('He') because irrelevant, leads to an Orphic scattering that despite its destructiveness resurrects and names him, in section III, as 'William Yeats' – one of many identities that might be associated with the generic 'poet' here invoked, although also recalling his own self-identification as 'the poet William Yeats' (similarly, the river of poetry described in section II suggests his 'living stream').[5] Section II remedies the absence of Yeats from section I as well as his purely iconic presence in section III, addressing him as a biographically embedded 'you', albeit with the presumptuous over-intimacy of one already embarked on that process whereby 'The words of a dead man/ Are modified in the guts of the living' – which, as a model of transmission, is in almost every aspect the reverse of Eliot's formulation in 'Burnt Norton' (1935): 'My words echo/ Thus, in your mind'. This ingestive modification of Yeats's writing, by a readership that now becomes the sole determinant of its meanings, is earthily comparable to worms' supposed consumption of dead bodies in the grave and, sacramentally, to the reception by participants at the Eucharist of 'the body of Christ', also associated with 'the Word'. The individual poet dies, but poetry collectively 'survives'; Yeats's corpse goes the way of all flesh, while his *corpus* comes alive.

It does so because he was one of those by whom the language 'lives' – which resembles but is crucially different from merely being someone who lives by language like, say, a journalist. In his contemporary essay, 'The Public v. the Late Mr William Butler Yeats', Auden clinched the case for the Defence by asserting that 'there is one field in which the poet is a man of action, the field of language, and it is precisely in this that the greatness of the deceased is most obviously shown' (*EA*, p. 393). The separation of art from agency separates it not only from 'executives' who don't see its point, but also from the earlier Auden intrigued by heroes or tempted to Spain; but poetry's making nothing happen doesn't consign it to irrelevance or complacent inactivity. Instead, as 'a way of happening', it finds itself at the close of the elegy charged with an agenda scarcely less ambitious than that with which, ten years earlier, 'Sir, no man's enemy' (which he later disavowed; *EA*, p. 36) had closed: if there 'the house of the dead' required harrowing, here the 'poet' must descend 'right/ To the bottom of the night'. The successful completion of these assignments would evidently see poetry rectify deficiencies of feeling underlying both individual pitilessness and collective 'hate'. Auden's poem closes in resonant semi-paradoxes: poetry cannot constrain but must persuade. Not the least paradoxical aspect of this elegy, curiously unresponsive to the human dimensions of Yeats's death, is its deployment of verbs such as 'rejoice' and 'praise' (different from the sadness and weeping with which Auden's Freud commemoration would close).

Within twelve months, composing 'New Year Letter', he would acknowledge that 'No words men write can stop the war / Or measure up to the relief / Of its intolerable grief' (*CP* 2007, p. 204); but in February 1939, Auden comes close to implying that poetry, when most true to itself, *might* help avert impending 'nightmare'. Any such belief had vanished by the time, in 'Prologue at Sixty' (1967), he recalled the Nazi 'torturers/ who read *Rilke* in their rest periods' (*CP* 2007, p. 832); but if the Yeats elegy looks backward – despite appearances to the contrary – in its inferences about the power and place of art, it is forward-looking in its recognition of the ways art and artists become cultural consumables. Its lesson about the manner in which the historically actual figure of Yeats is irrecoverably elided in contexts to which he and his work are assigned by successive readers is an apt reminder that the 'Auden' I have been discussing is an imagined figure, of whom it is largely irrelevant to enquire what did it mean to him 'there, then', as opposed to 'what does it mean to us, here now?' (*EA*, p. 61).

The contexts proposed in these essays offer a series of instigations for thinking about what Marsha Bryant has usefully termed 'the signifier "Auden"' – denoting ways in which he continues to be imbued with meaning by successive communities of readers.[6] Of course, this does not occur in complete disconnection from what our instruments of historical recovery agree that W. H. Auden (1907–73) did and wrote; but it also involves, as the Yeats elegy saw (not without foreboding), some quasi-predatory readerly modifications that, equally, are inseparable from processes of poetic survival. It is unquestionable that Auden *has* survived – and not simply as an object of literary study on university courses. Notably, he is regularly mentioned in serious journalism, even when the subject is not directly literary: 'September 1, 1939' came into renewed prominence in Internet discussions, after New York's Twin Towers were destroyed and, more recently, a letter-writer to the *Guardian* cited 'The Shield of Achilles' in connection with the serious riots that had affected some English cities. If these uses of Auden's work exemplify the significance of poetry's ways of happening suggested by the Yeats elegy, they also indicate the variance between poet and readership this poem also foretold: for such high valuation of 'September 1, 1939' directly contradicts the contempt and rejection Auden later directed toward it. Contributors to this volume continue to unbury poems he dispraised, finding not only 'September 1, 1939' but also 'Spain' and 'Sir, no man's enemy' necessary to an assessment of his work.

What, then, is Auden in our times? In some ways he is of the past, offering a kind of literary career it is difficult to imagine for the twenty-first century, even if his stupendous talents were to be replicated: is poetry ever going to seem quite so centrally important as his continuing eminence implies it was? But even his eminence was something which in his own lifetime he subverted, dismissing poetry as 'small beer'; it seems as if, once he had fulfilled and exhausted his undergraduate ambition to become a 'great' poet, what survived was the belief that poetry was the most important unimportant activity imaginable. One of the challenges he poses is just how to combine this sense of seriousness with this sense of levity – as when in 1932 he responded to Geoffrey Grigson's proposal to start *New Verse*: 'Why do you want to start a poetry review Is it as important as all that? I'm glad you like poetry but can't we take it a little more lightly' (*sic*; quoted RD-H 1995, p. 127). The registers adopted in Auden's poems can perplex, by the difference between them and the language of 'a man speaking to men', in Wordsworth's formulation; so that in the very late 'Lullaby' we encounter archaizing diction of 'another day has westered / and mantling darkness arrived', closely followed by 'you've gotten the garbage out' (*CP* 2007, p. 877). Many readers have found irritating such a *mélange* of idioms and the attitude implied by it; but this is a poem about the inherent wisdom of submitting to the body's desire for sleep (sleepiness, therefore, producing the poem's strange lexical mish-mash), of attending to 'the belly-mind', without whose sub-linguistic admonitions 'the verbalising I / becomes a vicious despot' (*CP* 2007, p. 878).

The dangers of despotism and the need for subversion of its importance and noise (which sometimes included the wrong kind of poetry) became a constant concern – heard, for example, in 'Under Which Lyre' (1946), whose subtitle, 'A Reactionary Tract for the Times', indicates Auden's continuing desire to notice the date. The war just ended ushers in renewal of the conflict between Hermes and 'Pompous Apollo' (*CP* 2007, p. 334), respectively the spirit of play and the spirit of self-aggrandizing responsibility. It is obvious Apollo is winning, despite Auden's declared affiliation with the losers; but perhaps what his poem yearns for is balance rather than Hermetic victory, the pun lurking beneath 'lyre' (liar) suggesting that a despotism of playfulness would be every bit as intolerable: 'The earth would soon, did Hermes run it, / Be like the Balkans' (*CP* 2007, p. 335). Taken to extremes, any position contains the potential for falsifying damage to human nature; thus it may be that Auden came to hear and despise the voice of the sloganeer in his famous line, 'We must love one another or die' (from 'September 1, 1939'), which elsewhere I have seen as encoding a totalitarianism of love.[7]

Auden's temptation by totalizing explanations – political, psychological, historical, and religious – generated an equal and opposite reaction against them, seen, for example, in his foreword to *The Dyer's Hand*, with its aversion for 'systematic criticism' (*DH*, p. xii). Although I hope the structure within which the following essays are grouped is largely self-explanatory,[8] and although this book is substantial, it does not attempt exhaustiveness: as Robert Frost saw, the chosen road implies the road not taken, and other contexts could with equal plausibility have found place within. To take merely two examples, Auden's sense of literary lineage could easily justify an essay covering poets like Hardy, Edward Thomas, and others; but the need for such is perhaps made less pressing by the great helpfulness of Katherine Bucknell's edition of the *Juvenilia*. A topic like 'Auden and Music' would be tempting, but would be difficult to treat adequately within an essay's format. So 'chance and my own choice' have made the book this is; although the overall design and basic conception of its topics has been mine, what contributors have chosen to make of their subject has been theirs to decide: the plurality of voices and approaches heard here is an important part of the collection's richness and vigour. It was no part of anybody's remit to agree with me or with each other, so no embarrassment need follow from encountering divergent views, as these do not detract from the collective contextual orientation around Auden, approached 'Arm in arm, but never, thank God, in step' (*CP* 2007, p. 539).

A focus purely on 'context' might, taken to extremes, omit the subject centred in it altogether: Auden, like Yeats, could 'disappear'. Such rigorous exactitude is not characteristic of these essays, which in various ways explore what is revealed when 'Auden' is considered within a particular setting; some are placed closer to setting, others to 'Auden'. The expertise of those writing them speaks, I trust, for itself and needs no puffery from me. It is a source of particular pleasure that many have been written by those who are also published poets in their own right – an appropriate mark of the professional respect which Auden continues to command. By the same token, however, I am obliged to regret the low proportion of women contributors, which does not accurately reflect the overall state of criticism. To any reader who, like me, is dissatisfied with this, I can only offer the assurance that more women were invited to contribute than felt able to accept the invitation; and more accepted the invitation than were enabled by events to submit their essay.

NOTES

1 'Auden Askew', reprinted in Barbara Everett, *Poets in Their Time* (Faber and Faber, 1986), pp. 228–29. Hereafter cited as 'Everett 1986'.
2 '*Ulysses*, Order, and Myth', in *Selected Prose of T. S. Eliot*, ed. Frank Kermode (Faber and Faber, 1975), p. 177.
3 Letters to E. R. Dodds in Bodleian Library, Ms Eng.Lett.c.464.
4 Mendelson sees this 'bleak new mode' as Auden's transformation of the traditional elegy (*LA*, p. 4 *et seq.*).
5 See, respectively, 'To be Carved on a Stone at Thoor Ballylee' and 'Easter, 1916'.
6 Marsha Bryant, *Auden and Documentary in the 1930s* (University of Virginia Press, 1997), p. 4; see also Stan Smith, *W. H. Auden* (Blackwell, 1985), pp. 5–6.
7 Tony Sharpe, *W. H. Auden* (Routledge, 2007), p. 90.
8 The description of Auden as 'the most professional poet in the world' was Randall Jarrell's, in his review of *The Shield of Achilles* (Haffenden, p. 400).

PART I

Contexts of Place

CHAPTER I

Auden's Northerliness

Tony Sharpe

When, soon after going up to Oxford in autumn 1925, Auden sat in Christ Church's junior common room composing 'The Carter's Funeral' (*Juv*, pp. 109–10), it probably wasn't what the college had anticipated from its new Exhibitioner in Natural Sciences, and it probably wasn't the sort of thing the room's other occupants were doing. Indeed, his gloomily imagining the obsequies of an agricultural worker may have implied reproach of their more privileged lives. Auden's choice of a communal area for what most would consider an antithetical activity seems self-conscious, even ostentatious; and early and late, whether swishing about Oxford in frock-coat or padding around New York dressed with a negligence increasingly divergent from the exactitudes of his personal routine, he could appear as someone over-committed to the role of being himself. But to defy expectation (as a scientist writing poetry) and to assert separateness within sociability (the private act within the public space) can be more positively conceived as strategies by which he fended off contexts others might propose. What I describe as Auden's 'northerliness' was a more consistent and deeply felt tactic of resistance: a geographical preference emphatically at odds with the prevailing view. This chosen affiliation implied difference, within which the relation between private and public spheres became an active issue: as he told Isherwood, 'North means to all: "Reject!"' (*Prose I*, p. 185).[1]

Had he been gifted in cricket rather than poetry, his birth in York could have entitled him to consideration for the county team; but his relocation near Birmingham in infancy meant that he lived mostly in the Midlands, and his schooling in Surrey and then Norfolk, followed by Oxford, did little to reinforce connections with the North. From the early 1920s he was a regular visitor to the Lake District, where his family kept a holiday cottage near Threlkeld, but he showed little affection for Wordsworthian scenery, provocatively preferring the industrialized view between Birmingham and Wolverhampton in 'Letter to Lord Byron' (written in 1936). Nevertheless, what the North meant to him and his attachment to it form a constant in his writing, in which literary, political, sexual and religious elements are at various times visible, grafted onto some obscure – but, for him, resonant – locations. Thus Rookhope, a remote Weardale village that was formerly the site of vigorous lead-mining activity, has a claim to being one of the most important places on what, in 'Prologue at Sixty', he would call his numinous map.

'The North', he lectured MacNeice in Iceland, 'begins inside' (*Prose I*, p. 375): initially such locations were imagined rather than experienced. Auden's attachment began in childhood, when his 'nursery library' included the work of Westmorland's Beatrix Potter as well as the Icelandic sagas which his father read to him: 'with Northern myths', he told Lord Byron, 'my little brain was laden' (*Prose I*, p. 329). But it also contained more technical books about the geology of lead mining, the various machines by which ore was processed and the northern English locations in which that industry was dwindlingly pursued. Although these reinforced his boyhood's intensively developed personal mythology – 'I spent a great many of my waking hours in the construction and elaboration of a private sacred world, the basic elements of which were a landscape, northern and limestone, and an industry, lead mining' (*F&A*, p. 502) – they also gave it geographical specificity and a practical focus, seeming even to indicate a possible career. Auden as mining engineer was really no more plausible than Auden as cricketer; but although that professional trajectory was unfulfilled, the mythological trajectory continued, sustained by an almost passionate identification with North Pennine places. '(Y)ears before I ever went there', he recalled in 1947, 'the North of England was the Never-Never land of my dreams'; nor did its potent unreality become prosaic on acquaintance, for 'to this day Crewe Junction marks the wildly exciting frontier where the alien South ends and the North, my world, begins' (*Prose II*, p. 335).

What, then, were the attributes of 'his' world, how was it transformed from being 'inside' or even, to use another adjective, 'autistic' (*CW*, p. 423), to intersect with shareable perceptions? 'North and South', he continued in 1947, were for him 'the foci of two sharply contrasted clusters of images and emotions'; among others, 'North' suggested 'heroic conquest of dangerous obstacles' contrasting with the South's 'life of ignoble ease' (*Prose II*, p. 335). His association of northernness with heroism was partly a consequence of the sagas; but because heroism is essentially a public phenomenon, its visualization meant progressing beyond the unpopulated privacy of his fantasy world toward an actually encountered landscape – this coinciding, according to a 1939 retrospect, with his own personal development: 'Besides words, I was interested almost exclusively in mines and their machinery. An interest in people did not begin till adolescence' (*Prose II*, p. 414). By his own account, he first set eyes on the North Pennine orefields he would later describe as his 'sacred landscape' at the age of twelve; although most powerfully compelled by scenes of desolation and desertion, by rusting machines littering abandoned workings typically situated in bleak moorland, he also visited operating mines and so observed the lead miners who, for a while, offered versions of a heroism that partly consisted in confronting the imminence of its own extinction. They were conscripted by some early poems as exemplars of stoical affirmativeness, such as the 'splendid generous Soul, the simple Mind' (*Juv*, p. 54) patronizingly approved at the end of 'Rookhope (Weardale, Summer 1922)' (1924); more convincingly, they were evoked by snatches of conversation overheard in 'Lead's the Best' (1926), tantalizingly naming places: 'They only keep a heading open still / At Cashwell' (*Juv*, p. 127). Here the poet's position, outside an inn whose suddenly closed door prevents his further eavesdropping, is significant: for if in his boyhood fantasy he had been 'the sole autocratic inhabitant' (*Prose II*, p. 42), its transformation from a solitary imaginary to an actual landscape, inhabited by others, posed urgent questions of precisely where, in respect of it, he stood.

'Who stands' were the opening words of the 1927 poem in which he first heard his own authentic voice ('The Watershed', as subsequently titled); its further reference to Cashwell, a lead mine near the summit of Cross Fell, locates it on Alston Moor in Cumberland. He came to love this locality, according to his brother John, more than any other, and a map of it found its way, twenty years later, to the unlikely setting of his beach shack on Fire Island (where presumably it, too, functioned as a marker of contrastive identity).[2] The poem also alludes to an incident that occurred in 1916 at the Nenthead complex of mines when an injured miner had to be transported underground to the doctor, because of snow, but subsequently died. Such details indicated interiority with place, and Auden had almost certainly visited Cashwell's extremely remote location; yet his poem's presumptuous onlooker turns out to be a 'stranger', belatedly fascinated but excluded as he contemplates acts of valiant endurance beyond his powers of emulation. The resemblance between heroic miners repairing a 'damaged shaft' and combatants' exploits in the Great War's trenches is pertinent. Auden, then, used his North to explain himself to himself, and as it developed alongside his own self-awareness, its potency became that, in part, of a paradise lost: for, despite what he would tell

Isherwood, he had already suspected that the North might do its own rejecting. 'I was never so emotionally happy as when I was underground' (*Prose II*, p. 415; *EA*, p. 398), he recalled; being 'underground' is also a potential metaphor for being concealed or clandestine, and if Auden later defined poetry as 'a game of knowledge' (*Prose II*, p. 345), that game included withholding as well as disclosing it. This underlies the teasing insolubility of the poem later called 'The Secret Agent' (1928; *EA*, p. 25), whose 'trained spy' reads the lie of the land but may not have been straight with those he deals with and is, perhaps, not 'straight' in other senses: Richard Bozorth convincingly reads this in the context of Auden's homosexuality, in *Auden's Games of Knowledge*. The predicament of one who knew himself 'Different or with a different love' (*EA*, p. 25) – in the words of another early poem describing an emotional impasse in an identifiably northern landscape – was surely intensified in relation to the lead-mining confraternity, homosocial within strict limits.

The rejections implicit in Auden's northerliness were, however, principally active rather than passive. Most subscribers to the January 1930 *Criterion* would have found an unfamiliar author's name attached to a work, 'Paid on Both Sides', containing place names of almost certainly equal unfamiliarity, but which denoted actual locations westward and eastward of Alston Moor: Garrigill, Nattrass, Lintzgarth, Rookhope, Brandon Walls. All were connected with lead mining, like Cashwell and, in 'The Secret Agent', 'Greenhearth' (for 'Greenhurth'); but here they enclose a landscape, not of longing, but across which is fought a serio-comic feud producing the defeat of love. This was another example of Auden's self-explanation; he later described it as 'A parable of English Middle Class (professional) family life 1907–1929' (*Plays*, p. xv: the dates defined his lifespan, up to the work's final revision). The virtual impossibility of anyone's appreciating that hidden dimension was paralleled by the unlikelihood of their connecting names with locations – such naming, therefore, had an exclusionary effect, defining ignorance rather than imparting knowledge: who, with any probability, would get it?[3]

This, in turn, was part of a strategy deployed against a cultural and economic dominant: the self-contented and self-centred Southeast, its 'Home Counties' nestling around London. It was hardly surprising that an essentially metropolitan spirit like Cyril Connolly should recall the Auden of this period as 'insularly devoted to northern England' (*Tribute*, p. 71); repudiation of settled geographical priorities was precisely the point, and, later, Auden's dedication to *The Dyer's Hand* (1962) expressed gratitude for 'a childhood spent in country provinces'. His first literary love was

Thomas Hardy, and the first poem he remembered writing had been a Wordsworthian effusion about Blea Tarn in the Lake District. Hardy spoke to him through his inhabitation of 'a world which had nothing to do with London, the stage, or French literature' (*Prose II*, p. 45), but both his Wessex and Wordsworth's Cumberland were regions whose resources had effectively been exhausted by their literary prospecting; such examples, however, suggested the advantages of exploiting a personal terrain. Wilfrid Gibson, Georgian poet and 'bard of Hexham', had some influence on 'Paid on Both Sides' and had prior squatter's rights over Auden's area, but was not a talent of a magnitude to repel subsequent settlers. This is not to dismiss Auden's undoubted preference for his particular limestone landscape as mere opportunism; but it should equally be remembered that his was to a high degree an elective affinity: he had chosen this lean country.

What Connolly dismissed as an insular attitude involved the aesthetic valorization of an identifiably northern landscape in which scar, fell and stone wall challenged the established iconographical supremacy of downland, hedgerow and thatched cottage; or slagheaps and slatternly tenements opposed the brightly lit metropolis: but, even for Auden, they could not replace them. Insular as it may have seemed, it could not represent 'this island': attempting that, or proposing a transformational politics, the Malverns or the Isle of Wight were his loci of visualization. When Auden tried to utilize lead-mining details and places for quasi-political purposes, for example in precedent versions of *The Dog Beneath the Skin*, Isherwood rejected them; they were replaced by material whose political incertitude has been well described as 'a Leftism charged with old Deserted Village nostalgias' (Cunningham 1988, p. 235). Auden's 'North' was not, in fact, a politically disambiguated place; the 'leader looking over' from his heroically ascetic fellside on the southern-seeming 'valley' (*EA*, p. 28), with its picture-postcard vista of orchard and river, might well prefer guns to butter, and be in spiritual sympathy with those Nazis who saw Iceland as the cradle of Germanic culture – about which Auden commented: 'Well, if they want a community like that of the sagas they are welcome to it. I love the sagas, but what a rotten society they describe, a society with only the gangster virtues' (*Prose I*, p. 265).

Closing his 1934 travelogue 'In Search of Dracula', Auden noted that he drove out of London 'past the new factories on the Great West Road, past the Old College, to Colwall. Dropped Peter in the road and turned north' (*Prose I*, p. 77). The details are suggestive: those 'new factories', erected along Brentford's 'golden mile' in the late 1920s and early 1930s, were evidence of the unequal effects of the Slump, with expansion still possible near London. Turning north, he took his preferred direction, the '"good" direction' (*Prose III*, p. 431) as he later defined it; but it was a journey toward deprivation, passing the Warrington and Wigan where forecasts of an 'Eotechnic Phase' were glaringly mendacious. These plate-glassed London factories, widely celebrated for exemplifying the new styles of architecture Auden later disavowed, contrasted with the gaunt, square-windowed northern mills whose appearance he preferred, but which offered evidence of a vanished prosperity and a persisting class struggle, its scars 'as yet unhealed' (*Prose I*, p. 209). The 'north' evoked in 'Letter to Lord Byron' (II), conflating its industrialized aesthetic with the Black Country scenery familiar from Auden's childhood, was one southerners understood: it was the region out of which hunger marchers rather than heroes descended on the capital, to mixed responses (they were baton-charged by mounted police in 1932); it was the land of mass unemployment and post-industrial malaise. This North, then, was congruent with some conventional perceptions, and even Auden's dislike for London invites comparison with the ruralist movement's distrust of the corrupting metropolis. Although the car-driving 'stranger' of 'The Watershed' may stand to the 'left', he spectates the landscape and its inhabitants across an ideological and social gulf. Its existence explains the difficulty Auden had in putting his particular 'North' to work in the service of an explicitly political programme: pointed up by the apparent paradox that a poet whose work so effortlessly admitted the ambient clutter of modernity – its arterial roads, wirelesses and power stations – was attached, in his vision of the North Pennines, to obsolete machinery and retrospection.

Although over the length of his career Auden was a true devotee of what MacNeice termed 'the obscure but powerful ethics of going North' (*Prose I*, p. 191), there was a period in the mid-1930s, Nicholas Jenkins suggests, when he defected: 'Auden in the early years of his career attempted to write the poetry of revived and redefined Englishness, of life in small, rural and often same-sex collectives in the southern half of the country, where he hoped a revitalization of the national spirit might take place'.[4] Such revitalization could hardly come from the depleted North, nor could that provide what Jenkins elsewhere terms the 'emblems of social totality and cognitive completeness' (*CCWHA*, p. 40) distinguishing such poetry – seen, for example, in the panoptic scenic choruses for *The Dog Beneath the Skin*, which replaced rejected lead-mining material. If Auden's North was continuously ethical – offering him, even in the fantasy stage of his attachment, a crucially educative choice between realism and magic when deciding what sort of machinery to imagine for his mine (see *F&A*, p. 502; *CW*, pp. 424–25) – it was also conflicted, whether in the melodramatic blood feud of 'Paid on Both Sides' or as the realm of an authenticity from which he felt debarred, as stranger or tourist. Auden acquired considerable knowledge of his North Pennines and was evidently well acquainted with particular places; it would hardly be too much to say that lead mining was to him what bullfighting was to Hemingway; but it may be significant that, in *A Certain World*, the extract by which he chose to represent his *afición* described the tour of a lead mine by a group of genteel outsiders.

Both the constancy and changingness of Auden's North can be seen in his deployment of Rookhope, first evoked in 'Rookhope (Weardale, Summer 1922)', then used in 'Paid on Both Sides' and intermittently present in his work up to 1965. Clearly a name of significant power, an early letter to Isherwood used it as title for 'The Watershed' – this despite the fact that internal evidence strongly suggests that the poem's imagined location would be westward across the county line, near Nenthead in Cumberland. The most extended and specific evocation occurred in 'New Year Letter' (III) in 1940; he named it in his 1954 travelogue, 'England: Six Unexpected Days', and nine years later, in his diary, referred to 'Amor Loci' as 'the Rookhope poem' (*LA*, p. 473). He associated it, personally, with the 'criminal leisure of a boy' (in Robert Lowell's phrase) experiencing an epiphanic moment when dropping a stone down a flooded shaft and, pictorially, with imagery of desertion and decay. This latter was a slight simplification; although lead mining had certainly been in decline since the later nineteenth century, Rookhope, along with Nenthead where a new shaft was sunk in 1925, was a site of its persistence: the Boltsburn mine near the centre of the village was still busy. There were abandoned workings elsewhere along the valley and up on the high fells beyond, and some of the railway connections were no longer used; but even though activity had been reduced, the place would still have had a certain bustle. Away from that, down the road at Lintzgarth, the impressive smelt mill had been in use until 1919, with its horizontal flue carried across stream and road on substantial masonry arches – thence continuing a diagonal ascent of Bolts Law for a mile (featured on the one-inch map). The mill remained more or less intact into the 1930s, and would have been so whether Auden first saw it in 1919 or 1922: it was – in the exact sense of his chosen adjective – 'derelict', but not dilapidated. It is difficult to resist the thought that this stone building with its cloister-like archway and becalmed rurality offered a secular, industrial equivalent of some post-Dissolution abbey: that would account for the powerful association, in 'New Year Letter', between such relics and vanished systems of belief.

It might also explain the sacramental air with which Auden increasingly invested his landscape, most prominently in applying to it the epithet 'sacred'. This marked a change. After its initial appropriation by his juvenile verse, the 'North' predominating in his early mature poetry was the site of exclusion produced by thwarted desire (whether for rights of association or another's love) or of conflict: in both, it literally set the scene for the 'restlessness of intercepted growth' (a formulation he filched from Trigant Burrow). It was also, in ways already indicated, connected with a hiddenness that unfitted it for the task of embodying 'the full view' (*EA*, p. 158) aimed at by Auden's period of English study, culminating in *Look, Stranger!* (1936), that 'strangely patriotic volume' (*CCWHA*, p. 41), as Jenkins styles it. It was only with the abandonment of his project for a totalizing version of Englishness and, indeed, after his abandonment of England itself, that Auden rediscovered his North, reinterpreting it in the light of his new relationship with Chester Kallman and the resumption of his relationship with God. 'The Prophets' (April 1939), written soon after meeting Kallman, rehearses the sequence of his attachment to lead-mining landscapes, explicitly resolving problems of belatedness, secrecy and non-reciprocation that afflicted 'The Secret Agent': what was covert, there, here becomes manifest, and what was latent, achieved.

If the unmoderated affirmativeness of 'The Prophets' could not be sustained, the expanding interpretability of Auden's 'North' was. Ironically, its unsuitability for use in any vision of English 'social totality' was what enabled it to function, next, in a far more capacious symbology, matching the encyclopaedic ambitions of the poem it appeared in. Justifying his decision to leave England, to E. R. Dodds in March 1940, Auden disclaimed any overall concern for the nation as such, advancing instead particular and limiting concerns: 'To me England is bits of the country like the Pennine Moors and my english (*sic*) friends' (*AS I*, p. 113). Yet this defensively reductive geographical definition was, simultaneously, forming the basis of an infinitely wider vision in part III of 'New Year Letter', where Auden, considering 'the human creature', summoned to mind 'An English area': 'I see the nature of my kind / As a locality I love, / Those limestone moors that stretch from BROUGH / To HEXHAM and the ROMAN WALL, / There is my symbol of us all' (*CP* 2007, p. 225). In the ensuing passage, punctuated by the proper names of various Pennine places, Auden used his landscape's geology to recapitulate the story of a (fortunate) Fall, then offered an account of his boyhood coming-into-consciousness, in a setting that necessitated rather than intercepted growth: 'There / In ROOKHOPE I was first aware' (p. 226). Although elements of (maternal) rejection in this latter narrative echo earlier aspects of his 'North', the differences are more marked: rather than being riddling, this is explanatory, and rather than being exclusive and delimiting, as a 'symbol of us all' it is supranationally admissive. North now means to all: accept – although just who might not be conscriptable to 'us all', in the context of world war, was an unacknowledged question.

In his Freud Memorial Lecture, 'Phantasy and Reality in Poetry' (1971), Auden offered this part of the poem as his 'first attempt' to engage with his childhood lead-mining world, describing 'what I had felt at the age of 12, when I first saw my sacred landscape with my own eyes'; he candidly admitted that this description was 'historically a fiction: what I wrote was an interpretation of [my experiences], in the light of … later reading in Theology and Psycho-analytic literature' (*AS III*, p. 191). The further sequence of engagements with his 'sacred landscape' he represented by 'In Praise of Limestone' (1948) and 'Amor Loci' (1965); but to begin such a list as late as 1940 overlooks not only a poem like 'The Prophets' but all the work of his early maturity in which that landscape was featured. As in much of Auden's revisionism, the omissions are glaring; but its underlying logic seems to derive from this landscape's accruing public as well as private meaning through its sacredness. Thus it changed from being the object of (internalizing) childhood fixation to that of (externalizing) religious devotion, in the sense, as he later put it, that 'To pray is to pay attention to something or someone other than oneself. Whenever a man so concentrates his attention – on a landscape, a poem, a geometrical problem, an idol, or the True God – that he completely forgets his own ego and desires, he is praying' (*CW*, p. 306).

Although Auden's northerliness was generic, to the extent that it included places like Iceland and Hammerfest because of their latitudes, it was most identifiable with a specific location, defined by the coordinates given in 'New Year Letter' or a 1950 letter to Geoffrey Grigson: '*My* Great Good Place is the part of the Pennines bounded on the S by Swaledale, on the North by the Romans Wall and on the W by the Eden Valley' (quoted RD-H 1995, p. 236). The link between specific places named in the 'New Year Letter' passage and the universalizing symbolism attached to them was a kind of incarnationalist manoeuvre, expressing an eternal principle in actual rocks and stones. The exemplification of 'the human creature' by a landscape, there, is congruent with the impulse to see place as semi-interchangeable with body, evident in the Italo-Pennine landscape of 'In Praise of Limestone', where sacramental attitudes relaxedly combine with an incipient if modified eroticism recalling 'The Prophets' – a poem readable as concerning Kallman or concerning Christ. Auden noted that beneath his own adolescent 'pseudo-devout phase' had lurked 'a quite straightforward and unredeemed eroticism' (*MCP*, p. 34); within the devotionalism of these mid-period poems a more redeemable eroticism is perhaps detectable, which contrasts with the predicament of the secret agent in his frustrate landscape.

The forthrightness that named and defined his sacred landscape in 'New Year Letter' and the relaxed forgivingness of 'In Praise of Limestone' were, on the whole, uncharacteristic. Although Auden became increasingly voluble about it in his prose, his 'great good place' reverted to an allusive rather than stated presence in his poetry. One of his photographs in *Letters from Iceland* had been captioned 'What the Tourist Does Not See', and the very title of his 1949 poem 'Not in Baedeker' highlights the inward aspects of place that superficial sightseers – amongst whom he includes his earlier self – take no interest in. It, too, is an Italo-Pennine setting, but the story it tells, of how somewhere specific becomes nowhere in particular – 'A certain place' reverts to being 'in the country somewhere' (*CP* 2007, p. 550) – foreshadows the lowered visibility of the North Pennines in his subsequent poetry. Revived, occasionally, by naming (Swaledale is an example), it was not evoked as a coherent landscape until 'Amor Loci'. This Latin title echoes his earlier formulation of 'a locality I love', but the poem is much less affirmative, connecting more to the disappointed tone of 'Not in Baedeker' than the hopefulness of 'In Praise of Limestone'. If 'The Prophets' simultaneously evoked the presence of Kallman and Christ, this poem's evacuated landscape implies the absence of any consoling vision, offering instead a 'real focus / of desolation' (*CP* 2007, p. 780). Its unpeopled scenery recalls Auden's solitary childhood imaginings, adding the lesson of necessary death; yet from his English area's very persistence and reinterpretability he gathered, albeit in a flinty register, what he often asked for: the truth about love.

NOTES

1 I refer to the text of *Letters from Iceland* in *Prose I*, which includes Auden's photographs and MacNeice's contributions.
2 For John Auden's comment see *Tribute* (p. 27); for the map displayed on Fire Island and other Pennine-related material, see my 'Paysage Moralisé: W. H. Auden and Maps', *AN* 29 (December 2007), pp. 5–12.

3 Edward Callan, in *Auden: A Carnival of Intellect* (Oxford University Press, 1983), was among the first to relate the names in 'Paid on Both Sides' to a map of Alston Moor; John Fuller, Katherine Bucknell, Alan Myers, Robert Forsythe and I have all written about the link between Auden's names and North Pennine places.

4 'Historical as Munich', *Times Literary Supplement* 9 February 2007, pp. 12–15 (at 15).

CHAPTER II

Two Cities: Berlin and New York

Patrick Deer

Unmistakably urbane, W. H. Auden's poetry stubbornly resists the urban. Auden's celebrated Thirties imaginary is bookended by his stay in Berlin in 1928–29 and by his controversial emigration to New York in January 1939 on the eve of World War II. The legend is that decadent Weimar Berlin freed Auden sexually and imaginatively, enabling the political impostures and commitments of his Thirties poetic; whereas New York ushered the poet into exile and 'later' style as an increasingly private and religious citizen in the alienating American 'megalopolis'. But the fugitive traces left by these cities in his poetry reveal a more complex story. His unpublished Berlin Journal declares, in an entry on Freud, 'Creative pleasure is, like pain, an increase in tension' (*EA*, p. 299): the two cities, their pleasures and pains, produced both extraordinary bursts of creativity and a profound increase in tension. Yet Auden's poetry refuses to be rooted in any metropolis, pushing instead towards a more abstracting exploration of the possibilities of 'the City' for modern life.

There were other cities that marked his imagination. Auden's family moved from the northern city of York near industrial Birmingham in the midlands, which already placed him off center as a 'provincial.' Oxford provided him with a reputation, coterie and Left politics; London propelled him to fame. Warring Shanghai and republican Barcelona haunted him. But it was Berlin and New York that offered staging posts for Auden's distinctive raids on the prolix imagination of the twentieth century. Both were cities in flux, discovered before the storm: Weimar Berlin in the artistic and political ferment before the Nazis came to power in 1933, and New York amongst the European refugees in the neutral United States after the defeat of the Spanish Republic and on the eve of the Second World War.

Arriving in Berlin in October 1928, W. H. Auden was one of a stream of British literary tourists to the Weimar Republic. He stayed ten months, of which seven were spent in Berlin, moving briskly from suburban lodgings in the Potsdamer Chaussée in Nikolassee with a respectable bourgeois family to an apartment house at 8 Furbringerstrasse, in the working-class neighbourhood of Hallesches Tor (see Page 2000, pp. 68–70 and also Weitz 2007, pp. 71–73).[1] Across the street was the Cozy Corner rent bar and its male prostitutes and rough trade, one of a hundred and seventy such establishments according to Auden's excited letters home (Page 2000, pp. 13–18). 'Is Berlin very wicked?' he had written to a friend knowing full well the answer. But British censorship and laws against homosexuality meant that the city's vibrant demi-monde appears only fleetingly in the poetry.

The city was a place that catalyzed his imagination, but where Auden could not remain imaginatively. John Fuller pithily sums up this crucial year, 'during which he (a) found personal liberation among the male prostitutes of Berlin; (b) established his critique of Freud's conventional morality; and (c) broke off his engagement' (Fuller 1998, p. 60). What Berlin offered was not quite liberation, however, despite Auden's vigorous immersion in the city's gay sex trade or his troubled friendship with John Layard, a student of W. H. Rivers who introduced him to the theories of educator and psychologist Homer Lane. Rather, the city offered a prism through which to defamiliarize the English landscape and body politic. The 'illness' of English culture could be manifested through a series of Weimar tropes that revealed the foreignness of home. Berlin rendered permeable his rather austere and abstract poetic imagination, but it did not permeate it.

In Weimar Berlin political violence converged thrillingly with psychological and sexual disturbance. This left its mark on Auden's dramatic 'charade', 'Paid on Both Sides', which he revised during his first months there. As the earlier version reveals, the poet grafted a German versus Jewish cast of gangsters, toughs and spies onto a northern saga of the warring Shaw and Nower clans (*EA*, pp. 1–17, 410–16). The hero John Nower's struggle to break with his mother's influence produces a psychic malaise fatally reproduced in the warring society around him. This expressionist blending of locales is both exhilarating and unnerving, reminiscent of early Brecht; but Auden's other poetry of the time is closer to the cool, cynical surfaces of the *Neue Sachlichkeit* (New Objectivity) than the more political German Expressionism it supplanted. In 'The strings' excitement, the applauding drum', the 'assaulted city', like the psyche, is under siege, offering 'no peace' but instead 'speeches at the corners, hope for news, / Outside the watchfires of a stronger army'. The poem then imagines repression overcome, as 'all emotions to expression come, / Recovering the archaic imagery' (*EA*, p. 32).

Returning to Britain, Auden found the foreign strains of political intrigue, incipient fascism, militarized masculinity, and revolutionary gesture at work at home. The exhilarating coup-plotting of 'We made all possible preparations', anticipates the dystopian vision of Rex Warner's *The Aerodrome* and Orwell's *Nineteen Eighty-Four*. In part I of *The Orators*, the 'great creative sequel' to his Berlin stay (RD-H 1995, p. 88), the Prize Day speaker declares hair-raisingly: 'Take a look around this hall, for instance. What do you think? What do you think about England, this country of ours where nobody is well?' (*EA*, p. 62). The Weimar political ferment encouraged Auden's Thirties vision of the poet as outsider and social diagnostician.

Weimar Berlin's sexual reform movement and de facto toleration of homosexuality offered him a glimpse of a possible future, an alternative sexual politics to the "Mediterranean" freedoms celebrated by writers like Wilde or Forster (Bozorth, p. 22; Weitz, pp. 297–305). In Berlin, his passionate encounter with Layard and the psychological reflections of D. H. Lawrence, Lane, Georg Groddeck and Nietzsche provided an intoxicating intellectual counterpart for his sexual experimentation. This re-reading of Freud eschewed repression in favour of the liberation of desire, and it declared all forms of physical illness psychosomatic. In this spirit, Auden's Berlin Journal lists lovers and sexual adventures on one side of the page and more philosophical reflections on the other. Anticipating the dark ironies of 'Miss Gee', 'Sir, no man's enemy …' subjects the call for psychic and bodily liberation to the awkward disciplines of the sonnet form. The Berlin poems are haunted by the awareness that sexual and psychological experimentation was loosening his ties to England, as in 'Love by Ambition', offering 'views from the rail' without yielding an alternative structure of feeling. The poem also shows the alienation of the sex trade queering the narcissistic love of 'Likeness to likeness' and opening up the painful pleasures of cross-class desire, 'Love is not there / Love has moved to another chair' (*EA*, p. 30). On his return, Auden broke off his engagement.

The most important poem of the period, later titled '1929' (*EA*, pp. 37–40), evokes Auden's Berlin experience as a 'season' rather than a place, carefully contained in a complicated series of temporal shifts and spatial displacements. In four sections the city is dematerialized, mediated by the cycle of the seasons, by clipped 'Audenesque' syntax and a phenomenological obsession with consciousness. Berlin provides the stage both for a modernist redescription of the world and a liberating reinvention of the self: 'Season when lovers and writers find / An altering speech for altering things'. The image of 'A fresh hand with fresh power' on the arm evokes tactfully Auden's sexual experimentation. Yet in the glimpse of a weeping solitary man 'Hanging his head down, with his mouth distorted / Helpless and ugly as an embryo chicken', an indiscreet reference to Layard's abortive suicide attempt, the city also confronts the reader with alienation and failure. The poem contrasts this with the 'success of others' in the 'happiness' of 'my friend Kurt Groote' and the 'absence of fear in Gerhart Meyer / From the sea, the truly strong man'. Here Berlin is personified unforgettably in the German rent boys with whom Auden had brief and disastrous affairs, leaving a 'fairly unpleasant whiff of Strength Through Joy' (*Early Auden*, p. 74). This strained defiance is counterpointed by the moving final lines evoking a bus running home and 'fallen bicycles like huddled corpses' (transposed from a 1927 verse letter written for an unrequited Oxford love).

The Berlin 'season' shifts into a record of recollected inner states in the second section of '1929'. The city is represented as a continuous present in a series of gerunds that pulse through the poem, beginning, 'Coming out of me living is always thinking, / Thinking changing and changing living'. A brief description of Weimar Berlin's political violence is compressed between the vista of ducks in a harbour and a detached interior monologue on Auden's theory of individuation as weaning: 'Am feeling as it was seeing'. As 'homesick foreigner', he observes the class war and street fighting – 'All this time was anxiety at night / Shooting and barricade in street' – reacting ambiguously to his friend's apocalyptic excitement: 'said I was pleased'. Amidst this metropolitan turbulence the desired epiphany of peace, 'To love my life, not as other', is significantly sought in 'field and distance', on a 'hill-top' above 'village square' amid singing larks (his difference from which the section's final line surreally acknowledges: '"being no child now nor a bird"').

The balance of '1929' leaves Berlin behind. The third section charts a return from Germany to rural England, 'In month of August to a cottage coming', where Auden's persona must begin 'the difficult work of mourning'. Leaving the city, the speaker is imagined as a weaned but faltering child, 'Happy only to find home, a place / Where no tax is levied for being there'. Images of colonization as 'mispronunciation' and 'intermarriage' give a further ironic twist to the return journey and to Auden's modernist experimentation in life and art, as the poet imagines 'foreign settlers to a strange country come' who 'By mispronunciation of native words / And by intermarriage create a new race and a new language'. The final section of '1929' makes no reference to Germany. Yet Berlin continues to work like a conspiracy on Auden's poetic, as the poem apocalyptically announces, 'This is the dragon's day, the devourer's'. A fascistic 'enemy' at home seeks to 'destroy the efflorescence of the flesh' and 'censor the play of the mind', enforcing 'Conformity with the orthodox bone'. Against this enemy the poem mobilizes the third-person plural, but its last lines resonate with apocalyptic traces of his 'season' abroad: 'we know that love … / Needs death, death of the grain, our death. / Death of the old gang'. Berlin the city has left its mark.

This is the highly seductive structure of poetic address that worked so effectively for Auden in the 1930s, but which he later rejected as manipulative and 'untrue': 'you' the reader might not travel to Berlin (or Shanghai or Spain), but could share like a secret agent in the coded knowledge with which Auden's poetic 'I' returned. His poetics diagnosed 'our' society's collective illness and projected an ethical counter-coup against the 'old gang', allowing his readers to participate in their imagined violent destruction. This is an incisively worldly, even cynical poetics befitting a turbulent historical moment.

His poem '1929' struggles to work through the 'season' he spent in Berlin, exercising a mix of discretion and exhibitionism. The traces of Germany needed to be dematerialized and displaced in favour of the familiar yet estranging Audenesque vision of Englishness in the 1930s. After returning, he found refuge in the straitened life of a private schoolmaster. Apart from a 'few days' in 1933 and a still more mysterious visit to Nazi Berlin in January 1939,[2] Auden did not return to Germany until 1945 when he interviewed bombed civilians for the U.S. Strategic Survey, but he stayed silent in print about the devastation he encountered until 'Memorial for the City' (1951). This foreshadowed the Berlin divided by the infamous 'Wall' to which he returned for a last stay in 1964, on a Ford Foundation residency.

New York, unlike Berlin, provided both a point of departure and a place to return. If Weimar Berlin had to be derealized and displaced, Auden turned to New York at first as a gritty fantasy of urban alienation, an austere retreat from political commitment and militarization into the abstraction of the modern metropolis. He promoted the myth of his exile in 'Refugee Blues' (March 1939), where the city with 'ten million souls' still has 'no place for us, my dear' (*CP* 2007, p. 253). He explored it further in a trilogy of precisely dated New York poems, 'September 1, 1939', 'New Year Letter' (set on 1 January 1940, published in *The Double Man* 1941), and '*The Age of Anxiety*' (set on All Souls' Night 1944, published 1946). This myth has powerfully shaped the critical reception of Auden's later work, counterpointing as Stan Smith observes 'the post-1939 estranged New York Auden' to 'the pre-1939 English provincial Auden' and the 'stateless post-1948 Auden' (*CCWHA*, p. 21).

Yet Auden's self-mortifying idea of New York can be read as an alibi for the emigrant who had ignobly left Britain to a chorus of disapproval. In truth, Auden arrived as an émigré; the harsh attacks on him during the war were to transform him temporarily into an exile. Like many a European's first impressions of the city, his were soon to change under the 'terrible honesty' of New York living. As a fatigued and ailing Albert Camus recorded in March 1946: 'At first glance, a hideous, inhuman city. But I know that one changes one's mind'.[3] For one thing, New York was much too hospitable.

Auden and Isherwood arrived in January 1939 on a liner via Ellis Island, met on a launch by Erika and Klaus Mann. Like many expatriates before them, they took a room in the somewhat shabby George Washington Hotel on Lexington Avenue. As in Berlin, his trajectory led him pro-ductively astray, from the thin air of upper-middle-class Manhattan to a more demotic education in middle-class Jewish Brooklyn, then to Greenwich Village and points beyond. Instead of solitude he found love and employment, and home in a series of apartments in Brooklyn and Greenwich Village. His literary reputation led to almost immediate pub-lication, to public appearances, paid reviewing, and also to teaching jobs, first at a prep school and then at colleges outside the city. At a talk at the League of American Writers, Auden met and soon fell in love with young Chester Kallman. He was productive: his last English volume, *Another Time* (1940), included a trove of poetic leave-takings written in neutral America: 'In Memory of W.B. Yeats', 'In Memory of Sigmund Freud', 'Refugee Blues', 'The Unknown Citizen', and 'September 1, 1939'.

After a 'honeymoon' on the eve of war, Auden took up residence in an apartment on 1 Montague Terrace in Brooklyn Heights, with a view across the East River to Manhattan. The poem 'September 1, 1939' (*EA*, pp. 245–47) opens in a Midtown locale: 'I sit in one of the dives / On Fifty-Second Street'. This has been identified as a gay club called 'Dizzy's', the scene that night of riotous behaviour on a street famous for its jazz clubs, yet in the poem it is not clearly placed. Nor are the generic 'blind skyscrapers' reaching arrogantly into 'this neutral air' as they 'use / Their full height to proclaim / The strength of Collective Man'. Greater specificity might have detracted from the poem's global reach and ambiguous politics, that 'There is no such thing as the State' or 'We must love one another or die'. Rather, the poem gains power from its own 'uses' of rhetoric, emotional ambivalence, and play of 'the folded lie' against poetic affirmation. As Tony Sharpe has observed, 'strong on love' the poem masks a profound political evasiveness (Sharpe 2007, pp. 88–90). Unsentimental about this famous New York poem, Auden cut it from his *Collected Poems* (see *LA*, pp. 477–78).

The Brooklyn view offered a more affectionate point of departure for the 'Purely random thinking' of the speaker of 'Heavy Date' (October 1939) as he waits for his lover: 'Sharp and silent … / The great city lies; / And I at a window / Looking over water / At the world of Business / With a lover's eyes' (*CP* 2007, p. 257). Images of Wall Street and the 'looking over / Faces in the subway' are displaced by freewheeling inter-textual references to Malinowski, Rivers and Spinoza. High rent drove the poet seven blocks north to a rooming house on 7 Middagh Street close to the Brooklyn Bridge, where he lived from October 1940 into the following summer with George Davis, Carson McCullers, Paul Bowles, Gypsy Rose Lee, Benjamin Britten and Peter Pears (Tippins 2006, pp. 62–77). In his embrace of philo-Semitism in New York, he found strong resonances between queerness and Jewishness (Roberts 2005, pp. 92–93). With Kallmann, Auden discovered opera but was less interested in the bebop jazz revolution going on uptown at 52nd Street and in Harlem. His operetta collaboration with Benjamin Britten, *Paul Bunyan*, was performed by Columbia University's music department to poor reviews in 1941. Richard Davenport-Hines notes that the early years of 'life crisis' and 'resettlement' were 'perhaps the richest of his life' (RD-H 1995, p. 228).

Middagh Street's chaotic collegiality prepared Auden for life in Greenwich Village, where he lived at 7 Cornelia Street from 1946 until 1951. Visitors were shocked by the austere squalor of his Cornelia Street rooms, with cots and work tables overflowing with books, an oasis of calm off the rowdy thoroughfare of West 4th Street, which linked the 'gay enclave' of the West Village (see Chauncey 1995, pp. 232–44) to Washington Square Park and the Bohemian cafes, bars and clubs to the south along MacDougal Street. Auden evaded the city summers, first through a shared beach house on Fire Island (1946–47), and from 1948 by a spring and summer rental on Ischia in the Bay of Naples, until in 1958 he bought his Austrian 'habitat'. Between 1953 and 1971 his winters were spent at his apartment on St. Mark's Place in the East Village.

In his New York poems, time is more clearly defined than place. Auden did not replace his 'archaic' English imagery with a new found urban imagery. For Auden, New York provided both a personal refuge and a staging post for his speculations about 'the City', even as he continued to resist the particularity of the urban in his poetry. Philip Larkin's famously brutal review, 'What's Become of Wystan?' (1960), which criticized Auden for failing to be a 'New Yorker Walt Whitman viewing the American scene through lenses coated with European irony' (Haffenden, p. 416), rings true but also misses the point. Auden is closer in this respect to the 'New York School' of abstract expressionism, which shared the formal conventions of abstraction and 'the identification of New York City as the embodiment of the modern' rather than an urban imaginary drawn from the everyday life of the city (Scott and Rutkoff 2001, p. 308).

The opening of 'New Year Letter' (1941) projects a vision of universal 'good cheer, / Love, language, loneliness and fear' as the city celebrates the passing of the year, echoing Eliot: 'Along the streets the people flow, / Singing or sighing as they go'. But the specifics of New York are displaced by the strained attempt to link metonymically Europe's war-torn 'haunted house' and neutral America, by noting that 'the same sun' that had observed the outbreak of war 'lit up America' (*DM* ll, pp.32–46; *CP* 2007, pp. 197–8). Part 1 of the poem follows in the same vein; its brisk tetrameter couplets subordinating place to literary reflection on the position of the poet in war-time and on the autonomy of literature: 'Art is not life and cannot be / A midwife to society' (*DM* ll, pp. 78–79; *CP* 2007, p. 199). The volume's British title, *New Year Letter*, suggested both a fresh start in the New World and a continuing correspondence with wartime England, but U.S. neutrality casts a disturbing shadow. Part II of the poem shifts to a more theological and philosophical register, signalled by the move from city to an archetypal landscape, to 'The signpost on the barren heath / Where the rough mountain track divides' (*DM* ll, pp. 322–33; *CP* 2007, p. 205).

Part III returns the reader to the cityscape: 'Across East River in the night / Manhattan is ablaze with light' (*DM* ll, pp. 833–34; *CP* 2007, p. 218). Again Auden contrasts the view from Brooklyn with 'Our privileged community' at Elizabeth Mayer's Long Island house, but this time the idealized memory is distanced in time and space. His poem is like a 'flare' in the desperate urban night: 'Around me pausing as I write / A tiny object in the night' (*DM* ll, pp. 975–76; *CP* 2007, p. 222). After paying his dues to the English imaginary of his early poetry

> I can but think our talk in terms
> Of images that I have seen
> And England tells me what we mean.
> (*DM* ll, pp. 1074–76;
> *CP* 2007, p. 225)

Auden later evokes the fallen present of America's 'machine' civilization. But 'New Year Letter' frames these bleak reflections in a series of restless historical and spatial shifts reminiscent of his Berlin poem, '1929', that describe the alienation that afflicts both warring Europe and the neutral United States: 'An earth made common by the means / Of hunger, money, and machines' (*DM* ll, pp. 1158–61; *CP* 2007, p. 227). The poem offers a European genealogy for the instrumental reason of 'Empiric Economic Man' (*DM* l, p. 1221; *CP* 2007, p. 228), which is 'without pity / Destroying the historic city'. Here the 'historic city' (*DM* l, p. 1307; *CP* 2007, p. 231) represents both the capitalist United States of 'Industrial man' (*DM* l, p. 1329) and Europe under siege from fascism. 'New Year Letter' is, as Edward Mendelson observes, an epic meditation on Auden's Faustian pact with America in which 'the dialectic is still at its constructive work' (*LA*, p. 121; see also pp. 101–03). The poem's Goethean references, like the host of citations in the eighty pages of notes, also link the New World both intertextually and historically with the Old.

In answer to 'September 1 1939', 'New Year Letter' challenges the 'lie' of Manhattan's 'secular cathedrals' that stand 'like rebel angels' denying 'that man is weak and has to die' (*DM* ll, pp. 1457–60; *CP* 2007, p. 235). This is still possible because, even in 1940, the alienating reign of *Homo economicus* is not hegemonic: 'He never won complete support / However many votes he bought' (*DM* ll, pp. 1253–54; *CP* 2007, p. 229). The poem explores a vision of U.S. history from the pilgrims through Jefferson and Hamilton, of 'the great Rome / To all those who lost or hated home' (*DM* ll, pp. 1469–70; *CP* 2007, p. 235), to modern New York, the refuge both of 'Artistic souls' and migrating Negroes 'east to hard New York they come', and to 'tolerant' California and fantastic Texas (*DM* ll, pp. 1500–03).

> More even than in Europe, here
> The choice of patterns is made clear
> Which the machine imposes, what
> Is possible and what is not,
> To what conditions we must bow
> In building the Just City now.
> (*DM* ll, pp. 1519–25; *CP*
> 2007, p. 236)

Auden then seems to retreat from this nuanced description of the conditions for building the Just City, 'the machine has now destroyed / The local customs we enjoyed'. Yet he observes more optimistically that the 'bonds of blood and nation' that have plunged Europe into war have been replaced here 'By personal confederation' (*DM* ll, pp. 1525–30).

The section's notes cite Kafka, Eliot, Jessie Weston, Whitman, Melville and Henry James, making clear the transatlantic reach of Auden's vision (*DM*, pp. 150–52). Ironically, the alienated present has forced a common knowledge of the city's privatized existential condition on all citizens: 'Compelling all to the admission, / Aloneness is man's real condition' (*DM* ll, pp. 1541–42; *CP* 2007, p. 237). Only in a city like New York could Auden have distanced himself from his ties with a wartime Britain inclined to see in him a defecting *persona non grata*, to find protection in the vast anonymity of its streets and intimacy in its throng of refugees, emigrants, businessmen, artists and workers.

Typical of Auden's New York poems, *The Age of Anxiety* (1946) travels onto a radically different terrain. Set on All Souls' Night 1944, the long poem opens in a Manhattan bar where four wartime strangers convert a brief encounter into a hallucinatory spiritual journey. The hybrid hard-boiled baroque prose style of the 'Prologue' promises an ironic urban vision (*CP* 2007, p. 447), but the poem shifts into an intensely subjective and expressionistic register. As the Canadian airman Malin reflects

> Here we sit
> Our bodies bound to these bar-room lights,
> The night's odors, the noise of the El on
> Third Avenue, but our thoughts are free …
> Where shall they wander?
> (*CP* 2007, p. 460)

The poem leads him and his three companions through a Dantesque adventure, punctuated only by wartime radio bulletins and brief returns to the bar and the streets. Although the poem gave apt title to Auden's New York exile and the years of the early Cold War, *The Age of Anxiety* met with a mixed reception. Yet it earned him the Pulitzer Prize. Auden returned phlegmatically to the myth of urban alienation in 'City Without Walls' (1967), less a New York poem than a jeremiad against suburban America, mass society and consumerism, '"Still monied, immune, stands Megalopolis …"' (*CP* 2007, p. 750). The comically absurd conclusion, in which inner voices cheekily interrupt the rant, draws attention to the polyvocal nature of Auden's engagement with New York. After the terrorist attacks of September 11, 2001, he was celebrated as the author of a quintessential New York poem, 'September 1, 1939'.

His Berlin apartment building survived the bombing in World War II. But thanks to the modernizing drive of Robert Moses, Auden's Middagh Street home was demolished in the 1950s and replaced by the Brooklyn-Queens Expressway. His other New York apartments have thus far survived the peace. The poet's need for the alienated 'megalopolis' was at odds with the nuances of Auden's personal vision of New York as 'civitas' or potential 'Just City'. It is to his credit that his poetry sustains this contradiction between ethical abstraction and urban everyday life. But his commitment to an expansive, sprawling speculative poetics forced out the particularity of city living from his poetry. There was to be relatively little Berlin or New York imagery to match the English imagery of his early poetry. Even though these two cities transformed his poetry and gave him refuge, the urban imaginary of Auden's poetry, both early and late, is fleeting.

NOTES

1 Details for all books referred to can be found in the 'Further Reading' for this chapter, at the end of the volume.
2 See Nicholas Jenkins, 'The Traveling Auden', *AN* 24 (July 2004), p. 8; 'Historical as Munich', *Times Literary Supplement*, 9 Feb 2007, p. 13.
3 Albert Camus, *American Journals*, tr. Hugh Levick, (Abacus, 1990), p. 32.

CHAPTER III

Ideas about England

Stan Smith

'What do you think about England, this country of ours where nobody is well?' asks the Old Boy addressing a school prize day at the start of Auden's *The Orators* in 1932 (*EA*, pp. 59–110). The question is as ambiguous as the speaker and as the context in which it's asked. Subtitled *An English Study*, the book was written and set in a minor private school in the salubrious Scottish town of Helensburgh on the Clyde, where Auden taught for two years from 1930. Although the Old Boy expresses an abiding opinion of Auden's in the 1930s, that individuals and societies are racked by psychosomatic illnesses which reveal their individual and collective repressions, he is not simply a mouthpiece for the poet's views. On the contrary, he is a figure of fun, to be parodied and reviled as a spokesman of patriarchal authority, engaged in the manipulation of the boys into guilty submission to the forces of order: school, civil society, and state. Yet his speech ends with an apparent volte-face, inciting his youthful audience of 'initiates' to stage what is virtually a pogrom against all the 'rotters and slackers … proscribed persons' in the school (he helpfully provides a list of undesirable schoolmaster types), who have all 'got to die without issue' and are to be thrust into the stoke hole under the floor of the school hall, which he recalls from the bullying initiation rites of his own school days.

It's a disturbingly abrupt transition from congenial old buffer mouthing patronizing commonplaces to the hate-filled rant of a fascist dictator in the course of a single speech; but it's clearly intended to express Auden's sense of a fragile cultural and political situation in which a respectable bourgeois order could rapidly degenerate into totalitarian irrationality. After all, when the book ran to a second edition in 1934, Adolf Hitler had already come to power by 'democratic' means and was rapidly converting the once liberal Germany of the Weimar Republic, beloved by the young Auden and his friends, into one vast concentration camp for those who did not share the Nazi ideology.

Auden had few doubts that his own native land could easily go the same way under the pressure of economic depression, mass unemployment, and the collapse of Ramsay MacDonald's short-lived Labour administration, beset by a bankers' ramp, into a Conservative-dominated 'National Government' coalition which received a huge mandate in the general election of October 1931. MacDonald briefly remained Prime Minister, until replaced by the Tory Stanley Baldwin. Meanwhile, a more sinister 'national' force waited in the wings, in the form of that Mosleyite fascism satirized throughout *The Orators*. Oswald Mosley had stalked out of MacDonald's Cabinet to found the 'New Party', originally touted as an ultra-left alternative to Labourism. His often leftist disciples readily donned, however, the black shirts of the British Union of Fascists into which the party rapidly mutated.

Such easy shifting between Left and Right radicalism was widespread at the start of the 1930s, and the young Auden was not immune. Much of his poetry derives its frequently near-hysterical tone from the same political equivocation. In the introduction to a revised *Orators* in 1966, Auden admitted as much: 'My name on the title-page seems a pseudonym for someone else, someone talented but near the border of sanity, who might well, in a year or two, become a Nazi'.[1] Only a couple of months after Hitler came to power, reviewing books on education by Leavis, Denys Thompson and L. C. Knights (*EA*, pp. 317–18), Auden toyed with the prospect of an authoritarian revolution from above: 'We live in an age in which the collapse of all previous standards coincides with the perfection in technique for the 'centralised' distribution of ideas; some kind of revolution is inevitable, and will as inevitably be imposed from above by a minority'. But it was Lenin's classic question, 'What is to be done?', which he invoked to remind those 'people who are usually called highbrows' of their civic responsibilities when 'the loudest voice' prevails and 'Mass production, advertising, the divorce between mental and manual labour, magazine stories, the abuse of leisure … are symptoms of an invalid society [which] can only be finally cured by attending to the cause'. In words that recall *The Orators*, he attributed to the liberal intellectual tradition represented by Leavis's journal *Scrutiny* the danger of 'making the invalid fascinated by his disease, of enabling the responsible minority to derive such intellectual satisfaction from contemplating the process of decay, from which by the nature of consciousness itself they feel insulated, that they lose the will and power to arrest it'. A month earlier, writing in the Labour newspaper *The Daily Herald*, he had been more forthright. In theory, Auden argued, machines had made possible for everyone a standard of living previously denied even to the very rich. But in practice, they have made the majority of mankind wretched, and reduced a supposedly privileged minority to 'unhappy, spoiled children':

If you are to make the theory fact, you must first establish a Socialist State in which everyone can feel secure, and, secondly, have enough self-knowledge and common sense to ensure that machines are employed by your needs, and not your needs by the machinery. (*EA*, pp. 315–17)

'Everyone': the addressees targeted by Auden's inclusivist rhetoric are not only the factory worker 'too old at thirty' but also the shareholder, whom 'the fierceness of competition and the constant trade booms and depressions keep … in a perpetual state of anxiety'. 'Half the machinery of the world is running to-day not to satisfy any real want', he argued, 'but to stop us remembering that we are afraid'.

It sometimes seemed that the main purpose of Auden's poetry was precisely to remind his readers to be afraid, very afraid, with that deliciously flesh-creeping frisson which accompanies the contemplation of catastrophe. 'Get there if you can', he wrote in one poem that addressed a propertied audience, 'and see the land you once were proud to own' (*EA*, pp. 48–49), a land now of abandoned mines, factories and power stations, deserted roads and railways, broken bridges, rotting wharves and weed-choked canals. It's not the thought of working-class lives ruined by economic collapse that invests the diatribe with its intensest emotion, but the prospect of retribution for the rentier classes, among whom Auden reluctantly numbers himself. Now, finally, they hear 'doom's approaching footsteps' as the mob begins to smash and engine drivers and factory girls start blowing up department stores and 'destroying intellectuals' – intellectuals like himself, who have spent their time 'Lecturing on navigation while the ship is going down'.

The contradiction is ubiquitous in Auden's vision of contemporary Britain. On the one hand, reproducing a leftist trope, the vast majority of all classes are victims of the capitalist system now apparently in terminal decline. On the other hand, we are all alike guilty, by omission or commission, and deserve what we're going to get. As 'The Witnesses' predicts, 'The sky is darkening like a stain, / Something is going to fall like rain / and it won't be flowers' (*EA*, pp. 126–30). The sense of a diffuse collective guilt transforms an historical conjuncture into a metaphysical condition, summed up in his adaptation of the Anglo-Saxon poem 'The Wanderer': 'Doom is dark and deeper than any sea-dingle'. In a corrupt and corrupting society, we are all equally doomed. Despite the prayer for a new dawn with which the poem ends, it is 'gradual ruin spreading like a stain' in an 'anxious house where days are counted' in which this poetry revels (*EA*, pp. 55–56).

Auden's early verse is suffused with an Old Testament prophet's fury of indictment and rebuke. 'Consider this and in our time' draws on a rote imagery of silted harbours, moribund factories and strangled orchards, to foster 'immeasurable neurotic dread' in the reader and in all 'seekers after happiness', warning stereotyped financier and Oxford don alike that 'the game is up for you and for the others', for 'It is later than you think' (*EA*, pp. 46–47). The 'immeasurable neurotic dread' and the mental fugues, 'explosion of mania' and 'classic fatigue' with which the poem closes are the psychological symptoms of a society paralysed by the prospect of its supersession. Packing to leave within the hour, his addressees are warned that they 'cannot be away'. Another poem advises in urgent pararhyme: 'Do not imagine you can abdicate; / Before you reach the frontier you are caught' (*EA*, pp. 44–45). The poem later called '1929' declares with gloating *Schadenfreude* in its closing October sequence that 'It is time for the destruction of error'. October 1929 was the month of the Wall Street Crash. The poem had opened with recollections of the street riots, shootings and barricades Auden had witnessed on his Berlin visit the previous Easter, a time of 'anxiety at night' with a friend 'Talking excitedly of final war / Of proletariat against police'. The 'choice' that seemed 'a necessary error' then now emerges clearly in the recognition that 'love / ... needs death ... our death, / Death of the old gang' (*EA*, pp. 37–40).

The 'old gang' was not Auden's coinage. The phrase was already current in the later 1920s to designate those responsible for the Great War and the wasted decade that followed. In March 1929 the Communist *Sunday Worker* denounced a left-wing Labour trade union leader as a 'renegade' and 'social fascist', under the headline 'A.J. Cook joins the Old Gang'. Reflecting Auden's own political ambivalence, the phrase allowed radicals of both Left and Right to justify what Oswald Mosley's 1932 polemic, *The Greater Britain*, called that 'surging discontent with a regime where nothing can be achieved', from which his British Union of Fascists was born. In Mosley's words:

The enemy is the 'Old Gang' of our present political system. No matter what their Party label, the old parliamentarians have proved themselves to be all the same; no matter what policy they are elected to carry out, their policy when elected is invariably the same. That policy is a policy of subservience to sectional interests and of national lethargy.[2]

The Orators, published the same year, also indicts a ubiquitous 'Enemy', differing from Mosley only in adding to the names of MacDonald and Baldwin those of 'the Simonites, the Mosleyites and the I.L.P.' outside the National coalition – the first a faction of breakaway Liberals, the last an Independent Labour Party to the left of traditional Labour. Auden's insurrectionary rhetoric hardly differs from Mosley's demand that 'the Old Gang Government must be overthrown and effective measures ... adopted before the situation has gone too far. The enemy today is the Old Gang of present parliamentarianism'.

The 'social fascist' label was de rigueur in Communist denunciations of non-Communist leftists before the Comintern adopted in the mid-1930s the conciliatory 'Popular Front' strategy of anti-fascist, interclass collaboration. It is an indication of how close Auden sailed to the Communist Party of Great Britain (CPGB) in the first half of the decade that the original title of 'Honour', his contribution to Graham Greene's 1934 collection *The Old School*, was 'The Liberal Fascist'. He claimed there that 'The best reason I have for opposing Fascism is that at school I lived in a Fascist state' (*EA*, pp. 321–27, at p. 325). He had already argued, in reviewing books on progressive education in *Scrutiny* in 1932, that the school system, both state and private, was geared to the production of pliable functionaries and compliant citizens. In this process 'unconsciously the liberal becomes the secret service of the ruling class, its most powerful weapon against social revolution'. His politically ambiguous justification for this assertion owes as much to D. H. Lawrence as to the Comintern's 'Third Period' strategy:

Every child responds to the love smarm – for a bit. But emotionally it withers. Before a man wants to understand, he wants to command or obey instinctively, to live with others in a relation of power: but all power is anathema to the liberal. He hasn't any. He can only bully the spirit.

Auden's conclusion is unequivocal: 'the freedom they boast of is bogus, management by flattery, persuading people that your suggestions are really their own. Its power lies in the inexhaustible vanity of the human heart' (*EA*, p. 313). It is only a little step from this to the self-congratulating denunciations of a poem he later suppressed in some embarrassment, 'A Communist to Others', which versified many topoi from this and similar essays, reserving its most stinging contempt for 'That army intellectual / Of every kind of liberal / Smarmy with friendship but of all / There are none falser' (*EA*, p. 122).

'The Group Movement and the Middle Classes', Auden's contribution to Richard Crossman's 1934 collection *Oxford and the Groups*, asseverates that 'we do not think until we are defeated, until the power of action is taken from us' (*Prose I*, p. 50). Frank Buchman's evangelical crusade, renamed 'Moral Rearmament' after 1938, was seen by many on the Left as the recruiting sergeant for a full-blown British fascism, a mass movement more threatening because it was more insidious than Mosley's un-British histrionics and capable, as Auden asserted, of tapping the unconscious of the masses. Sensitive to the 'unconscious hypocrisy' of the petty bourgeoisie, he saw opportunity as well as danger in the middle-class enthusiasm for Buchman's Movement. 'Anyone who has spoken to a young Nazi or Communist convert', he wrote, 'will know that they exhibit the same symptoms' as the Oxford Groupers. 'The Movement has certainly succeeded in effecting a psychological revolution in many people', and the middle class, 'given a crisis of real importance and a compulsory choice ... would seem likely to choose Fascism'. Nevertheless, if it became 'fully aware of the ambivalency of love' and acquired 'a definite material and political programme', it might be deflected in a more progressive direction (*Prose I*, pp. 52–54). Looking back on the low, dishonest decade of the 1930s from his American expatriation in 1940, Auden concluded that Hitler came 'uncomfortably near being the unconscious of most of us' (*Prose II*, p. 69). He would shortly categorize that epoch in the title of his mid-1940s allegory, *The Age of Anxiety*.

Mid-1930s Britain assumed a serio-comic aspect in the long epistolary poem written at the geographical and mental remove afforded by the poet's trip to Iceland. 'Letter to Lord Byron' links the Oxford Groupers and 'honest Oswald's call' to join his storm troopers as siren voices for a middle class '[B]egot on Hire-Purchase by Insurance'. No longer John Bull, but rather Disney's 'little Mickey with the hidden grudge', this cartoon caricature petty bourgeois 'straphangs in the tube, / And kicks the tyrant only in his dreams'. He dreads authority; but 'he dreads yet more / Those who conceivably might set him free', by which is meant, as the reiteration of Lenin's famous formula indicates, the Party that offers 'the choice of what is to be done' (*EA*, pp. 178–81). That choice is presented equally starkly in the first play Auden co-authored with Christopher Isherwood, *The Dog Beneath the Skin* (1935). Francis Crewe, the young absconding heir to the estate of Pressan Ambo, chooses there 'to be a unit in the army of the other side'. In agitprop mode, the original published version closed with an Epilogue that invited the audience, 'Whose hours of self-hatred and contempt were all your majesty and crisis', to join him and 'Choose ... that you may recover: both your charity and your place' in 'another country / Where grace may grow outward'. The closing line invoked a familiar formula from the *Communist Manifesto* to clarify what that choice entailed: 'To each his need: from each his power' (*Plays*, pp. 582, 585).

The sense of metaphysical displacement and dispossession was for Auden intimately bound up with the fear of being exposed in a corruption and hypocrisy at once personal and collective. Yet, paradoxically, such fear could be overcome by a deliberate act of public self-outing and renunciation such as Francis Crewe's, an exposure which, at once feared and desired, carried a libidinal thrill. A chorus from *The Ascent of F6*, the 1936 play co-authored with Isherwood, spells this out:

> At last the secret is out, as it always must come in the end,
> The delicious story is ripe to tell to the intimate friend;
> Over the tea-cups and in the square the tongue has its desire;
> Still waters run deep, my dear, there's never smoke without fire.

Behind all the symptoms of middle-class anxiety, from the corpse in the reservoir to the migraine attack and the sigh, 'There is always another story, there is more than meets the eye'; but it's not always clear whether the 'wicked secret', the 'private reason for this', is truly private or originates in a wider, societal disorder (*Plays*, pp. 352–53). A 1933 review of Winston Churchill in *Scrutiny* attributed just such a self-deceiving (and gendered) duplicity to the English as

a feminine race, the perfect spies and intriguers, with an illimitable capacity for not letting the right hand know what the left hand is doing, and believing so genuinely in their self-created legend of themselves as the straight-forward no-nonsense, stupid male that at first others are taken in. (*Prose I*, p. 31)

To deconstruct this mindset the writer must recognize his own complicity, becoming, as 'The Wanderer' puts it, a 'stranger to strangers', assuming what 'August for the people' calls 'the spies' career' (*EA*, p. 156). It's hard to say how much his emotional ambivalence, the discourse of the double agent, can be attributed to Auden's homosexuality. An unpublished passage from his last co-authored play, *On the Frontier*, suggests as much, observing how 'quick and furtive is the lovers' night', under 'The moon's accusing lantern', which 'brings to light / The sleepers ruined in a brief embrace' (*Plays*, p. 660). Active homosexuality carried a prison sentence in Britain until 1967, a mere six years before the poet's death, and his sense of oppositional marginality, of being on the frontier, a stranger and spy in his own country, in conflict with the established order, doubtless owed much to this situation. In a 1936 article for the Birmingham socialist newspaper *The Highway*, he confided that 'The artist is the person who stands outside and looks, stands even outside himself and looks at his daydreams'. He is 'a mixture of spy and gossip', a spiritual espionage with political implications, as the repetition of the Communist catchphrase indicated: '"To each according to his needs, from each according to his powers", in fact' (*Prose I*, pp. 162–65).

An early poem envisages a deracinated self, addressing an unidentified stranger, 'proud of [his] young stock', confronting a land that, 'cut off, will not communicate', and advised to 'turn back again, frustrate and vexed' in the face of a world 'already comatose, / yet sparsely living' (*EA*, p. 22). Written in August 1927 and predating, therefore, the economic catastrophe that drove so many of his generation to Communism, 'Who stands' prefigures Auden's dominant 1930s theme: the need for an existential leap of faith which would liberate him from complicity with those '[H]olders of one position, wrong for years' dismissed at the end of 'Since you are going to begin today' (*EA*, pp. 44–45). A writer with emotional antennae as acute as Auden's didn't need the cruder catastrophes of what '1929' calls 'the dragon's day, the devourer's' to alert him to the coming storm. Already, during the nine days of the General Strike in 1926, when his fellow Oxford undergraduates were playing at strikebreaking as special constables or bus drivers, Auden had driven a car on behalf of the workers. He later recalled being thrown out of a cousin's house for such blatant class treachery. The enigmatic subject of 'Who stands', hovering between being a mere interrogative pronoun and a generic, anonymized point of view, thus confronts a moral and political as well as geological watershed. In choosing a direction he will be constructing the self he is to become, retrospectively giving an identity to that empty indeterminate pronoun with which the poem opens, finding in the process what another poem calls 'New styles of architecture, a change of heart' (*EA*, p. 36).

"'O who can ever praise enough / The world of his belief?' asks a poem in *Letters from Iceland*. Another poem has farmer and fisherman ask, 'O who can ever gaze his fill … / On native shore and local hill …?'" (*EA*, pp. 205–6). But neither poem fulfils the idyllic promise of its opening lines. The 'harum-scarum' play of childhood in the meadows of home of the first rapidly sees its protagonist thrown into 'the pit of terror'. In the second, the 'fortunate heyday' of farmer and fisherman mutates into 'empty catch' and 'harvest loss'. The 'guilty world' is never forgiven, for 'The desires of the heart are as crooked as corkscrews'. Fear and the 'nesting lie' preside over all, in a dance of death that ends only when you drop. Three years earlier the opening announcement of Auden's play *The Dance of Death* had declared the poet's heuristic purpose: 'We present to you this evening a picture of the decline of a class … Of how its members dream of a new life … But secretly desire the old, for there is death inside them' (*Plays*, p. 83).

Yet, if his Thirties poems indict the physical and moral dereliction of his 'native shore', they also delight in the apocalyptic vision of a broken Britain, claiming in 'Letter to Lord Byron' that 'the old historic battle-field' of the industrial North and Midlands is 'the most lovely country that I know'. As he confesses there, 'Tramlines and slagheap, pieces of machinery, / That was, and still is, my ideal scenery', recalling that, as a four-year-old, seeing a coalfield from the train, he had envied those who lived there, thinking '"how I wish that situation mine"' (*EA*, p. 175). Indeed, it is not the scenes of industrial decline that draw Auden's venom in this poem, but a modernity that is far from run down: the fast cars, Aertex underwear, plate glass windows and chromium-plated furniture, salads and swimming pools of 'well to do' Home Counties Britain.

In Auden's most explicit depiction of the condition of England, *Look, Stranger!* (1936), the title poem invites another mysterious stranger, spy and gossip to turn his gaze on 'this island now'. The book seemed for many first-time readers a patriotic celebration of England, and indeed it brought him not only national but even royal recognition in 1937, in the form of the King's Gold Medal for Poetry, acceptance of which moved many of his leftist literary comrades to personal recrimination. But *Look, Stranger!* is a decidedly unsettling account of Britain in what 'August for the people' dubs 'this hour of crisis and dismay' (*EA*, p. 157). Between the book's publication and Auden's medal ceremony the neophyte King Edward VIII had been eased into abdication by Prime Minister Baldwin, ostensibly for seeking to marry an American divorcee, Wallis Simpson, but also, it now appears, for his Nazi sympathies and contacts. The book's 'Prologue', although written much earlier, in 1932, inevitably aroused echoes of previous succession crises, evoking John of Gaunt's deathbed speech about 'this England' in the apparently patriotic blason of 'This fortress perched on the edge of the Atlantic scarp, / The mole between all Europe and the exile-crowded sea'. But the beatific vision of England rap-idly shifts to the depiction of a disintegrating island, its 'furnaces gasp-ing in the impossible air, / The flotsam at which Dumbarton gapes and hungers'. It ends by imagining 'Some possible dream', which with 'its sur-geon's idea of pain' will burst 'out of the Future into actual History' to excise the rot (*EA*, pp. 118–19).

That the surgery prefigured is a Communist one is confirmed by the book's 'Epilogue' (*EA*, p. 165), which cryptically invokes 'the neat man /

To their east' who ordered the city of Gorki to be electrified as one of those who 'towards the really better / World had turned their face' (*EA*, pp. 165–6). This enigmatic saviour is none other than Lenin, who described Communism as 'soviets plus electricity', and Lenin appears anonymously in various disguises throughout the text – in, for example, the unattributed quotation in 'Our Hunting Fathers', which speaks of the revolutionary's vocation 'To hunger, work illegally, / And be anonymous' (*EA*, p. 151). Auden's 1934 review of Liddell Hart's biography of T. E. Lawrence ('Lawrence of Arabia') had unexpectedly cited the same text, attributing it explicitly to Lenin and comparing the men as 'two whose lives exemplify most completely what is best and significant in our time, our nearest approach to a synthesis of feeling and reason, act and thought, the most potent agents of freedom and to us, egotistical underlings, the most relevant accusation and hope'. It also cited that other Lawrence, D. H., as one also able to see through 'the Western-romantic conception of personal love [as] a neurotic symptom, only inflaming our loneliness, a bad answer to our real wish to be united to and rooted in life' (*EA*, pp. 320–21). These improbable couplings suggest that Auden's own political ambivalence, a desire to be 'rooted in life' which teeters on a knife edge between Left and Right, remained unresolved in the mid-1930s. T. E. Lawrence, 'Aircraftsman Shaw', widely regarded before his premature death as a potential British Mussolini who might cure the English sickness, is a clear prototype for the mysterious Airman who attempts a revolution in *The Orators*.

Look, Stranger!, like the island it depicts, is riven by class conflict, a place of perpetual unsettlement and transit torn between antagonistic world views, of which the split subjectivity of its title poem is one symptom. The beautiful sestina later called 'Paysage Moralisé' is a dysfunctional pastoral that inverts all the traditional tropes to present a series of cameos of 'starving cities' awaiting redemption (*EA*, pp. 135–36). 'Out on the lawn', doctored in its truncated post-war version, 'A Summer Night', into a 'vision of Agape', offers a far less condign vision of 'The gathering multitudes outside', hungry and poor, who look in on '[O]ur freedom in this English house' and 'Our metaphysical distress' with an indignation that projects the poet's own class guilt (*EA*, pp. 136–38). The volume ends with a witheringly bleak assessment of this England where 'The feverish prejudiced lives do not care', answering its own rhetorical questions: 'Can / Hate so securely bind? Are they dead here? Yes' (*EA*, pp. 165–66). En route in 1938 to China, to report in *Journey to a War* on what now seem the opening shots of World War II, Auden penned a sonnet that indicted Britain as 'the false island where the heart cannot act and will not suffer'

(*EA*, pp. 231–32). The conditions for his and Isherwood's departure to the United States in January 1939, with war or surrender to Hitler on the horizon, are apparent in this last undeniably 'English' travelogue.

In American expatriation in 1940, Auden thought more fondly of the island he had abandoned, writing in 'New Year Letter' that 'England to me is my own tongue / And what I did when I was young'. This section of his long epistolary poem rehearses a litany of personalized place names, epitomes of a stereotypical Englishness, which mix affection and contempt in equal measure, speaking of 'squalid, beery Burton', which stands for 'shoddy thinking of all brands', 'the wreck of Rhondda', 'graceless Bournemouth' and a shabby fantasy England represented by the archly pseudo-archaic 'Ye Oldë Tudor Teashoppe'. He set against this an image of Eden – specifically, the valley of the Cumbrian river Eden and the limestone moors stretching from Brough to Hexham and the Roman Wall, a geological analogy for that locus where human beings first 'faulted into consciousness' (*NYL*, pp. 54–55; *CP* 2007, p. 225). Auden had already experienced his own *felix culpa*, consummated by naturalization as an American citizen in 1946. In a 1965 interview he claimed that his decision to leave England had already been made in 1936: '*F6* was the end. I knew I must leave when I wrote it.... I knew it because I knew then that if I stayed, I would inevitably become a member of the British establishment'.[3] Significantly, in an unpublished letter to his brother John in September 1939, urging him not to join the RAF but to stay in India or go to America, he described the coming conflict in terms that drew on Marxist orthodoxy even as, in the wake of the Nazi-Soviet Pact, he pronounced a plague on both the houses which had dominated that 'low dishonest decade' terminated by Hitler's invasion of Poland:

Apart from all this, the war is not our war, (even if I hadn't become a pacifist before now …). On the purely political line, it is a war between Big Business imperialism and Nazi-Soviet bureaucracy and I have no use for either.[4]

Auden's 1964 elegy for Louis MacNeice, 'The Cave of Making' (*AtH*, pp. 18–21; *CP* 2007, pp. 690–93), recalls the England into which they had both been born, coming to consciousness at a time when railway engines were still named after Arthurian knights, schoolboys called science 'Stinks', and 'the Manor still was politically numinous', a culture of deference where individuals knew their place. They had seen in their time 'the sack of Silence' in a world of omnipresent, perpetual noise, emptying churches, the disappearance of the cavalry, replaced by mechanized warfare, the triumph of German metaphysics (Marx, Nietzsche,

Heidegger) and of a relativistic polity in which the concept of 'immanent virtue' had died, murdered by the amoral tyrannies of Nazism and Soviet Communism. But the greatest disenchantment lay in the loss of faith in one's own moral judgment, the recognition that 'we shan't, not since Stalin and Hitler, / trust ourselves ever again: we know that, subjectively, / all is possible'. This is Auden's final judgment on the time and place that had made him, and on the self it had made.

NOTES

1 W. H. Auden, *The Orators: An English Study* (Faber and Faber, 1966), p. 7.
2 Oswald Mosley, *The Greater Britain* (BUF Publications, 1932), 'Conclusion'. The unpaginated text is available at http://www.freespeechproject.com/britain.html.
3 Quoted in John Matthias, *Reading Old Friends: Essays, Reviews, and Poems on Poetics, 1975–1990* (SUNY Press, 1992), p. 98.
4 I am grateful to Anita Money, John Auden's daughter, for permission to quote this unpublished material, © The W. H. Auden Estate.

CHAPTER IV

Ideas of America

Aidan Wasley

Auden's emigration to America in January 1939 marks an obvious and crucial pivot point in his career. Every account of his poetic development necessarily reckons with Auden's decision to leave England, coming on the apparent eve of a cataclysmic war about which he'd spent the previous decade sounding the alarm in his poems. That decision brought with it, not only a profound change of scene, but a fundamental turn in poetic aspiration and identity. If Auden had spent much of the 1930s seeking, through the power of his art, to heal 'England, this country of ours where nobody is well' (*EA*, p. 62), he would spend his next American decades reflecting on the failure of that ambition and actively revising his notion of what poetry could and should be in a world where, as he puts it in 'New Year Letter', his first long poem in America, 'No words men write can stop the war' (*CP* 2007, p. 204). But the connection between Auden's new poetry and the country in which it was written is more than circumstantial. The meaning of the United States itself to Auden and his poems is an essential aspect of his post-1939 poetics, and Auden's ideas of America – even as they evolved over the more than thirty years he made his home there – would play a central imaginative role in his work until the end of his career.

   In the first poem he wrote in the United States, his famous elegy for Yeats (*EA*, pp. 241–43), Auden sounds a conflicted note on the purpose and power of poetry as embodied in the celebrated, recently expired senior poet of the age. Yeats's death followed two days after Auden and Christopher Isherwood had disembarked in a snowy Manhattan in the appropriately funereal 'dead of winter'. But the world and its indifferent meteorological instruments agree that the winter's chill is entirely unrelated to any mourning for the great poet; and even among those few who do mourn, they will merely recall this day, if at all, as 'a day when one did something slightly unusual'. If the world doesn't care about the death of renowned poets, the poem indirectly suggests, it certainly would ignore the migration of two young writers from one country to another (a wish-ful deflection, perhaps, of the sharp public criticism he and Isherwood would receive for seeming to have abandoned their nation in its hour of need). And in the central stanza of the poem, noting that for all of Yeats's passionate intensity 'Ireland has her madness and her weather still', Auden homes in on the larger, melancholy point: 'For poetry makes nothing happen'. In the context of this moment in Auden's career, such a conclu-sion seems overdetermined. Like the plunging Icarus of 'Musée des Beaux Arts' (written a month before his departure for America), Auden's poetic futility in the face of the guns of Franco, Mussolini and Hitler seems not even an important failure to an oblivious, bloody-minded world. His res-ignation to the fact of poetry's practical and political impotence bids fare-well to his public fame as the literary standard-bearer of the English Left and seems to inaugurate a new American career of retreat and diminished ambition.

Yet the poem ends on a striking note of optimism, as Yeats, for all his flaws, is invoked as a humane farmer (revising the unsympathetic plough-man of 'Musée'), a liberating singer and a teacher who can guide his readers toward freedom, hope and communion. Auden's dream of being England's heroic poetic healer is translated into the depersonalized civic image of a 'healing fountain', which in turn transforms, in that central section (which was actually composed last of the poem's three parts), into a vast, life-giving river. This river is Auden's new sign of poetic purpose and his hopeful answer to his own gloomy assertion, only a few lines earlier, of poetry's incapacity to make anything happen: '[I]t survives, / A way of happening, a mouth'. Significantly, this river flows south through an identifiably American landscape of 'ranches of isolation' and 'raw towns' until it reaches, like the iconic Mississippi, the delta of its 'mouth'. For Auden, in this first American poem and in many subsequent ones, America – its landscape, its history and its idea of itself – provides him with a living emblem for how his own poetry – and art generally – can change, survive and, in the face of war and despair, still be a way of happening.

Amid the global darkness, it is Yeats's 'unconstraining voice' that Auden hears, like Keats's nightingale or Hardy's darkling thrush, singing of rea-sons to hope. But Auden's distinctive choice of adjective has a notably American tinge, appearing prominently as it does in Whitman's preface to *Leaves of Grass* as one of the defining features of true 'American bards': 'The old red blood and stainless gentility of great poets will be proved by their unconstraint'.[1] Auden had been reading Whitman while writing the

Yeats elegy, publishing an essay on Whitman and Matthew Arnold the same month that his completed elegy was first publicly printed in April 1939. In the essay, he praises Whitman for his 'formless originality', for being 'at home in his country and his age' and for his conviction that 'Everything comes out of the dirt, everything – everything comes from the people, the everyday people' (*Prose II*, p. 12). He compares Whitman to Arnold's 'disciplined and fastidious abstractions', and presents each poet as representing 'approaches to life which are eternally hostile, but both necessary'.

In the conflict between the two poets (who, Auden tells us, 'detested each other'), we can see Auden articulating his own sense of self-division, with Arnold speaking for his English past and Whitman for his American present. In works like *The Orators* and 'Spain' he had seemingly privileged intellectual abstraction over individual feeling, and in his new writing he aimed to resist that temptation and open his work to the human particular and the plain-spokenly earthbound. However, as he suggests at the essay's conclusion, '[I]f democracy is not to be overwhelmed by an authoritarianism under which poetry would be impossible, it must listen not only to Whitman's congratulations but also to Arnold's cold accusing voice' (*Prose II*, p. 13). Even if poetry makes nothing happen, Auden still apparently believes that democracy itself somehow depends on the world's listening to the wisdom of poets. And further, Auden here presents his vision of his new American project, not necessarily in terms of an absolute rejection of his old English self, but rather as a dialectical incorporation of different selves into an ever-evolving community of selfhood. 'Each great I / Is but a process in a process / Within a field that never closes', as he puts it in 'New Year Letter' (*CP* 2007, p. 206), which was itself published in America in a volume titled *The Double Man*. Auden's poetic self, in true Whitmanic fashion, can contain multitudes.

Just as the Yeats elegy recognizes the duelling truths of poetry's powerlessness and potential, placing the examples of Arnold and Whitman in relation offers Auden a richer insight – what he calls in 'New Year Letter' the 'gift of double-focus' (*CP* 2007, p. 218) – into the world's complexities and his difficult time's specific demands. And significantly, if seemingly paradoxically, he associates that dialectical perspective with America itself. 'More even than in Europe, here / The choice of pattern is made clear', he writes of what he sees as America's special capacity to present us starkly with our existential options: '[W]hat / Is possible and what is not, / To what conditions we must bow / In building the Just City now' (p. 236). As he tells an audience of graduating Smith College students in 1940, 'If coming to the United States has been for me one of the most significant experiences of my life, it is because … I think I have learned here what I could have learned nowhere else: what the special demands and dangers of an open society are' (*Prose II*, p. 66). Repeatedly in his American writing, and especially during his first years in the United States, Auden presents America as an open ground where the realities of modernity and the self are most nakedly exposed. It is, he continually suggests, a fundamentally pedagogical space in its continual revelation of modern man's private moral predicament. In 'Atlantis', in a poem that announces both his transatlantic perspective and his sense of his new country as a source of special existential insight, Auden articulates his American poetic vision: 'O remember the noble dead / And honour the fate you are, / Travelling and tormented, / Dialectic and bizarre' (*CP* 2007, p. 314).

As Auden sees it, America confronts its citizens – and he officially became one in 1946 – with the constant awareness of the inescapability of moral choice and existential solitude. In his introduction that same year to Henry James's *The American Scene*, he used his famously transatlantic precursor's analysis of America to offer his own views on how his adopted country imposes on its inhabitants 'the loneliness and anxiety of having to choose himself, his faith, his vocation, his tastes'. Channelling the voice of America itself, he tells us, 'It's no good your running to me and asking me to make you into someone. You must choose. I won't try to prevent your choice, but I can't and won't help you make it' (*Prose II*, p. 279). Unlike in Europe, where the forces of history, class, religion and region combine to dictate from birth a sense of a self already implicated in a preexisting cultural narrative that tells you who you are, Auden's America is a nation of isolated individuals, solitary questers each in search of their own identities.

There are several implications, both personal and poetic, of this idea of America in Auden's work. First, his image of America as a land of unrooted seekers, burdened by the task of self-construction, clearly reflects his own private crisis of vocation and transition from his English past. If Auden felt both the exhilaration and anxiety of a new life without roots, he could take comfort in imagining everyone around him in his new home as facing the same predicament. Second, America becomes synonymous for Auden with modernity itself. The existential lessons America teaches are ones that the rest of the world will eventually learn, for better or ill. Third, Auden's vision of America is not that of a romanticizing immigrant, dazzled by democratic vistas and myths of progress. Even when he first arrives, he sees America through a nonidealizing lens, with its raw towns, isolated ranches and dense commuters, and tells the Smith students, 'Let me try, then, to paint America not, alas, as it is, but as it might or ought to be' (*Prose II*, p. 66). As he confides to a friend in 1941, 'America is one of the loneliest places on this planet'.[2] And fourth, Auden finds, or constructs, a notion of America that exactly mirrors his new poetic aspirations. In his move away from his earlier poetic mode, he was seeking a 'way of happening' that would offer himself and his readers an open field where the contending complexities of the world were made explicit, rather than elided by abstractions or political wish fulfillment. And in encouraging his readers to grapple (along with himself) with the inescapability of interpretive, moral, and existential choice, his poems were to have a didactic function, illuminating a path, however long and bumpy, toward the Just City. America and his poems teach the same lessons and reflect back on each other. 'The United States are themselves essentially the greatest poem', Whitman declares in *Leaves of Grass*.[3] Auden follows Whitman in seeing America in explicitly poetic terms.

Another important aspect of Auden's view of America is its relation to the question of national identity. Isherwood, reflecting later on what drew himself and Auden to the United States, recalled the paradoxical attraction: 'America is the anti-country; that was why I had to join it'.[4] In 'New Year Letter', Auden makes similarly clear that his definition of America as an assemblage of solitary necessity questers has broader consequences, asserting that the conditions of modernity, epitomized by America, have 'Replaced the bonds of blood and nation / By personal confederation' (*CP* 2007, p. 236). To be an American, Auden argues, it to be fundamentally nationless, an unknown citizen in a land of fellow pilgrim souls. His ambition to find a home in America doesn't require the rejection of his Englishness so much as a conviction that the very idea of nationality no longer matters, and a recognition that the notion of home itself is – in America and increasingly everywhere else – a matter of self-will and personal choice, not of cultural expectation or ancestry. In coming to New York in 1939, he was not merely leaving England behind; he was expressing his wish to escape any national identity at all.[5]

Much of Auden's sense of America as a vast stage on which mankind's existential plight is enacted had to do with his response to the American landscape, which was a continual source of revelation, and anxiety, to him. From the minescapes of his early poems, to his emblematic cities, to the later limestone landscapes and domestic geographies, Auden always looked to the topography of specific places meaningful to himself for broader metaphorical and symbolic significance. And starting with the

Yeats elegy, he found in America's epic natural terrain both a reflection of his private narrative of personal rootlessness and vocational renewal and a projection of that narrative in a more universal register. The winding American river of the Yeats elegy revises the indifferent ever-running river from his earlier 'As I Walked Out One Evening' and turns it into a restorative image of human connection and poetic survival. But the inhuman scale and limitless horizons of the American continent, which he regularly traversed first by train and later by plane on his many teaching, reading, and lecturing tours, deeply impressed on him the relation between the land and the American character. 'There is indeed an American mentality which is new and unique in the world', he observed in 1955, 'but it is the product less of conscious political action than of nature, of the new and unique environment of the American continent' (*Prose III*, p. 511). In America, unlike in Europe, 'Nature is seen as the Other, the blind neuter savage realm of necessity against which man must pit his will and his wits; nature, so to speak, is the dragon and Man St. George' (*Prose III*, p. 373). Describing flying across the country as 'an unforgettable experience' for someone used to the densely populated, historically imbricated European landscape, he sees in the inconceivably large stretches of blankness between ironic points of light below a clearly revealed human truth: '[T]his is still a continent only partially settled and developed, where human activity seems a tiny thing in comparison to the magnitude of the earth, and the equality of men not some dogma of politics or jurisprudence but a self-evident fact' (*Prose III*, p. 508). And the consequence of this truth is not entirely comforting. Citing and revising Whitman once again, he notes the cost of trying to connect across such huge distances: '[T]he Open Road has its own forms of misery, in particular loneliness and anxiety' (*Prose III*, p. 523). Auden found the American landscape powerfully illuminating, but it often provoked in him only further feelings of isolation, which he then extrapolated onto the rest of its citizens. Temperamentally he preferred cosyness and the road more travelled: 'Now when I go to Europe from the States, the great relief is escaping from a non-humanised, non-mythologized nature and getting back to a landscape where every acre is hallowed' (*Prose III*, p. 525).

Auden's views on the meaning of America also evolved over time, as his experience with it changed and deepened. We can almost chart his attitudes toward the United States through its explicit appearance in his poems at different points in his poetic career. One of the very first poems Auden ever wrote was in fact called 'California', although its title refers to an English village and not the American west coast (*Juv*, p. 3). But the fifteen-year-old budding poet surely enjoyed the dissonance between his account of a homely English landscape presided over by 'A round moon like a Stilton cheese' and the exotic, sun-soaked American landscape the title would also ironically invoke. Four years later in 1926, while a student at Oxford, the word 'America' makes its first known appearance in his poetry, in a poem called 'Thomas Epilogizes'. The lines are characteristically obscure, referring to 'The mindless wind, the trumpeter of April, / Thrusting the grass blades into their America, / Like bowler hats before a passing hearse', connoting principally perhaps the national origin of the author of *The Waste Land*, whose style the poem pointedly apes (*Juv*, pp. 147–48). More than a decade later, after a meteoric career and much international travel, but before he had yet crossed the Atlantic, it becomes 'shrill America' in 'The Sphinx' (January 1938), signalling both disdain and distance from any notion of America as a possible future creative refuge. In sonnet XXII of 'In Time of War' (concerning a later phase in that same 'journey to a war', whose homecoming stages saw Auden and Isherwood pay their first brief but intoxicating visit to the United States in summer 1938), we hear the voice of America asking, 'Do you love me as I love you?' (*EA*, p. 260). The poem's tone seems sarcastic, but the question nonetheless foreshadows the requited affection that would bring both writers to America a few months later, this time to stay. By 1939, as he embraces his new life and a new poetic way of happening, the eponymous epic hero of his operetta *Paul Bunyan* declares, 'America is what you do, / America is I and you, / America is what we choose to make it' (*Lib*, p. 46). Other poems from this period, such as 'In Memory of Ernst Toller', 'September 1, 1939', and 'New Year Letter', evoke 'neutral' America, reflecting both the wartime neutrality of Auden's new home as well as his sense of America as a country defined by its absence of national identity. In 1947's *Age of Anxiety*, an English émigré character wonders, 'Yes, America was the best place on earth to come to if you had to earn your living, but did it have to be so big and empty and noisy and messy?' (*CP* 2007, p. 448), expressing Auden's own private feelings that one of America's chief values was in furnishing him with a steady income from his various teaching and reviewing jobs, and also his frequent public theme of America as a site of continuous existential challenge. That poem gives voice to noisy America itself in the form of a blaring radio, screaming nonsensical advertising slogans that distill Auden's discomfort with modern mass commercial culture and his vision of America as the harbinger of man's increasingly technologized future: '*Lasts a lifetime. Leaves no odor. / American made. A modern product / Of nerve and know-how with a new thrill'* (p. 460). In 'A Walk After Dark' from 1948, Auden says goodbye to his first life-altering decade in America and points the way to further changes (he would spend his summers for the next eight years in Italy) with an anxious prayer, 'Asking what judgment waits / My person, all my friends, / And these United States' (p. 345). In 1958, he brings a bit of that American technological modernity with him back across the Atlantic, installing in his recently purchased Kirchstetten cottage a new kitchen designed in 'do-it-yourself America' (p. 703), hinting at the double edge of invention and isolation implicit in that phrase. By age sixty in 1967, he is in retreat from the country that had fired his imagination for three decades, asking, 'Who am I now? / An American? No, a New Yorker' (p. 832). He would leave New York permanently for Oxford and Austria in 1972 and die the following year.

One of the first things Auden wrote when he arrived in America in 1939 was a draft synopsis, with Isherwood, for a film to be called 'The Life of an American'. It told the story – through the perspective a single camera taking the point of view of the never-seen protagonist – of an 'average American' as he went through the various milestones of his representative life. It was, for the newly arrived Auden, an effort at understanding the defining character of his new home and projecting his own private drama onto an American everyman. That film was never made, but interestingly, and forming a kind of bookend to his American career, one of the last things Auden wrote about America was also a film script, and this one was completed. Commissioned in 1968 for an international exposition in San Antonio, Texas, called HemisFair, the film was called *US* and featured documentary images of American history and landscape, set to a poetic text by Auden, for visitors to the United States Pavilion at the fair. The poem is profoundly unsentimental about the meaning of America, walking the viewer through the competing narratives of American promise and moral failure, from hope-filled immigrants to the 'Luckless millions who were made to come / Torn from their African homes by force' (*Lib*, p. 415). 'We have pinned our hopes on our machines', he warns, and he enumerates the gathering blights of poverty, industrial devastation, and toxic waste. 'We are free in our greed', he tells the Texas tourists, to 'Let noxious effluvia fill the air, polluting our lungs'. The poem ends with a rewriting of 1948's 'A Walk After Dark', where the anxious open question of the original finds an answer in his fellow citizens of 1968: 'On each of us depends / What sort of judgment waits / For you, for me, our friends, / And these United States'. The poem is clearly suggestive of the elder Auden's increasing personal disaffection with, and disappointment in, the country that he had found so exciting thirty years earlier. The 1960s were a bewildering, depressing time for Auden, and he felt exhausted by America and by life. It's worth noting, however, not only that the poem ends on the same note of exhortation and faith in the possibility of redemptive human connection that he struck long before in his elegy for Yeats, his first American poem. Also, and just as significantly, even here at the nadir of his American experience, when his idea of America seems most jaundiced, he still uses the pronoun 'we' and unhesitatingly embraces the double meaning of the poem's title: When describing the hard moral obligations facing the people of his adopted nation, that 'Us' includes him.

NOTES

1 Walt Whitman, *Poetry and Prose* (Library of America, 1996), p. 14.
2 Charles Miller, *Auden: An American Friendship* (Paragon House, 1989), p. 33.
3 Whitman, *Poetry and Prose*, p. 5.
4 Christopher Isherwood, notes to lecture, 'Influences,' 1963, Huntington Library. Here I am correcting p. 212, n. 14, of my *Age of Auden* (Princeton University Press, 2011).
5 For a related discussion see Nicholas Jenkins, 'Auden in America,' *CCWHA*, pp. 39–54.

CHAPTER V

At Home in Italy and Austria, 1948–1973

Justin Quinn

I

In the summer of 1948, W. H. Auden rented a house at Forio on the island of Ischia in the Bay of Naples. He would spend his holidays there for the next ten years, before purchasing a house in Kirchstetten in Austria, which became the summer retreat for the remainder of his life. These two European domiciles affected his poetry in ways that this chapter explores – their landscapes, communities and climates imprinting themselves on the intellectual contours of the poetry and providing much incidental imagery. Given his busy life as a lecturer in the United States and UK in the period 1948–1973, his summer homes afforded him greater opportunities to write poetry. More generally, however, his European domiciles contrasted sharply with the geographical immensities of America, and they also offered him denser historical textures, which he knew more intimately. Some of that texture was fresh, and this provided Auden with an opportunity to meditate on the relations of art, guilt and landscape in the wake of World War II, opportunities which he found hard to encounter in the United States.

Yet Auden was never a poet of place in the different ways that, say, Thomas Kinsella, John Betjeman and Charles Olson are. If the details of these domiciles enter his poetry, they mostly do so as part of larger narratives even when, as in 'Ischia', he speaks directly to the island. As Ladislav Vít remarks, 'with a few exceptions, the more than one hundred poems written after the late 1940s reveal very little sign of trying to capture the specificity or *genius loci* of, say, the Mediterranean landscape'.[1] It is instructive then to counterpoint those large narratives with both Ischia and Kirchstetten, as one can assess all the more precisely the growth of what I will call the 'generic' mode in Auden, by which I mean a poetry of generalization, or abstraction that strives to encompass the world and the age, that is not restricted to any one nation or class.

The generic Auden depends, above all, on tone, that is, how he gauges which group he speaks for when he uses the first-person plural. Implicit here is Auden's sense that he was the spokesperson for his generation, that he could find the best expression for what his peers presumed and that, as he progresses, no single individual can fall outside his generalizing statements. Integral to this mode of address is the presumption that the people of the world live in one 'age', the salient features of which are shared by all. We might differ in contingent features such as language, Christmas traditions and so forth, but the fundamental structures are the same. This was not particular to Auden but was a feature of much intellectual work of the period, as writers saw themselves as addressing what Louise Bogan, in a review of Auden, referred to as 'the spiritual illness of the age' (quoted RD-H 1995, p. 226). In the wake of historicist criticism, our own 'age' is suspicious of such generalizing. Thus, in addition to the counterpoints of the summer homes, I will also look at the other images and ideological structures that animate Auden's thought of the post-war period and fuel his tendency to address the world, or the 'age', in toto.

II

In a review of Eleanor Clark's *Rome and a Villa*, he praised the American novelist thus: 'Miss Clark's real service to us had been, I think, to make each of us ask ourselves a question which is perhaps unanswerable, but which will not let us rest: "Why did I come here? Why here rather than somewhere else?"' Why did Auden come to Italy? Not for intellectual stimulation ('one had better stay in New York'), nor for looser morals ('lax everywhere today'), and the contrast between Protestant and Catholic cultures is no longer so pronounced (*Prose III*, pp. 320–21). Perhaps for the classical ruins, which remind one of the parallels between the Roman Empire and our present civilization:

To Miss Clark and to all of us, I believe, in the middle of the twentieth century, the Roman Empire is like a mirror in which we see reflected the brutal, vulgar, powerful yet despairing image of our own technological civilization, an imperium which now covers the entire globe, for all nations, capitalist, socialist and communist, are united in their worship of mass, technique and temporal power. What fascinates and terrifies us about the Roman Empire is not that it finally went smash, but that, away from the start, it managed to last for four centuries without creativity, warmth or hope.

The Emperor Hadrian was individually what we now are collectively, Lord of the World; what we are collectively, each of us can in fantasy see himself as individually. (*Prose III*, pp. 321–22)

Although this review was published in 1952, the parallel Auden draws
between imperial Rome and the world of his time informed his poetry
before his move to Italy (e.g., 'The Fall of Rome', written in 1947). What is
instructive is Auden's image of his 'age'. Although Europe had been effectively carved up by the superpowers by this point, he refuses to accept
the East/West divide as definitive for an understanding of the modern
world (arguably, his historical instincts let him down here). Variations on
the phrase 'our own technological civilization' are frequent in his critical
prose of the period, emphasizing the force of the image for Auden. In his
view, the lives of the people of the world, no matter how far apart culturally, politically and geographically, all share certain characteristics and
are thus bound together in a common 'age', or 'civilization', which can be
invoked with little explanation.

One of the main features of this 'age' is a preoccupation with the self.
Here Auden's intense lifelong engagement with psychology and existentialism come into play. Roughly speaking, the 'self' that Freud and
Kierkegaard presented was outside history and society: its economy was
unaffected by differences of language and nation. This self is not disinterested or detached from the contingencies of existence – it is immersed in
them – but its structure and economy are the same from the Arctic to the
Gobi Desert. For many of Auden's generation, it seemed as though Freud
had laid bare the fundamental structures of humanity, and he did so by
isolating the self. It is not that Auden was ignorant of other languages or
lacked detailed historical knowledge, rather he chose to set those aside in
order to concentrate on the grand commonalities.

The 'self' became Auden's key to the 'age': such selves face technology
in New York, Tivoli, Radnorshire or a small Central European village,
and they share the same reactions. This fuels much of Auden's poetry
of the period: the 'self' is a portmanteau idea for a writer who travelled
through the world, in one place for an airport stopover (e.g., 'In Transit'),
in another for ten summers. It was always to hand as subject matter, available for imaginative examination. The work of Martin Heidegger provides a good foil for defining Auden's interest in the self. In his major
early work, *Being and Time* (1927), the German philosopher concentrates
on the self outside historical and linguistic contexts (there is a vague
acknowledgment of the social context in the concept of *Gerede*), but as
his engagement in Nazism strengthens in the 1930s, he increasingly sees
Being, or the self as it participates in Being, as grounded in particular
historical and national fates (with the necessary privileging of Germany).
This is an existential turn that Auden does not, or cannot, countenance.

Faced with an 'age', or a 'civilization', shared by all, Auden tried to make poetry out of a generic experience of the self, and concomitant with this was a particular use of the first-person plural (John Fuller calls this mode 'generalised symbolic form' [Fuller 1998, p. 485]). Having searched out commonalities, Auden then felt justified in his employment of this mode of speech, which erases tribal, national or linguistic affiliations. This is apparent, for instance, at the beginning of 'Bucolics': 'Deep, deep below our violences, / Quite still, lie our First Dad, his watch / And many little maids' (*CP* 2007, p. 554). Announcing the deep structures of experience as revealed by psychology, the poem wishes to draw all readers, no matter where they are from, into its purview. The scope of this first-person plural is profoundly different from that of Auden's early work: there he tends to speak for a coterie, those in the know, who might be supposed to share the same background as the poet. But by the early 1950s, that coterie has become the world. Moreover, 'Bucolics' was written in Ischia in the summers of 1952 and 1953, and yet it deliberately avoids limiting itself to that particular insular landscape: he writes not of a wood or a lake or a mountain on the island, but rather of 'woods', 'lakes' and 'mountains' in general. A further index of the global scope of the poem is in the dedicatees, indeed in their very names – Alexis Leger, Nicholas Nabokov, Hedwig Petzold, Isaiah Berlin, Giovanni Maresca, Wendell Johnson and Elizabeth Drew. The major 'generic' poems of the period are 'Bucolics', 'Memorial for the City', 'In Praise of Limestone', 'The Shield of Achilles', 'Horae Canonicae' and 'Thanksgiving for a Habitat'. The term 'generic' when used in literature is usually pejorative, but here we should be careful not to imply a contrast with a consistently more 'rooted' poetry: these poems are no less authentic, although not set in particular locales (even 'Thanksgiving for Habitat', which uses the rooms of his house in Kirchstetten).

The shift to the generic is accompanied by Auden's attempt to overhaul his style. As Edward Mendelson remarks, 'In 1948 Auden began summering in Italy, partly because he wanted to write a different kind of poetry from the kind he had been writing in America' ('The European Auden', *CCWHA*, p. 55). That entailed a shift from accentual metre to syllable count: thus on a fundamental level his enjambments become deliberately more ragged, as Auden tried to break open the brilliance of his own style. Louis MacNeice in the early 1940s remarked that 'Auden has purged his world-view of certain ready-made, second-hand over-simplifications and is now attempting a new synthesis of his material'.[2] The style is the man and also the man's ideas.

The island of Ischia enters the poetry primarily as a kind of idyllic 'nowhere' (strangely similar to Fire Island, where Auden had summered before his move to Italy[3]) – an example adduced in a grand philosophical argument. But the generic mode in post-war Auden is offset by an occasional engagement with the particular, not as illustration of larger structures of thought, but for itself: there is an encounter between poet and place that bears the inimitable stamp of each, and thus engenders singular images and emotions. Although there is little sense of necessity in the choice of Ischia as domicile, despite the point about the Roman Empire mentioned previously (after all, England or France might serve just as well for this), his experience on the island, and of the island, provoked meditations that could not have occurred elsewhere. Towards the end of the review of Clark's book he is much more persuasive when he subtly contradicts himself: 'no wonder we are drawn to Italy as to an Eden, idyllic because it is poor and its public life is intimate and local, and the eyes that meet ours are friendly but distant, like those of a grandmother who has survived too much to entertain false hopes' (*Prose III*, pp. 322–23). Having come from New York, Auden enjoys the 'intimate and local' aspects of this contrasting public life: here Italy is viewed in contrast to global 'civilization'; here is a qualitative difference in the life of the place; here we do not have 'selves' encountering 'technology' but an apprehension of history that is visible in the eyes of the inhabitants (and elsewhere palpable in their bodies).

Auden insisted that Italy was a kind of retreat from intellectual life, in contrast to the intensity of New York City, where he mostly continued to winter. Yet he was sought out in Ischia by both friends and acolytes (one of the latter, James Merrill, contented himself with a visit to the island itself and not its poetic master[4]). Robert Craft has described his own arrival:

The boat to Ischia, a packet steamer, absurdly class-segregated, is crowded and excruciatingly smelly. [...] At Forio I transfer to a scavenger-like trawler and am rowed ashore. Wystan meets me at the pier, barefoot and with the 'bottoms of his trousers rolled', and he carries my bag through the toylike town to his house on the Via Santa Lucia. At street level this is an empty stable and carriage room, but the upstairs rooms are ample, bright, and immaculate, except for the burnt offerings in unemptied ashtrays, which may very well represent a protest against the sterility of American cleanliness. [...] We walk to a beach in the afternoon, Wystan at high speed (he is now wearing Plimsolls) in spite of the heat, and, himself excepted, universal indolence. (quoted RD-H 1995, pp. 277–78)

Poetry Auden wrote here is suffused with bright sunlight but also an overwhelming sense of aftermath. The poem 'Ischia' balances between the generic and particular. It begins by bidding farewell to the grand military gestures that shape history, focusing on those who 'broke / with our aggressive habit' (*CP* 2007, p. 541). He contrasts the island with the idea of a 'birthplace', but he says this is not his theme today:

> I am presently moved
> by sun-drenched Parthenopea, my thanks are for you,
> Ischia, to whom a fair wind has
> brought me rejoicing with dear friends
>
> from soiled productive cities.
>
> (*CP* 2007, p. 541)

Auden announces the temporary nature of his emotion in the first line here. He implies that this place is a kind of stopover, where he can have certain realizations and enjoy the company of certain friends before moving on. Ischia is restorative, a retreat from 'our own technological civilization', not a reminder of it. The enjambment across the stanza break especially emphasizes the contrast between the good values in life on the island (friends, celebration, and, later in the poem, improved sex), and the modern 'age' on the horizon, with its 'soiled productive cities'.

Construction work on this modern idyll is, fortunately, halted at the end of the poem, as Auden tempers his description with negative elements:

> Not that you lie about pain or pretend that a time
> of darkness and outcry will not come back; upon
> your quays, reminding the happy
> stranger that all is never well,
>
> sometimes a lonely donkey breaks out into a choking wail
> of utter protest at what is the case or his
> master sighs for a Brooklyn
> where shirts are silk and pants are new,
>
> far from tall Restituta's all-too-watchful eye,
> whose annual patronage, they say, is bought with blood.
> That, blessed and formidable
> Lady, we hope is not true; but, since
>
> nothing is free, whatever you charge shall be paid,
> that these days of exotic splendor may stand out
> in each lifetime like marble
> mileposts in an alluvial land.
>
> (*CP* 2007, pp. 542–43)

The fourth line here is Auden's usual knee-jerk reaction to Victorian consolation: specifically, in the form it took in Tennyson's *In Memoriam*

(CXXVII). Restituta's claim on the people's blood resonates with the price paid by millions in the preceding war, which sets off the 'exotic splendor' of Auden's days on the island. Mention of 'days' reminds us of the temporary nature of his stay there, declared at the poem's opening. 'Ischia' then provides an opportunity to celebrate the pleasures of friendship and the flesh, while simultaneously acknowledging the forces that are inimical to them, a paradox that is compressed in the final two lines. The juxtaposition of 'days' with 'lifetime' suggests the ways in which a 'lifetime' becomes embedded in a greater number of such places but also reminds us of it as a finite span. Moreover, it is not clear if the donkey's owner has returned from Brooklyn or dreams of going there. In either case, the lines are a further healthy realistic complication of Ischia, which was drifting dangerously close to idealized landscape.

'Ischia' is an occasional poem in the best sense, and the occasion was one of arrival. 'Good-Bye to the Mezzogiorno' is a poem of farewell, in which Auden considers differences in climate and theology. It is deeply influenced by Victorian characterizations of northern and southern culture, a good expression of which occurs in John Ruskin's account of Gothic in *The Stones of Venice* (1851):

[W]e should err grievously in refusing either to recognize as an essential character of the existing architecture of the North, or to admit as a desirable character in that which it yet may be, this wildness of thought, and roughness of work; this look of mountain brotherhood between the cathedral and the Alp; this magnificence of sturdy power, put forth only the more energetically because the fine finger-touch was chilled away by the frosty wind, and the eye dimmed by the moor-mist, or blinded by the hail; this out-speaking of the strong spirit of men who may not gather redundant fruitage from the earth, nor bask in dreamy benignity of sunshine, but must break the rock for bread, and cleave the forest for fire, and show, even in what they did for their delight, some of the hard habits of the arm and heart that grew on them as they swung the axe or pressed the plough.[5]

The element that Auden adds is the idea that guilt pervades northern culture (perhaps Ruskin was whispering in his ear, spurring him on, as he walked at high speed through the heat of the beach): 'Out of a gothic North, the pallid children / Of a potato, beer-or-whisky / Guilt culture, we behave like our fathers and come / Southward into a sunburnt otherwhere // Of vineyards, baroque, *la bella figura*' (*CP* 2007, pp. 640–41). As I implied previously, Ischia begins as an 'otherwhere' and then familiarity deepens its particular effects on Auden's imagination. 'Good-Bye to the Mezzogiorno' (written in September 1958) makes some of the same points that the review of 1952 makes more wittily, but the extra element is the entrance of Goethe towards the end, as Auden looks northward to his new domicile in Austria.

III

One of the illustrative quotations in the *Oxford English Dictionary* for the adjective 'Horatian' is 'the bland Horatian life of friends and wine', which comes from Auden's poem 'Christmas 1940' (in the 1945 *Collected Poems*, but subsequently purged from his works). Like 'generic', 'bland' is now rarely used for approbation, yet the *OED* has yet to note its pejorative denotation and records its meanings as 'soft, mild, pleasing to the senses; gentle, genial, balmy, soothing'. For his friend MacNeice, embracing the Horatian mode entailed a retreat from earlier ambition, a détente with the Establishment (as in 'Memoranda to Horace'), but in Auden it takes on different contours. He bought his latter-day Sabine farm, a house in Kirchstetten, about 40 km from Vienna, in October 1957. According to one biographer, the period 1957–63 was the least exciting of Auden's life (RD-H 1995, p. 307); subsequently, Chester Kallman's long summer absences (in Greece) caused him unhappiness. Living in Kirchstetten also meant that Auden spoke German regularly, and several poems of the post-war period dwell on language difference, especially as projected onto the relationship of humans with fauna. But his Central European domicile was no Horatian retreat; rather, this locale had cradled Fascism and thus confronted Auden with issues of guilt and complicity: to consider his neighbours and the immediate landscape beyond his garden became a way of broaching these themes.

In 'The Horatians' (1968), Auden addresses a poet, Flaccus (Horace's last name), who has 'a love for some particular // place and stretch of country, a farm near Tivoli / or a Radnorshire village' (*CP* 2007, p. 772). On one hand, Auden seems to condescend to him (whose 'knowledge of local topography' makes him a likely figure to appear in, at best, a Whodunit), but at the end of the poem he accords Flaccus an admirable, sturdy modesty, as the latter declares: '"We can only / do what it seems to us we were made for, look at / this world with a happy eye / but from a sober perspective"' (p. 773). Auden's Horatianism is not uncritical, but it is profound.

The large work in the Horatian mode is 'Thanksgiving for a Habitat', which takes in turn the rooms of the house in Kirchstetten and meditates on their historical and cultural resonances. Although they are particular rooms in a particular house in a particular village, Auden presents them as archetypes, loading them with his accumulated experience in England, America and Europe; they become the occasion for elegy, disquisition, diaristic remarks and gossip. Location is noted more as illustration as, for instance, when 'The Cave of Making' anticipates MacNeice's scholarly 'interest'

> in facts I could tell you (for instance,
> four miles to our east, at a wood palisade, Carolingian
>   Bavaria stopped, beyond it
> unknowable nomads).   (*CP* 2007, p. 690)

The parentheses are telling, implying that these details are of secondary importance in the archetypal discourse of the poem. John Fuller praises the 'symbolic suggestiveness and allusive range of the later style', and that very range, in 'Thanksgiving' and other poems, assigns the particulars of Kirchstetten to illustration (Fuller 1998, p. 485). Auden's continued exploration of the grandstanding 'generic' poetic mode accompanies an increasing experimentalism, which is especially evident in section VII, as he scatters the words across the page in a 'retreat from rhyme and reason into some mallarmesque / syllabic fog' (*CP* 2007, p. 702).

In 'Josef Weinheber' (1965; *CP* 2007, pp. 756–59), we see greater engagement with the particularities of Auden's summer home, in writing about the Austrian poet who formerly inhabited a neighbouring property, but had committed suicide in 1945. Mid-way through, Auden turns to his familiar theme of historical disaster moving across the world, touching different places at particular times, identified here as 'the Shadow'. Repeatedly, he locates his meditation in personal experience and the place of Kirchstetten. The poem begins:

> Reaching my gate, a narrow
> lane from the village
> passes on into a wood:
> when I walk that way
> it seems befitting to stop
> and look through the fence
> of your garden where (under
> the circs they had to)
> they buried you like a loved
> old family dog.

The tone is signally different from the beginning of 'Bucolics' described previously: the syllabics here give an air of artlessness and relaxed delivery, almost of a letter (especially with the colloquialism of 'circs'). In his edition, Edward Mendelson groups this as one of 'Eleven Occasional Poems': where 'occasional' carries the connotation of 'lesser'. Without making outsized claims for 'Josef Weinheber', I would remark that its lack of grandstanding hardly necessitates demotion. Instead, what is at stake is a view of Auden's late style as not merely 'generic'. The poem is one of the most successful of his last two decades, notable for its lack of historical and psychological caricature and its clear-eyed humanism:

> Looking across our valley
> where, hidden from view,
> Sichelbach tottles westward
> to join the Perschling,
> humanely modest in scale
> and mild in contour,
> conscious of grander neighbors
> to bow to, mountains
> soaring behind me, ahead
> a noble river,

Thus, Auden grounds himself in 'our' valley: where the first-person plural seems to refer to Weinheber and himself rather than the denizens of the 'age'. He lightly touches on the anti-Romanticism that preoccupied him throughout his career in his description of those smaller tributaries, and also in the force of approbation behind the words 'modest' and 'mild'. The 'generic' mode, as I described it previously, erased national and linguistic boundaries, but this poem is notable for the way that it foregrounds those very differences in the final verse, where 'my English ear' contrasts with 'your German', the language that replaces English in the final line, which is handed over to Weinheber, *'den / Abgrund zu nennen'* ('to name the abyss': see the translation at *CW*, p. 58).

Kirchstetten was the scene of many meetings and reunions (also of the unachieved meeting with MacNeice that underlies 'The Cave of Making'). One of the most important occurred in 1972, when Joseph Brodsky first met Auden there (Brodsky provides a moving account of this in 'To Please a Shadow'). A link was forged between the English and Russian traditions that would have profound ramifications for both poetic cultures for decades to come. The Austrian village, like the Italian island before it, at first provided illustrations to grand arguments and then asserted its singular characteristics as Auden stayed on. Thus they provide useful indices of conflicting forces in his imagination: the ambition to write an all-encompassing poetry of the 'age' and the 'world' and an attention to the details of existence that cannot easily be inducted into the former.

NOTES

1 Ladislav Vít, forthcoming essay on Auden and place. I am grateful to him and
   Peter McDonald for commenting on an earlier draft.
2 Louis MacNeice, *Selected Prose of Louis MacNeice*, ed. Alan Heuser (Oxford
   University Press, 1990), p. 90.
3 This is also emphasized by Auden's positioning of 'Pleasure Island' (written
   about Fire Island in 1948) after 'Ischia' in the original publication of *Nones*.
4 James Merrill, *Collected Prose*, eds. J. D. McClatchy and Stephen Yenser
   (Alfred A. Knopf, 2004), p. 646.
5 John Ruskin, *The Works of John Ruskin*, eds. E. T. Cook and Alexander
   Wedderburn, vol. 10 (George Allen, 1904), p. 188.

PART II

Social and Cultural Contexts

CHAPTER VI

Auden and the Class System

Adrian Caesar

In 'New Year Letter', (1940) Auden writes, 'For we are conscripts to our age / Simply by being born; we wage / The war we are' (*CP* 2007, p. 227): thereby demonstrating that despite his recent reversion to Christianity he had not jettisoned the idea derived from Marx that the specific historical circumstances of one's birth are constitutive. In this essay I suggest that part of the war Auden waged with himself was a class war and demonstrate how this quarrel with his family background and upbringing manifests itself not only in his poetry of the 1930s but throughout his oeuvre.

Auden was born into the professional middle classes in 1907. His grandparents on both sides were Anglican clergymen. His father, educated at Repton and Cambridge, became a doctor. His mother, unusually for her times, had gained a degree in French prior to her marriage, graduating with a gold medal from Royal Holloway College. Although both parents were solidly middle class, Constance Auden considered her family connections to be superior to her husband's, and she boasted several relatives who had held high office and enjoyed patronage by royalty and aristocracy. Auden admired his gentle father, inheriting from him a keen interest in illness and the role of the healer, but it is arguable that his mother had the more profound psychological influence: 'We imitate our loves: well, neighbours say / I grow more like my mother every day', Auden wrote in 'Letter to Lord Byron', written in 1936 (*EA*, p. 191). After his mother's death in 1941, her presence lived on as the voice of Auden's conscience: 'mother wouldn't like it' became a catchphrase (RD-H 1995, p. 11).

During his childhood, Constance Auden was the purveyor of 'Edwardian virtues' and Anglo-Catholic religiosity. There were prayers before breakfast with the servants in attendance, and at Christmas a crèche was displayed in the dining room around which the family gathered to sing hymns. The atmosphere of the family home was bookish; Auden was encouraged to read from an early age. By his own account, he also imbibed from home 'prejudices' that he declared he would 'never lose'. These included 'an interest in medicine and disease and theology' as well as 'a contempt for businessmen and all who work for profit rather than a salary' (*EA*, p. 397).

Both his intellectual interests as they are articulated here and his revulsion from large sections of the middle classes are significant for an understanding of his poetry. Although he wished to disown the 'preacher's loose immodest tone' (*CP* 2007, p. 202) and declared that poetry couldn't be a 'midwife to society' (p. 199), nevertheless the roles of priest and doctor attracted him, and the confident, pedagogic tonality of much of his work might be related to his predilection for diagnosis and his search for cures, his ethical analysis and spiritual advice. At the heart of society's ills, Auden perceived industrialization and all that had followed from it; in particular, he regarded large sections of the middle classes as psychologically and spiritually diseased, hypocritical and morally bankrupt. His insistence that he came from the 'professional' middle class, repeated as late as 1971 (RD-H 1995, p. 179), is an attempt to differentiate himself from the bourgeois – those in trade, management or business.

But this is to travel too far, too fast. Auden's quarrel with his own class started with his formal education undertaken at St. Edmund's prep school in Surrey followed by his public school, Gresham's in Norfolk. From there, he progressed to Christ Church, Oxford, but by this time he had already found his vocation as a poet. Although he averred he was 'very happy' throughout his time at Gresham's, Auden in the 1930s more than once suggested he was anti-Fascist because at school he had 'lived in a Fascist state' (*EA*, pp. 322, 325). He was also of the view that most English writers rebelled against their education (RD-H 1995, p. 34). Yet between 1930 and 1935 Auden worked as a schoolmaster within the system he identified as the training ground of the English ruling class, and a significant proportion of his early work is ambivalently obsessed with the world of school.

In a journal entry of 1929, speaking about drama, Auden wrote: 'The Prep School atmosphere: that is what I want' (*EA*, p. 301). Unfortunately, he didn't go on to make plain why he wanted to recreate this inevitably immature ambience. Taken together with his other remarks about his education made in the 1930s, the implication is that he wished to anatomize the education of the ruling classes in order to expose the parallels between the politics of school and those of the broader society. But the resulting tonalities are very difficult to read with any confidence. Far from straightforwardly satirical, in keeping with the equivocal tone of the whole work, the 'Address for a Prize Day' and 'Six Odes' from *The Orators*

(1932), for instance, articulate his deep ambivalence towards the world of the prep and public school. There is a knowing, arch, self-delighting schoolboy cleverness in the writing that at once seeks to provide a critique of the middle class, yet recruits leaders and healers from within it to save 'this country of ours where nobody is well' (*EA*, p. 62).

That phrase 'of ours' is telling. England belongs to the upper-middle and upper classes, and any future political leadership, it is implied, will have to come from that class. In the 'Journal of an Airman' section of *The Orators*, the poem 'Beethameer, Beethameer, bully of Britain', provides a barely disguised attack on the newspaper magnates, Lords Rothermere and Beaverbrook. Here, the 'public' said to be 'poisoned' by Beethameer's paper are described as 'pretty well dumb'. Although it's said they will turn on their betrayer when the time comes, it's Beethameer's cousins who will lead the way by 'recovering their nerve' and delivering to the peer in good public school fashion 'the thrashing' he so 'richly deserves' (*EA*, pp. 86–87).

Even though it can (and has) been argued that the melange of modes within *The Orators* has the effect of providing a radical critique through destabilizing the dominant tones and discourses of political rhetoric,[1] nevertheless it still seems to me that the direction of the radicalism is very questionable and I find myself resistant to the text because I'm not one of 'The Initiates' to whom the writing seems to be primarily addressed. Although the analogy of a public school to a Fascist state seems highly questionable (the progress of boys through the school whereby they gain power and status seems contrary to class relationships under Fascism) there is in *The Orators*, as Auden himself later discerned (RD-H 1995, p. 108), much that might be related to that political ideology. The misogyny, the interest in strong leadership and the address to a small elite group all tend in that direction. Advocates for the work will point to the jokiness, the camp frivolity, in the writing as providing a saving irony. I'm not so sure.

In 1929 Auden wrote, 'the real "life wish" is the desire for separation, from family, from one's literary predecessors' (*EA*, p. 299), and as I have argued elsewhere, it's clear that this struggle for separation forms the central conflict of some of the early poems.[2] But the real social and political problem that bedevils the rest of the oeuvre is once having effected a partial separation, how to rejoin, to reconnect? In both the prose and poetry of the 1930s (notably in 'Letter to Lord Byron'), Auden deployed a Marxian analysis to speak of alienation in general and the artist's alienation in particular. The poet no longer had a confident sense of an

audience with shared values, which left him entertaining his friends, as
he said (*EA*, p. 185) – a rather exclusive circle. On one occasion, he went
so far as to say that poets formed a social class of their own (*EA*, p. 370).
Under these circumstances it is not surprising that Auden could not in
any unequivocal way endorse a Marxist solution to the ills he diagnosed.

If bourgeois decadence and decay is the primary subject of his 1930s
work, his own position in relation to the middle class remains conflicted
throughout the decade. Many of the difficulties of his early poetry stem
from the uncertain attribution of pronouns; who 'we' are as opposed to
'they' and 'you' provide puzzles that might be explained by Auden's own
struggle to position himself as a middle-class dissenter who nevertheless
couldn't make common cause with either the working class or the aristocracy. No wonder Auden was attracted to the figure of the spy reconnoi-
tring new territory on behalf of the old regime.

In a letter of 1932, Auden said he was 'bourgeois' and so would not join
the Communist Party (RD-H 1995, p. 157). Two years later in an essay
about his public school, he glossed further the reasons for his distance
from the working class: 'The fact remains that the public school boy's
attitude to the working class and the not-quite-quite has altered very little
since the war. He is taught to be fairly kind and polite, provided of course
they return the compliment, but their lives and needs remain as remote
to him as those of another species' (*EA*, p. 323). This last remark tends to
rob the working class of their full humanity. In the same essay Auden's
own 'kindness' does not extend to 'the problem of school maids', which,
he says, 'no one seems ever to have solved': 'they are invariably slatternly
and inefficient' (*EA*, p. 322).

In Auden's poetry of the 1930s, the working classes are largely conspicuous by their absence. When he speaks of northern industrial landscapes, it's the machinery that attracts Auden rather than the people.
'Who Stands the Crux left of the Watershed' (*EA*, p. 22) exemplifies this.
The ruined machinery is located in a depopulated landscape. The miners
whose exploits are noticed are by inference villagers; they do not really
belong to the industrial proletariat of the northern cities. It is a poem
about alienation; the middle-class 'stranger, proud of [his] young stock'
is 'frustrate and vexed' because although he looks at the land it will not
communicate with him. The sense of foreboding with which the poem
ends signals Auden fears for the consequences of this separation.

When the working classes do appear in Auden's poems they are either
condescendingly stereotyped as unthinking imbibers of popular culture
or portrayed as the potential purveyors of a threatening violence. The

idea that 'the mob' will realize 'something's up' and 'start to smash' (*EA*, p. 49) articulates a traditional middle-class fear of working-class insurrection that can be traced back to the time of the French Revolution.³ Auden is clearly not immune. And as the conflicted speaking position in poems like 'A Communist to Others' and 'I have a handsome profile' indicates, any easy coalition between the middle and working classes is not envisaged. Indeed the latter poem seems to rule out the possibility altogether.

In other poems, Auden's distance from the working and lower-middle classes is indicated in different ways. 'Here on the cropped grass of the narrow ridge I stand' begins as several other of Auden's 1930s poems do, with the speaker looking 'down' upon England. Later in the poem, he becomes for a moment 'a digit of the crowd' who would, 'like to know / Them better whom the shops and trams are full of, / The little men and their mothers, not plain but / Dreadfully ugly' (*EA*, p. 142). This tendency to prejudice and to speak *de haut en bas* can be seen elsewhere. The Epilogue to *Look, Stranger!* (1936) begins with a line about 'our city – with the byres of poverty down to / The river's edge' where 'rumours woo and terrify the crowd' (*EA*, p. 165). 'Byres' dehumanizes the poor, making them as cattle; 'the crowd' are the faceless masses, incapable – it is implied – of rational analysis or response. In a love poem addressed to Benjamin Britten from the same volume, we hear gratuitously of 'night' that 'shadows with a tolerant hand / The ugly and the poor' (*EA*, p. 162). Although the syntax makes it unclear whether the ugly and poor are the same people or two different categories, the effect is the same: Auden and his beloved are above and beyond.

It is evident from this that Auden's experiences with working-class boys in Berlin brothels had not brought about any sympathetic identification with the working class. On the contrary, as Richard Davenport-Hines has shown, in the time Auden spent in Berlin living on an allowance from his father, he came to see himself as 'the king of Berlin' and was proud that a previous client of one of his rent boys had been Lord Revelstoke (RD-H 1995, pp. 60, 87ff.). It would be wrong to make too much of this youthful *braggadocio*, but it is important to make clear that having sex with the working class wasn't necessarily a radical or revolutionary act; it may have been liberating for Auden but could well be seen as exploitation of the boys concerned.

However this may be, as Davenport-Hines says, Auden's 'snobbishness proved ineradicable', a contention that is nicely illustrated by two quotations: one from the 1940s, to the effect that Auden held 'the European attitude that the lower classes simply ought to go to bed when asked', and the other taken from Auden's 1964 'Introduction' to Shakespeare's Sonnets in which the 'Vision of Eros' is said to be inflected with 'Class feelings': 'no one, apparently, can have such a vision about an individual who belongs to a social group which he has been brought up to regard as inferior to his own, so that its members are not, for him, fully persons' (RD-H 1995, p. 60).

It is this sense of the 'otherness' of the working classes that Auden grappled with in his work. 'They' haunt his poems as problems; he is acutely aware of 'the poor' and 'the hungry', but what to do about the economic system that generates such inequalities remains a vexed question. Following the tradition of nineteenth-century writers whose only answer to the depredations of industrial capitalism was 'love', Auden's 1930s poems, influenced by his reading of Freud and Lawrence among others, wrestle with new modes of loving which might lead to social and political advances. His reversion to Christianity was a culmination of these investigations, prefigured by one of his most important poems of the decade, 'Out on the lawn I lie in bed'.

Written in 1933 while he was working as a schoolmaster at the Downs School, the poem records summer evenings of beatitude spent with his colleagues in a peaceful atmosphere of affectionate belonging. The poet, however, is very much aware that this experience depends on literally and metaphorically shutting out political 'violence' in Europe and closer to home: 'The creepered wall stands up to hide / The gathering multitudes outside / Whose glances hunger worsens' (*EA*, p. 137). The rest of the poem dwells on the conflict between his inherited values and the possibility of revolutionary change instigated by those threatening 'multitudes'. The poem ends with a plea (or a prayer) that the inherited values and institutions that underwrite the private pleasures of the evening might survive and become part of any reformed society.

Auden much later identified the circumstances that provoked this poem as his first experience of Agape – he felt himself invaded by a power that enabled him to know what it meant 'to love one's neighbour as oneself', by which, the account makes clear, he meant his colleagues rather than those beyond the 'creepered walls' (*F&A*, pp. 69–70). It was one of the 'crucial' experiences in his gradual movement back to the Anglican communion that may be traced through his poems of the later thirties. This process also coincided with a number of restless and difficult journeys, most notably to Iceland, and to the wars in Spain and China, Auden having left teaching in 1935. These physical separations from England might be seen as Auden's attempts to distance himself from the psychological and emotional conflicts of 'home' that were gaining intensity as the political situation deteriorated in Europe. They culminated in the joint decision with Isherwood to emigrate to the United States.

Auden later described this move as an attempt to 'break away' from English provincialism. 'Become an American citizen', he said, 'and you've crossed to the wrong side of the tracks' (quoted RD-H 1995, p. 179) – a point of view that, ironically, is English and middle class. The move to America may have provided Auden with immediate relief from the constraints and tensions of the English class system, but predictably it neither eradicated his ambivalence towards his own class or resolved his distance from the 'masses'. Although in some poems from the American period there is an abstract and theoretical concern for the poor and oppressed, 'they' are often portrayed by means of negative stereotypes and characterized as passive, unthinking dupes of propaganda and dominant ideology. The Shepherds in 'For the Time Being' provide a good example. It can, of course, be argued that these are a symbolic group and that Auden is speaking on behalf of their plight; nevertheless it is hard not to feel that the experience of working-class people is demeaned through this portrait as the possibility of independent thought or action to better themselves is denied. The Shepherds wait for the revelation that will release them from 'the filth of habit' (*CP* 2007, p. 381).

Auden's Christianity also didn't prevent snobbery from erupting on occasion, often in relation to art. In 'At the Grave of Henry James' the novelist is praised for ignoring the 'Resentful muttering Mass, // Whose ruminant hatred of all that cannot / Be simplified or stolen is yet at large' (*CP* 2007, p. 309). Auden asks the 'Master' to inspire in him a similar immunity. The 'mass' here might be said to be as much middle as working class – although elsewhere Auden praises the English 'middle-class' and identifies the poor with stealing (*CW*, pp. 258–59). But the most damaging word here is the dehumanizing 'ruminant' with its suggestion of sheep and cattle. We are reminded again of 'the byres of poverty'.

In a 1947 essay, 'Yeats as an Example', Auden exports and extends his class consciousness to the United States. Speaking of Yeats's attraction to the occult, Auden wrote, 'How could Yeats with his great aesthetic appreciation of aristocracy, ancestral houses, ceremonious tradition, take up something so essentially lower-middle-class – or should I say Southern Californian – so ineluctably associated with suburban villas and clearly unattractive faces? A. E. Housman's pessimistic stoicism seems to me nonsense too, but at least it is a kind of nonsense that can be believed by a gentleman' (*Prose II*, p. 385). This passage (which he accepts may reflect an English 'snobbery') recalls Auden's earlier lines about the 'ugly' faces of the little men and their mothers, quoted earlier in this chapter. The sneer at Southern Californians is also evidence of his penchant for slick generalizations. The word 'gentleman' marks Auden's upper-middle-class Englishness.

It is hard to say whether Auden has more distaste for the lower-middle class (the 'lower-ordersy' of the poem 'Woods') or the working class. In 'The Cave of Making', a poem from the sequence 'Thanksgiving for a Habitat' dedicated to his fellow poet Louis MacNeice, Auden refers to the 'remnant' of society 'still able to listen' to poetry. In this context, he goes on, 'as Nietzsche said they would, the *plebs* have got steadily / denser' (*CP* 2007, p. 692), a line as gratuitous as it is ill-founded. In 'We Too Had Known Golden Hours', 'the crowd' is blamed for the departure of 'golden hours' wherein it was possible 'in the old grand manner' to sing 'from a resonant heart'. But 'pawed at and gossiped over / By the promiscuous crowd', the poet's manner and language have been debased: 'All words like Peace and Love, / All sane affirmative speech, / Had been soiled, profaned, debased / To a horrid mechanical screech' (*CP* 2007, p. 620). Even though the rhetoric here is reminiscent of Yeats, the word 'mechanical' harks back to D. H. Lawrence and the idea that industrialization has stifled instinctual responses and 'mechanized' people – an idea that influenced Auden in the 1930s. In the 'suburb of dissent' inhabited by the poet, Auden argues, the only possible voice has to be 'sotto voce, / Ironic and monochrome'.

Happily, this isn't an entirely accurate description of all Auden's poetry of the 1950s. In poems like 'The Shield of Achilles' and 'Horae Canonicae' there are passages of great force, which are hardly monochrome whispers. But the 'crowd' in 'The Shield of Achilles' is seen either marching off to do the dictator's bidding in unthinking obedience or passively gawking at atrocity. In part three of 'Sext' from 'Horae Canonicae', Auden provides a meditation on the mass of people witnessing the crucifixion. The eyes and mouths of the crowd are 'perfectly blank'. A richly ambivalent gloss on 'brotherhood' is given when we are told that 'joining the crowd' 'is the only thing all men can do'. Only this enables us to say, 'all men are brothers'. The possibility of the crowd worshipping 'The Prince of this world' is all that makes them potentially 'superior' to the 'social exoskeletons' (*CP* 2007, pp. 630–31). But we, as an audience, know that the crowd watching the death of Christ were not so worshipping; 'brotherhood' for Auden remains an abstract possibility, but it depends on the individuals within the crowd to join in belief.

Redemption, the attainment of the Just City, then, depends on faith. It is symptomatic of Auden's inability to shuck off the prejudices of his inheritance that when, in the first poem of 'Bucolics', he imagines 'our Authentic City', it is in terms of an Edwardian idyll: he sees, 'a lawn over which, / The first thing after breakfast, / A paterfamilias / Hurries to inspect his rain-gauge' (*CP* 2007, p. 555). It's as if Auden is recalling his father and his own childhood.

In 'Letter to Lord Byron' he wrote, 'You can't, at least in this world, change your class' (*EA*, p. 199); the caveat perhaps indicating that he never strayed very far from the Christianity of his upbringing. As if to reprise this comment, in 1971, two years before he died, Auden wrote to Geoffrey Gorer, 'I am much more conscious now of being British and Upper Middle Class Professional than I ever was when I lived in England' (quoted RD-H 1995, p. 179). In the same year, Auden's commonplace book, *A Certain World*, was published. Here there is an entry on 'Middle-Class, English' in which Auden thanks God that the term doesn't have the 'pejorative associations of the label bourgeois' and, he avers, that English artists, scientists and philosophers don't have to apologize for their middle-class origins as their French colleagues do. Auden continues: 'One may sneer as one will at its narrow-mindedness, its repression, its dullness, but let it be remembered that it was the middle-class who first practised, if it did not invent, the virtue of financial honesty ... The aristocracy paid its gambling debts but not its tailor's bills; the poor stole' (*CW*, pp. 258–59).

Auden did his fair share of sneering at the middle classes, particularly in the 1930s, and later poems like 'Under which Lyre' and 'The Managers' make clear that he never lost his distrust of the managerial and entrepreneurial bourgeoisie. But by the same token, many of his received values travelled with him, however hard he may have kicked against them. Imagining an alternative career for himself, Auden wrote, 'I like to fancy that, had I taken Holy orders, I might by now be a bishop, politically liberal I hope, theologically and liturgically conservative I know' (*CW*, p. 38). Mother would have approved.

Auden is a great poet. His technical brilliance together with his intellectual breadth and reach contribute to his stature, as does the depth and ferocity of the quarrel he waged with himself, from which the work arises. That social class remained an issue throughout his life is nicely encapsulated in the following vignette, in which Auden imagines himself as a 'Hellenized Jew from Alexandria' in Jerusalem on the first Good Friday. He is visiting an intellectual friend and passes beneath Golgotha where he sees three crosses and a 'jeering crowd'. He describes his imagined reaction: 'Frowning with prim distaste I say, "it's disgusting the way the mob enjoy such things. Why can't the authorities execute criminals humanely and in private by giving them hemlock to drink like Socrates?" Then, averting my eyes from the disagreeable spectacle, I resume our fascinating discussion about the nature of the True, the Good and the Beautiful' (*CW*, p. 169). This passage shows him to be aware of his sense of distant superiority to 'the mob' and his tendency to retreat with upper-middle-class fastidiousness from 'unpleasantness' into the safe and fascinating world of abstractions. He also makes fun of his own 'liberalism', implicitly pointing us towards Christ as the only source of hope for social justice. Auden's irony here, directed at himself, provides perhaps a saving grace, but it doesn't entirely dispel the force of his inherited prejudices.

NOTES

1 Stan Smith, *W. H. Auden* (Blackwell, 1985), pp. 52–69.
2 A. Caesar, *Dividing Lines: Poetry, Class and Ideology in the 1930s* (Manchester University Press, 1991).
3 R. Williams, *Culture and Society 1780–1950* (Penguin, 1979).

CHAPTER VII

The Church of England: Auden's Anglicanism

Tony Sharpe

A study of *Auden and Christianity* concludes that 'American Auden is emphatically a Christian Auden'.[1] Leaving England, he found religion; their seeming simultaneity suggests that each demonstrates the same radical severance. His expatriation and his Christianity have both been cited, by astonished critics, as reasons why his work grew worse; an opposite view argues that they brought about improvement; here, however, I want to consider the significance of the fact that, less emphatically, 'American Auden' was also an Anglican Auden.

His was not a sudden conversion; its roots lay in the past, and the more he reflected on them later, the further back they went: if in 1956 he saw first portents in his discomfiture before the locked churches of Barcelona in 1937, by 1964 he included the experience that in 1933 had prompted 'Summer Night'. Later stages involved his exposure to individual 'sanctity' on meeting Charles Williams and to collective loathsomeness, hearing the anti-Polish vociferation of German-Americans watching a Nazi propaganda newsreel. Mendelson has argued that he went to that Manhattan cinema precisely to be shocked (*LA*, pp. 89–90), which suggests the somewhat constructed nature of such episodes, both at the time and in retrospection. Although Auden recalled having drifted away from faith soon after confirmation, at thirteen, only two years later Robert Medley offended him by attacking the Church and so changed the subject to poetry; a letter to an Oxford friend on Good Friday 1927 noted lugubriously 'Jesus died today' (*Juv*, p. 187); Isherwood said he struggled to prevent Auden's religiose tendencies from infiltrating their plays. To see all this is to appreciate what differentiated Auden's 'Americanness' from his Christianity, particularly when both were chosen. Writing to his friend Professor E. R. Dodds in January 1940, he explained his expatriation as the attempt 'to live deliberately without roots' (*AS I*, p. 111) – the echo of Thoreau giving added point; but if his choice of nationality expressed severance, his religious choice had aspects of re-racination.

'There is', Auden wrote in 1944, paraphrasing Kierkegaard, 'no time-less, disinterested I who stands outside my finite temporal self and serenely knows whatever there is to know; cognition is always a specific historical act accompanied by hope and fear' (*Prose II*, p. 214); not-withstanding its antecedent impulses, his readherence to the Church of England was also a specific historical act involving contemporary contexts. In November 1939 he took the first step toward U.S. citizenship, crossing to Canada in order to re-enter as a prospective immigrant. His ambitious long poem 'New Year Letter' was written between January and April 1940; during its composition, in letters to Dodds, Auden was defending his decision to stay in America after the outbreak of war. He also read enthusiastically Williams's *The Descent of the Dove* (1939), sub-titled 'A Short History of the Holy Spirit in the Church', where he first encountered Kierkegaard – as well as finding the title for *The Double Man* (1941), in which 'New Year Letter' was first collected. Dodds in Oxford was, in effect, pressing the claims of historical immediacy from wartime England and enjoining him to look at this island now, whereas Williams's book opens observing that 'The beginning of Christendom is, strictly, a point out of time' (p. 1). Auden had finished his poem before the 'phoney' war was decisively ended by German incursions through the Low Countries, the improvised evacuation from Dunkirk and the rapidly ensuing fall of France (May, June); that June, writing within an hour of hearing radio reports of the occupation of Paris, Auden told Mrs. Dodds he had already consulted the British Embassy, to be advised that only those with relevant technical skills need return. During this period he started experimentally attending Episcopalian services in New York City, the tentativeness ending when he began taking communion, around the same time he was readying *The Double Man* for publication. In December 1940 he wrote to Eliot that 'thanks to Charles Williams and Kierkegaard, I have come to pretty much the same position as your-self, which I was brought up in anyway. (Please don't tell anyone about this)' (quoted *LA*, p. 159). The secret became open with the publication of *The Double Man*: one reviewer described him as 'a profoundly Christian poet' (Haffenden, p. 311).

Auden's reference to his upbringing in that letter to Eliot seems to modify a position adopted in 'New Year Letter' where, echoing some of his debate with Dodds, he had examined the meanings of 'England' and the nature of its claim on him. 'England to me is my own tongue', he asserted, 'And what I did when I was young' (*CP* 2007, p. 224), as if to imply an obligation to put away childish things, and anticipating his later view that he had needed to get out in order to grow up properly. The poem then pays tribute to the enduring significance of his boyhood's beloved 'English area', but even that apparently heartfelt evocation ends enforcing the need for maternal separation – producing the slightly prim rebuttal that 'such a bond is not an Ought, / Only a given mode of thought' (p. 227). Yet, if never doubting the abiding personal importance of his mother tongue, Auden seems also quickly to have recognized continuing claims of what he did when he was young and its given modes of thought. For the desire to disconnect from the mother country evident in his emigration was accompanied, perhaps surprisingly, by reaffiliation to the liturgy familiar from boyhood, associated with the mother church (after his own mother's death he would take pains to recover her crucifix). This is not to underestimate the decisive influence of non-Anglican Protestant theologians, from Kierkegaard through Barth, Niebuhr and Tillich, but it is to draw attention to some continuity within discontinuity; a double man, indeed: an Anglican-American.

The Church of England is historically and politically bound up with the national identity, but Auden deplored this. In 1935 he alluded to adverse effects when, under Constantine, Christianity had ceased to be antithetical to empire but was instead assimilated to it – 'Men are Christian, not necessarily because of a revelation, but because their parents were' (*Prose I*, p. 116) – and he consistently expressed disapproval: 'I consider the adoption of Christianity as the official state religion, backed by the coercive powers of the state, however desirable it may have seemed at the time, to have been (...) an un-Christian thing' (*F&A*, p. 41). One attraction of those radical Protestant thinkers lay in the challenge they posed to such an accommodation, as Mendelson has suggested: 'The theology he learned from Tillich did not recommend a comforting return to the religion of his childhood. Christians of every faith, Tillich wrote, must obey God's command to Abraham to go out from his country "into a land that I shall show thee"' (*LA*, p. 152). The deracination implied by this distantly recalls the Leninist formula Auden twice quoted in 1934 (in a book review and in 'Our Hunting Fathers'): 'to hunger, work illegally, and be anonymous'. He himself saw, or retrospectively constructed, continuities between his earlier political and later religious phases, when asserting in 1956 the proto-Christianity of those thinkers by whom he had been formatively influenced: 'In all the figures I have mentioned [Blake, D. H. Lawrence, Freud and Marx], I have come to realize that what is true in what they say is implicit in the Christian doctrine of the nature of man, and what is not Christian is not true' (*MCP*, p. 39).

Yet, formally at least, Auden returned as nearly as possible to the religious practice of his childhood – albeit that there was, as in Lichtenberg's formulation, 'a great difference between believing something *still* and believing it *again*' (quoted *F&A*, p. 87). He did not identify himself as a 'Christian' (for constant aspiration rather than achievement) but as an 'Episcopalian', 'Anglican' or, with friends, 'Anglo-Catholic': the liturgical persuasion of his parents, as well as Eliot. On one hand this had given him a powerful and abiding sense of the value of ritual: 'it implanted in me what I believe to be the correct notion of worship, namely that it is first and foremost a community in action, a thing done together, and only secondarily a matter of individual feeling or thinking' (*MCP*, p. 33). On the other hand, however, it introduced him to ecclesiastical controversy and snobbery: his mother execrated the Bishop of Birmingham, Ernest Barnes, who was virtually at war with the Anglo-Catholic faction in his diocese to which she belonged (Auden negatively name-checked Barnes in *The Orators* (1932) and his 1970 introduction to G. K. Chesterton); and he certainly knew about the Prayer Book controversy of 1928, when Parliament rejected a revised version seen to lean too far toward Romish practice (see Ansen, p. 78). For, of the Protestant denominations repudiating papal authority, the Church of England is doctrinally closest to the Roman Catholic position; within Anglicanism, the Anglo-Catholic or 'High Church' persuasion is nearest to Rome, and the 'Low Church' farthest from (Dissenters were even further afield). These metaphorical positionings elided into perceptions *de haut en bas*; from childhood, Auden was initiated into a contempt for 'Prot' behaviour and a knowingness about its placing on the social scale: 'When I was young, for an Anglican to "go over to Rome" was (...) something which can happen in the best families. But for an Anglican to become a Baptist would have been unthinkable: Baptists were persons who came to the back door, not the front' (*F&A*, p. 77).

Older Auden found such overlappings of class prejudice with religious punctilio amusing, but his sense of being 'in the same position' as Eliot was modified, Mendelson suggests, by his coming to suspect that a certain snobbery inhered in Eliot's (see *LA*, p. 150n). He later wrote that it was 'no insult to say that Anglicanism is the Christianity of a gentleman, but we know what a tiny hairbreadth there is between a gentleman and a genteel snob' (*F&A*, p. 71). A poet more congenially attuned to the resonances of Auden's Anglicanism was John Betjeman, for the first American selection of whose work he provided an enthusiastic if offbeat introduction in 1947, waxing lyrical about the world they shared:

(T)he provincial gaslit towns, the seaside lodgings, the bicycles, the harmonium, above all, the atmosphere of ritualistic controversy[.] By the time I could walk,

I had learned to look down with distaste on 'Prots' (...), to detest the modernism of our Bishop, and mildly deplore the spikyness of Aunt Mill, who attended a church where they had the Silent Canon and Benediction. (*Prose II*, p. 304)

Aunt Mill was 'definitely over the Roman border' (*MCP*, p. 33); but in Betjeman, met and indeed bedded at Oxford, he encountered a kindred spirit with whom, in the mid-thirties, he sought out eccentric pulpit performers and who, like him, knew which tunes accompanied which hymns. Betjeman, too, was alert to the gradations of worship: the undisclosed title of the poem Auden enviously quoted in his introduction is 'Calvinistic Evensong'. All this was bound up with ideas of Englishness, where he felt Betjeman had a faultless if limited register ('really a minor poet, of course': Ansen, p. 60): other samples Auden praised were his 'technically brilliant' description of the ghost of Captain Webb appearing at 'the Congregational Hall' (to be recited, Betjeman directs, 'with a Midland accent') and lines from 'Margate, 1940', which contrast innocently English pleasures of that formerly twinkling seaside resort with its darkened, invasion-menaced present. Although the previous year Auden had been granted U.S. citizenship, England was on his mind (partly because of his impending visit), for he told Ansen he intended to write a guidebook in collaboration with Betjeman. Interestingly, *The Age of Anxiety* (1947), which he wanted 'to be completely American in language' (Ansen, p. 22), was dedicated to Betjeman and took its opening epigraph from a hymn. At one point, two of its characters ride bicycles through an imaginary England; Auden confided to Ansen about Betjeman, 'that's really my world – bicycles and harmoniums. (...) The real thing is the Church. It's what separates England from the Continent as well as America' (p. 60).

Auden's Christianity may have invoked existential dimensions of hope and fear, but it more light-heartedly included bicycles and harmoniums: a 'curate's bicycle' was one of the bequests proposed to the Church of England by 'Auden and MacNeice: Their Last Will and Testament' (*Prose I*, p. 360). He saw 'humor' as an important component of Anglican piety (*F&A*, p. 71), and throughout his life the Church of England furnished his comic repertoire, from the mock sermons he composed to the impromptu clerical impersonations he enjoyed throwing off and the 'English parsonage' jokes he shared – sometimes with baffled auditors. When Caliban imagines his audience begging to be carried back 'to the cathedral town where the canons run through the water meadows with butterfly nets' (*CP* 2007, p. 436), the vignette is parodically but affectionately Anglican: 'wouldn't it be nice', Auden asked Ursula Niebuhr in 1947, 'to be a minor

canon in a cathedral close?' (*Tribute*, p. 116). With her he shared reminiscences of their Anglican upbringings and 'sometimes became very nostalgic for the nineteenth-century hymns of our childhood' (p. 110): a copy of
The English Hymnal (1906) remained in his library at his death. Neither a
connoisseur of ecclesiastical architecture like Betjeman nor a churchwar-
den like Eliot, Auden became a member of the Guild of Episcopal Studies
and participated in discussions of an informal ecumenical group calling
itself 'The Third Hour' (when the Pentecostal miracle occurred). This ecumenical interest probably best represented his religious stance; Mendelson
cites a 1947 letter in which Auden suggested that his Anglicanism was
essentially a given mode of thought – albeit one connecting faith with
nationality: 'As I was born an Englishman, I returned to a Church whose
split with Rome is largely an historical accident' (quoted *LA*, p. 280).

By 1956 he was audibly less sanguine about ecumenical prospects: 'Into
the question of why I should have returned to Canterbury instead of pro-
ceeding to Rome, I have no wish to go in print. The scandal of Christian
disunity is too serious' (*MCP*, p. 43). Although he expressly wished not
to emulate his aunt's 'spikyness' ('Liturgically, I am Anglo-Catholic
though not too spiky, I hope': quoted *Tribute*, p. 106), he could subject
the Roman Church to disapproving scrutiny. In 1938, writing to Mrs.
Dodds from Brussels, he described Belgian newspapers as 'terribly reactionary and Catholic'; in 1939 he noted that 'its political record has been
consistently evil, (...) its hierarchy is perhaps the most corrupt'; he also
offered the 'coarse generalisation (...) that Catholicism betrays the reason, Protestantism the heart' (*Prose II*, pp. 444, 445). In 1970, disputing
Chesterton, he even explained the genesis of Nazism as 'the revenge of
Catholic Bavaria and Austria for their previous subordination to Protestant
Bismarckian Prussia' (*F&A*, p. 402). Although he toyed with the idea of
becoming Roman Catholic, he more consistently regretted its adoption of
Thomism as its official philosophy (see *Prose II*, p. 134), offering his own
Augustinian convictions as one reason for not 'going over', and annoyed
his brother John, who had, by alleging that the doctrine of Immaculate
Conception betrayed a latent anti-Semitism. In multi-denominational
America and Roman Catholic Italy and Austria alike, his Anglicanism
may have forestalled assimilation by maintaining difference.

Auden's dislike of hearing sermons – deploring in his own work 'The
preacher's loose immodest tone' (*CP* 2007, p. 202) – and his affirmation
of communitarian worship aligned him more with Catholicism, but his
suspicion of hierarchical authority and his individualism were markedly
Protestant traits: 'one might say that, in conjugating the present tense of

the verb *to be*, Catholicism concentrates on the plural, Protestantism on the singular' (*F&A*, p. 87). Reviewing Niebuhr's *The Nature and Destiny of Man* in 1941, he offered the differentiation that, whereas both affirm the doctrine of Incarnation as the entry of the divine into historical time, 'The Catholic emphasizes the initial act of intellectual assent, the Protestant the continuous process of voluntary assent' (*Prose II*, p.134): thus underlining the need to 'believe *again*'. He associated Anglicanism with liturgical practice that enabled such reaffirmation of individual faith within a verbal structure that was communal: 'I am an Anglican. Of all the Christian Churches, not excluding the Roman Catholic, the Anglican Church has laid the most stress upon the institutional aspect of religion. Uniformity of rite has always seemed to her more important than unity of doctrine, and the private devotions of her members have been left to their own direction without much instruction or encouragement from her' (*F&A*, p. 71). Such benign neglect, or disinclination to police her faithful, tolerated a broad spectrum of belief, licensing the Auden of 'In Praise of Limestone' (1948) both to evoke and gently doubt closing affirmations from the Apostles' Creed: '*if* / Sins can be forgiven, *if* bodies rise from the dead' (*SP* 1979, p. 187: my emphases).

Whatever scepticism regarding 'the life everlasting' that poem presents, it is, in the person of its 'nude young male', convinced in one aspect at least of the flesh that rises, celebrating it (more coyly after Auden's revisions) in a logical extension of the holiness conferred by Incarnation. Auden, for whom 'public worship' meant that 'we bring our bodies to God' (*CW*, p. 175), was dismayed when 'flesh' became 'our lower nature' in crass liturgical modernisation: 'not Christian, but Manichean' (p. 226); to rhyme, as once he did, 'urinals' with 'miracles' was to acknowledge and annul a gap (*CP* 2007, p. 316). The importance of the body to his Christianity also finds reflection in Auden's emphasis on the Crucifixion, that tormenting of the holiest body which expresses the inherent brokenness of being and, in its cruelty and violence, accurately reflects the world that is the case; in 1964 he expressed agreement with Simone Weil's words: 'If the Gospels omitted all mention of Christ's resurrection, faith would be easier for me. The Cross by itself suffices me' (quoted in *F&A*, p. 52). His own identification with that event underlay his choice of faith: 'Why Jesus and not Socrates or Buddha or Confucius or Mahomet? Perhaps all one can say is: "None of the others arouse *all* sides of my being to cry 'Crucify him'"' (*Prose II*, p. 197). He himself experienced love's destructive repudiation and accompanying loss of self, in becoming 'the prey of demonic powers' (*MCP*, p. 41), through his own momentarily murderous despair confronting Chester Kallman's infidelity in 1941. This led to Auden's sympathy for Joseph's predicament, in 'For the Time Being', but also to the Christmas salutation he addressed to Kallman that year: in a kind of idiosyncratic litany, secular and devout, heartfelt and humorous, components of the Christmas story were sequentially linked to aspects of their own relationship, ending with the declaration, 'As this morning I think of the Good Friday and the Easter Sunday already implicit in Christmas Day, I think of you' (quoted *LA*, p. 183).

Auden's Anglicanism was precisely that: his unauthorized version of a Church of England that condoned conscientious discrepancies, 'a community in which wide divergences of doctrine and rite can and do exist without leading necessarily to schism or excommunication' (*MCP*, p. 33). The nature of his allegiance is shown in 'Whitsunday in Kirchstetten' (1962), in which he defined himself as 'obedient to Canterbury'; *About the House* (1965) opened celebrating his Austrian 'habitat' but closed here, at the house of God (Auden's poetry, unlike either Eliot's or Betjeman's, seldom involved churches). The poem models an unmilitant sectarian obedience, concerned as it is both to evoke and question a series of boundaries. On Whitsunday, Christians celebrate Pentecost, for Williams 'the visible beginning of the Church' (*The Descent of the Dove*, p. 1) and for Auden the breaking down of linguistic barriers, a gift of 'ears' rather than 'tongues' in 'a miracle of instantaneous translation': 'The curse of Babel, one might say, was redeemed because for the first time men were willing in absolute fullness of heart to speak and to listen, not merely to their sort of person but to total strangers' (*SW*, p. 139). The feast suggests inclusiveness and universal intelligibility, but 'Whitsunday in Kirchstetten' (*CP* 2007, pp. 742–44) observes a disharmonious world. Its dedicatee, a German Catholic priest who had fled the Nazis, involved himself in liturgical issues as a modernizer rather than, like Auden, a traditionalist; John Auden recalled that his treatment by the Church (he seems to have clashed with his American bishop) influenced Wystan against becoming Roman Catholic: therefore even this ecumenical dedication conceals discords. The epigraph quotes 'The Hymn of Jesus' in 'The Acts of John', which, from the New Testament apocrypha, stands outside the canon: leading into the poem's structural concern with things inside (the act of worship) and outside (the nearby autobahn and, beyond, a Europe politically divided 'East' versus 'West', and an Africa then in process of emerging from colonialist exploitation). Although literally inside, the poet is, he acknowledges, a 'metic'; this poem opens in a foreign tongue (his first to do so) and whilst its inclusion of non-English words and phrases suggests

Pentecostal receptivity, these may denote 'tribal formulae', defended on old historic battlefields that persist in territorial demarcations – religious, economic, social and military – also registered. This Anglican poet is accepted by this Roman Catholic congregation, but how far he is really 'their sort of person' leads to the more broadly based ethnic inquisition of 'my kind' and its rights of ownership, now that the 'Big White Christian upstairs' seems to have died and can no longer be invoked – the poem over-optimistically hopes – to 'bless our bombs' (*A Certain World* includes Chaplain Downey's prayer preceding the Nagasaki bombing). Auden had once mocked himself, corn-afflicted as he was, for imagining himself dancing, and his final image acknowledges an absurdity appropriate to the poem's part-resolved contrarieties: like his bellowed participation in the opening hymn, this closing 'Grace' may be ungainly as well as amazing.

Private devotion was important to Auden, as the friend who interrupted it attested; but so were the public prescriptions of *The Book of Common Prayer*, defining 'a community in action' renewed by repetition through the centuries. The relation of the individual worshipper to liturgical tradition resembles the reader's relation to canonical literary texts; Auden had hinted at the parallel between the ingestion of Yeats's corpus by its future readers and the communicant's receiving 'the body of Christ': both are a means of breaking bread with the dead without which, he opined, 'a fully human life is impossible' (*SW*, p. 141). The utterance of the self through liturgical formulations also offered a distant model for *A Certain World* (1970), an indirect autobiography in which Auden self-effacingly expressed his sense of his world principally through the writings of others and that ended citing St. Augustine: 'The truth is neither mine nor his nor another's; but belongs to us all whom Thou callest to partake of it, warning us terribly, not to account it private to ourselves, lest we be deprived of it' (*CW*, p. 425). Or, rather, it would have ended in that resonantly appropriate way had not Auden thought of extra items necessitating an ensuing 'Addenda' that, like the pious carpet weaver's intentional flaw, forestalls any presumptuousness inherent in perfection.

'The imperfect is our paradise', asserted Wallace Stevens (in 'The Poems of Our Climate') – with which the author of 'In Praise of Limestone' would agree, notwithstanding its sideswipe at Stevens.[2] Niebuhr, in a passage Auden singled out for its brilliance, wrote that 'Man contradicts himself within the terms of his true essence' (*Prose II*, p. 133): if invariably we 'fall down in the dance' (at the end of 'New Year Letter'), we affirm the possibility of faultless performance even by marring it. Such imperfections and self-contradictions were characteristic, too, of England's Church: 'Its credentials are its incompleteness', its future Archbishop wrote in 1936, 'It is clumsy and untidy, it baffles neatness and logic. For it is not sent to commend itself as "the best type of Christianity", but by its very brokenness to point to the universal Church'.[3] The Auden who in 1939 wished never to see England again but in 1953 was moved by listening to a broadcast of the Coronation[4] – that ceremonial of nationhood – was well accommodated within the dear old bag of Anglicanism, an institution silly like us, its clumsy aspects seemingly inseparable from its grace; 'People don't understand', he once declared, 'that it's possible to believe in a thing and ridicule it at the same time'.[5] He prefaced his essay about his own Anglicanism with the remark, 'The way in is sometimes the way round' (*MCP*, p. 31), but he perhaps came to think that the way round was, finally, the true and only way. His Kirchstetten Sundays, joining an imperfect community imperfectly in action, seem as appropriate to the faith he professed as to the church where he worshipped under a foreign code of conscience and was interred, an honoured guest, in a tactfully negotiated ecumenical ceremony.

NOTES

1 Arthur Kirsch, *Auden and Christianity* (Yale University Press, 2005), p. 170.
2 For an extended consideration of this connection, see my essay 'Final Beliefs: Stevens and Auden', *Literature and Theology* vol. 25 no. 1, March 2011, pp. 64–78.
3 A. M. Ramsey, *The Gospel and the Catholic Church* (1936), quoted in S. W. Sykes, *The Integrity of Anglicanism* (Mowbrays, 1978), p. 3.
4 Remarks made, respectively, in letters to Margaret Gardiner (19 November 1939) and Elizabeth Mayer ('Corpus Christi', 1953); both in the Berg Collection, New York Public Library.
5 Quoted in a review of *Age of Anxiety*, *Time*, vol. 50 no. 3 (21 July 1947), p. 100.

CHAPTER VIII

British Homosexuality, 1920–1939

Gregory Woods

'Between the two German wars of the present century the fashionable vice was probably homosexuality'. So wrote T. H. White in 1950.[1] From the perspective of the twentieth century's midpoint, it had become clear that this was no longer going to be the case – indeed, that it was going to become fashionable to denounce homosexuality as the worst of the vices. But the interwar period was another matter: two public models of the visible homosexual (frivolous and serious) had appeared and lingered, almost to the extent of becoming tolerable – if only to the literati, and if only to some of them. In their 1941 social history of the same period in Britain, Robert Graves and Alan Hodge wrote:

Homosexuality had been on the increase among the upper classes for a couple of generations, though almost unknown among working people. The upper-class boarding-school system of keeping boy and girl away from any contact with each other was responsible. In most cases the adolescent homosexual became sexually normal on leaving school; but a large minority of the more emotional young people could not shake off the fascination of perversity. In post-war university circles, where Oscar Wilde was considered both a great poet and a martyr to the spirit of intolerance, homosexuality no longer seemed a sign of continued adolescence … [Male] homosexuals spent a great deal of their time preaching the aesthetic virtues of the habit, and made more and more converts.[2]

They added, with apparent approval, that lesbians 'were more quiet about their aberrations at first' – until they heard of the example of Weimar Berlin: 'in certain Berlin dancing-halls, it was pointed out, women danced only with women and men with men. Germany, land of the free! The Lesbians took heart and followed suit, first in Chelsea and St. John's Wood and then in the less exotic suburbs of London'.

Looking back at the 1930s from the vantage point of the 1970s, Julian Symons wrote:

The Thirties might also be called the homosexual decade, in the sense that in these years homosexuality became accepted as a personal idiosyncrasy: and became, too, a sort of password, so that several homosexual writers of little talent found their work accepted by magazines simply on a basis of personal friendship. It would probably be untrue to say that any writer of heterosexual instincts suffered seriously through this homosexual literary tendency among the young, but the assessment of writers on the basis of their sexual attractiveness can hardly be anything but damaging to literary standards.

Symons clearly had no conception of the difficulties a homosexual writer might have faced if he or she had chosen to write openly, rather than obliquely, about homosexual relationships – think of the undissembling openness of Radclyffe Hall's *The Well of Loneliness*, as against the complex codes of Isherwood's Berlin stories. He added:

About all this, it may seem, there is nothing specifically new ... A, B and C, those well-known homosexual writers, were firmly established with their young men for years before the Thirties. That is true enough: the unique contribution made by the intelligentsia in the Thirties to the change in our sexual ethic rested in the attitude they adopted, by which the assertion of sexual freedom appeared to be a social duty.[3]

If to some limited extent 'fashionable', then, between the wars, male homosexuality adopted different styles in the two decades. The symbolic queer figure of the 1920s was an affluent and whimsical queen, dedicated to aestheticism and leisure, with a wandering eye for a burly sportsman. As this figure went out of fashion in the 1930s he was replaced by the more masculine and politicized artist, espouser of causes and befriender of workers. Middle class rather than upper class himself, he nevertheless moved between exalted circles – having met the right people at Oxford or Cambridge – and the pubs and meeting rooms of the working class, romanticizing the working man as the emblematic figure in an ideal future of social equality. It was to the latter group, broadly speaking, that W. H. Auden and his closest literary friends belonged.

Looming over all homosexual men in Britain was the fate of Oscar Wilde in 1895. What had seemed smart and risqué to a metropolitan audience of the arts became, to the courts and the press, the deepest of scandals. The death penalty for buggery had been replaced, in 1861 in England and Wales and in 1889 in Scotland, by penal servitude for between ten years and life. But section 11 of the Criminal Law Amendment Act 1885 then criminalized all male homosexual acts short of buggery. This section, the so-called Labouchère Amendment, introduced into law the concept of 'gross indecency' – a crime far broader and easier both to commit and to prove than buggery – for which the penalty was to be imprisonment for up to two years, 'with or without hard labour'. It was for this that Oscar

Wilde was convicted.[4] In 1947 Auden remarked to Alan Ansen that he'd 'like to throw shit on [Labouchère's] grave' (quoted RD-H 1995, p. 243).

Wilde was godfather to the 1920s aesthete queen. Men like Ronald Firbank, Brian Howard, Harold Acton, Stephen Tennant and Cecil Beaton – although each unique in his way – and fictional characters like Reginald (in Saki's short stories), Anthony Blanche (in Evelyn Waugh's *Brideshead Revisited*), Ambrose Silk (in Waugh's *Put Out More Flags*) and Cedric Hampton (in Nancy Mitford's *Love in a Cold Climate*) – made a significant contribution to the visibility of homosexuality in English society. Their variety boiled down to the unity of a popular, and not so popular, stereotype: the effeminate, arty, upper-class pansy.

Waugh's novels are scattered with representations of such men, all of them located somewhere beside, or even astride, a fault line between frivolity and seriousness. Towards the end of *Black Mischief* (1932), Sonia says to Basil Seal, 'people have gone serious lately'. Basil has been away in East Africa, attempting to modernize the island nation of Azania; on his return he has begun to notice the social consequences of the Wall Street Crash. Soon after a brief conversation with Seal, Sonia says to her husband, 'D'you know, deep down in my heart I've got a tiny fear that Basil is going to turn serious on us too!'[5] For all but the uppermost crust, turning 'serious' meant coping with economic reality – mainly by finding a way of earning a living. It meant, as in any period, growing up, settling down, perhaps getting married and starting a family. For some – like Waugh himself – it meant leaving their bisexuality behind. Yet when the Bright Young People looked back on their prime from the more sober times of the 1930s and 1940s, they often lit on their gaudiest homosexual friends as epitomes of all that was most vibrant and exciting about the 1920s. In Waugh's *Put Out More Flags* (1942), Ambrose Silk personifies modern culture, and his homosexuality is crucial to his modernity. Yet his heyday is past, as is that of the age he represents:

It had been a primrose path in the days of Diaghilev; … at Oxford he had recited *In Memoriam* through a megaphone to an accompaniment hummed on combs and tissue paper; in Paris he had frequented Jean Cocteau and Gertrude Stein; he had written and published his first book there, a study of Montparnasse Negroes that had been banned in England by Sir William Joynson-Hicks [the Home Secretary from 1924 to 1929]. That way the primrose path led gently downhill to the world of fashionable photographers, stage sets for [C.B.] Cochrane, Cedric Lyne and his Neapolitan grottoes.

In 1929, the year of the Wall Street Crash, Silk turns from dalliance to austerity, moves to Germany and – ignoring the promiscuous pleasures for which so many Englishmen would have gone there – quietly falls in love with a Brownshirt called Hans. When the Nazis subsequently find out that Silk is a Jew, Hans is sent to a concentration camp: for them he represents 'something personal and private in a world where only the mob and the hunting pack had the right to live'.[6] So Modernism degenerates in two distinct ways: in England its aesthetic is watered down to the frivolous level of the Cochrane revues and fashion magazines (Waugh is mainly getting at men like Noël Coward and Cecil Beaton), whereas in Germany its aesthetic side is discarded in favour of the drive for the industrial and military efficiency of fascism.

In *Brideshead Revisited* (1945), it is again the homosexual man who best represents international modernity: Anthony Blanche never succumbs to the nostalgia that afflicts the book's narrator (and, indeed, its author). Blanche, too, like Ambrose Silk, has experienced Modernism at first hand; and his Modernism, too, is of a distinctly homosexual sort:

[H]e dined with Proust and Gide and was on closer terms with Cocteau and Diaghilev; Firbank sent him novels with fervent inscriptions; he had aroused three irreconcilable feuds in Capri; by his own account he had practised black art in Cefalù [presumably with Aleister Crowley] and had been cured of drug-taking in California and of an Oedipus complex in Vienna.[7]

He has recited not *In Memoriam* but *The Waste Land* through a megaphone across an Oxford quad. And, like Ambrose Silk, he has sought love not among the boys of Oxford, whose homoeroticism is represented as being a sign of arrested development (embodied in Sebastian Flyte's teddy bear, Aloysius), but among the men of Germany: he has a relationship with an unnamed policeman in Munich, and later lives with a man in Morocco. This man, Kurt, eventually returns to Germany and becomes a storm trooper, but he is not allowed to withdraw when he has second thoughts; eventually he hangs himself in a concentration camp.

Yet one should not underestimate the willingness of a class content to be amused rather than offended, to ignore potential affront in favour of more palatable amusement. For, despite everything one might assume about the Wilde scandal's having irreversibly linked effeminacy and homosexuality in the general consciousness, it was still possible to play the aesthete without being fingered as a sodomite. Speaking of an occasion when he appeared at a party in the 1920s in a tunic embroidered with chincherinchee and narcissus, Robert Medley (one of Auden's early affections) said, 'Nobody thought I was gay, dear, they just enjoyed the smell'.[8]

Jocelyn Brooke heard England's transition from the 1920s to the 1930s in the sounds of male voices. In *The Military Orchid* (1948), he wrote of the earlier decade:

The Roaring Twenties …! But the label, perhaps, is a mistake. The true voice of the epoch was, surely, not so much a full-throated roar as a kind of exacerbated yelping; a false-virile voice tending, in moments of stress, to rise to an equivocal falsetto – half-revealing (like the voice of M. de Charlus [in Proust's *Recherche*]) behind its ill-assumed masculinity a whole bevy of *jeunes filles en fleurs*.

When Brooke went on to speak of the decade's end, it is clear that he was thinking of one generation taking over from its predecessor. Having described the 1920s as a crowd of sissies verbally cross-dressing as men, he cast the 1930s, too, in terms of a homosexual style – but a very different one:

The intellectual *chichi* which had marked the vanishing era was sternly rebuked; and the strident war-cries of homocommunism echoed from Russell Square [in Bloomsbury] all the way to Keats Grove [in Hampstead]. A number of ageing Peter Pansies wisely fled to the country, there to cultivate their Olde Worlde Gardens among the pylons and the petrol pumps; and an epoch which had begun with a bang came to an end, all too appropriately, with a whimper.[9]

In essence, what he was describing was the ceding of cultural power by what was left, in the 1920s, of the pre-war Belle Époque to the brash young intellectuals of Modernism, the 'pylon poets' and the followers of Eliot (whose 'The Hollow Men' had ended 'Not with a bang but a whimper' in 1925). It was Stephen Spender who famously published the poem 'The Pylons' in 1933, but it was to the wider Auden group, and the Zeitgeist in general, that Brooke referred. When Louis MacNeice visited Cambridge in April 1936, he found that university 'still full of Peter Pans but all the Peter Pans were now talking Marx'. Stephen Spender later wrote of 'the Thirties when everything became politics'. The camp styles of the 1920s aesthete had given way to the more down-to-earth, in some respects duller, masculinity of the Auden group and those who followed in their wake. By the end of the 1930s the aesthetes would seem dated and irrelevant survivors of a less complicated era. On 27 October 1939, Spender lunched with the ex–Bright Young Thing Brian Howard and then fixed him in his diary: 'rather silly, I thought, with his feminine way of tilting his head up as though under a cloche hat, and looking at you through half-closed eyelids'.[10]

Similar changes, in both style and substance, were taking place across Europe. Curzio Malaparte outlined the changes in his novel *The Skin* (first published in 1949 as *La Pelle*):

Those same noble apostles of Narcissus who had hitherto posed as decadent aesthetes, as the last representatives of a weary civilization, sated with pleasures and sensations, and who had looked to such as Novalis, the Comte de Lautréamont and Oscar Wilde, to Diaghilev, Rainer Maria Rilke, D'Annunzio, Gide, Cocteau, Marcel Proust, Jacques Maritain, Stravinsky and even Barrès to furnish the motifs of their played-out '*bourgeois*' aestheticism, now posed as Marxist aesthetes; and they preached Marxism just as hitherto they had preached the most effete narcissism, borrowing the motifs of their new aestheticism from Marx, Lenin, Stalin and Shostakovich, and referring contemptuously to bourgeois sexual conventionalism as a debased form of Trotskyism. They deluded themselves that they had found in Communism a point of contact with the ephebes of the proletariat – a secret conspiracy, a new covenant, moral and social as well as sexual in character. From '*ennemis de la nature*,' as Mathurin Régnier called them, they had changed into '*ennemis du capitalisme*.' Who would ever have thought that among other things the [First World] war would have bred a race of Marxist pederasts?[11]

In Britain, it was the Auden group that most visibly exemplified this cultural tendency; and as the supposed leader of the group, and its most authoritatively vocal member, he was himself its embodiment.

The schoolboy Auden was already talking easily and dispassionately about homosexuality when he met the first adult homosexual he knew as such, Michael Davidson, who helped him get his first poem published. Already a fully paid-up Freudian, Auden had a tendency to treat the matter as being worthy more of analysis than of shame or embarrassment. In his final school year, when he fell in love with John Pudney, he lectured the younger boy about homosexuality, self-abuse, D. H. Lawrence, socialism and Sigmund Freud. When he went up to Christ Church, Oxford, he did not become an aesthete, in part because he could not have afforded the necessary display of fine living. He did, however, become sexually active, and, within the bounds of sanity, was open about it. Uninhibited and apparently guiltless, he might have enjoyed himself more had he not been in the habit of falling in love with sturdily heterosexual athletes. Not until his trip to Germany, and to Berlin in particular, between October 1928 and July 1929 did he have the access to such men's bodies that an economic depression afforded relatively wealthy, foreign visitors.

Often flippant, most of his early writing's references to homosexuality are, by the standards of a later era, negative. He used the epithets 'poof', 'pansy', 'pathic', 'bugger' and 'queer', and he consistently referred to homosexuality as a weakness, or as a 'crooked' deviation from 'straight' logic. However, such references, each in itself apparently only glancing, do build up to a clear demonstration of interest – so much so, indeed, that as early as 1938 the American critic James G. Southworth wrote an essay characterizing Auden as a campaigner on behalf of homosexuals (or Urnings, in the terminology of K. H. Ulrichs), among whom he was himself to be numbered: 'Aware of the anomalous position of the Urning in modern society he has sought by his frankness of utterance to rid himself of any guilt or inferiority'. On the evidence of *Poems* (1930), *The Orators* (1932) and *Look, Stranger!* (1936) he concluded that Auden had made 'an impassioned plea for tolerance toward the Urning whose position in society is anomalous even though he is the product of that society'.[12]

His sexual boldness notwithstanding, Auden was aware of the need for strategic discretion. He had several scares, some involving written indiscretions. One was in 1923, when his mother found and read a homoerotic poem he had written about his school friend Robert Medley. She passed the poem to her husband, who lectured the two boys about schoolboy intimacy and destroyed the poem. Another, at Oxford, saw him obliged to buy his college bedmaker's silence, after having been caught in bed with John Betjeman (RD-H 1995, pp. 48–49, 108). Potentially far more serious was the incident in 1934, when he and Isherwood went to meet the latter's German lover, Heinz, at Harwich. An immigration officer, having read one of Isherwood's letters to Heinz, doggedly and suspiciously questioned him about the nature of his family's relationship with this working-class foreigner before finally refusing to allow Heinz into the country. Auden's diagnosis of the situation was that the officer had seen through Isherwood at once because he was himself homosexual.[13]

The modern history of homosexuality is also, perforce, a history of homophobic responses to homosexuality. In *The Road to Wigan Pier* (1937), George Orwell casually distances himself from current English poetry with a pair of references to 'the Nancy poets'. He apparently expects his reader, the typical subscriber to Victor Gollancz's Left Book Club, not only to know whom he means, but also to agree with him about them. He does not mean the effeteness of poets in general but the homosexuality of a particular clique. In both passages, Orwell implicitly vaporizes the claims of the writers in question to a socialist conscience.

Practically everything we do, from eating an ice to crossing the Atlantic, and from baking a loaf to writing a novel, involves the use of coal, directly or indirectly. For all the arts of peace coal is needed; if war breaks out it is needed all the more. [...] In order that Hitler may march the goosestep, that the Pope may denounce Bolshevism, that the cricket crowds may assemble at Lord's, that the Nancy poets may scratch one another's backs, coal has got to be forthcoming.

In the second passage, he casts his net even wider.

You and I and the editor of the *Times Lit. Supp.*, and the Nancy poets and the Archbishop of Canterbury and Comrade X, author of *Marxism for Infants* – all of us really owe the comparative decency of our lives to poor drudges underground, blackened to the eyes, with their throats full of coal dust, driving their shovels forward with arms and belly muscles of steel.[14]

One of the implied crimes of the poets is that the 'arms and belly muscles of steel' were apt to be noticed by them as the erotic outcomes of toil. On receiving Nancy Cunard's 1937 petition to British writers about the civil war in Spain – 'Are you for, or against, the legal Government and the People of Republican Spain?' – Orwell replied, 'Will you please stop sending me this bloody rubbish … I am not one of your fashionable pansies like Auden and Spender'. He added, for good measure, 'By the way, tell your pansy friend Spender that I am preserving specimens of his war-heroics' in order to shame him later. At no point did Orwell show any awareness that such accusations might put the accused in a position of danger, threatening his employability if not his liberty.[15]

Roy Campbell's similarly ostentatious determination to distance himself from homosexual men, their neuroses and their literature extended to his forthright poetry. In his 'Georgian Spring' he boils the supposed blandness of Georgian poetry down to one dismissive sentence: 'A thousand meek soprano voices carol / The loves of homosexuals or plants'. Although happy to celebrate the possibility of a healthy bisexuality, he insistently did so to the detriment of mere homosexual infirmity. In the first part of 'The Georgiad' he celebrates the figure of the heroic Androgyne: 'This was no neuter of a doubtful gender, / But both in him attained their fullest splendour, / Unlike our modern homos who are neither, / He could be homosexual with either / And heterosexual with either, too – / A damn sight more than you or I could do!' Not for him the pathetic pathic's reliance on the support of book learning: 'With Edward Carpenter he had no patience / Nor from the Sonnets [of Shakespeare] would he make quotations'. This Androgyne is a creature of instinct, with no need to excuse his own identity or actions. 'He read no text-books: took himself for granted / And often did precisely what he wanted'. Besides, even if a man were to identify with or seek solidarity among fellow homosexuals – more fool him – he would only be betrayed, for 'Cain had more Christian mercy on his brother / Than literary nancies on each other'.[16]

Writing about the new generation of poets, Campbell insisted on their interconnectedness to the extent of giving them the portmanteau surnames Spauden (Spender, Auden), Spaunday (Spender, Auden, Day Lewis) and MacSpaunday (MacNeice, Spender, Auden, Day Lewis). Even when naming them as individuals he did so only to meld them into a clique with a single brain: 'What Auden chants by Spender shall be wept'; 'the fat snuggery of Auden, Spender, / And others of the selfsame breed and gender'. Campbell had come to regard the whole of English literary life as an effeminate and emasculate conspiracy against real men – and real poets – like himself. All around him he saw the effects of the 'All-Castrating Knife / Of London and its literary life'; and every lesser male writer than himself he regarded as a 'literary catamite / Who stands aghast at beauty and delight'.[17] Among an already hostile audience for whom their shared homosexuality was an open secret, Auden and Isherwood's pre-war emigration to the United States would only reinforce such impressions of intense and misplaced loyalties.

NOTES

1 T. H. White, *The Age of Scandal* (Folio, 1993), p. 102.
2 Robert Graves and Alan Hodge, *The Long Week-End: A Social History of Great Britain, 1918–1939* (Penguin, 1971), pp. 97–98.
3 Julian Symons, *The Thirties: A Dream Revolved* (Faber and Faber, 1975), pp. 40–41.
4 The 1861 law was partially rescinded in 1967; the 1889 law was rescinded in 1980. The Labouchère Amendment was not killed off until 2004.
5 Evelyn Waugh, *Black Mischief* (Penguin, 2000), pp. 231–232, 233.
6 Evelyn Waugh, *Put Out More Flags* (Penguin, 1943), pp. 43, 42.
7 Evelyn Waugh, *Brideshead Revisited* (Penguin, 1962), p. 47.
8 Keith Howes, *Outspoken: Keith Howes' Gay News Interviews* (Cassell, 1995), p. 39.
9 Jocelyn Brooke, *The Orchid Trilogy* (Penguin, 1981), pp. 57, 58.
10 Louis MacNeice, *The Strings Are False* (Faber and Faber, 1965), p. 156. Stephen Spender, 'Introduction' to *The Temple* (Faber and Faber, 1988), p. xi. Stephen Spender, *Journals 1939–1983* (London: Faber and Faber, 1992), p. 53.
11 Curzio Malaparte, *The Skin* (Panther, 1964), p. 91.
12 James G. Southworth, *Sowing the Spring: Studies in British Poets from Hopkins to MacNiece* (Blackwell, 1940), pp. 136, 142.
13 Christopher Isherwood, *Christopher and His Kind, 1929–1939* (Eyre Methuen, 1977), pp. 123–125.
14 George Orwell, *The Road to Wigan Pier* (Penguin, 1962), pp. 29–30, 31.
15 George Orwell, *Essays* (Everyman, 2002), p. 74.

16 Roy Campbell, *The Collected Poems of Roy Campbell, Volume One* (Bodley Head, 1949), pp. 181, 203–204, 232.

17 Roy Campbell, *The Collected Poems of Roy Campbell, Volume Two* (Bodley Head, 1957), Spauden: p. 49; Spaunday: pp. 85, 92; MacSpaunday: pp. 86, 87, 89, 90; 'What Auden chants': p. 45; 'the fat snuggery': p. 143; 'All-Castrating Knife': p. 133.

CHAPTER IX

American Homosexuality, 1939–1972

Richard R. Bozorth

When Auden portrayed himself as 'sit[ting] in one of the dives / On Fifty-Second Street' (*EA*, p. 245) to elegize the 1930s, this act of self-location was in keeping with his great occasional poetry of the period: the elegies for Yeats, Freud and James; the sonnets 'In Time of War'. Even so, the power of 'September 1, 1939' comes in some measure from transcending the distance between Thucydides to this moment and between Europe again at war and neutral America. This expansiveness had much to do with Auden's later suppression of the poem for its 'incurable dishonesty' – its indulgence, as he saw it, of the kind of rhetorical immodesty that his celebrity in Britain had tempted him with and that he had left there in part to escape (quoted *Early Auden*, p. 201). At the same time, in its expression of a solitary consciousness reaching out to other 'ironic points of light' (*EA*, p. 247), 'September 1, 1939' anticipates the existentialism of his work in coming years. Auden saw America as the land of modern, rootless individuality and Manhattan as its epitome. Moving there was his own way of being absolutely modern.

Such are the kinds of observations found in standard accounts of Auden's career, which typically contextualize his emigration to the United States in terms of an intellectual shift from the secular to the sacred – from Freud and Marx in the 1930s to Kierkegaard, Tillich and Niebuhr.[1] So what happens when we refocus context on time and place more precisely – when we consider that the 'dive' of the poem was named Dizzy's, one of a number of jazz clubs on Fifty-Second Street with a gay clientele; that it was a cruising spot known for quick pickups; and that Auden had learned about it a day or two earlier from Harold Norse, who had gone there with Auden's lover, Chester Kallman, perhaps a day or two before? Auden and Kallman had recently returned to the city from a cross-country trip that Auden had referred to as their honeymoon, but Kallman was evidently not (as Auden may have suspected but eventually learned for certain) committed to marital fidelity: his affair with an English merchant seaman would soon precipitate a crisis in the relationship (see Carpenter, pp. 303–17). That this bar was, as Norse put it, 'the sex addict's quick fix, packed to the rafters with college boys and working-class youths' – 'like an orgy-room for the fully clad' – provides an angle on Auden's meditation rather different from what we would otherwise have: it is the start of World War II contemplated from a gay pickup joint.[2]

Nevertheless, to contextualize 'September 1, 1939' – and Auden more broadly – in American sexual politics and social history presents some challenges. Not least is that like most of his writing, it may be read 'without any knowledge of its author's homosexuality'.[3] It is true that this 'dive' was a gay bar, but is it relevant? Auden's own stated views would consign such matters to literary gossip that tells us nothing useful for a valid aesthetic response – trivia at best; at worst, fodder for indecent prurience (see, for example, his introduction to Shakespeare's sonnets, *F&A*, p. 90). We might respond, to be sure, that no less than Yeats, Auden has 'bec[o]me his admirers', his own words inevitably 'modified in the guts of the living' (*EA*, p. 242). And anyway, he violated his own claims on the irrelevance of artists' lives to their work as often as he issued them. We might condemn him for hypocrisy and evasion, but there is ample reason instead to see him as engaging in a game of secrecy and innuendo that he had long been playing with his readers, becoming in the process the greatest practitioner of a pre-Stonewall queer literary tradition dating back to Byron and Wilde.[4] Auden garbed himself in a poetic rhetoric of universality, but as Thomas Yingling observed, we should ask 'from what vantage point' the apparently 'universal' is rendered in his work.[5] From this angle, the setting of 'September 1, 1939' in a cruisy gay bar is not biographical trivia but an emblem of how the social and sexual-political fabric of homosexual life in mid-century America was to inform Auden's writing in coming years.

Academic study of queer history makes clear that the decades before gay liberation were ones neither of utter repression nor of gradual progress culminating in the Stonewall Rebellion of 1969. In New York City, relative tolerance seems to have prevailed from the late 1800s through the 1930s. Notwithstanding periodic moral crackdowns, the men's clubs and dance halls of lower Manhattan provided a thriving scene for 'fairies' (the common usage of the time) and those who loved them. The coming of the Harlem Renaissance coincided with a measure of sexual openness in Times Square and the theatrical venues of midtown, and Prohibition actually permitted even more freedom: because alcohol was illegal, places for its consumption had no official control. With Prohibition's repeal in

1933, the power of the New York State Liquor Authority to regulate alcohol sales provided a new mechanism for enforcing sexual crime laws, as
courts recognized its right to prosecute establishments for allowing sexual 'deviants' to congregate. Survival of such places meant bribing the
police – that is, it depended on the precarious hypocrisy of official authority – but there was the constant threat of undercover agents seeking targets to entrap, and the lifespan of bars like Dizzy's was relatively brief.
Although the influx of men and women from all over during World War
II brought a loosening of sexual attitudes, the threatening conditions for
gay bars continued into the 1960s, ultimately, of course, provoking the
riots outside the Stonewall Tavern of June 1969.[6]

So it is worth considering how the great themes of 'September 1, 1939' –
aloneness, escapist intoxication, alienation from civic life, anxiety about
state power and the position of the individual in mass society – resonate with the conditions of homosexual life in Manhattan at the time.
It may be that Auden on that night thought of dives he had frequented
in Weimar Berlin a decade before – sites of gay culture since obliterated
by the Nazis.[7] But the tone with which he observes this scene is mor-
dant, not elegiac, as he moves from history and the cityscape outside to
the enclosure of this probably windowless space. For the patrons, the
bar mirror is a device for seeing and being seen; for Auden, the mirror
reveals a moral condition just as real here as in Europe, visible in faces
desperately 'crave[ing] ... Not universal love / But to be loved alone' (*EA*,
p. 246). This, he writes, is the desire of 'the normal heart', and although
credited to 'mad Nijinsky' writing of his former lover Diaghilev, the
conviction that gay love is implicated in emotional authoritarianism is
something Auden had explored a great deal in the 1930s.[8] Accordingly, to
hear in 'normal' a resonance of its usage to mean heterosexual (a usage
Auden himself employed) is to realize that the poem's moral judgment
on humanity is shaped by its perspective on the psychic dynamics of a
gay pickup bar. The wish to be 'loved alone' may belong to 'each woman
and each man', but Auden derives it from observing the anxious aloneness in this place. Whatever its inhabitants pretend, the bar is not a
'home' but, as Auden sees it, an illusory 'fort' against a hostile world.
The threat is no less present here in the desperate narcissism feeding and
fed by homosexual desire.

Auden's later rejection of the poem fixed on what he felt was the fraud-
ulence of his stirring declaration, 'We must love one another or die' (*EA*,
p. 246). The line occurs after the poem has moved back outside the bar
in its closing stanzas. From a sexual-political point of view, what seems

problematic is that the rhetorical power of the line cannot resolve the crisis of relation between individual and state, 'citizen' and 'police', that Auden confronts outside the bar. So the tentativeness of the closing stanzas is as significant as their moments of sonorous pronouncement: 'All I have is a voice'; 'Ironic points of light'; 'May I show' – these are hardly examples of Yeatsian rhetoric. Instead they bespeak Auden's uncertainty about his own poetic authority once he exits the gay bar, as it were, and tries to speak to (or for) society as a whole. After declaring that 'We must love one another or die', he never uses 'we' again: its implication of community – of a common voice – is unsustainable. Accordingly, the 'messages' of 'the Just' are imaginable only as 'ironic points of light' coming from socially marginal isolates like those inside the dive (*EA*, p. 247). The gay bar may be in the city, and the city in the wider world. But the location of homosexual life in a larger context is itself (one might say) ironic: geographically but culturally marginal, emblematic of broader cultural dysfunction but officially ostracized.

The belief that to be homosexual is to be exiled or marginalized pervades Auden's writing from the 1940s on, in ways both obvious and subtle, in longer works like 'For the Time Being' (1942) and *The Age of Anxiety* (1948) – as Robert Caserio has powerfully shown – and in a variety of shorter poems.[9] It shaped his views of eros, of home, of spirituality and of nationality itself. Much of the reason involved his relationship with Kallman, which evolved with difficulty into a committed but non-sexual relationship, following his discovery of Kallman's infidelity in 1941. Auden's early poems inspired by Kallman, like 'The Prophets' (1939), portray falling in love as leading to a marriage that would mean the end of loneliness, but Kallman's hesitation drove Auden to write poems that see love as requiring an existential embrace of uncertainty and solitude as a condition for commitment: 'Leap Before You Look', 'Time Will Say Nothing' and 'In Sickness and In Health' (all written in 1940). If Kallman's rejection of sexual exclusivity figured as the proximate cause for what became their non-sexual relationship, an ultimate cause may be seen in the fabric of homosexual life at the time. This was, after all, decades before state-sanctioned gay marriage became something even imaginable, much less actual – necessarily rendering marital bonds dependent almost entirely on personal commitment. So when Auden wrote in 'Leap Before You Look', 'A solitude ten thousand fathoms deep / Sustains the bed on which we lie, my dear' (*CP* 2007, p. 311), the lines reflected not just his own existentialist outlook but the social forces arrayed at such a time against committed marital fidelity between men.

It is difficult to imagine how such a poem would not exacerbate Kallman's hesitation, particularly because he enjoyed casual sex and was simply not inclined to any sexual commitment to Auden. By 1944, in 'Few and Simple', Auden acknowledged himself as 'the one who would but didn't get you' (*CP* 2007, p. 324). The relationship continued for the rest of his life, each of them finding sexual partners elsewhere; and when read in this light, Auden's later poetry about love constitutes a remarkable pre-Stonewall document of a long-term relationship that is not modelled on monogamous heterosexual marriage. At his more self-pitying moments, Auden characterized his love for Kallman as a quasi-religious burden, and in a way that reflected his sense that homosexuality itself condemned him to emotional exile. In a 1945 letter he wrote that 'Being "anders wie die Andern" has its troubles': 'There are days when the knowledge that there will never be a place which I can call home, that there will never be a person with whom I shall be one flesh, seems more than I can bear' (quoted *LA*, p. 227). He was living with Kallman as he would, on and off, for the rest of his life, but it was not 'home' because they were not 'one flesh'. In invoking the 1919 German film *Anders als die Andern* ('Different From The Others'), Auden implied that this was a consequence both of social restrictions that, as in the film, frustrate gay love and condemn it to tragedy and of intrinsic sexual 'difference'. Much of this difference, he believed – in keeping with longstanding homophobic truisms – lay in the constitutional drive to promiscuity of gay men. Thus he claimed in conversation (as recorded by Alan Ansen in 1947) that '[s]exual fidelity is more important in a homosexual relationship than in any other' because otherwise there was nothing else to hold two people together (Ansen, p. 81). Like Don Juan, whom he regarded as the type for the male homosexual, gay men were in Auden's view motivated by quantity, not quality; and the fantasy of a homosexual subculture, as he saw it, was that it could form a community organized around the freedom to pursue sexual pleasure.[10]

Such attitudes infuse his most direct poem to address homosexual culture in America, the ironically titled 'Pleasure Island' (1948). The poem is an ode to Fire Island, which, as a barrier island off Long Island, existed at several removes from the mainland and mainstream culture. It is on the margin of a margin, and as in 'September 1, 1939' Auden's perspective on homosexual subculture is conveyed by space and locale. In the 1940s, Fire Island's Cherry Grove was already evolving into a mecca for gays and lesbians, and like other such places – Provincetown, Massachusetts, or New Hope, Pennsylvania – it historically went on to serve, not just the desire for escape from the squalor and policing of the city, but also something of a utopian ambition. Esther Newton has written that '[b]ecause Cherry Grove was the first, and for years the *only* gay-controlled geography, the resort was a key venue in the historic movement of gay identity from furtive and fearful friendship networks to a universalizing gay nationalism'.[11] Auden's skepticism about any such gay utopia is easily imagined, both in light of his temperament and in the context of the 1940s. The attraction of Cherry Grove, where he and some friends owned a cabin, was rather more recreational – according to Dorothy Farnan (later to become Kallman's stepmother), Auden and Kallman were drawn by 'its gay bar and the uninhibited homosexual ambiance'; Auden could wear a full bishop's regalia to a street carnival, and boys could be seen in haute couture ladies' beach outfits.[12] 'Pleasure Island' conveys the attraction but with sardonic ambivalence. The impulses catered to here are not, in this rendering, socially utopian but fundamentally anti-social, because they are purely sexual and physical: 'churches and routines' are absent in this 'outpost where nothing is wicked / But to be sorry or sick' (*CP* 2007, p. 342). In its devotion to the body, the beach licenses a lassitude interrupted only to worship 'bosom, backside, crotch / Or other sacred trophy', but the pagan paradise of parties, sex and bars that Auden calls 'our place' is actually, in his judgment, where real love goes to die: 'this / Place of a skull, a place where the rose of / Self-punishment will grow' (p. 343). Although the context of Auden's spiritual concerns has shaped critics' comment on 'Pleasure Island', it is also one of the most pointed poetic contemplations of gay male sexual culture in America of its period, as powerful in its own way as poems like Frank O'Hara's 'Homosexuality' (1954), John Wieners' 'A Poem for Cocksuckers' (1958) or Allen Ginsberg's 'Chances "R"' (1966). But it is hardly celebratory: Auden's ode to Fire Island concludes by envisioning exile and alienation after the party is over: outside the bar, in the night, is a 'decaying / Spirit' on the beach, 'excusing itself / To itself with evangelical gestures / For having failed the test', and the next morning 'Miss Lovely, life and soul of the party / Wakes with a dreadful start' as the dream of gay paradise yields to hangover.

The hint of existential dread here points to a religious element in Auden's ambivalence about a gay devotion to pleasure, sexual and otherwise. This is not a matter of puritanism but of his sense of the moral and psychological effects of homosexual marginality in American society at large. Written also in 1948, 'In Praise of Limestone' portrays the pleasures of the male body not as pathological but as innocent, and in a way that the Mediterranean locale of Ischia enabled him to envision as America did not. As against the uncaring sea and sky of 'Pleasure Island', here he traces a landscape that is cozy in its Freudian homoeroticism:

> What could be more like Mother or a fitter background
> For her son, for the nude young male who lounges
> Against a rock displaying his dildo, never doubting
> That for all his faults he is loved ...?
>
> (*SP* 2007, p. 189)

Auden reworks a long European tradition here of homoerotic idealization of the Mediterranean; the poem is a rich, complex meditation, not just on homosexuality and love, but on salvation – a vision of gay heaven, where 'The blessed will not care what angle they are regarded from, / Having nothing to hide', which contrasts with the hell of 'Pleasure Island'.[13] The attraction of this vision for Auden – indeed its very possibility – was that in Ischia he found a culture where homoeroticism neither hid in the dark nor thrived anxiously at the margins. It is out in the open and the day-light, visible in the 'band of rivals as they climb up and down' this land-scape, 'sometimes / Arm in arm', or 'Or engaged / On the shady side of a square at midday in / Voluble discourse'. There is a utopian element in this vision, not in the modern progressivist form of liberation from the closet, but in its idealization of homoeroticism that is simply, innocently there because in this place it always has been.

Auden's mock-lecture idioms – 'Mark these rounded slopes', 'examine this region', 'Watch, then, the band of rivals' – serve as campy gestures of pseudo-detachment belied by his obvious erotic investments. But ulti-mately, the poem concedes a profound alienation just as intense here as inside Dizzy's or on Fire Island: 'this land is not the sweet home that it looks'. He and Kallman were to spend a decade of summers on Ischia, but even at the beginning Auden felt himself an exile. The home from which he is exiled is at once religious, personal and political. It is heaven: 'the life to come' where 'the blessed' have 'nothing to hide'. It is domes-tic and erotic – a 'faultless' personal love unachieved in his relationship with Kallman, for which Auden admits himself 'reproached, for what / And how much you know'. But it is also a gay political vision, although not of a sort that accords either with the rebellious utopianism of the era that began with Stonewall or with the drive for mainstream recognition that has since come to animate the lesbian, gay, bisexual and transgen-der (LGBT) push for civil marriage and other legal rights in the United States. As post-war Italy stands to the rest of the world – 'A backward / And dilapidated province, connected / To the big busy world by a tunnel, with a certain / Seedy appeal' – so too, this poem suggests, the political significance of gay subculture defined by desire consists in its exilic ambivalence. We can visit but cannot live in this site of 'seedy appeal'. But in its continuing marginal existence according to its own 'backward' norms, it denies the ultimate authority of dominant culture: it 'calls into question / All the Great Powers assume; it disturbs our rights'. Legally an American citizen, Auden nonetheless suggested that it is the province of homosexuality not to be at home in the United States, and to question 'our rights' everywhere.

NOTES

 1 See, for example, Edward Mendelson, *LA*, pp. 129–41. A valuably complicating treatment of Auden's intellectual shifts can be found in Justin Replogle, *Auden's Poetry* (University of Washington Press, 1969), pp. 50–57.
 2 Harold Norse, *Memoirs of a Bastard Angel* (Morrow, 1989), p. 78. See also Sherrill Tippins, *February House* (Mifflin, 2005), pp. 55–56.
 3 Edward Callan, *Auden: A Carnival of Intellect* (Oxford University Press, 1983), p. 36.
 4 See Richard R. Bozorth, *Auden's Games of Knowledge: Poetry and the Meanings of Homosexuality* (Columbia University Press, 2001), pp. 3–4, 233–36, 253–54.
 5 Thomas E. Yingling, *Hart Crane and the Homosexual Text: New Thresholds, New Anatomies* (University of Chicago Press, 1990), p. 16.
 6 For a history of pre–World War II homosexual life in New York City, see George Chauncey, *Gay New York* (Basic Books, 1994). On the war's effects on sexual mores and behavior, see Charles Kaiser, *The Gay Metropolis, 1940–1996* (Houghton Mifflin, 1997), pp. 27–51.
 7 See Tippins, *February House*, p. 56.
 8 See Bozorth, *Auden's Games of Knowledge*, pp. 174–95.
 9 On the extensive interconnections among sexual politics, nationality and citizenship in Auden's life in the 1940s and in 'For the Time Being' and *The Age of Anxiety*, see Robert Caserio, 'Auden's New Citizenship', *Raritan* 17 (1997), pp. 90–103.
10 For an analysis of 'Numbers and Faces' (1950) in terms of sexual promiscuity and fidelity, see Bozorth, *Auden's Games of Knowledge*, pp. 211–13.
11 Esther Newton, *Cherry Grove, Fire Island: Sixty Years in America's First Gay and Lesbian Town* (Beacon, 1993), p. 11.
12 Dorothy J. Farnan, *Auden In Love* (Simon and Schuster, 1984), p. 116.
13 For the wider context of this tradition, see Robert Aldrich, *The Seduction of the Mediterranean: Writing, Art, and Homosexual Fantasy* (Routledge, 1993); see also Bozorth, *Auden's Games of Knowledge*, pp. 246–47.

CHAPTER X

Auden among Women

Janet Montefiore

'His mother and her mother won' (*EA*, p. 17): to write about Auden and women means primarily writing about Auden and mothers whose symbolic representation is crucial to his identity as a homosexual and a poet. Mothers may be thwarting and destructive, as in 'Paid on Both Sides'; or sources of wounding inspiration, as in 'the deep *Urmutterfurcht* that drives / Us into knowledge all our lives'[1] of 'New Year Letter' (*NYL*, p. 56; *CP* 2007, p. 226); or benign presences enabling happiness as (with reservations) in the post-war 'In Praise of Limestone'; or means of grace like Mary in 'For The Time Being' or Clio the 'Madonna of silences' (*CP* 2007, p. 610); but they are always central to the poet's world.

This does not mean that the only significant woman in Auden's life was Constance Rosalie Auden, important though her maternal influence was. Apart from his abortive 1928 engagement to Sheilah Richardson and 1947 affair with Rhoda Jaffé (see RD-H 1995, pp. 73–74, 243–45), Auden was friendly in the 1930s with Naomi Mitchison and Annie Dodds. After moving to the United States in 1939, he made close and lasting friendships with highly intelligent and talented married women: Elisabeth Mayer (addressee of 'New Year Letter'), Tania Stern, Ursula Niebuhr, Hannah Arendt, and Thekla Clark, author of the warm, illuminating memoir *Wystan and Chester* (1995). That some of Auden's recorded opinions of women are extremely negative is unsurprising from the poet who notoriously prophesied that in a healthy England 'All of the women and most of the men / Shall work with their hands and not think again' (*EA*, p. 105), and whose final instruction to the lady bound on her impossible quest is to 'Find the penknife ... and plunge it / Into your false heart' (*CP* 2007, p. 278). His 'table talk' includes some indefensible misogyny: 'Women should be quiet. When people are talking, they ought to retire to the kitchen ... Women shouldn't be talked to on intellectual subjects' (Ansen, pp. 65–66).[2] Against this hostility can be set Auden's warm friendships with high achieving women and his later admiration of the feminine imagination, 'which accepts facts and is coolly realistic' (quoted *LA*, p. 441). Later, Auden can sound positively feminist, praising women for being free from the phallic rivalry that produces ever bigger guns and bombs: 'I see little hope for a peaceful world until men are excluded from foreign policy altogether and all decisions concerning international relations are reserved for women, preferably married ones' (*CW*, p. 299), while his wry poem 'Moon Landing' unenthusiastically commemorates 'an adventure / it would not have occurred to women / to think worth while' (*CP* 2007, p. 844).

There is a parallel change in Auden's writing from the devouring mothers, frustrated spinsters and glamorous airheads of his early work, through the friendly maternal landscape of 'In Praise of Limestone' and the 'Steatopygous, sow-dugged' Dame Kind (*CP* 2007, p. 665), alias Mother Nature as a 'grim old She' ('Plains', p. 564), to the benign deities Gaea and Clio. True, the destructive mother reappears in Queen Agave who unknowingly kills her son Pentheus in the 1963 Auden/Kallmann libretto *The Bassarids*. But Agave, sympathetically rendered as a victim of Dionysus' malice, achieves dignity and self-knowledge as she faces her crime, quite unlike the lethal mothers of Auden's earlier plays and poems who thwart a hero bent on escape from 'the immense bat-shadow of home' (*EA*, p. 66) and the forces of bourgeois repression. Girls in Auden's early work are typecast, as brides the hero fails to marry (Anne Nower in 'Paid on Both Sides', Anna in *On the Frontier)* or as sirens (Lou Vipond in *The Dog Beneath the Skin* who briefly distracts the hero Alan from his quest, Alan's fiancée Iris who treacherously marries the industrialist Trunnion-James, Anna the unfaithful wife in 'Victor', and 'Sue' the pretty nonentity). None holds anything like the power wielded by Auden's mothers.

In the 1929 'charade', 'Paid on Both Sides', the hero John Nower, born when his father is killed by the enemy family and hailed by his vengeful mother Joan as a future killer, attempts reconciliation by marrying his enemy's daughter, and is himself killed at the urging of her vengeful mother. John's enthralment to a fierce maternal superego appears in the play's central dream scene where a spy (whom in reality John had shot) is put on trial, guarded by 'Joan as his warder with a gigantic feeding bottle'. John's 'accusation' consists of a patriotic speech, eliciting groans from his repressed self, at which 'Joan brandishes her bottle: "Be quiet or I'll give you a taste of this"' (*EA*, p. 8). The play thus dramatizes the internal conflicts of sons in thrall to dominating, angry mother-figures who will not allow them to stop being boys among aggressive boys and have heterosexual lives of their own. Auden himself called it 'a parable of

English middle class family life 1907–1929' (quoted *Plays*, p. xv): in other words, of his own lifetime. The gang warfare between the two families, suggesting the war between the wealthy industrialised nations of England and Germany, represents the ongoing trauma of the First World War. Fathers are killed off young and their bitter widows make sure that the sons carry on the feud. Because his own father returned home from war service, this scenario does not directly correspond to Auden's own experiences; nevertheless, he felt that 'though I did not ... lose my father physically by death, to some degree I lost him psychologically' (*F&A*, p. 500).

Neither 'Paid on Both Sides' nor the later plays Auden wrote with Christopher Isherwood, set in cartoon versions of the actual social world of bourgeois Britain, make any distinction between real mothers and nightmare mother-figures. Thus Mildred Luce in *The Dog Beneath the Skin,* is a hysterical bereaved mother who wants to destroy Germany ('Strew all her fields / With arsenic!') and hates young men for being alive when her sons are dead. At the end of the play when the capitalist Right takes over, she shrieks before stabbing the lost heir Francis that their followers are cannon-fodder for the next war: 'And I'm glad! What does it matter to me if you're all murdered? My sons were murdered and they were taller and stronger and handsomer than you'll ever be!' (*Plays*, p. 579). More insidiously destructive is Mrs Ransom in *The Ascent of F6* who colludes with the leaders of the Empire to destroy her son, the hero Michael Ransom. He is chosen to lead a British expedition to climb the famous haunted mountain 'F6' so as to secure Britain's colonial prestige. Aware that this is a jingo stunt, he refuses but is subdued by maternal emotional blackmail. When, after the deaths of his companions, Michael dies encountering the 'Demon' of the mountain in a dream sequence recalling the Spy's death and resurrection in *Paid* (both are trial scenes), the Demon/Dragon turns out to be 'Mrs Ransom as a young mother' crying 'My Boy! At last!' (*Plays*, p. 353). Her sinister influence is underlined at the end of Act I where, after the expedition has set off, she appears 'talking to herself in a hoarse and penetrating whisper', promising that 'Mother's with you. Of course she won't leave you alone, Michael, never.... Wasn't she with you from the very beginning, when you were a tiny baby? Of course she was. And she'll be with you at the very end'. She ends these gruesome reassurances with a lullaby:

> When the Demon is dead,
> You shall have a lovely clean bed...
> A saint am I and a saint are you,
> It's perfectly, perfectly, perfectly true.
> (*Plays*, p. 318)

If the Demon turns out be a projection of Michael Ransom's own Oedipal desire, Mrs Ransom is evidently to blame for his plight. He is the victim of her deadly maternal possessiveness, imaged in that 'lovely clean bed'; she wants him dead because only so can he be a hero whom she can fully possess 'at the very end'.

More alarming still is the old woman who kills her goose Nana in Auden's 1940 radio play 'The Dark Valley' (based on an earlier cabaret sketch 'Alfred'), making her doomed pet the scapegoat for everything she envies and resents – youth, energy, the modern world which has forgotten her, even her own wasted potential. Even as she strangles it, she identifies herself with the 'precious goose' whose father's 'loving hands are gripping her so tightly that she gasps for air' as he looks down furiously while she protests 'I'm young, I don't want to die!' (*Lib*, p. 381). The real culprit turns out, unsurprisingly, to be yet another life-denying mother. The old woman had loved and identified with her Lawrentian miner father, 'first of them all with drill and dynamite and daring', and after he died, her 'prim and pious' mother 'watched every movement I made', so that 'father's passionate blood' (*Lib*, pp. 371, 376) became a passion to destroy. Her threatening, cajoling, murderous voice represents both Fascism and, more widely, humanity's addiction to the death drive.[3]

The figure of the destructive mother haunts Auden's great surrealist fantasy book *The Orators*. This simultaneously dramatizes and satirizes the life-denying attitudes of English culture as represented by all-male institutions: public schools, groups of youth in search of a 'Leader', the lonely heroic 'airman' who is the book's homosexual, flawed hero. The only women actually mentioned are the twisted types prayed for in the joke Litany: 'the virgin afraid of thunder … the wife obeyed by her husband … the spinster in love with Africa'. Mothers appear obliquely as 'the immense bat-shadow of home', or as the source of disease: 'Man is the sufferer, woman the carrier. "What a wonderful woman she is! Not so fast, wait till you see her son"' (*EA*, pp. 66, 73). What the son suffers from is sketched in the book's 'Prologue', about a man 'by landscape reminded once of his mother's figure' whose sham heroic exploits derive from this infantile fixation. Recalling this maternal scenery with nostalgia for 'all the family names in the familiar places', the son goes out into the world with apparent success, but returns 'homing the day is ended', to nightmares in which he is reproached for cowardice while 'the giantess shuffles nearer, cries Deceiver' (*EA*, p. 61). Like Michael Ransom, he stands accused of cheating, not his mother who knows about his weakness and grotesquely embodies it, but the people who accept him as a hero.

When early Auden writes about women who are not mothers, his most vigorous and memorable work is hostile or mocking or both, and is most notable in his 1937 black comic ballads invariably culminating in the deaths of women. In 'Victor' and 'James Honeyman', wives get killed; 'Miss Gee', the plain pious spinster who dreams of being chased by 'a bull with the face of the Vicar', dies of repressed desire turned cancerous, and 'Sue' is destroyed by the clothes and make-up which constitute her identity. There is some pity for Miss Gee who like the Owl in Lear's 'The Owl and the Pussy-Cat' 'looked up in the starlight / And said, "Does anyone care?"' and hears the church choir singing 'so sweetly / At the ending of the day' but not to her; yet she ends up mocked by the students who dissect her (*EA*, pp. 214–16). There is none for the rich, empty-headed Sue (a female figure common in left-wing 1930s rhetoric[4]), with her wardrobe out of *Vogue*, her jewels, her sports car, her 'five half-empty boxes of expensive sweets', her boyfriends and her pointless occupations. Unlike Miss Gee's squint, thin lips and sloping shoulders, Sue's face and body are a blank; when she realizes her own emptiness, her mirror tells her 'You're right, die' and her clothes and make-up join in.[5] Persecuted by the possessions which are all the self she has, Sue obediently takes an overdose. It is not surprising that when Auden showed the manuscript of this funny, inventive, spiteful poem to a woman friend, she 'felt it was an outrage on her sex' and tore it up (Ansen, p. 11).

Auden's poetry looks simply misogynist up to this point. Something changes, however, in his attitude towards women after 1941. His poems featuring women become notably warmer: 'The Model' contemplates a picture of an old lady who has come into the face she deserves, becoming 'the essential human element', while 'In Schrafft's' contemplates a 'shapeless' middle-aged woman stirring her coffee who looks up and smiles as if she has just encountered a god (*CP* 2007, pp. 332–33). This change in tone is part of Auden's reinvention of his poetry in response to certain crucial events in his life: his move to New York where he met his lifelong love Chester Kallmann; their difficult relationship which led him into deeper self-questioning than any of his previous affairs and became central to his life and thought; his return to Christianity in 1940; and the death of his mother in 1941. Equally crucial was the Second World War, in response to which he insisted for the rest of his life that poetry should not, as he had written in 1935, 'make action urgent and its nature clear' (*EA*, p. 157) but '*Bless what there is for being*' (*CP* 2007, p. 589). I surmise that Auden's experiences, first of falling for Kallmann and then of feeling murderous rage at Kallmann's infidelity while loving him nonetheless, are of crucial importance here. That they moved Auden towards self-scrutiny is clear from the beautiful, outrageous 'Letter' to Kallmann on Christmas Day, 1941, two years into their relationship.

Because, suffering on your account the torments of sexual jealousy, I have had a glimpse of the infinite vileness of masculine conceit,
As this morning I think of Joseph, I think of you.
Because mothers have much to do with your queerness and mine, because we both have lost ours, and because Mary is a camp name,
As this morning I think of Mary, I think of you.
Because the necessarily serious relation of a child to its parents is the symbol, pattern and warning of any serious love that may later depend upon its choice, because you are to me emotionally a father, physically mother and intellectually a son,
As this morning I think of the Holy Family, I think of you. (Quoted *LA*, pp. 182–83)

Exploring the complexities of his relationship, Auden invokes different true images of love, jealousy, and dependence in the trinity of Mary, Joseph, infant Jesus, finding these time-honoured figures in his own mind and life. This prose-poem is a beautiful instance of Auden's new conception of art as consciously distanced from the life it portrays. The figures from the Christmas story carry the punch they do because they are surprising, unexpected, and outrageous. This is art as Auden described it in 'Squares and Oblongs', a serious 'game of knowledge, a bringing to consciousness, by naming them, of emotions and their hidden relationships' (*Prose II*, p. 345).

In Auden's later poetry, women still appear as mothers, but far more diversely. Maternal divinity, playfully featured in 'Plains' and 'Ode to Gaea', first appears in a meditation on Auden's beloved Pennine moors and their mineshafts in 'New Year Letter', a long poem which returns through philosophical argument and allegory to the Christian beliefs which meant so much to his mother (and which is also the first major work Auden dedicated to a woman). In a key passage whose intensity recalls Wordsworth blessing the 'Wisdom and Spirit of the Universe' for a childhood experience of a threatening mountain that moved him to a guilt-ridden yet deeply creative apprehension of 'unknown modes of being',[6] Auden recalls his early encounter with awe-inspiring, empty mineshafts. These made him aware 'Of Self and Not-Self, Death and Dread':

> Adits were entrances that led
> Down to the Outlawed, to the Others,

The Terrible, the Merciful, the Mothers;
Alone in the hot day I knelt
Upon the edge of shafts and felt
The deep *Urmutterfurcht* that drives
Us into knowledge all our lives,
The far interior of our fate
To civilize and to create,
Das Weibliche that bids us come
To find what we're escaping from.
(*NYL*, p. 56; *CP* 2007, p. 226)

In 'Pleasing Ma', John Fuller has untangled the Heideggerian, Wagnerian, and Goethean allusions in this apprehension of the 'unconscious sexual drive behind art'.[7] But the female presence (*Das Weibliche*) beside whom the boy Auden kneels in alarmed fascination is not only a maternal Muse, although she is that too. The terror of her threatening, life-giving energy, comprising both the 'Not-Self' world which engenders the poet and the depths of his own unconscious, is – as with the experience of 'pain and fear' granted the young Wordsworth by the 'Spirit of the Universe ' – the beginning of self-knowledge. This vision inaugurates a new poetry in which images of gender grow flexible in ways signalled by the 1941 Christmas letter-poem to Kallmann. Thus, the early fables of the devouring mother whose son cannot free himself are inverted in the allegorical poem 'A Household' (1948), which overtly describes a success- ful widowed businessman who boasts about his 'young scamp' son and his 'saintly mother, calm and kind and wise', but in the evening goes to a wretched home inhabited by 'a miserable runt / who wets his bed (. . .) / a crybaby and a failure' and 'a slatternly hag / Who caches bottles in her mattress, spits / And shouts obscenities from the landing'. It turns out that the successful master (namely, the poet's ego) needs these unfor- tunates to be his captives: 'Should they unmask and show themselves worth loving … he would die' (*CP* 2007, pp. 616–17). The man's iden- tity depends on bullying and imprisoning the mother and the vulnerable child in himself.

Mothers remain important, appearing in the title-poems of two later collections: Thetis in 'The Shield of Achilles' who 'cried out in dismay' at the terrible sights created for her son the 'iron-hearted man-slaying Achilles' (*CP* 2007, p. 596); and conversely Clio, whose gaze redeems the casualties of history in 'Homage to Clio'. A maternal landscape is famously addressed at the start of 'In Praise of Limestone': 'Mark these rounded slopes / With their surface fragrance of thyme, and beneath / A secret system of caves and conduits'; 'examine this region / Of short

distances and definite places: / What could be more like Mother (…)?'
(*N*, p. 11; *CP* 2007, p. 538).

The Mediterranean 'rounded slopes', the underground streams, and
the tiny, ideal landscape that forms a home for small decorative animals,
is clearly related to yet different from the 'familiar places' beloved of the
flawed hero of *The Orators*; whereas the 'secret system of caves and conduits' sounds like a benign version of the 'reservoir of darkness' in 'New
Year Letter', into which the boy Auden had guiltily dropped pebbles
(*NYL*, p. 56; *CP* 2007, p. 226). The limestone landscape is an Oedipal
childhood idyll, with its 'private pool' (an obvious womb symbol) and
the little ravines 'whose cliffs entertain / The butterfly and the lizard'
suggesting the small-scale, enchanted landscape of childhood. The nude
son 'displaying his dildo', (meaning an artificial phallus or possibly a figurative erection: either way, a nice image for art as a game) will reappear
at the end as an 'innocent athlete' carved from marble locally quarried
and thus truly a child of the hills which he adorns. As a multiplicity of
critical readings has demonstrated, the poem's landscape has wonderfully various, shifting meanings[8]; the point is not that the limestone hills
and valleys *are* the mother but that they can be seen as *like* her, the camp
question 'what could be more like Mother?' making a point of its own
artificiality. And unlike the mountain heights of *The Orators* and the
lonely moors of 'New Year Letter', this limestone region is inhabited –
by butterflies and lizards, by youths and their statues, and by easy-go-
ing individualists strolling 'arm in arm, but never, thank God, in step'
(*N*, p. 11; *CP* 2007, p. 539). Life can be lived here on a human scale –
which is why the landscape is essentially maternal, because it is mothers
who first give humans a place in the world, tempting us to believe that
happiness and virtue can be easily achieved. But although it looks like a
'sweet home', nowhere inhabited by humans 'the inconstant ones' can be
that.[9] The countryside is backward, even seedy; its sons don't have deep
spiritual lives and can go to the bad in petty ways, 'ruin[ing] a fine tenor
voice / for effects that bring down the house'. The powerful for good or
ill find this life too easy, leaving to find the clays they can dominate or
the granite wastes where they can contemplate eternity free from human
distractions – although conversely, limestone's enduring virtue lies in
confronting arrogant visionaries with their human limitations. But the
ending, where limestone and its underground streams image forgiveness
and 'the life to come', not only as in the Nicene Creed's 'the life of the
world to come' but in the Lawrentian sense of the body coming alive in a
place where love (including the homosexual love implied in the repeated

address to 'my dear') can find itself, is also an implicit tribute to the mother whose body gave life to the poet.

That said, women are conspicuous by their absence from a poem whose symbolic maternal realm is inhabited exclusively by sons. It is not that women and mothers in Auden's late poetry are nothing but imagined landscapes or what John Fuller, discussing the way the older Auden feminizes his own body, calls 'the female irresponsible matter of the last poems'.[10] Certainly, Auden's later poems often invoke natural forces and instinctual drives by the names of goddesses, hunger and love being represented by Artemis and Aphrodite, and the created world by 'Dame Kind', in his prose and his poetry. This is not a bow to animism, for the patterning of raw nature into classical culture or medieval allegory intimates the distance between the poet's language and the forces made thinkable by being named as deities: a point made in 'Ode to Gaea' which addresses 'our Mother, the / nicest daughter of Chaos' as her face is viewed from a plane while the poet, gazing down at the great masses of seas and continents, realizes how irrelevant we who think 'six foot is tall' are to the Earth, to whom our messy and miserable history is a matter of complete, but presumably benign, indifference and our 'good landscapes' merely lies (*CP* 2007, pp. 551, 553, 554). Auden's syllabics are exceeded by their subject to whom his metres can mean as little as the 'farms unroofed and harbour-works wrecked' (p. 553) by a recent war.

Whereas Gaea is a goddess of space with a mind of her own, Clio – the muse of history – belongs to time, though not the time of geologists or even of historians recording the fall of princes and the rise of empires. Her concern is for the unimportant, unique human lives that don't get into the history books, to whom she offers forgiveness, when it is 'your eyes, Clio, into which / We look for recognition after / We have been found out'. Unlike the ruthless natural drives of sexuality (Aphrodite) and hunger (Artemis), represented in statues – 'one recognises at once from the perfect buttocks, / The flawless mouth too grand to have corners, whom the colossus must be', Clio the 'Madonna of silences … who look[s] like any / Girl one has not noticed' cannot be represented, though she can be glimpsed in newspaper photographs of women 'nursing / a baby or mourning a corpse' with total concentration: 'You had nothing to say and did not, one could see / Observe where you were' (*CP* 2007, p. 610). Clio's silent gaze in these secular nativities and *pietas* attends to human lives beginning or ending. Her deep, unspeaking attention is a sacred space, not unlike the good place of 'In Praise of Limestone', where maternal love gives being and meaning to a son's existence. But that was an ideal arcadia, or anyway an image of one, whereas Clio's concern is precisely our fallen human world: all that, later, in 'Moon Landing' Auden called 'the usual squalid mess called History' (*CP* 2007, p. 845). As Edward Mendelson has argued, she embodies, 'the feminine principle ... [which] values unique particulars, unlike the boastful repetitive cock 'pronouncing himself himself' (*LA*, p. 196). In this 'hymn to Our Lady', as Auden described this poem in a letter to J. R. R. Tolkien,[11] the maternal deity is neither a symbolic landscape nor an aspect of the poet's own identity; she becomes a means of grace 'whose kindness never / Is taken in', transcending the game of the poetry in which Auden celebrates her:

> Muse of the unique
> Historical fact, defending with silence
> Some world of your beholding, a silence
>
> No explosion can conquer but a lover's Yes
> Has been known to fill.
>
> (*CP* 2007, p. 610)

The misogynist who wrote that 'Women should be quiet' has now come to acknowledge, and even to idealize, the redeeming silence of a divine feminine gaze.

NOTES

1 *Urmutterfurcht* is glossed by John Fuller as 'fear of the primeval mother' (Fuller 1998, pp. 330–31).
2 Auden's hostility to women intellectuals was triggered by Mary MacCarthy speaking of 'the burden of bisexuality' (Ansen, p. 65).
3 Auden wrote in a letter that 'she's really Knut Hamsun' (quoted Fuller 1998, p. 306); the Norwegian novelist Hamsun notoriously admired the Nazis.
4 Janet Montefiore *Men and Women Writers of the 1930s: The Dangerous Flood of History* (Routledge 1996), pp. 94–97.
5 Auden 'Sue', Oxford, Sycamore Press 1977. There exists no fair copy of this poem, which was reconstructed from draft material in a notebook belonging to Christopher Isherwood.
6 Wordsworth *Prelude* (1805), book I lines 428, 440.
7 John Fuller, 'Pleasing Ma: the poetry of W.H. Auden', Kenneth Allott Memorial Lecture no. 9, *Liverpool Classical Monthly vol. 20, 1995* (p. 5); Fuller 1998, p. 332.
8 See, for example, the 'Symposium' on this poem in *AS III* (pp. 243–72). See also Lyndsey Stonebridge's analysis in *The Destructive Element: British Psychoanalysis and Modernism* (MacMillan 1998, pp. 120–25) of the way Auden 'writes back' to Adrian Stokes' *The Stones of Rimini* 'acknowledg[ing] the beauty of limestone while resisting its mythical import' (p. 124).

9 The 'inconstant ones' – glossed as 'intellectuals' in John Fuller's *Reader's Guide to W. H. Auden* (Thames and Hudson, 1970), p. 213 – may also be a Freudian pun, because the three Auden brothers grew to life 'in Constance'.

10 Fuller 'Pleasing Ma' p. 7 Fuller argues that in Auden's thought matter is female: 'if consciousness is male and therefore [a] paternal principle, our loss of it at death redeems us from the Fall and restores us to Mother Nature' (p. 2).

11 Auden to J. R. R. Tolkien, 14 June 1955, quoted *LA*, p. 396. Auden also wrote to Ursula Niebuhr around this time about the 'Anglican problem of composing a hymn to the B.V.M.' (ibid.).

CHAPTER XI

Auden and the American Literary World

Aidan Wasley

Auden was a major figure in American literary life for more than three decades. Between his arrival in the United States in 1939 and his departure in 1972 to live out the remaining year of his life in Oxford and Austria, his American impact and presence were significant and multifarious. Auden was, above all, a poet whose influence could be heard in countless younger American poets, from the early 1930s on. But he also played a remarkable range of roles in mid-century literary culture. He was a teacher, a lecturer, and an early emblem of poetry's post-war move into the institutions of academia. He was also an influential and prolific reviewer, editor, literary prize-giver, and public intellectual. On the page and in person, Auden powerfully shaped and defined American letters in ways that went well beyond his reputation as a distinguished poetic import, as expressed by Malcolm Cowley in 1941: 'It's as if we had sent T. S. Eliot to England before the war on a lend-lease arrangement. Now, with Auden, we are being repaid in kind'.[1]

Auden's effect on American poetry and literary culture began well before his 1939 emigration. In the Random House editions of his *Poems* (1934), *On This Island* (1937), and his enigmatic verse plays, younger American poets like Randall Jarrell and Elizabeth Bishop had already found an exciting and seductive voice that seemed to speak not only to the concerns and landscape of his anxious British generation, but to their own as well. Jarrell first read 'Paid on Both Sides' as a teenager in 1932 and later confessed to 'know[ing] Auden by heart, practically'.[2] Auden's distinctive 1930s poetic mix of knowingness and vulnerability, formal mastery and rhetorical surprise, public engagement and private elusiveness was assimilated and emulated in Jarrell's own poems, as it was in that of others of his generation, including Karl Shapiro, Delmore Schwartz, Theodore Roethke, and Louise Bogan. John Berryman summarized his own early career in terms that reflected his generation's embrace of Auden's influential poetic mode: '[F]or several fumbling years I wrote in what it is convenient to call "period style", the Anglo-American style of the 1930s, with no voice of my own, learning chiefly from middle and later Yeats and from the brilliant young Englishman W. H. Auden'.³ For Bishop, Auden's influence was felt so strongly by herself and her peers that, she later recalled, it took a conscious effort of will to resist it: 'All through my college years, Auden was publishing his early books, and I and my friends, a few of us, were very much interested in him. His first books made a tremendous impression on me ... I think I tried not to write like him then, because everybody did'.⁴

As Auden settled into his American life, first in Brooklyn (including a celebrated stint living in a rooming house with a startling panoply of creative characters like Benjamin Britten, Carson McCullers, Richard Wright, Paul Bowles, and Gypsy Rose Lee) and later in Greenwich Village, he threw himself into the local literary scene and finding income to pay his way in his new home. He had spent the earlier 1930s working as a teacher in England and he soon found steady employment as a visiting teacher and lecturer on college campuses in America. His first American teaching job was a month-long stay at St. Mark's prep school in Massachusetts in May 1939, at the invitation of Richard Eberhart, the school's resident poet. Eberhart later recalled Auden's unorthodox pedagogical methods (including asking his students to write essays in which every sentence contained a lie); his copious tea, wine, and Benzedrine consumption; his cheerful dishevelment; and his productivity: 'He was writing his early poems and would change a line on the instant if you suggested it and what you suggested seemed better. I think I watched him write "Voltaire at Ferney". He was lively and high-spirited, very much alive, well-mannered in a friendly British way'.⁵ After St. Mark's, Auden went on to teach and lecture at numerous American universities, beginning in 1940 with a year-long engagement at the New School in New York. He spent the next year teaching at the University of Michigan, and from 1942 until 1945 taught fulltime at Swarthmore and Bryn Mawr outside Philadelphia. During the 1940s and 1950s, he also held visiting positions of various durations at Penn State, Olivet College, Bennington, Barnard, Mount Holyoke, and Smith, among others, along with frequent appearances on other campuses across the country. He was a familiar academic presence throughout the decades of his life in America, from his Turnbull Lecture at Johns Hopkins in 1940, to numerous appearances over the years at Harvard, including the performance in 1946 of his Phi Beta Kappa poem, 'Under Which Lyre', which waggishly exhorted the students, many of whom had recently returned to school after service in the war, to 'read *The New Yorker*, trust in God; / And take short views' (*CP 2007*, p. 338). He offered the 1949 Page-Barbour Lectures at the University of Virginia (which produced *The Enchafèd Flood*), a Gauss Seminar at Princeton in 1957 (Randall Jarrell's own, earlier Gauss lectures in 1951 had been dedicated entirely to discussion of Auden's poems), and presided over countless other pedagogical occasions, including the poetry tutorials he offered at Columbia in 1971 just a few months before his final departure from New York. His various lengthy reading and lecture tours also took him to myriad schools and cities across the country. 'God bless the lot of them, although / I don't remember which was which', he reflected ruefully in his comic poem, 'On the Circuit' (1963): 'God bless the U.S.A., so large, / So friendly, and so rich' (*CP* 2007, p. 730).

Auden's extensive American teaching and lecturing career, while helping to pay his bills, also served as a pioneering and influential example in the increasing academic institutionalization of poetry in American post-war literary culture. As the convention of the celebrity poetry circuit took hold – epitomized by Dylan Thomas's American tours of the early 1950s – and poets increasingly found their chief sources of income in the nascent industry of the many university creative writing programs that were established after the war, Auden was a prominent figure in both developments. And perhaps most importantly, it was in his role as itinerant pedagogue that he met and influenced many younger American poets whose first encounter with Auden and his poems was often as a student in one of his classes or an audience member at one of his readings. Robert Hayden, who studied with Auden while he was teaching at the University of Michigan, recalled Auden's effect on his students' poetic development: '[S]omehow or other he stimulated us to learn more about poetry in a way that we never would have been had it not been for him'. For Hayden, Auden's influence was more than literary: 'He came to see my daughter when she was born ... He was eager to see what she looked like, and so he looked down on her in her crib. I've told her, "You must remember always W. H. Auden came to look at you"'.[6] Auden also helped Hayden get a job at the Michigan library and facilitated the publication of some of his earliest poems. During Auden's semester at Smith in the spring of 1953, one his most impressionable and eager student acolytes was a 20-year-old Sylvia Plath:

The great W. H. Auden spoke in chapel this week, and I saw him for the first time. He is my conception of the perfect poet: tall, with a big leonine head and a sandy mane of hair, and a lyrically gigantic stride. Needless to say he has a wonderfully textured British accent, and I adore him with a big Hero Worship.

I would someday like to touch the Hem of his Garment and say in a very small adoring voice: Mr. Auden, I haveapome for you: 'I found my God in Auden'.⁷

New York was Auden's home until 1972 when he wasn't teaching, travelling, or summering abroad, and his notable public and private presence in the city was a significant aspect of his American influence. He was an eager participant in the cultural life of the city, an active creator and consumer of its intellectual and artistic energies, and was fond of describing his nationality as a 'New Yorker', rather than English or American. An opera fan, he could often be seen, and occasionally heard, in the audience at the Met (where his own *The Rake's Progress* would have its American premiere in 1953), as remembered by Auden's friend and fellow opera-lover, the poet William Meredith, who had the amusingly awkward misfortune of accompanying Auden on a night when he disapproved of the musical offerings: 'As the applause faded, a high British voice which I was proud and horrified to realize was my guest's voice – we were in the box of the Metropolitan Opera Club – was heard through the house calling *Shame! Shame!*'⁸ He was just as readily encountered on the streets of Greenwich Village, shambling from his apartment to a nearby coffee shop in his famous carpet slippers, and became a well-known neighbourhood fixture and an almost talismanic local presence for many younger New York artists, including Jack Kerouac and the Beats, who had amiable relations with Auden in part through his social connections with members of the scene like the poets Harold Norse and Alan Ansen, both of whom worked as Auden's secretary for several years.

In fact, Auden's social life was itself an element of his local legend and cultural impact. For decades, throughout his life in New York, he routinely made himself available to younger poets, often inviting them to tea or cocktails in his notoriously messy apartment. Marilyn Hacker remembered one such visit in 1961, when she was still a 19-year-old student poet: 'We sit in a cold room. A. pours the tea. / A gaudy twilight helps us hide ourselves. / I try to read the titles on the shelves / and juggle cup and saucer on my knee. / A. tells me anecdotes that I have read'.⁹ Many other young New York poets, especially those who were studying at Columbia in the 1940s and 1950s (like John Hollander, Richard Howard, Daniel Hoffman, Louis Simpson, and Allen Ginsberg), had similar experiences and absorbed Auden's human, pedagogical influence in tandem with that of his poems. The elaborate annual birthday parties that Auden threw for himself – with formal invitations pointedly asserting 'carriages at one a.m.' in a stern alert to guests when they would be leaving so the host could keep to his rigidly enforced bedtime – were also significant artistic occasions where Auden's festive assemblage of cultural luminaries would mingle with his younger literary friends. James Schuyler, another young New York poet who worked as Auden's secretary for a time, recalled in a 1974 elegy the heady intellectual opportunities on offer to visitors of Auden's modest flat: 'It was in / that apartment I just missed / meeting Brecht and T. S. Eliot'.[10] As Richard Howard put it, Auden's New York presence was a crucial part of his and his peers' poetic and personal educations: 'For all of us, he represented a kind of conscience that was both literary and social and, of course, for gay people like myself, sexual as well'.[11] In fact, Auden's prominence as a well-known gay artist and intellectual was another aspect of his American presence, and many younger gay and lesbian writers from Bishop to Ginsberg to James Merrill found in Auden's relative openness about his sexuality an encouraging model for their own aspirations for honest artistic self-expression. And Auden's pornographic poem, 'The Platonic Blow', written privately for friends in 1948 and describing in frank and delighted detail an idealized homoerotic encounter, became a celebrated underground emblem of sexual freedom and gay pride in 1965 when it found its way – against Auden's will – into public print in the New York counterculture journal *Fuck You, A Magazine of the Arts.*

Even while Auden was on vacation in Europe, his influence on American literary life exerted itself. From 1948 until 1957, Auden summered in Forio on Ischia, off the coast of Naples, and there he played host – sometimes reluctantly – to literary visitors like Ginsberg, who travelled specifically to Ischia in 1957 to see Auden and argue with him about the need for a new American poetic revolution. The two poets had known each other in New York and Ginsberg's earliest verse had been written in earnest imitation of Auden's, but with the 1956 publication and notoriety of *Howl*, Ginsberg now saw his early mentor as a conservative obstacle to his grander poetic ambitions. The meeting, involving considerable alcohol and shouting, did not go well – Ginsberg stalked off, calling Auden and his friends 'a bunch of shits'[12] – although the two poets soon reconciled and maintained friendly and respectful relations until Auden's death. Anthony Hecht, another young poet who spent time on Ischia in Auden's company in the early 1950s, remembered a milder scene around the tables of Maria's Café, Auden's preferred Ischian haunt: 'He was a generous man and a shy one ... He certainly had more to say, and on more topics, than any of us; he had read more widely and had thought more clearly'.[13]

Auden's centrality to American poetic culture in the 1940s and 1950s was not met with universal approval, however, as Ginsberg's Ischian quarrel with

Auden exemplified. Younger poets like Charles Olson and Robert Creeley, who positioned themselves as inheritors of Ezra Pound and William Carlos Williams's open-form poetics, saw Auden as a frustrating successor to Eliot in his importation of an alien British sensibility and formalism into the mainstream of American poetry. Williams himself had forcibly condemned Auden in his influential 1948 essay, 'The Poem as a Field of Action', attributing Auden's emigration to his having 'come to an end of some sort in his poetic means – something that England could no longer supply, and that he came here implicitly to find an answer – in another language. As yet I see no evidence that he has found it'.[14] Nonetheless, Williams's disapproval of Auden's poetics did not keep the two poets from establishing a cordial collegiality and Auden always acknowledged Williams's importance, allying himself as early as 1939 with a group of American writers calling themselves 'Les Amis de William Carlos Williams' that advocated for greater public recognition of the poet. Auden's sense of engagement with the community of American poets – even ones very different in mode and sensibility – expressed itself in other ways as well, as in his helping to organize a fundraising effort for Kenneth Patchen's medical assistance in 1951, and serving as best man at Theodore Roethke's wedding and loaning him his Ischia house for the honeymoon.

One of Auden's most significant roles in American literary culture was his function as a prominent arbiter of literary taste and achievement. In his frequent position as a judge for the many literary contests and prizes that further reflected poetry's increasing mid-century institutionalization, Auden did much to both shape the American literary terrain and serve as a kind of poetic gate-keeper. Perhaps most controversially, he served on the panel of judges who awarded the first Bollingen Prize, established by the Library of Congress in 1949 to honour major achievement in American poetry, to Ezra Pound. Pound had narrowly avoided being tried for treason for his role as a propagandist for Mussolini, having instead been declared insane and confined to St. Elizabeth's hospital after the war. The decision to give him the country's biggest poetry prize provoked a national outcry and Congressional condemnation, resulting in the Library discontinuing its sponsorship of the prize, spinning it off to be privately administered by Yale in subsequent years. Auden publicly defended the Pound award, however, maintaining – as he had in his Yeats elegy – that a poet's art outlasts his perhaps unadmirable life. Auden was named a Chancellor of the Academy of American Poets in 1954 and also served on the committee that awarded the Pulitzer Prize, receiving one of his own for *The Age of Anxiety* in 1948.

Auden's most lasting contribution as an institutional prize-giver was his tenure as the judge for the Yale Younger Poets Prize from 1946 to 1958. As one of the few avenues at the time for young poets to have their first book published by a major press, the Yale series held an outsize significance in establishing poetic careers in the 1940s and 1950s, and in the twelve years Auden served as judge, he selected for publication the first books by a remarkable range of poets who would go on to have among the most distinguished careers in post-war American poetry, including W. S. Merwin, Adrienne Rich, Daniel Hoffman, John Ashbery, James Wright, John Hollander, and William Dickey. The notable stylistic diversity of these poets, even at the beginnings of their careers, testifies to Auden's catholicity of taste and keen eye for talent, even if he was prone to offering backhanded praise to the prize winners in his introductions to their volumes, as in his condescending preface to Rich's *A Change of World* in 1951, which treats the poet like a polite, precocious schoolgirl: 'The poems a reader will encounter in this book are neatly and modestly dressed, speak quietly but do not mumble, respect their elders but are not cowed by them, and do not tell fibs'.[15] The 1956 award to Ashbery resulted from Auden's personal solicitation of manuscripts from Ashbery and Frank O'Hara, both young poets Auden had known in New York, because he had found the rest of that year's submissions to be unsatisfactory. Ashbery and O'Hara were close friends and firm devotees of Auden's work, Ashbery having written his senior thesis at Harvard on Auden in 1949. Along with Schuyler and Kenneth Koch, they formed the nucleus of what would later be called the 'New York School' of poets, reflecting their allegiances to the modern painters who were reshaping the New York art scene in the 1950s. Auden chose Ashbery over O'Hara, although Auden pointedly remarked to both of them that he found their shared tendency toward surrealism excessive and ill-considered. The formal rivalry imposed on them by Auden did not damage the poets' friendship and each went on to major poetic careers: O'Hara, until his untimely death in 1966, as a central figure in New York's swirling poetry scene; and Ashbery as, eventually, the most renowned and influential American poet of his generation.

Along with his poetry, Auden also generated a prodigious amount of critical prose for American publications of every kind, beginning almost as soon as he arrived in New York. The poet Robert Fitzgerald remembered Auden's eagerness to find journalistic employment in America and his boldness in self-introduction:

One summer day in 1939 the phone rang in my office at *TIME* and the receptionist announced 'Mr. Auden to see you.' I went down and greeted him, looking bony and boyish in his tennis shoes and flannels, a Saxon with a blond cowlick, a touch of the hayseed, very bright-eyed and good-mannered. He was just off the boat, so to speak, [and] he wanted work.[16]

Auden didn't end up writing for *TIME*, but that magazine was perhaps the only major American publication that did not print something by Auden in the succeeding decades. Beginning with the appearance in the *Partisan Review* in early 1939 of 'The Public v. the Late Mr. W. B. Yeats' (the prose exploration of the Irish poet's flaws and virtues that would find fuller poetic expression in his first American poem, 'In Memory of W. B. Yeats'), a torrent of book reviews, essays, and topical commentaries followed in journals ranging from *The New Republic* and *The Nation* to *Vogue* and *Harper's Bazaar*. He wrote pieces for *Common Sense, Junior League Magazine, Mademoiselle, House and Garden, The Kenyon Review, Town and Country, Encounter, Shenandoah, Esquire, The Atlantic,* and *Reader's Digest*, among dozens of others. Richard Howard, like many of Auden's American readers, found his apparent omnipresence in book reviews and magazines almost as essential a part of his cultural importance as his poems: 'He was writing all that criticism all the time, and it was wonderful ... We all fell upon it whenever he wrote in *The New Yorker* or in the papers. He was everywhere, in the *Times*, in *The New York Review of Books*, and we read all those things'.[17] Other poets, like Anthony Hecht, also paid close attention to Auden's voluminous journalism:

I think I was almost never disappointed in a discovery of Auden's. His taste, his acumen, was as near to infallible as one could want ... I read virtually every book review that he wrote and on his say-so I'd go out and buy anything that he recommended. If he said it was good then I was sure I would like it.[18]

Under the pseudonym 'Didymus' Auden also contributed a series of articles to the Catholic opinion journal *Commonweal*, in which he wrestled – under the cover of anonymity – with spiritual and theological questions that reflected his private (and eventually public) turn toward Christianity following his move to America. He even wrote reviews of amateur theatre productions for the Swarthmore College student newspaper, and penned pieces in undergraduate publications at the University of Michigan and Bennington.

Auden was also something of a literary entrepreneur later in his American career, founding – along with Lionel Trilling and Jacques Barzun – his own subscription book club in 1951. Originally called Readers' Subscription until a 1959 name-change to the Mid-Century Book Club, the organization lasted twelve years during which Auden and the two other distinguished editors selected and distributed (for a fee) notable books for an educated general readership. He also contributed essays to the club's magazine on recent books that caught his interest, like Arendt's *The Human Condition*, Faulkner's *The Mansion*, Tolkein's *Lord of the Rings*, and poetry collections by Graves, Eliot, Betjeman, and Larkin. The club folded in 1963 due to financial difficulties and editorial fatigue, but had at its height more than 40,000 subscribers. Auden also individually edited a wide range of books, including a 1946 edition of Henry James's *The American Scene*, which he enthusiastically lobbied Scribners to republish (the book had never been reprinted since its first publication in 1907) and for which he wrote an introduction and selected illustrations. He edited collections of ancient Greek literature, Kierkegaard's essays, works by Poe and Byron, and anthologies of nineteenth-century British and modern American verse, among numerous others, along with providing prose prefaces and introductions to an enormous assortment of other books, including Shakespeare's sonnets, Baudelaire's journals, Cavafy's poems, and *The Art of Eating* by M. F. K. Fisher.

His friendships and connections with other major American artists and thinkers – many of them European émigrés like himself – also placed Auden firmly within the pantheon of post-war American public intellectuals, a well-known mandarin of the cultural establishment. He wrote operas with Stravinsky, socialized with Dag Hammarskjöld, debated books with Lionel Trilling, read theology with Reinhold Niebuhr, and proposed marriage (unsuccessfully) to Hannah Arendt. Auden's national prominence as a public face of art and ideas was further manifested in his numerous appearances on American radio and television, both as a creator of work for broadcast and as an interview subject and social commentator. He scripted three radio plays (one of them an adaptation of *Pride and Prejudice*) for CBS in 1940 and 1941, and was commissioned by NBC to translate for television *The Magic Flute* in 1956 and *Don Giovanni* in 1960. He was interviewed on national television several times, including a two-part programme devoted to his life and work in 1958 on the CBS network, and in 1962 was featured as a celebrity guest on Merv Griffin's Hollywood chat-show.

Even after his death, Auden's impact on the American literary world continued to be felt, especially in the work of younger writers who had found his voice essential to the development of their own. James Merrill's 1982 occult epic *The Changing Light at Sandover* conjured Auden's ghost – via the Ouija board – as Merrill's Virgilian guide to an underworld of dead poets and cosmological spirits and even offers readers 'new' Auden poems from beyond the grave. Notable elegies by Richard Wilbur, Derek

Walcott, and Joseph Brodsky pointed to Auden's importance in their own work, whereas succeeding generations of younger American poets attested to their own Audenesque inheritance in poems like Paul Muldoon's '7, Middagh St.' (1987), J. D. McClatchy's 'Auden's OED' (1995), and Rachel Wetzsteon's 'In Memory of W. H. Auden' (1998), the last of which – addressing Auden as Auden had once addressed Yeats – concludes with an apt summation of Auden's ongoing influence and utility for American writers: 'You have taught us / not how to follow in your footsteps, but / how to carve out a path for ourselves'.[19]

NOTES

1 Malcolm Cowley, *The Flower and the Leaf: A Contemporary Record of American Writing Since 1941* (Viking, 1985), p. 269.
2 Randall Jarrell, *Pictures from an Institution* (University of Chicago Press, 1986), p. 243.
3 John Berryman, *The Freedom of the Poet* (Farrar Straus & Giroux, 1976), p. 324.
4 Elizabeth Bishop, '"The Work!": A Conversation with Elizabeth Bishop', *Ploughshares* 3 (1977), p. 19.
5 Richard Eberhart, 'A Tribute to W. H. Auden', *The Harvard Advocate* 108.2–3 (Special Issue, 1973), p. 30.
6 Robert Hayden, *Collected Prose* (University of Michigan Press, 1984), pp. 100–01.
7 Sylvia Plath, *Letters Home: Correspondence 1950–1963* (Harper & Row, 1975), pp. 107–08.
8 William Meredith, *Poems Are Hard to Read* (University of Michigan Press, 1990), p. 10.
9 Marilyn Hacker, quoted in Samuel R. Delany, *The Motion of Light in Water: Sex and Science Fiction Writing in the East Village* (Masquerade, 1988), p. 143.
10 James Schuyler, 'Wystan Auden', *Selected Poems* (Farrar Straus and Giroux, 1993), p. 242.
11 Richard Howard, interview with the author, 2 April 1997.
12 Quoted in Barry Miles, *Ginsberg: A Biography* (Viking, 1990), p. 230.
13 Anthony Hecht, 'Discovering Auden', *Harvard Advocate*, p. 49.
14 William Carlos Williams, *Selected Essays of William Carlos Williams* (Random House, 1954), p. 288.
15 W. H. Auden, foreword to Adrienne Rich, *A Change of World* (Yale University Press, 1951), p. 11.
16 Robert Fitzgerald, 'W. H. Auden', *Harvard Advocate*, p. 52.
17 Howard, interview with the author.
18 Anthony Hecht, interview with the author, 29 December 1996.
19 Rachel Wetzsteon, 'In Memory of W. H. Auden', *Home and Away: Poems* (New York: Penguin, 1998), pp. 40–41.

CHAPTER XII

Atlantic Auden

Michael Wood

Auden perhaps meant to say that the achieved work of art is its own sufficient act of witness.[1]

I

'He has gone in the right direction', Randall Jarrell wrote of Auden in 1940, 'and a great deal too far'.[2] The joke is quick and perhaps too easy, but we might take it as a pointer to a more complex thought. The suggestion may be that the right direction cannot be entirely or exclusively right and that even if it were it one could still go too far. The fact that Jarrell probably borrowed this thought from Auden before holding it against him makes it all the more interesting.

But what was Auden's direction in 1940, and did he have only one? He had travelled westward from Southampton to New York in January 1939; and by the following year was perhaps already thinking of staying in America.[3] He became a citizen of the United States in 1946. In October 1940, he returned to a version of the Anglican fold he had left long ago and began to realize that when he explained the meaning of the death of God, it would be the word 'dead' rather than the word God that he needed to frame in quotation marks (see *CW*, p. 175).

Had he become plainer in his poetry, as Jarrell suggested, less 'oracular', more committed to 'responsibility'? *Another Time*, Jarrell said of the volume of poems Auden published in 1940, 'is Auden's eighteenth century; rational, didactic, social, full of abstractions, comment, light verse'. Within a year, Jarrell found himself eating his words. 'New Year Letter' was Auden's eighteenth century, making *Another Time* look like faithful modernism, and Jarrell jokingly pretended that Alexander Pope's ghost had appeared to him in order to give him the news.[4] Barbara Everett notes that 'the direction in which Auden's meditations are moving' takes him to an 'almost dizzying distance from the actual'; and still thinking of

'New Year Letter', identifies 'the poetical anonymity that he has chosen as his American role'.⁵ Nicholas Jenkins has another view, suggesting that in 'New Year Letter', along with 'The Unknown Citizen' and 'September 1, 1939', Auden was writing 'hybrids, stylistically displaced both from "Old World" clarity and restraint and from "New World" inwardness and liberation' ('Auden in America', *CCWHA*, p. 44). This is an elegant move, because it refuses the familiar division and pretty much inverts Jarrell's and Everett's definitions of the new and the old (Audens and worlds), and their relations to clarity and inwardness. The very possibility of this plausible inversion tells us much about the difficulty of naming what Auden was up to, and makes us think we should think again.

Auden himself said, 'I don't think you could tell which works in *Another Time* were written over here' (Ansen, p. 70). We could and we couldn't. 'Lay your sleeping head' surely belongs to England, and so do 'Law, say the gardeners' and 'As I walked out one evening'. That's two out of three. The dates of the poems, respectively, are January 1937, September 1939, and November 1937. 'In Memory of W B Yeats' was written 'over here', but only just. Yeats died three days after Auden and Isherwood arrived in New York; the poem was written in February 1939. We are a little more secure with 'In Memory of Sigmund Freud' (November 1939), because the whole poem breathes an air of distance from darkened Europe, and is written in American syllabics. But is this a direction or an option, a perspective?

It would be shallow to suggest nothing changed in Auden's work in the 1940s, even if the changes do not correspond closely with his move to America or his return to the Christian church. But it is not clear that he ever abandoned the actual, or became thoroughly rational or abstract or anonymous in the sense of these descriptions; it is not even clear that his non-hybrid poems do not have elements of the hybrid in them. Auden certainly shifted his ground and his tone and his diction, but he shifted them often, and there is much to be said for resisting the temptation to split him in two, wherever and however we cast the halves. Patrick Deane puts the transatlantic matter very well when he says, 'As a "secondary world", a body of ideas, images and linguistic practices out of which Auden's identity was formed, England would travel with him. As the milieu in relation to which that identity would unfold historically, England would – must – be left behind' ('Auden's England', *CCWHA*, p. 37). To this I would add that America would be welcomed and lived in but never quite cease to be imaginary, for reasons that have to do both with Auden and with America's idea of itself – 'this new yet unapproachable America', as Emerson called it. Jarrell was right in a way he cannot have intended. Auden always thought (and showed) that the right direction could be the wrong direction; and always, when he could, went too far.

II

It is curious but perhaps not surprising that Auden is remembered as hav-ing said he wanted to be a minor mid-Atlantic Goethe.[6] The notion of the mid-Atlantic, most often used of Anglo-American accents when it is not used to described certain states on the Eastern seaboard, suggests hesitation and incompletion, even deception, as if one wished to hang on to two identities by splitting them down the middle; to be both here and there by means of the odd expedient of being nowhere. There is sense in which Auden, at times at least, wanted to be nowhere, and there is a sense in which America for him had the advantage of being a sort of nowhere, 'the great Rome / To all who lost or hated home' (*CP* 2007, p. 235). But this is not a sense suggested by the term mid-Atlantic, and Auden didn't use the term. He said – and in a poem, not in an autobiographical aside or wisecrack – that he would like to become, 'if possible, / a minor atlan-tic Goethe' (p. 692).

There are all kinds of ambitions and ironies swirling in the phrase. How minor could you get and still be a Goethe of any kind? How small would the ocean have to be to suit such a figure? And what does 'atlantic' mean anyway? Nordic, perhaps; non-Mediterranean; looking towards the new world. It might mean 'transatlantic' in either of two interpretations: describing one who had crossed the Atlantic to his new home, or one whose continuing history included crossing and re-crossing the Atlantic. When Auden called himself a clown, his interlocutor corrected him by suggesting he was 'a sacred one'. Auden said, 'No, but a transatlantic one at least'.[7]

There is also the possibility that an 'atlantic Goethe' would be a citi-zen of Atlantis as Auden memorably describes it in a poem of that name (*CP* 2007, pp. 313–15). Getting to this fabulous (and ultimately hostile-seeming) place, a paradise that perhaps cannot be inhabited, involves a whole series of trials: passing as 'one of The Boys', learning belief through doubt, forgetting about one's goal in order to be able to continue the jour-ney, acquiring real knowledge of 'each refuge that tries to / Counterfeit Atlantis'. Auden's tone at the beginning of the poem – 'Only the Ship of Fools is / Making the voyage this year' – seems a long way from anything we associate with Goethe, but it matches the role of the clown, and Goethe did say, in the *Italian Journey* Auden was soon to translate, that he might have 'become deranged' if he had not been so interested in the observation of the natural world he associated with science. A 'minor atlantic Goethe', then, if we try to pull some of these threads together, could be a major writer at least in hope (minor only when compared to Goethe), a citizen of two countries connected by a sea – it was Tocqueville who said 'I do not think the intervening ocean really separates America from Europe' – and a person whose uncertain home is somewhere between an imaginary Eden and an actual but not yet accessible promised land. It is important too that Auden thinks of Goethe as a man with 'a passion for weather and stones', a 'silliness / re the Cross', and the knowledge that 'Speech can at best, a shadow echoing / the silent light, bear witness / to the Truth it is not, he wished it were' (*CP* 2007, p. 692). The phrasing and rhythms are awkward, but the thought is delicate. What Goethe wishes and what he knows are at odds, but both matter. The suggestion of truth's shyness was already hovering in 'New Year Letter':

> Yet truth, like love and sleep, resents
> Approaches that are too intense,
> And often when the searcher stood
> Before the Oracle, it would
> Ignore his grown-up earnestness
> But not the child of his distress.
>
> (*CP* 2007, p. 204)

III

How are we to pronounce the word 'clerk'? To rime with lark or with work? When he was sounding American (in poetry) Auden opted for the latter (as in 'The Fall of Rome'); but he also believed that the transatlantic meanings of the word were different. An American clerk would be like Bartleby, a member of no group except those who say they prefer not to, whereas a poet in Europe might see himself as a 'clerk' of sorts, the kind who could commit the betrayal named in Julien Benda's *La Trahison des clercs* and translated at the end of Auden's poem 'At the Grave of Henry James': 'because there is no end / To the vanity of our calling, make intercession / For the treason of all clerks' (*CP* 2007, p. 310). Still, even a treasonous clerk would be, in Auden's words 'a member of a professional brotherhood, with a certain social status irrespective of the number of his readers, and ... taking his place in an unbroken historical succession'. 'In the States', Auden goes on, 'poets have never had or imagined they had such a status, and it is up to each individual poet to justify his existence by offering a unique product'. He cites a well-known remark of Eliot's ('Tradition cannot be inherited, and if you want it you must obtain it by great labour') as a mark of Eliot's Americanness, and argues that a European critic 'would not, of course, deny that every poet must work hard but the suggestion ... that no sense of tradition is acquired except by conscious effort would seem strange to him' (*DH*, pp. 365–66). As it seems strange to Auden, no doubt. He continues speaking of the 'advantages and disadvantages in both attitudes', but the important point here is the difference between the *made* and the *self-made* artist, which corresponds exactly to a larger, more philosophical difference Auden identifies between a European idea of virtue and an American idea of liberty.

These are familiar ideas in one sense, part of the lexicon of anyone who has ever tried to think about the old and the new worlds together. They take on fresh life in Auden's analysis because they are not simple opposites but versions of emphasis, and because Auden clearly understands how symbolic, even allegorical, these contrasts are. What is missing in America, Auden says, 'what has been consciously rejected ... is the *romanitas* upon which Europe was founded and which she has not ceased attempting to preserve' (*DH*, p. 318). We may note in passing that English thinkers in America invariably think of themselves as European, however un-continental they may feel at home. They weren't conquered by the Romans and the Normans for nothing. And now, a longer quotation:

> The fundamental presupposition of *romanitas,* secular or sacred, is that virtue is prior to liberty, i.e., what matters most is that people should think and act rightly; of course it is preferable that they should do so consciously of their own free will, but if they cannot or will not, they must be made to. ... The antagonistic presupposition ... is that liberty is prior to virtue, i.e., liberty cannot be distinguished from license, for freedom of choice is neither good nor bad but the human prerequisite without which virtue and vice have no meaning. Virtue is, of course, preferable to vice, but to choose vice is preferable to having virtue chosen for one. (*DH*, p. 318)

In the middle of this paragraph, Auden makes an important concession. The priority of liberty over virtue is not a presupposition 'peculiar to America and would probably not be accepted by many Americans' (*DH*, p. 318). Even so, America has come to stand symbolically for this presupposition, just as Europe stands for its opposite. In a postscript to his essay, Auden becomes even more worried about the gap between symbol and human fact – how many Americans fail to be Americans philosophically, how many Europeans are Americans at heart – and suggests we all act on both presuppositions at different times. 'In everyday life we instinctively adopt the Roman position in relation to strangers and the Liberal position in relation to our friends' (*DH*, p. 324). We want, in other words, law enforcement for some and freedom of action for others.

But this attempt at improved complexity is itself still too rigid, and loses the interest and authority of the grand simplification. *Romanitas* and its counterpart are powerful instruments for thinking about our moral and political worlds, they correspond in significant proportions to the cultures of Europe and America, and every person, every country, is going to have to make a deal with the demands of both of these principles. Both as a matter of emphasis, as I have said, and as a matter of choice. There might be, as Auden says in 'New Year Letter', 'An abstract model of events / Derived from past experiments', but then 'Each life must itself decide / To what and how it be applied'(*CP* 2007, p. 199). There is no middle ground, no mid-Atlantic, but neither principle is ever fully in abeyance anywhere. It is because he works so thoroughly and so lucidly through these questions in his poetry that we can think of Auden as he wanted us to: as an atlantic poet who understands the reigning preferences of both of the ocean's coasts.

This sounds rather heavy-going, but the effect is very different in the poetry, and usually in the prose. Auden's examples or tests of such balancing acts are complex, quirky, and concrete. 'Even a limerick', he says, 'ought to be something a man of / honor, awaiting death from cancer or a firing squad, / could read without contempt' (*CP* 2007, p. 692). And in the essay 'The Poet and the City' we read: 'among the half dozen or so things for which a man of honor should be prepared, if necessary, to die, the right to play, the right to frivolity, is not the least' (*DH*, p. 89). In the first case, the man of honour is the implied judge of the poet as clerk, the craftsman for whom labour and skill are a tradition and a morality. Liberty has been subordinated to virtue, in a 'European' fashion, but the result of that virtue is a light, perhaps immoral verse. And in the second case, we are invited to think of dying not for our country – as Europeans and Americans regularly feel called on to do, or at least to ask others to do – but for the opposite of work. In this case, an extreme virtue serves a slender liberty, one that no American would seek at such price but that nevertheless lurks, Auden is suggesting, in the logic of the American notion of freedom. Who could be freer than the person freed into frivolity? No middle ground, as you can see; but an extraordinarily agile conjugation of conflicting moral allegiances.

Here is another instance, again rather intricate. Auden suggests that Raymond Chandler 'could not be more mistaken' than he is about the nature of the detective story, because professional criminals cannot offer an image of a good society, threatened by the murder in its midst and redeemed at last by the discovery of who the murderer is. Everyone else, whatever their appearances, is innocent, and that is why, according to Auden, these theological fables are so satisfying. Auden thinks, or at least says, that Chandler is a better writer than most authors of (real) detective stories, 'and his powerful but extremely depressing books should be read and judged, not as escape literature, but as art' (*DH*, p. 151). This remark is of a piece with Auden's view that twentieth-century American literature (literature as art) is all depressing (*Prose* II, p. 297). But then a page or so later he pretends to offer Chandler a subject, a way into the detective story even through his criminals.

Among a group of efficient professional killers who murder for strictly professional reasons, there is one to whom ... murder is an *acte gratuite* [sic]. Presently murders begin to occur which have not been commissioned. The group is morally outraged and bewildered; it has to call in the police to detect the amateur murderer, rescue professionals from a mutual suspicion which threatens to disrupt their organization, and restore their capacity to murder. (*DH*, pp. 152–53)

The premise is precisely an invasion of professional *romanitas* by anarchic personal freedom, and cops and criminals join forces to detect and expel the intruder. Earlier in the essay, Auden has said that he finds it 'very difficult' to read a detective story 'that is not set in rural England', but here, with characteristic devious ingenuity, he has converted rural England into an American underworld (or vice versa), and the murderer into a figure who in almost any other context, especially an American one, would be a hero: 'to choose vice is preferable to having virtue chosen for one'.

IV

The difficult dialogue between virtue and liberty is not everywhere in Auden, but it does appear in many forms which are not those of the intercontinental allegory: in the thought of England's precarious historical privilege, ended in 1939 ('what doubtful act allows / Our freedom in this English house, / Our picnics in the sun' (*EA*, p. 137)); in the fear of what Tony Sharpe calls the 'unearthly, dangerously magical' powers' of a 'freedom unconditioned by necessity' ('Auden's Prose', *CCWHA*, p. 122) as well as in the horrors of a necessity undiluted by freedom. America was always edging towards anarchy, in Auden's view. He wasn't entirely serious when he said it was easy to commit murder in America (see Ansen, p. 13), but he was serious about the scary license of which this would be an exaggerated expression. But then in England, among all those writers who absorb tradition without working at it or knowing it, he could find only memories, a usable past, an unworkable present.

'September 1, 1939' is in many ways the perfect example of an 'atlantic' poem, ostensibly American, secretly European, and ultimately belonging to the private world of a writer who left one place without quite arriving in another. The poem becomes more (rather than less) significant, I want to suggest, through its very privacy, its lack of any direct relation to violent, dated history.

The more one looks at it, the more private it gets. As many critics have noted, Auden's poem echoes Yeats' 'Easter, 1916' in its form. Actually the echoes are rather slight: trimeters and a long stanza. The stanza length and rhyme schemes are quite different. What is striking is that both poems offer remarkably unpolitical reflections on political events, and both begin with a person in a city: 'I have met them at close of day / Coming with vivid faces / From counter or desk among grey / Eighteenth century houses'[8]; 'I sit in one of the dives / On Fifty-Second Street / Uncertain and afraid' (*EA*, p. 245). For Yeats, a violent local history transfigures glamorous and vicious acquaintances alike (they are 'transformed utterly') and prompts him to what is effectively an antipolitical question: do we really want to have 'hearts with one purpose alone', resistant to change, resembling stones rather than birds or horses or human riders? Yeats doesn't answer this question, but just returns to a historical (rather than a political) perception: 'A terrible beauty is born', the Rising has altered the Irish (and English) world irrevocably, whether Yeats has his doubts about it or not.

Yeats starts with himself and ends with history, effectively bracketing both the moral and the political. Auden starts with himself and ends with a company of the Just, which may, with any luck, include him. He has more questions and worries than Yeats, and it soon becomes clear that there is a deep indirectness in the poem, in spite of its title and ostensible occasion.

The immediate question for Auden, as for Yeats, seems to be: what has happened? This is where the stanzas about Luther and Hitler and Thucydides take us, and perhaps even the stanza about imperialism and the blind skyscrapers. Germany, tyranny, 'Collective Man': the imago of our time. But we are less than halfway through the poem. The later stanzas are not about the historical event and how or why it happened, but our shock at the event and every doubt the event awakens in us. We are 'children afraid of the night', we crave 'to be loved alone', we make false promises, and we fail to understand the depths of our hunger or loneliness – of our shared hunger and loneliness, our communal isolation. Hitler has almost done us a favour, revealed the vast lies on which we construct our lives. No terrible beauty is born, but there is a chance of some sort of awareness. 'We must love one another or die' (*EA*, pp. 245–46).

There is no historical perception here, only a dream of justice and affirmation. History, even in the shape of the invasion of Poland, is a vast morality play in which we are all sinners. In this sense, we should note the courage of Auden's poem and its unlikely, willfully unpopular perspective. But the evasion of history, the reduction of the world to a moralizing mind on 52nd Street, is still striking, and the poem's conclusion is desperately unconvincing – so unconvincing as to be lyrically touching in an almost Yeatsian manner the expression not of a hope or a prayer but an already defeated fantasy.

As is well known, Auden dropped this poem from later editions of his work, classifying it among pieces he saw as 'dishonest, or bad-mannered, or boring'. He famously said the line 'We must love one another or die' was simply false, because we die anyway. But when a subtle and intelligent writer says something blunt and even rather silly – did Auden not know in 1939 that we die anyway? – we should always look again. It would be – it is – a good thing to love another, and it might even save us from several forms of moral death; but it won't stop Hitler from invading Poland, and for two excellent reasons. The invasion has already happened, and Hitler doesn't care whether we love one or another or not. Furthermore, our loving one another will not save Belgium or France or stave off the Blitz.

The thought of love in this context is neither dishonest nor bad-mannered nor boring – even if Auden said the work was 'the most dishonest poem I have ever written' (see RD-H 1995, p. 319). The thought is grand and sincerely deluded, a condition precisely identified in the poem itself, 'the romantic lie in the brain / Of the sensual man-in-the-street' (*EA*, p. 246). The same delusion, in its negative form, is beautifully revealed in one of the poem's finest lines, the one about the children, Hansels and Gretels lost in the forest of history, 'who have never been happy or good' (*EA*, p. 246). This may be the saddest inference ever drawn from a fairy story, and looks forward to the picture of the child in 'The Shield of Achilles' 'who'd never heard / Of any world where promises were kept, / Or one could weep because another wept' (*CP* 2007, p. 596). This world is all too imaginable, but such desolation would at least save us from decisions, because it wouldn't matter what we did. 'Never' sounds like a long time, but it isn't a time at all. It doesn't have a date; and no dictator can cause it or invade it.

'The Shield of Achilles' itself is a slightly different kind of atlantic poem, wiser and even more oblique, and one that engages more fully with the entanglements of virtue and liberty, because as Edward Mendelson shrewdly says, it attacks the very form of presentation that makes it so appealing to worried readers ('The European Auden', *CCWHA*, pp. 59–60). Hephaestos and Thetis, maker and watcher of what's on the warrior's shield, bear no responsibility for the distant horrors they craft and see; they are as helpless as the lost subjects of 'September 1, 1939'. But readers of the poem are not as lost as this – or we are lost if we choose to be, if we settle for the imagined safe side of an infinite Atlantic, as if there were a place that violence cannot reach, and as if its reaching our shores had nothing to do with our history.

NOTES

1 Geoffrey Hill, 'Language, Suffering, and Silence', *Collected Critical Writings* (Oxford University Press, 2008), p. 405.
2 Randall Jarrell, *Kipling, Auden & Co* (Carcanet, 1986), p. 36.
3 See Edward Mendelson, 'Introduction', *Prose* II, p. xv.
4 *Kipling, Auden & Co*, pp. 36, 55.
5 Barbara Everett, *Auden* (Oliver and Boyd, 1964), p. 73.
6 See Peter Porter, 'Auden's English', (*CCWHA* p. 127); and Rowan Williams's webpage, entry on Auden at www.archbishopofcanterbury.org/articles. php/2001/the-archbishop-on-poet-w.h.-auden.
7 Thekla Clark, *Wystan and Chester* (Columbia University Press, 1996), p. 26.
8 *Yeats's Poems*, ed. A. Norman Jeffares (Macmillan, 1989), pp. 287–89.

PART III

Political, Historical, and Theoretical Contexts

Communism and Fascism in 1920s and 1930s Britain

Matthew Worley

I

The year is 1930; the place is Swan Court, Chelsea. In a modern flat, gathered around an elaborate glass table in a state-of-the-art drawing room, a group of well-to-do young men and women discuss the ongoing ramifications of Wall Street's crash and the ponderous response of Ramsay MacDonald's beleaguered Labour government to the gathering economic problems. Talk turns to the apparent death of democracy, to the need for state intervention and strong leadership; terms such a 'totalitarian', 'corporatism' and 'planning' come to the fore. References to Hitler, Mussolini, and Stalin spark heated debates and disagreement, although all concur that a new form of politics must emerge to confront the challenges of the modern age. One of those present, Wyndham Lewis, makes the case for fascism, praising Mussolini and predicting a prosperous future for Germany's emergent National Socialist movement. Peter Eckersley, until recently the BBC's chief engineer, speaks enthusiastically about the proposals put forward by Sir Oswald Mosley on his resignation from the Labour government. Aldous Huxley, meanwhile, suggests that the Soviet Union provides a more suitable model for Britain to follow. To his side, the Labour MP and socialist cartoonist Frank Horrabin nods sagely as Dorothy Clark busily tends to her guests' drinks and deliberates on the relative merits of fascism and communism as a necessary alternative to a parliament entrapped by its outmoded customs and traditions.[1]

As this glimpse through the chintz suggests, W. H. Auden was not the only British intellectual responding to political and ideological currents that challenged mainstream thinking in the 1920s and 1930s.[2] In the aftermath of the Great War (1914–18), and especially amidst the political-economic dislocation of the Great Slump (1929–32), many writers, artists, and academics sought to shape public and establishment opinion by adopting new ideas and new means to transform the world of which they were part. Alternatives were sought to the 'old ways' that had led Britain into four years of unprecedented slaughter and had precipitated a post-war world of ever-worsening uncertainty, haunted or enticed by the spectre of alternate totalitarianisms. For Auden, communism came closest to providing a practical and visionary ideal; for others, fascism offered answers. But quite often, particularly in the years prior to Hitler's consolidation of power in the early to mid-1930s, the distinction between them was blurred. Mosley's conversion to fascism came after much discussion within his circle of the emergence of broadly analogous 'modern movements' such as Bolshevism, Italian Fascism, German National Socialism, the Young Turk movement, Austrian social democracy, the Kuomintang and also King Alexander's 'experiment towards the modern state' in Yugoslavia.[3] George Bernard Shaw famously complemented his commitment to socialism with a respect for fascism that extended well into the 1930s.[4] As for Auden, Graham Greene noted in his review of *The Orators* (1932) that it was difficult to tell 'whether the author's sympathies are Communist or Fascist', recognizing the apparent tension that existed between Auden's leftist sympathies and his ambiguous attraction to the figure of the Leader (Haffenden, pp. 115–16). In this, he was far from alone.

II

Intellectuals' interest in communism and fascism should not, however, suggest that either creed seriously threatened to overhaul Britain's liberal parliamentary democracy between the wars. In organized political terms, both the Communist Party of Great Britain (CPGB) and the various fascist groupings that came and went between 1923 and 1940 remained on the margins of British politics, serving as designated 'extremes' against which to measure mainstream opinion and practice. In particular, their confrontational politics of action began to rub against the grain of a British polity informed by an ever more peaceable political culture. As Jon Lawrence has shown, the inter-war years revealed a growing distaste for the unruly politics of the Victorian and Edwardian periods. The impact of the war and the extension of the franchise combined with changes to electoral procedure – an end to 'rolling' elections, redrawn constituency boundaries, the free use of school halls – to facilitate a recasting of political-cultural values and expectations. Broadly understood, the expression of public opinion in the years after the war was to be seen less in the midst of the unruly crowd and more in the rational choices of a mass electorate.[5]

The CPGB, formed in 1920, was affiliated with the Communist International established by the Bolsheviks following the 1917 revolution. Its membership in the 1920s averaged around 5,000, before the heightened political climate of the 1930s saw the party ranks slowly grow to 17,500 on the eve of the Second World War. To put this into context, the Labour Party emerged to provide the main alternative to Conservatism after 1918 with a moderate socialist programme that attracted more than 2,500,000 affiliated and individual members by 1939. Across the entire inter-war period, the CPGB boasted just four MPs and a political influence that sometimes appeared to exist more in the abstract – as a 'bogey' for Tories and Labour socialists to utilize as they saw fit – than in fact.

That said, the CPGB proved to be a visible and persistent political presence in Britain between the wars. As an overwhelmingly proletarian party, it formed bases of support in most urban and industrial areas and exerted a notable influence within the trade union movement and amongst the unemployed. For all the notoriety of the Jarrow Crusade organized by Labour's Ellen Wilkinson in 1936, it was the communist-led National Unemployed Workers' Movement (NUWM) that organized and mobilized the widespread unemployed demonstrations that took place in British towns and cities throughout the period, including the hunger march to Hyde Park in 1932 that culminated in a full-scale confrontation with baton-wielding mounted police. The party also fought its way to the forefront of the anti-fascist struggle during the 1930s, both in Britain and with regard to mobilizing support for republican Spain. Taken generally, therefore, between the wars, the CPGB established itself as the principal party to the left of Labour. Although understood to be bound to the Soviet Union, such a relationship provided the CPGB with funds and abundant kudos, once Stalin's Five-Year Plan appeared to provide a working alternative to the faltering capitalist systems of the early 1930s. It was, moreover, the self-appointed guardian of Marxism in Britain, albeit distorted by the Bolshevik lens.

Coming in the opposite direction, early British fascism enjoyed an awkward relationship with Britain's political establishment. Where communists clearly stated their intention to overhaul parliamentary democracy and establish a soviet state via the dictatorship of the proletariat, the British Fascisti (later the British Fascists (BF)) was formed in 1923 as an overtly patriotic organization concerned primarily with repelling the supposed threat of socialism. Its membership was small but well-connected; links to landed families (the Duke of Northumberland, the Eighth Earl

of Glasgow, Lord Garvagh, and Sir Ormand Winter), ex-military types
(Brigadier-General Robert Blakeney, Major-General T. D. Pilcher, and
Rear-Admiral A. E. Armstrong), Conservative MPs (Patrick Hannon, Sir
Burton Chadwick, and Colonel Charles Burn) and even MI5 (Charles
Maxwell Knight) have been well-documented.[6] Although inspired by
Mussolini's repression of the Italian left, the British Fascisti lent its sup-
port to the Conservative Party and for some time appeared fascist in name
only. As a consequence, more vigorously fascist groups had also emerged –
the National Fascisti and the vehemently racist Imperial Fascist League,
for example – before Mosley's foundation of the British Union of Fascists
(BUF) in 1932.

The BUF was a more serious proposition. Its contentious but cogent
basic programme envisaged a centrally planned economy and a corporate
state that claimed to reconcile class and sectional differences by asserting
the overarching primacy of the nation-state itself. Mosley, a baronet and
war veteran whose political journey had led him from the Conservative
Party through to the Independent Labour Party, Labour government
and New Party between 1918 and 1932, presented the BUF as a resolutely
modern organization, combining the 'dynamic urge to change and progress with the authority, the discipline and the order without which nothing great can be achieved'. Fascism, he said, was 'revolutionary, or it is
nothing'.[7] But although Mosley won support from Lord Rothermere's
Daily Mail, the implicit and actual violence of the BUF's paramilitary
organization and its open adoption of anti-Semitism diminished its
appeal. Estimated to have had up to 50,000 members in 1934, it ended the
decade devoid of 'respectable' support and ready to be crushed as a fifth
column.

Significantly, many of the intellectuals attracted by communist or
fascist ideology did not therefore join (or even align themselves with)
those political parties. Some, such as Stephen Spender, Cecil Day Lewis,
and John Strachey, joined briefly or served as 'fellow-travellers'; but others – including Auden – engaged more readily with the ferment of ideas
emerging out of the post-liberal 'modern movements', and sought rather
to define the political and cultural agenda, than to subscribe to pre-
determined doctrines. Nevertheless, many within Britain's intellectual
milieu empathized with efforts to transcend prevailing liberal-demo-
cratic ideas of social-economic and political organizations; they were
prepared to entertain the notion that democracy was a chimera and that
the future belonged to a modern, state-driven dictatorship. Why was
this so?

British intellectuals' sympathy for communism and fascism stemmed from a number of sources. The context of the time was important. The Great War had redrawn geographical, political, and psychological boundaries; as empires collapsed, political and ideological voids opened, receptive to a range of new and transformative ideas. Amongst these, fascism combined ultra-nationalism with glorification of the modern world: fascism, Mosley insisted, was a 'steel creed of an iron age. It cuts through the verbiage of illusion to the achievement of a new reality'.[8] Similarly, Marx's communist spectre took (for some) positive shape, in a Bolshevik Revolution fuelled largely by popular dissatisfaction with the War. Simultaneously, that war's trauma and upheavals provided a cultural 'space' in which modernist literary styles and artistic *avant gardes* could reimagine form and content. Across Europe (and beyond), this induced a sense of an era both ending and beginning; in consequence, the post-war future could inspire optimism as well as dread.

This political and ideological rupture served to provoke a contentious and transnational debate about future civilization. Communists inspired by the Russian revolutions came to see in Bolshevism, the Soviet Union, and Stalin's five-year plans the basis for a realized socialist future; elsewhere, as in Italy and Germany, ultra-nationalists imagined their nations reborn and purified. In the British context, such debate touched on a number of related themes. Most obviously, the rigours of war compounded earlier concerns for the well-being of the British economy and the effectiveness of parliamentary democracy in maintaining and advancing national status. In economic terms, Britain emerged from the war intact but damaged. Not only had it lost markets to overseas competition, but it owed money to the United States and relinquished its role as the world's leading financial centre. The foundations of Britain's pre-war economic growth – free trade and the staple industries of cotton, coal, and iron – appeared no longer to provide support for a modern post-war economy. In fact, the war itself had been won by means of a state-directed economy that seemed only to expose the shortcomings of *laissez faire* liberalism. Politically, meanwhile, the 1918 Representation of the People Act all but completed the extension of democracy across the British adult population, serving to reconfigure politics and usher in a period of reappraisal. As the Labour Party emerged to provide the principal alternative to Conservatism, so the fault lines of British politics shifted, encompassing questions of socialism, class and gender; debate about democracy gave way to concerns over the efficacy of parliamentary government and the deficiencies of the party system.

Even the relative calm of the mid-1920s was disturbed by the upheavals of the 1926 General Strike (which Auden supported, unlike many of his class), before the Wall Street crash exacerbated Britain's economic problems and rekindled debate about the sustainability of its economic and political norms. Journals such as *Political Quarterly* initiated a symposium of the 'failure of political parties', while politicians such as Bob Boothby and Lord Percy questioned whether democracy could survive so severe a period of economic turmoil.[9] Given such a context, it should be no surprise that many were politicized: for if many a 'bright young thing' turned to escapist frivolity in the 1920s, the darkening mood of the early 1930s prompted a more engaged response.

This, of course, was compounded and complemented by the widespread social-economic and political upheaval in inter-war Europe. Throughout the period, regular visits to the Soviet Union saw everyone from Sidney and Beatrice Webb to Aneurin Bevan, Cynthia Mosley, and Lady Astor journeying to the first workers' state. And even when the harsh realities of 'building socialism' were recognized in the repression and deprivation experienced within the Soviet Union, the rationale of socialist planning and the revolutionary core of the communist objective continued to offer a striking contrast to Britain's apparent malaise. Equally, however, some busy minds looked elsewhere. For Italophiles, such as the Sitwells, it was Mussolini who offered a solution to the liberal impasse; for Lewis, the aesthetics of Nazism held uncomfortable appeal. Fascism, as John Strachey later admitted, had an 'attractive entrance', and neither he nor Mosley was alone in drifting towards it in the inter-war period.[10]

In fact, Strachey's *The Coming Struggle for Power* (1932) endeavoured to capture those intertwining factors that encouraged intellectuals to wrestle with radical politics and to perceive the future in terms of a struggle between fascism and communism. He dissected in detail the contradictions of post-war capitalism, before going on to analyse the ongoing 'decay of capitalist culture'. This, he argued, resulted from reason, rationality, and science negating the value of religion and undermining the basic tenets of capitalism. In response, literary intellectuals, inspired by the mood of 'violence and despair' pioneered by Nietzsche, had committed themselves to revealing the 'shallow hypocritical optimism' of the pre-war period. Thus, H. G. Wells and George Bernard Shaw, both of whom combined critiques of parliamentary democracy with a sympathy for authoritarian alternatives, were offered by Strachey as examples of intellectuals who looked beyond liberalism in their visions of a new age. Equally, writers such as Lawrence and Huxley were noted for their reflecting the 'agonies of the epoch in which we live'.[11]

Furthermore, this debate potentially divided the generations. The Great War had thrown up a symbolic barrier, appearing to separate children of the British middle and upper classes born in the 1890s and early 1900s from their forebears. In fact, direct experience of war combined with its political consequences to deny that so-called war generation the relative socio-economic certainties of their parents. Many therefore rebelled against the perceived orthodoxies of the Victorian and Edwardian age, by living for the moment or seeking solace in moral and political creeds that claimed to explain the changing world around them.[12] For many who came of age during or in the wake of the Great War, the division between pre-war and post-war worlds was all too apparent. In the words of 29-year-old Bill Allen, writing in 1930 as a Unionist MP poised to join with Sir Oswald Mosley on his journey to fascism, 'we have no respect for the grey hairs, grey theories, methods and traditions' of the pre-war age, '[ours] is a world of aeroplanes, wireless, talkies, speedboats, of all things new and wonderful'.[13] His list includes some of the technological items also to be found in Auden's poem of the same year, 'Consider This...', which communicates a similar sense of violent rupture from the past leading towards the necessity for change. This suggests something of the appeal of the political extremes emerging in the aftermath of war, for the young intellectual whose radicalism served to reinforce generational distinction and to challenge the prevailing authority of an ageing and seemingly deficient liberal establishment.

Finally, it may be suggested, perhaps controversially, that both fascism and communism complemented the intellectual's supposition of innate superiority. Fascism, most obviously, rejected notions of human equality, preferring instead to celebrate the 'superman' and envisage a corporate ideal that bound together – instead of alleviating – socio-economic and intellectual differences. And although fascism's emphasis on spirit and physicality meant less regard was paid to political theory, both Mosley and his foreign counterparts retained an admiration for technical reasoning, science, and aesthetics that could flatter and excite the intelligentsia. The ideological foundations of fascism also built on many long-standing themes of debate, not least those of eugenics and theories of race.[14] Communism, meanwhile, combined its stated desire for a classless, egalitarian society with a political method that by the 1920s was defined by Lenin's conception of a revolutionary vanguard. Consequently, communist theory – not to mention the intellectual challenges of Marxism – offered much that appealed to those of a more cerebral bent. In a 1936 poem, Auden evoked Lenin, alongside figures as diverse as Freud and Schweitzer, as a neglected guide to 'the really better / World' (*EA*, p. 165). On one hand, it allowed intellectuals a designated role; on the other, its ideas overlapped with progressive opinions that had long been the preserve of at least a section of Britain's intellectual milieu.

Against the drab mediocrity offered by democracy and socio-economic decline, the utopias promised by fascism and communism provided an exciting alternative. Over time, they developed into polarized visions of modernity, alternative futures to be fought for intellectually and physically. In Spain, for example, the civil war of 1936–39 was understood in just such terms, not least by Auden (at first), who journeyed there both to lend support to the republic and to gain 'direct knowledge' of political events by which to inform his poetry and thereby enable him to 'speak to/for' the soldiers he fought beside (quoted *Early Auden*, pp. 195–96). As totalities, fascism and communism stimulated a range of intellectual interests, providing for an influence that extended beyond the relatively closed worlds of academia or literary society; simultaneously, of course, alignment with a political 'extreme' reinforced the intellectual's sense of existing outside the mainstream. In other words, the glamour of dissent combined with political fashion to endow the intellectual with a status that transcended alike the broader 'mass' and the bourgeoisie's stultified morality.

To suggest that Britain's intellectuals fell neatly into line behind the opposing banners of communism and fascism between the wars would be misleading. As Stefan Collini reminds us, the majority of British intellectuals did not become politically engaged or publicly express their political views at this time.[15] What is clear, however, is that many young intellectuals were attracted to the possibilities opened by the new political creeds that emerged in the aftermath of the Great War. At a time of great uncertainty, with the world seemingly poised on the brink, the competing ideologies of communism and fascism offered alternative futures to the apparent malaise of liberal democracy and capitalism. In their totality, these ideologies offered wholly re-imagined civilizations that challenged and animated thinking people. Both provided stinging critiques of the way things were and a combative approach to overcoming the problems of the post-war age. For the young, these ideologies offered a means of rebellion that licensed challenging ideas and new ways of living. That both creeds led, ultimately, to death and destruction is simply the darkly ironic aspect of what Richard Overy has recently described as a thoroughly 'morbid age'[16] – his formula chiming with Auden's judgment, in 'September 1, 1939', that the foregoing decade had been 'low' and 'dishonest', its 'hopes' revealed as speciously 'clever' (*EA*, p. 245).

NOTES

1 The description is drawn from reminiscences contained within M. Eckersley, *Prospero's Wireless: A Biography of Peter Pendleton Eckersley* (Myles Books, 1997), pp. 327–31.

2 For an analysis of the role played by intellectuals in Britain, see S. Collini, *Absent Minds: Intellectuals in Britain* (Oxford University Press, 2007).

3 BBK/C/254, O. Mosley, Untitled Memorandum, 19 November 1930 (Beaverbrook Papers); C. F. Melville, 'A Balkan Monarch Takes a Chance', *Action*, 12 November 1931, p. 11; M. Worley, *Oswald Mosley and the New Party* (Palgrave, 2010), pp. 29–32.

4 G. B. Shaw, *The Intelligent Woman's Guide to Socialism and Capitalism* (Penguin, 1928, reprinted in 1937).

5 J. Lawrence, 'The Transformation of British Public Politics after the First World War', *Past and Present*, 190/1 (2006), pp. 185–6.

6 M. Pugh, *Hurrah for the Blackshirts: Fascists and Fascism in Britain Between the Wars* (Jonathan Cape, 2005); T. Linehan, *British Fascism, 1918–39: Parties, ideology and Culture* (Manchester University Press, 2000); J. Hope, 'British Fascism and the State, 1917–27: A Re-Examination of the Documentary Evidence', *Labour History Review*, 57/3 (1992), pp. 72–83; R. Griffiths, *Fellow Travellers of the Right: British Enthusiasts for Nazi Germany, 1933–39* (Oxford University Press, 1983).

7 O. Mosley, *The Greater Britain* (London: BUF, 1932), pp. 15–16.

8 Mosley, *The Greater Britain*, p. 16.

9 *Political Quarterly*, 3/1 (1932); R. Boothby, 'Can Democracy Survive', *Nation and Athenaeum*, 3 May 1930; Lord E. Percy, *Democracy on Trial: A Preface to an Industrial Policy* (John Lane, 1931).

10 J. Strachey, *The Menace of Fascism* (Gollancz, 1933), p. 165.

11 J. Strachey, *The Coming Struggle for Power* (Gollancz, 1932), pp. 188–230.

12 D. J. Taylor, *Bright Young People: The Rise and Fall of a Generation, 1918–40* (Chatto & Windus, 2007); M. Green, *Children of the Sun: Narrative and Decadence in Britain in England After 1918* (London: Pimlico, 1992 edition).

13 *The Times*, 28 November 1930.

14 D. Stone, *Breeding Superman: Nietzsche, Race and Eugenics in Edwardian and Interwar Britain* (Liverpool University Press, 2002); J. Carey, *The Intellectuals and the Masses: Pride and Prejudice Among the Literary Intelligentsia, 1800–1939* (Faber and Faber, 1992).

15 Collini, *Absent Minds*, p. 86.

16 R. Overy, *The Morbid Age: Britain Between the Wars* (Allen Lane, 2009).

CHAPTER XIV

Auden and Wars

Patrick Deer

W. H. Auden's war poetry is most notable for the war he did not cover. By leaving Britain for New York on the eve of World War II, he was judged to have treacherously left the 'island fortress' in its hour of need. He may have refused the opportunity to contribute to British war culture between 1939 and 1945, but his exposure to the conflicts of the 'inter-war' period nevertheless gave him a powerful understanding of the importance of culture to the transformation of modern warfare. As he argued in a brief article on 'Poetry and Total War' for *The Chicago Sun* in March 1942, 'I think it not unlikely that the aspect of this war which will be most reflected in the poetry of the next few years is the danger that, in order to win it, the democracies will construct an anti-fascist political religion, and so, by becoming like their enemies, lose the peace' *(Prose II,* p. 153). His grasp of the usefulness of poetry and rhetoric to the war-makers made him especially wary of the aestheticization of violence and the seductions of patriotism. 'If the poet, qua poet, has any other social function than to give pleasure, it is, in the words of the greatest poet produced by the last war, "to warn", so that in one sense, the serious poetry of any given moment is always at odds with the conscious ideas of the majority' *(Prose II,* p. 153). Although here invoking the authority of Wilfred Owen, in the midst of World War II, Auden continued to refuse the conventional role of war poet in favour of a lonelier path, consistently skeptical of the modernizing culture of war.

Like George Orwell, Auden offered a profound critique of the manipulation of language in war. But Auden's poetry traces a more complicated understanding of the wartime corruptions of rhetoric: whereas Orwell advocated demystification and plain English against jargon and propaganda, the constant dialectical shifts of Auden's poetry make clear the twists and turns required to challenge official rhetoric and the tenacious grip of the war-makers over language. For Auden, 'war is an overt eruption of tensions and malaises which have long been present, and to which the poet has, or should have, long been sensitive. Thus changes in poetry both antedate and postdate historical events' (*Prose II*, p. 152). He refused both the seductive mythology of combat as a proving ground for the masculine poet and the Hobbesian vision of permanent warfare.

One of Auden's most penetrating explorations of the relation between poetry, politics, and violence, 'In Memory of W. B. Yeats' (1939), was written from the vantage point of neutral New York on the eve of war, hearing how 'In the nightmare of the dark / All the dogs of Europe bark' (*EA*, p. 243). Against warmongering nations 'sequestered' in 'hate', poetry is to be prized for its very lack of utility and instrumentality, 'For poetry makes nothing happen: it survives / In the valley of its saying where executives / Would never want to tamper' (*EA*, p. 242). This famous phrase, 'poetry makes nothing happen', would seem to reinforce the image of Auden dumping his politics overboard as he sailed to America, echoed as it is by the disturbing ambiguities of 'September 1, 1939', where the poet simultaneously contests 'the romantic lie' of the 'man-in-the-street' (that 'There is no such thing as the State') and 'the lie of Authority' (that 'no one exists alone'), seeking to override both by the equally famous formula, 'We must love one another or die' (*EA*, p. 246). In the elegy for Yeats, as in his longer meditation on the role of the poet in wartime, 'New Year Letter' (1941), there *is* such a thing as the state and it, like society, makes demands on expert practitioners of language. Like Yeats's, Auden's poetic voice is implicated, living out a privileged relationship to language, all too aware of its capacity to manipulate and sway emotion. 'Time', he asserted in lines he later removed, 'Worships language and forgives / Everyone by whom it lives' (*EA*, p. 242), irrespective of the odiousness of their political views (Auden's examples were Kipling and Claudel). Poetry might make 'nothing happen' as the elegy declares, but the stakes were extremely high, because 'language' also includes the wider uses of words by the official culture, mobilized in the service of a 'political religion' anxious to make *something* happen, as opposed to the narrower sense of 'poetry' as an autonomous, non-instrumental literary discourse. Auden's elegy for Yeats makes clear that the poet, like the citizen, must grapple with the contradiction between these two seemingly incompatible uses of language. Because Yeats was one by whom the language lived, he dies, but the fruits of his 'gift' do not. Through him, poetry 'survives' – the elegy insists – as 'a way of happening, a mouth' (*EA*, p. 242).

What were Auden's wars? Like others in his generation, Auden's childhood and adolescence were overshadowed by the Great War. His father, George Auden, served in the Royal Army Medical Corps in Gallipoli,

Egypt, and France between 1914 and 1918, during which time Auden saw
little of him, passing the war in boarding school and holidays amidst limestone and lead mines. In Berlin in 1928–29, the young poet was exposed
to revolutionary violence, fascist reaction, and the homoerotic force of 'the
Truly Strong Man'; the political violence in Weimar in 1928 gave the war
metaphors in his Berlin poetry a sharp edge. Returning to Britain, he diagnosed symptoms of authoritarianism within some prominent traditions and
institutions, most notably in the private schools where he found employment. In 'The Prolific and the Devourer' (1939) he observed, 'Politically a
private school is an absolute dictatorship where the assistant staff play, as
it were, Goering Roehm Goebbels Himmler (*sic*) to a headmaster Hitler.
There are the same intrigues for favour, the same gossip campaigns, and
from time to time the same purges' (*Prose II*, pp. 417–18).

Auden's fascination with imperial airpower, whose mythology had survived the bloody deadlock and disillusion of trench warfare, and with the
charismatic figure of 'the Truly Strong Man' converged in his exploration
of the figure of the Airman in general and of T. E. Lawrence in particular. This resulted in the extraordinarily unstable critique of militarized
masculinity and 'social illness' of *The Orators* (1932) and in the moun-
taineering drama, *The Ascent of F6* (1936). Auden's Leftism then inevitably drew him to the Spanish Civil War, where he spent January–March
1936, mainly in Barcelona and Valencia. As he wrote to E. R. Dodds,
'I am not one of those who believe that poetry need or even should be
directly political, but in a critical period such as ours, I do believe that the
poet must have direct knowledge of the major political events ... I shall
probably be a bloody bad soldier but how can I speak to/for them without becoming one?' (quoted *Early Auden*, pp. 195–96). Auden volunteered
as an ambulance driver with the Spanish Medical Aid Committee, but
instead he worked briefly in propaganda broadcasting. He wrote the celebrated pamphlet poem 'Spain', donating all proceeds to Medical Aid for
Spain; but he subsequently altered and finally repudiated this poem altogether. When he returned, he recorded little of his experiences, disturbed
by the political violence.

The desire for 'direct knowledge' of modern warfare persisted, and
the project of producing a travel book took Auden and Christopher
Isherwood to a China under attack by Japan. There he was exposed to
Japanese bombing, to the elusiveness of front-line combat, and to war
cultures that seemed opaque. Returning via the United States, the two
formed a plan to emigrate the following year, their arrival in New York in
January 1939 coinciding with the death-throes of the Spanish Republic.

From neutral America, Auden grappled with the consequences of his absence from beleaguered Britain, offering in 'New Year Letter' (1941) a skeptical vision of the political and aesthetic impact of the Second World War. Unsuccessful in earlier attempts to participate directly in the American war effort, after the end of European hostilities, he was sent to Germany with the rank of Major in the U.S. Strategic Bombing Survey, where he observed at close hand the effects of area bombing on the defeated German population.

'Consider This and In Our Time' provides a useful point of entry into his ambivalent relations with modern war culture. The poem famously surveys British society from a panoramic vantage point, 'As the hawk sees it or the helmeted airman' (*EA*, p. 46). This line brings various histories of war together in uneasy alliance. The combination of the 'hawk' and the 'helmeted airman' evokes the mythology of the Great War 'knights of the air', whose heroic reputation survived the disillusionment of trench warfare. The loftiness of vision notably foreshadows Auden's praise for Hardy's tragically panoramic 'hawk's vision' in his poetic epic of the Napoleonic Wars, *The Dynasts*, (*Prose II*, p. 46), as well as echoing D. H. Lawrence's modernist diagnosis of the psychological malaise of the post-war 'Waste Land' (see Fuller 1998, p. 74); the poem's imaginings of fascist militarism in English settings also draws on his experience of the revolutionary violence of Weimar Berlin in 1928–29.

Like other poets of the 1930s, Auden was obsessively 'airminded': the references to the aerial view in 'Consider This…' tap into the futuristic imaginary of a modernizing official war culture reinventing itself by projecting strategic fantasies of imperial air power. But Auden was to find this panoramic vision increasingly problematic; in the ambivalent figure of the 'Airman,' as in the real life contradictions of T. E. Lawrence, he explored the dream and nightmare of the period's obsession with imperial air power (see Deer 2009).[1] Nowhere is this more powerfully or presciently explored than in *The Orators* (1932). The armoured masculinity and panoramic gaze of the airman are embodied, and unevenly satirized, in the rise and fall of the tormented, proto-fascist figure of its 'Truly Strong Man' protagonist. But its contradictions exact a terrible cost, as Auden explores the dark side of the Airman's charismatic appeal.

Auden's complex ethical stance in relation to poetry and violence confronted its greatest challenges in The Spanish Civil War. His poem, 'Spain' offers a conspectus of political obsessions of the 1930s. The conflict has relegated to the past conventional martial heroics, 'Yesterday the belief in the absolute value of Greece, / The fall of the curtain upon the death of a hero'. It has also postponed the futurist aestheticization of violence, 'To-morrow for the young poets exploding like bombs' (*SP* 2007, p. 57). The poem insists repeatedly instead, 'But to-day the struggle'. In the twenty-fourth stanza of the original poem, readers encountered Auden's most famously problematic lines of war poetry: 'To-day the deliberate increase in the chances of death, / The conscious acceptance of guilt in the necessary murder' (*SP* 2007, p. 57). Despite asserting that the poem was 'one of the few decent things that have been written about the Spanish war', in his essay 'Inside the Whale' Orwell famously seized on the apparent amorality of 'necessary murder', associating it with Stalinist 'liquidation': 'It could only be written by a person to whom murder is at most a *word*. Personally I would not speak so lightly of murder … Mr. Auden's brand of amoralism is only possible if you're the kind of person who is elsewhere when the trigger is pulled'.[2] Auden was stung by Orwell's 'densely unjust' criticism, defending himself to Stephen Spender as late as 1963: 'I was *not* excusing totalitarian crimes but only trying to say, what, surely, every decent person thinks if he finds himself unable to adopt the absolute pacifist position … If there is such a thing as a just war, then murder can be necessary for the sake of justice' (RD-H 1995, p. 167). But revising the poem in *Another Time* (1940), he compressed three stanzas about the Republican cause into one and changed the notorious line to 'The conscious acceptance of guilt in the fact of murder'. Defending the ethical complexity of Auden's original line, Tim Kendall persuasively observes, 'The final version takes a small step back from courageous complication to blind conviction'.[3]

Within the intricate structure of the poem, Spain functions not as a pretext for violence, but instead as a screen on which fantasies of political action and violence are projected. At the very midpoint of the poem, the poem imagines 'the life' replying from 'the heart … of the city':

> What's your proposal? To build the just city? I will.
> I agree. Or is it the suicide pact, the romantic
> Death? Very well, I accept, for
> I am your choice, your decision. Yes, I am Spain.
> (*SP* 2007, p. 56)

The ironic framing of this image of Spain as a crucible for both political experiments and the death wish of combatants would seem to undercut any certainty about the ethical necessity of killing. But, of course, it is Auden's one-liner about 'necessary murder' that continues to outlive the poem, even though the whole lesson of his poetry about war and war culture teaches otherwise.

His fascination with the contradictory elements of modern war culture and his unstable relation with Englishness at war are temporarily resolved in the remarkable anthropological perspectives of Auden's sonnet sequence, 'In Time of War', which was published as part of *Journey to a War* (1939), the travelogue co-authored with Isherwood after their largely unsuccessful attempt to capture front-line experience of the Sino-Japanese war. Auden later extracted the sonnet sequence from the book, and as Mendelson notes, 'severely revised' and reduced its length (*Prose I*, p. 825), retitling it 'Sonnets from China'. But the sequence is best understood in its original form within the hybrid volume, *Journey to a War*, set between Auden's sixty-photograph 'Picture Commentary' and the much-maligned verse 'Commentary' and fold-out map that concludes the book (*Prose I*, pp. 667–89).

The title, 'In Time of War', is misleading, as the sequence offers a remarkably ambitious genealogy for the emergence of human consciousness in which the violence of the Sino-Japanese war is only a culminating event, a narrative present intruding into a vast synchronic perspective anchored in Auden's Orientalizing vision of Chinese history. The deliberately enigmatic, biblical simplicity of the language, influenced by the 'currently fashionable' Basic English movement of the 1930s (Fuller 1998, p. 235) at first resists interpretation. Sonnets I–XII chart the progress and fall into worldliness and violence of man, 'a childish creature' (Sonnet I), from creation into various states of human history. The parable-like simplicity suggests both the inevitability of conflict, 'the way back by angels was defended / Against the poet and the legislator' (Sonnet II) and the intimate relation between poetry and the will to power. 'In Time of War' thus tells the double story of man's anthropological capacity for violence and the poet's complicity with the seductive complexity of this fallen state. In Sonnet III, Auden evokes this double bind of one apparently trapped by his own constructed understanding of the world around him, who 'to his own creation became subject':

> And shook with hate for things he'd never seen,
> And knew of love without love's proper object,
> And was oppressed as he had never been.

Both poets and citizens are condemned to become oppressed by their 'own creation'; the difference is that, for Auden, poetry's alienated state allows the space for melancholy reflection: 'The poet wept and saw in him the truth, / And the oppressor held him up as an example' (Sonnet IV). The sequence turns around with Sonnet XIII, which offers one of Auden's panoramic visions of historic injustice: 'But hear the morning's injured weeping, and know why: / Cities and men have fallen; the will of the Unjust / Has never lost its power'.

The great originality of 'In Time of War' is to locate this longer temporality within the violence of the Sino-Japanese war. In the process, Auden both encapsulates and distances ironically the fears of bombing and aerial holocaust that haunted the 1930s, most famously captured in Prime Minister Stanley Baldwin's declaration that 'The bomber will always get through'. Sonnet XIV captures the grim cosmopolitan irony of these seemingly inevitable apocalyptic fears, 'Yes, we are going to suffer now; the sky / Throbs like a feverish forehead; pain is real' as the 'groping searchlights suddenly reveal / The little natures that will make us cry'. Yet, if 'pain' were 'real', we would not need to be reminded of it. And are these 'little natures' the bombers of Sonnet XV, 'free / And isolated like the very rich; / Remote like savants' (Sonnet XV), or is it the littleness of instrumental reason, that manufactures a culture of fear? Sonnet XVI, however, insists on the specific, declaring that 'maps can really point to places / Where life is evil now: / Nanking; Dachau' – a localized perspective individualized, albeit anonymously, in the Chinese soldier who dies unrecorded, 'Far from the heart of culture' (Sonnet XVIII).

The sequence moves towards a European present haunted by the echoes of distant war, existing in uneasy calm: 'We lie in the Present's unopened / Sorrow; its limits are what we are' (Sonnet XX). Monumental urban architecture only heightens the amnesia, 'No, not their names', nullifying Kipling's famous refrain in 'Recessional' 'Lest we forget'. (Sonnet XXIV); 'brass bands throbbing in the parks' (Sonnet XXV) foster the delusion of a 'future reign of happiness and peace'. Against this, Auden's concluding sonnets insist on the contingency of violence, 'Nothing is given: we must find our law', and on our common physical existence, 'We have no destiny assigned us / Nothing is certain but the body' (Sonnet XXV). The sequence's larger historical movement pitches Auden's calmly anamnestic logic against the forgetting that allows war to recur: 'We can't believe that we designed it' – to read these lines slightly against their grain – 'Disaster comes and we're amazed to find it' (Sonnet XXVI). While Europe slumbers, sighing 'for an ancient South', the final sonnet declares that 'we are articled to error' (Sonnet XXVII).

The sequence insists that in relation to the violence of the Sino-Japanese war, or to the apocalyptic fears of the 1930s, 'we stand elsewhere' (Sonnet XVII): this distance speaks both of our temporary insulation from total war and of our ethical responsibility to take a stand. 'In Time of War' suggests that poetry, for all its complicity with the rhetoric of power and domination, may contain the possibility for just such a stand, for an alternative imagining of human history beyond the reach of the 'bomb terror'.

The talkativeness of the verse 'Commentary' that follows undercuts the elevated tone of the sonnet sequence, but provides a helpful counterpoint. It aspires to Auden's panoramic mode, providing exhilarating glimpses of his imagination grappling with the political implications of what he and Isherwood have witnessed in China: 'one sector and one movement of the general war / ...Which ... / In essence is eternal' (*Prose I*, p. 682). By contrast, the sonnet sequence refuses this logic of permanent warfare. Instead, 'In Time of War' reveals to the reader a longer speculative history of the emergence of poetry and its relation to power and violence; but poetry must survive the corruptions of wartime, in order to continue to produce some other kind of knowledge. In this sense, the 'Commentary' can be read as *wartime* poetry, subordinated to the temporality and demands of a current emergency, whereas the sonnet sequence stages a temporality – 'In Time of War' – that is bounded by longer perspectives and other priorities: by creation, commemoration, collective mourning, and individual memory. In its dissonant elements, *Journey to A War* separates the contradictions explored 'In Memory of WB Yeats', offering its readers alternative possibilities for poetic discourse in what Walter Benjamin called 'a moment of danger'.

In 'New Year Letter' (1941), Auden maintained his skeptical stance towards wartime culture, detecting in the Second World War home front a conservative mood which demanded that 'All our reflections turn about / A common meditative norm, / Retrenchment, Sacrifice, Reform' (*DM* 15). His Pulitzer Prize-winning long poem, *The Age of Anxiety* (1947), also explored the disturbances wrought by total warfare. An expressionistic *psychomachia*, the poem offered a bridge from the Second World War into the early years of the Cold War, effectively naming an era characterized by anxiety, paranoia, and political Manicheanism. Auden remained largely silent about what he had seen of the ravages of Allied area bombing while serving with the U.S. Strategic Bombing Survey in Germany in 1945, abandoning a plan to write a book about it with his friend James Stern. Auden's official reports remain lost in the National Archives (*LA*, p. 285). In Stern's memoir of the trip, *The Hidden Damage* (1947), Auden's character 'Mervyn' is an elusive presence, maintaining a fugitive relation to the ruins and German refugees. In 'Refugee Blues' (1939), Auden had evoked the plight of German Jews fleeing from a murderous Hitler.

Imagery of the holocaust and a devastated Germany, newly partitioned by the Cold War, at last emerged in 'Memorial for the City' (June 1949).

> Across the square,
> Between the burnt-out Law Courts and Police Headquarters,
> Past the Cathedral too damaged to repair,
> Around the Grand Hotel patched up to hold reporters,
> Near huts of some Emergency Committee,
> The barbed wire runs through the abolished city.
>
> (*CP* 2007, p. 592)

Here Auden explores conditions of various political and Christian ideas of 'the City', in a poem 'consciously written in the years after Auschwitz' (Fuller 1998, p. 417). His 'Memorial' suggests these ideals may have been irreparably damaged by the violence required to defeat fascism. He insists, unforgettably, that the post-war era poses new ethical challenges that only modern poetry may fully explore: 'Our grief is not Greek: As we bury our dead / We know without knowing there is reason for what we bear' (*CP* 2007, p. 590).

After World War II, Auden observed the rise to supremacy of the 'Economic Man' in the managerial bureaucracies of a permanent war economy, which President Eisenhower warned of as the 'military industrial complex' in his Farewell Address in January 1961. As an American citizen who spent his summers in Europe, Auden observed the uses of literature as an instrument of U.S. Cold War cultural policy. As an openly gay poet, he also suffered from the pressures of Cold War witch hunting. Although he kept his political views on a tight rein, in 1966 at the height of the struggle for decolonization and anti-colonial nationalism in the Third World, he wrote a devastatingly ironic poem about the British architect of the 1947 Partition of India. Auden died in 1973 during a period of détente in the nuclear standoff between the United States and the Soviet Union, and the bloody end-phase of the Vietnam War. His first public utterances about Vietnam were too nuanced for those in the anti-war movement, but he privately expressed his distress over the conflict and finally went on the record denouncing the war in March 1968 (RD-H 1995, p. 329). Auden's poetry about war fared worse than his other poems in his own later revisions of his canon. He gained posthumous fame after September 11, 2001, as his poem 'September 1, 1939' circulated obsessively on the Internet – a poem that he said he loathed and had cut from his *Collected Poems*. Whereas war poetry is often shelved during peacetime, Auden's continues to resonate in war and peace, raising troubling questions about the degree to which we continue to live in a profoundly militarized world, 'sequestered in its hate' (*EA*, p. 243).

NOTES

1 See Patrick Deer, *Culture in Camouflage: War, Empire, and Modern British Literature* (full details in 'Further Reading' for this chapter, at the end of the volume).
2 'Inside the Whale', in *The Collected Essays, 30s Journalism and Letters of George Orwell*, Vol. I, p. 516.
3 Tim Kendall, *Modern English War Poetry*, p. 109 (see full details in 'Further Reading' for this chapter).

CHAPTER XV

Auden and Freud: The Psychoanalytic Text

John R. Boly

Auden's early commentators agree that he was influenced by psychology. Following a sensible guess, they assumed that Freud, the best known of the psychologists, was his major influence. But Auden, ever the contrarian, may owe as much to Freud's rebellious collaborator, Otto Rank, as to Freud himself. Coincidentally, at about the time Auden resolved to become a poet in 1926, Rank repudiated the Oedipal Complex, left Freud's inner circle, and moved to Paris. In retrospect, Auden's earliest criticism, his cryptic 1929 Journal, tracks Rank's heretical rejection of Freudian theory. For Rank, the great psychological event is the birth trauma, a metaphor for the individual's break with acculturated thought and attitudes. Auden concurs that 'The real "life-wish" is the desire for separation, from family, from one's literary predecessors' (*EA*, p. 299).

Despite his disagreements with Freud's theory, Auden admired Freud's therapeutic practices. In 'Psychology and Art To-Day', Auden notes that therapy and the fine arts share a common method.

The task of psychology, or art for that matter, is not to tell people how to behave, but by drawing attention to what the impersonal unconscious is trying to tell them ... to render them better able to choose, to become increasingly morally responsible for their destiny. (*EA*, p. 341)

Like psychoanalysis, poetry rejects the attitude of the passive spectator or 'man in the street'. Its challenge is to expose tactics of distortion which conceal a hidden field of experience. Whereas Auden had little patience for doctrines of innate depravity, he recognized the strong human tendency to deceive both others and oneself. In fact, the devious brilliance of human self-deception so fascinated Auden that it led him to craft poems whose analytical practices can be as rigorous as psychoanalysis. It is these vital practices, not the melancholy fatalism of the Oedipal complex, which inform Auden's tribute in the Freud elegy, more wistful than insistent, that the psychologist might engender 'a whole climate of opinion'

(*CP* 2007, p. 273). A good poem, like the addict's dream he found in Maurice Nicoll's *Dream Psychology* (*EA*, p. 335), does not replicate a general theory: it maps a specific complex.

Whereas Auden's critics have recognized his interest in psychoanalytic practice, this aspect of the poet's intellectual preoccupations has not been productive interpretatively. The reason can be traced to the romantic tradition, Auden's persistent nemesis and inspiration. Through the success of its sublime and visionary poets, romanticism established what was to become a prime directive of the English lyric: the poem must convey the poet's own unique and authentic voice. Wordsworth restricts the highest achievements of poetry to those passages 'where the Poet speaks to us in his own person and character'.[1]

Unfortunately, when transposed to a psychoanalytic context, the romantic assumption leads to misreading. The imperative that the lyric convey the poet's voice casts the speaker in the role of the analyst. From this, it follows that Auden's authoritative persona will penetrate the concealing defenses and unearth the unconscious complexes of an implied analysand, whether that be a political movement or a historical figure. But when the confrontation between a devious subject and an exhuming psychoanalyst is imposed on Auden's poetry, the results are often absurd. Unlike his intellectually credible prose speakers, Auden's poetic personas are often too enigmatic, exorbitant, or neurotic to play the expected role of authoritative therapist.

Consequently, critics interested in Auden and psychology have followed a path of lesser resistance and concentrated on the poet's themes and references. This is no small task. Unravelling the tangled allusions of a single phrase, 'liar's quinsy', might spin past John Layard, Homer Lane, and Georg Groddeck before winding back, more or less, to Freud. But the analytical scene itself, the cat and mouse game of concealment and discovery between analyst and patient, has not drawn sufficient critical interest. That could change, though, if more readers were to take Auden at his word. Regarding the poetic persona's authority, Auden suggests these skeptical prompts in 'Making, Knowing and Judging': 'What kind of a guy inhabits this poem? ... What does he conceal from the reader? What does he conceal from himself?' (*DH*, p. 51). Surely this indicates that the presumptive romantic role assignments need to be reversed. The poetic persona should be cast, not as the authoritative analyst, but as the neurotic analysand. This reframing of the poetic context opens a crucial dramatic irony. The hitherto embarrassing extravagances of Auden's lyric personae, so ill-suited to the dour disinterments of Freudian analysis, now emerge as the apt defenses of a wily analysand.

Like any clinical hypothesis, the proposal that some of Auden's lyrics cast the reader as doctor, the persona as patient, requires prediction and testing. Clinically, neurotics are talented at concealing their real motives, especially from themselves. Their self-deception is accomplished by an impressive array of cognitive strategies which excuse, distract, resituate, flip, camouflage, or otherwise misrepresent the actual source of misery. This habit of neurotic misrepresentation leads to several predictions. If some of Auden's poetic personas really do play the part of analysands, they will display inappropriate or self-destructive behaviours, remain unaware of their deeper motives, and shield their unawareness behind ingenious strategies of concealment.

Whereas these readily apparent predictions are a start, they neglect the complexity added by Auden's often ambiguous dramatic settings. Following Yeats, Auden adapted the English lyric's intimate address to the demands of public performance. His ambiguous rhetorical contexts often raise the possibility of multiple audiences, and this multiplicity suggests a further set of predictions. As students of history and politics know, public speakers commonly keep two audiences in mind: outsiders and insiders. The first group is more inclined to take the speaker at his word. Insiders, however, have mastered codes which can lend entirely different meanings to what is apparently said.

When the rhetorical complexity of Auden's orators is crossed with the self-deceptions of his neurotic personas, the result is a threefold structure of deceit. It begins with what the persona is concealing from outsiders, moves to insiders, and then shifts to himself. And for really ambitious readers/analysts, there might be a further level, deeper even than self-deception. This would be a state of cultural oblivion, its repressions enacted not by an individual but by an entire era.

If the predictions of our psychoanalytic model hold true, then one might proceed through a poem, like an analyst, peeling back each layer of deception. Because so many of Auden's poems mingle lyric subtlety with rhetorical deceit, it should be easy to find a test case for the psychoanalytic model's predictions. 'Sir, no man's enemy', written October 1929 (*EA*, p. 36), suggests that Auden understood the game from the very beginning. Later entitled 'Petition', the poem crosses the subtlety of a holy sonnet with the flourish of a public liturgy. As a speaker hiding something from outsiders, the persona might be pictured as an un-defrocked clergyman. Perhaps he has lost faith, a belated casualty of Bishop Colenso's too old rocks or Charles Darwin's too human apes. But trapped by circumstance or convenience in his pastoral role, the clergyman still needs to pay the bills. So his spoof of a petitionary prayer needs to be plausible enough to mollify his flock with the expected rituals, yet caustic enough to satisfy his own disbelief.

How does the sonnet manage its competing tasks? As an earnest effort at petitionary prayer, the poem offers what political handlers call plausible deniability. The clergyman follows a respectful rhetorical format for importuning the Almighty: direct personal address, praise of divine power and mercy, a wish list, confession, and a preview of anticipated blessings. True, some of his earlier requests may be indiscreetly specific, but eventually he resumes the orthodox path of asking for the wisdom to heed God's will. In terms of its literary heritage, the poem borrows from the conventions of holy sonnets from Donne to Hopkins. Its wide-flung imagery mixes military, regal, biblical, medical, and possibly even apocalyptic elements within an alternately archaic and modern setting. This kind of far-reaching eclecticism, a favourite technique among religious sonneteers, lets the poem physically dramatize the otherwise tenuous adventures of the soul, as well as demonstrate the inescapable reach of its spiritual theme. Nonetheless, a few of the clergyman's flock could suspect that the prominence of all those psychosomatic ailments might be a way of recruiting a satiric competitor against traditional spirituality. This is where plausible deniability kicks in: religious rhetoric routinely uses contemporary references to assert its big-tent relevance.

However reasonable its denial of any irreverent intentions, the poem is still a satire. It pokes fun not only at its mysterious 'Sir', but anyone addled enough to take such a figure seriously. The prayer's petitions mock their target divinity by soliciting him to cure a series of madcap maladies, including 'intolerable neural itch' and 'ingrown virginity'. The pleonasm, combined with the persistent clash in register, ensures the preposterousness of these conditions at both a literal and figurative level. Any itch will involve the nervous system, so the phrase 'neural itch' forces the anatomically technical to modify the crudely sensory. And whether 'ingrown virginity' refers to a bodily symptom of denied sexuality or a mental illness of morbid introspection, its mismatch between the trivial and the fateful generates a further comic effect.

To heighten the satire, the sonnet's order of illnesses suggests an Ages of Man sequence. If so, then the 'Sir' is petitioned to relieve the incurable malady otherwise known as life. The 'negative inversion' can be glossed as the emergence of self-consciousness, and the 'exhaustion of weaning' as a reference to Otto Rank's birth trauma or break with tradition. The 'coward's stance' may be Auden's version of D. H. Lawrence's critique, later described in *The Dyer's Hand*, of 'the laziness or fear which makes people prefer second-hand experience to the shock of looking and listening for themselves' (*DH*, p. 280). To confirm the jest, the verses revisit that favourite metre of the Age of Wit, heroic couplets. These are not silkily enjambed in the manner of a Keats or Browning, but closed, six with full stops. So the rhymes suggest the finality of judgment (all/prodigal), sense (touch/itch), and causal logic (quinsy/virginity).

But to the reader/analyst, these satiric features might confirm a diagnosis of neurotic displacement, concealed through distraction. Displacement shifts hostile emotions from a risky target to a safe target. For example, the persona might be hiding an unconscious motive, his resentment of the Superego or moral censor, by externalizing it as the satirized divinity. The 'Sir' is a safer target because, unlike the Superego, he cannot inflict the revenge of guilt, anxiety, obsession-compulsion, or illness. Meanwhile, to keep his pious flock from objecting to the satire, the clergyman distracts them by adhering to established literary and liturgical convention. These norms furnish the credible deniability shielding him from charges of irreverence or worse.

As would be expected from Auden, the ever-practical schoolmaster, the sonnet's initial challenge is modest. Only those immured in an impenetrable religionism would miss the persona's broad parody. But the sonnet's next challenge is more difficult. After the outsiders, the speaker's trusting flock, come the insiders. This group might consist of the pastor's confidantes, or the classmates of a schoolboy amusing his friends with a caricature of the chaplain.

In any case, the sonnet challenges its reader/analyst to figure out what the speaker is trying to hide from the insiders. Coiled within those jibes at the 'Sir' and his devotees, could there be a deeper resentment of the insiders themselves? If so, it had better be well concealed. To this end, the strongly externalized reference of the poetic apostrophe's 'Sir', the complicity between the satirist and his knowing audience, and of course the rationalization that it is all in jest, help to marginalize any deeper motive. But according to the psychoanalytic hypothesis, such plausible explanations could also facilitate an artful diversion. Analysts usually trust behaviours more than words. Accordingly, a verbal performative which might betray an unconscious motive is the speaker's sheer exorbitance, his expenditure of far more effort than is needed to achieve an easy goal. The Protean 'Sir' is by turns saddled with attributes of a public utility, king, physician, headmaster, prison warden, publisher, messiah, and solar god. These too elaborate manoeuvres to determine the 'Sir' may suggest that he serves as a metonymy for the satirist's confidantes.

Even the title itself is suspect. 'Sir' sounds like a term of respect. But it also situates the addressee in a prior and fixed hierarchy. Because the levels of this hierarchy are undefined, and because the precise rank of the 'Sir' is never indicated, the honorific entwines its subject in a net of ambiguous command. To announce that this figure is no one's enemy, and that he forgives everything, enlists the broad scope of 'man' and 'all' to fashion a double truism. While English teachers dutifully warn students about the emptiness of truisms, they can also perform an important rhetorical task – stifling dissent. In this way, the hapless 'Sir' becomes further entangled.

Each rhetorical turn draws the net tighter. In the intricate syntactic riddle of the second line's exception, 'But will his negative inversion', the grammatically ambiguous 'will' shuttles between a dual antecedence. If taken as an auxiliary verb, then the phrase becomes an elliptical construction. It might be paraphrased: Except the Sir will (keep? indulge?) his own negative inversion. But if 'will' is taken as a nominal, the paraphrase becomes: Except the Sir shall not forgive the human will's negative inversion. Auden's deliberately ensnared syntax carries out a frankly brilliant series of manipulations. Its initial confusion creates a sense of disorientation and hence dependency. Then, after each grammatical option is worked out, together they collude to put the 'Sir' in a double bind. Because each option contradicts the other, the Sir can comply with just one, not both. Further, regardless of which option he takes, the Sir is forced to contradict the previous line, in that he would not be 'forgiving all'. So the riddling phrase operates not only an internal double bind, in that each variant is incompatible with the other, but also an external double bind, in that both variants are incompatible with the previous line. Not even the god of this unholy sonnet can escape such a diabolical trap.

But the sonnet's entire first sestet is riddled with such artful devices. Rhetorically, these logical snares accumulate to perplex and outpace the intellect, which makes for a befuddled, hence easier to manipulate, audience. To the reader/analyst, such elaborate tactics, their intricacy so far beyond the requirements of satire, could disclose the speaker's efforts to dominate his audience of insiders. On this analysis, the persona's exorbitance might suggest a neurotic defense of acting out. This mechanism does not try to conceal the unconscious drive, a compulsion to control the social other. Instead, it disguises the drive's emotional tenor by shifting its mood from earnest to playful, thereby transforming unacceptable resentment into amusing fun.

How to hide things from audiences could almost serve as a concise definition of rhetoric. Lyric poems, however, more often focus on personas that hide something from themselves. As noted, the persona's robust externalization of the 'Sir', his choice of a public liturgical form, and his declamatory mode of address all work to locate the satiric target well beyond the self. But psychoanalysis holds that the unconscious complex often runs counter to the conscious intent. Thus, the aggressive externalization of the 'Sir' may indicate a defense of reversal. This mechanism turns the forbidden material inside out, or upside down. If so, then the sonnet's manifestly externalizing gestures might suggest that the satirized 'Sir' embodies a latent element within the self, a liberating social force, or both.

Because it is harder to hide something from oneself than from an external audience, the strategies of concealment need to be commensurately subtle. Within the perilous arena of his own thoughts, Auden's persona constructs a formidable linguistic barrier between himself and the 'Sir'. After the initial invocation, each following sentence and independent clause begins with a command. Although the 'Sir' is formally the grammatical subject, the imperative mood entails an implied ellipsis, as in 'Sir', (I order you to) 'Send'. These recurrent ellipses transform the addressee into a syntactic object. By depriving him of any capacity for action other than what is assigned by the persona, the sonnet pushes the 'Sir' away from the order of conscious beings, and nearer to the category of insentient things. Although the 'Sir' is nominally the most powerful figure in the sonnet, it is the always speaking yet constantly elided 'I' who occupies the centre of this universe.

From a psycho-interpretive perspective, such skilful efforts at concealment act as a summons to further analysis. The poem's initial rhetorical manoeuvres are so obstreperous that its first sestet might easily set the tone for the entire work. But sonnets are highly discrete texts whose dramas are often pieced together from different sensibilities. A likely arrangement for this poem would be a 6–6–2 variant of the English sonnet's traditional three quatrains and a couplet. When structured in this fashion, the sonnet's divisions trace an inner journey which begins with ridicule, shifts to entreaty, and ends with hope. And that would comprise, a decade before Auden's much-discussed conversion, as convincingly religious a design as anything fashioned by Donne or Hopkins.

In good sonnet fashion, each division marks a boundary between opposing sensibilities. Fully half of the first sestet is given over to the satiric litany of psychosomatic ailments. The overzealous tone and isolated viewpoint convey a bleak sense that while cultural institutions can sometimes be mocked, they can never be changed. With the second sestet, however, the perspective shifts so dramatically that its opening line, 'Prohibit sharply the rehearsed response', could imply a commentary on the previous section. Now the tone grows more earnest and the focus shifts from an inward obsession with psychosomatic paralysis to the publically available topics of 'response', 'stance', 'retreat', 'reverse', and 'lives'. The 'Sir', no longer a distant and ridiculed monarch, has somehow turned into a respected guide. Finally, the sonnet's last two lines leap, in mid-sentence, into a visionary and ecstatic mode. 'House of the dead', 'architecture', and 'heart' assemble the domains of the spiritual, the secular, and the personal, respectively. The tone grows upbeat and grateful, and the brightening mood is supported by a rapid shift in scene from 'city', to 'country houses', to the open-ended 'New styles of architecture'. A previously static and alien culture has become the malleable product of human creativity.

This trajectory of the sonnet's 6–6–2 structure might trace the deeper complex driving the persona's mechanisms of reversal. His frivolity masks an acute dissatisfaction with the unhappy being portrayed in his psychosomatic litany, namely himself, by turns nit-picking, timid, malcontent, clingy, and devious. But as with the dream of Maurice Nicoll's patient, the lyric's enactments are constructive. By dramatizing how the Sir's transformations enact the self's capacity to change, the sonnet also shows a way through the persona's/analysand's predicament.

After the third level of concealment, dedicated to what the persona hides from himself, the reader/analyst comes to an ominous threshold. One might go further, but this requires venturing into unconscious material which is not repressed by the individual ego, but obscured by the limits of an era's knowledge. At the deepest level, the personal unconscious fades into the culturally unthinkable. Freud's other heretical disciple, C. G. Jung, hoped to populate this utterly voided space with the masks and myths of his universal archetypes. Unfortunately, the deepest unconscious is both more historically contingent and more interpretively elusive than Jung thought. Its mechanisms of concealment are no longer driven by the shifts of the neurotic ego, but by an era's most respected and unquestionable traditions. Here one encounters gleams of insights that are neither disguised nor repressed, but incapable of signifying in any fashion, in that the context needed to grasp their meaning does not yet exist.

What textual clues might gesture towards such depths of cultural oblivion? As it turns out, in Auden they are often hidden in plain sight. Probably the poet's most quoted and least understood lines are from the Yeats elegy: 'For poetry makes nothing happen' (*EA*, p. 242). True enough. As both pragmatists and aesthetes concede, the poem, fixed on the page, just sits there. But the readers of poetry are stuck in history, try as they might to escape. So indirectly, by influencing its readers, poetry *can* make something happen. This influence is often thought of in terms of conveyed ideas or feelings, both of which Auden mistrusted. But there is also the force of what might be termed an analytical (as opposed to an emotional) transference. When this occurs, the skills developed by puzzling out the defensive riddles of a poem are transferred to a full range of other texts, not necessarily poetic.

The possibility of this unthinkable transference, from the frivolous poetic to an earnest historical text, may account for an otherwise obscure design woven into the sonnet's imagery. The poem distinguishes the prowess of the 'Sir' from the enfeeblement of its anonymous everyman. Asking the 'Sir' to send power and light, for example, presupposes that he commands kinaesthetic movement, autonomic vitality, and the capacity of sight. The etymologies of both 'prohibit' (to hold back), and 'correct' (to make straight) confirm this kinaesthetic might. With 'sovereign touch' his reach extends to actual contact. But most significant are the sonnet's instances of compound images, 'Curing', 'Publish', and 'Harrow', which coordinate multiple senses into a complex process.

Meanwhile, in a gesture which some readers might trace to Marvell's 'Dialogue between Soule and Body', the sonnet's everyman suffers that classic Auden curse, a rebellion by his physical self. He is plagued with exhaustion and anxiety, tormented by a sore throat, and isolated by deafness, blindness, and paralysis. This corporeal assault links the text to Auden's recurrent metaphor in which the workings of the body provide a trope for the poetic text. With that in mind, the contrast between the prowess of the 'Sir' and the weakness of the everyman could portray a variance in their skills as readers. Unlike the 'Sir' who understands intricate pathologies and can foster the natural healing which produces health, the everyman must endure mysterious symptoms. As long as an itch remains purely 'neural', neither its causes nor its effects can be known. Similarly, the fatigue of weaning and the distortions of ingrown virginity are determined by uncontrollable agents such as the withheld breast or a mutinous internal organ, hence beyond conscious reach.

As an extended metaphor for the poetic text, then, the contrast in the sonnet's corporeal imagery might suggest that while the 'Sir' understands how poetic patterns can reveal an array of subtle processes, the persona does not. One is a strong reader, the other weak. One can decipher and redirect textual defenses. The other is their hapless victim.

Auden's psychoanalytic model of the text, with its shift of authority from persona/analysand to reader/analyst, offers a useful approach to many of his works, particularly the parodies and satires. But what about the more serious poems? Could Auden's analytical irony be so pervasive that even the spellbinding personas of 'In Memory of W. B. Yeats' and 'September 1, 1939', or the disillusioned ciceroni of 'Musée des Beaux Arts', have something to hide? That question, along with many more riddles, still awaits Auden's readers/analysts.

NOTES

1 Walter Jackson Bate, ed., *Criticism: The Major Texts* (Harcourt, Brace and World, 1952), p. 342.

CHAPTER XVI

Auden's Theology

Alan Jacobs

I

Theology seems always to have been of interest to Auden. Anne Fremantle reported having intense theological debates with him – especially about Patripassianism, the belief that the Father shared in the sufferings of the Son on the Cross – in 1931, when Auden almost certainly had no religious beliefs. Fremantle, then a committed Anglican, 'passionately believed' that the Father did indeed so suffer; but Auden reminded her that the first of the Articles of Religion in the Book of Common Prayer affirms that God is 'without body, parts, or passions'. Fremantle commented, 'Wystan [was] always more theologically sound than I' (*Tribute*, p. 80).

If such debates were for Auden a kind of intellectual game, it is note-worthy that he found the game worth playing. He seems to have thought it desirable to have an articulate theology even when he had no beliefs or experiences to which the theology needed to correspond. This tells us, among other things, that whereas an essay on Auden's theology will not necessarily reveal much about Auden's religious experience, the two simply cannot be severed.

Auden was raised in the Church of England, and the chief mover of his family's devotional life was his mother. She was strongly Anglo-Catholic, and he later remembered with fondness his time serving as 'boat-boy' – bearer of the incense-container – at Mass. This early love of ceremony was accompanied, for a time, by actual belief, and even 'a period of eccle-siastical *Schwärmerei*' (*F&A*, p. 517) – 'a pseudo-devout phase' (*Prose III*, p. 575). But this enthusiasm did not last, and by the time he came up to Oxford in 1925, Auden had been an unbeliever for at least three years.

This condition would last for about another decade, although it is difficult to make secure affirmations about such matters. Christopher Isherwood, who collaborated with Auden on plays through much of the 1930s, thought that he always had Christian leanings: 'When we collaborate ... I have to keep a sharp eye on him – or down flop the characters on their knees; another constant danger is that of choral interruptions by angel-voices' (*Tribute*, p. 74). Isherwood's account is worth noting, in large part because it differs from Auden's own. In the story Auden consistently told about his return to the Christian faith, four events stood out. First, during the Spanish Civil War, he surprised himself by being 'profoundly shocked and disturbed', encountering Barcelona's closed churches: 'I could not escape acknowledging that, however I had consciously ignored and rejected the Church for sixteen years, the existence of churches and what went on in them had all the time been very important to me. If that was the case, what then?' (*Prose III*, p. 578). The second event was his meeting Charles Williams, an editor at Oxford University Press and a devout, if highly eccentric, Christian. 'For the first time in my life', Auden later wrote, '[I] felt myself in the presence of personal sanctity ... I felt transformed into a person who was incapable of doing or thinking anything base or unloving' (pp. 578–79). His description of the third event made veiled reference to his jealousy on discovering Chester Kallman's infidelity: 'I was forced to know in person what it is like to feel oneself the prey of demonic powers, in both the Greek and the Christian sense, stripped of self-control and self-respect, behaving like a ham actor in a Strindberg play' (p. 579).

The fourth event is not quite an event, but instead an increasingly insistent question that confronted him as Hitler rose to European dominance: 'If, as I am convinced, the Nazis are wrong and we are right, what is it that validates our values and invalidates theirs?' (p. 578). In an interview he gave near the end of his life, Auden would link this question with a particular moment: the viewing in Manhattan, in November 1939, of a documentary film that celebrated the Nazi conquest of Poland. He was 'shocked' by the largely German-speaking audience's open hatred of the Poles and celebration of the Wehrmacht's power.[1]

So the key experiences that led Auden to Christian belief involved a conviction of his own sinfulness, a feeling of someone else's sanctity, and the pressing sense that some acts truly and always deserve to be called evil. The theology he espoused early in his life as a Christian centred largely on the first of these.

II

It was soon after meeting Williams that Auden 'started to read some theological works, Kierkegaard in particular' (*Prose III*, p. 579). The juxtaposition is unlikely to have been accidental: as editor, Williams sponsored the earliest English translations of Kierkegaard, including the large selection from the journals that appeared in 1938; and he celebrated Kierkegaard in his 1939 book *The Descent of the Dove*, for which Auden later wrote an enthusiastic introduction. Writing in 1968 about his first encounter with Kierkegaard, Auden would comment, 'Like Pascal, Nietzsche, and Simone Weil, Kierkegaard is one of those writers whom it is very difficult to estimate justly. When one reads them for the first time, one is bowled over by their originality (they speak in a voice one has never heard before) and by the sharpness of their insights (they say things which no one before them has said, and which, henceforward, no reader will ever forget)' (*F&A*, pp. 182–83). What seems to have bowled Auden over above all else is the thought expressed in the title of the final section of *Either/Or*: 'The Edifying in the Thought that Against God We Are Always in the Wrong'. In this sermon, an unnamed fictional priest (clearly speaking for Kierkegaard) writes,

> If … you claim, and are convinced, that you are always in the wrong, you are hidden in God. This is your divine worship, your religious devotion, your reverence for God. … Never shall any anxious doubt tear me away from him, never will the thought terrify me that I might prove to be in the right against Him, against God I am always in the wrong.[2]

For Kierkegaard – as for Augustine, Luther, and Calvin before him – this thought is 'edifying', encouraging, and reassuring, because it reminds believers that nothing they do can earn the favour of God, and therefore nothing they do can lose that favour. As the reformers put it, echoing St. Paul in Ephesians 2:8, Christians are saved by God's grace alone (*sola gratia*), which they appropriate by faith alone (*sola fides*). This is for such Christians more deeply reassuring than the view, often called Pelagianism, that salvation can be earned through good works – because if salvation *can* be so earned, then it *should* be, and the person who fails to earn it is infinitely and eternally culpable.

This insight seems to have struck Auden with great force, perhaps because of its paradoxical quality: the idea of being in right relation to God *because* before Him one is always in the wrong has a certain absurd appeal. In one of the first poems he produced as a Christian, 'In Sickness and In Health', Auden wrote,

> Beloved, we are always in the wrong,
> Handling so clumsily our stupid lives,
> Suffering too little or too long,

Too careful even in our selfish loves:
The decorative manias we obey
Die in grimaces round us every day,
Yet through their tohu-bohu comes a voice
Which utters an absurd command – Rejoice.

(*CP* 2007, p. 317)

Being 'always in the wrong' is then the very cause and engine of rejoicing. (The logic of paradox infuses the whole poem: the lover here prays, not that he be preserved from temptation, as in the Lord's Prayer, but that he and his beloved *will* be endangered by temptations.)

Similarly, Auden's Caliban, at the end of his long, baroque declamation in 'The Sea and the Mirror', imagines a primal scene of self-knowledge for himself and his fellow actors: 'Beating about for some large loose image to define' the experience, recorded in *The Tempest,* of the disillusion of magic and the acceptance of bounds, Caliban finally settles on the thought of 'the greatest grandest opera rendered by a very provincial touring company indeed'. It is the very poverty and ineptitude of the production that makes it spiritually and morally valuable to its actors, for even though 'there was not a single aspect of our whole performance, not even the huge stuffed bird of happiness, for which a kind word could, however patronisingly, be said', nevertheless it is 'at this very moment [that] we do at last see ourselves as we are'. And, more important still, 'for the first time in our lives we hear … the real Word which is our only raison d'être'. At the moment when all pretence to aesthetic achievement falls away and the actors are confronted with the authentic selves that they had used their performances to escape, they come to see God precisely in their distance from Him:

… we are blessed by that Wholly Other Life from which we are separated by an essential emphatic gulf of which our contrived fissures of mirror and proscenium arch – we understand them at last – are feebly figurative signs … it is just here, among the ruins and the bones, that we may rejoice in the perfected Work that is not ours. (*CP* 2007, p. 442)

The phrase 'Wholly Other' is an acknowledgement of the great Swiss theologian Karl Barth, who was known for his insistence that God is *Ganz Andere*: between God and humanity there is an 'infinite qualitative distinction'. Significantly, Barth came to this theological position as a young pastor as a result of reading Kierkegaard.[3] In a 1943 letter, Auden described his own theological position as 'Neo-Calvinist (i.e. Barthian)', but he had been aware of the emphasis of Barth's work since 1934 at the latest – another indication that his serious interest in theology predated his religious belief (see *LA*, p. 149).

This absolute self-abasement, this comfort in being 'always in the wrong', did not constitute the whole of Auden's theology in the first few years of his life as a Christian; but it certainly dominated his account of how the believer, on a purely individual and personal level, is always ethically situated. And it may have been especially attractive to him as he considered Christianity's traditional repudiation of homosexuality: his sexuality might be 'crooked' – to use a word he sometimes employed – but his inmost being was and could be no more crooked than anyone else's.

III

At the same time that Auden was articulating this distinctively Kierkegaardian version of Augustinian *moral* theology, he was also developing a *political* theology. There was a distinct urgency to Auden's early endeavours in this field, for his return to Christianity was coincident with war in Europe, and he needed to figure out how one might think in a genuinely Christian way about the circumstances in which war might be justified. Throughout 1939 and 1940 – as war approached and then arrived – Auden acknowledged the appeal of pacifism. In a lengthy collection of his own *pensées* that he worked on for some months, but never published, he staged a dialogue with himself in which he says, 'Certainly my position forbids me to act as a combatant in any war'; but then he goes on to say that he 'has very little use' for pacifism as 'simply the refusal to bear arms'. 'To think that it is enough to refuse to be a soldier and that one can behave as one chooses as a private citizen, is to be quite willing to cause a war but only unwilling to suffer the consequences. I have more respect for Hitler' (*Prose II*, p. 451).

But what was this 'position' that forbade Auden to be a combatant? At the time, it was not quite Christianity: the *pensées* are full of admiration for Jesus but suspicious of much orthodox theology and of the church. When Auden came to embrace Christianity itself, this 'position' became rather less secure, less clear. It was at this point that he began to read the work of Reinhold Niebuhr; and through Niebuhr and certain other scholars – especially Charles Norris Cochrane and, somewhat later, Eugen Rosenstock-Huessy – he developed a political theology that centred on a sophisticated evaluation of the project typically called Constantinianism, or Christendom.

The process took some time. In Auden's early reviews of Niebuhr's books, his focus was on the moral situation described in the previous section of this essay. About *The Nature and Destiny of Man* he writes, 'The most brilliant chapters of Dr Niebuhr's book are those dealing with the Christian conception of sin' (*Prose II*, p. 133); and even in reviewing a book called *Christianity and Power Politics*, Auden's chief concern is to agree with Niebuhr's claim that 'Pacifism … blasphemes by denying original sin and pretending that perfection can be acquired in a progressive school' (p. 109).

So although Niebuhr is often cited as a major influence on Auden's theology, a more significant driver of Auden's Christian thinking about politics was probably Cochrane's magisterial *Christianity and Classical Culture: A Study of Thought and Action from Augustus to Augustine*. Writing about this book in *The New Republic* in 1944, Auden opened with a remarkable statement: 'Since the appearance of the first edition in 1940, I have read this book many times, and my conviction of its importance to the understanding not only of the epoch with which it is concerned, but also of our own, has increased with each rereading' (*Prose II*, p. 226).

Auden learned a great deal from Cochrane, but the heart of it may be found in these lines from the concluding paragraph of his (quite extensive) review:

Our period is not so unlike the age of Augustine: the planned society, caesarism of thugs or bureaucracies, paideia, scientia, religious persecution, are all with us. Nor is there even lacking the possibility of a new Constantinism; letters have already begun to appear in the press, recommending religious instruction in schools as a cure for juvenile delinquency; Mr Cochrane's terrifying description of the 'Christian' empire under Theodosius should discourage such hopes of using Christianity as a spiritual benzedrine for the earthly city. (*Prose II*, p. 231)

Jesus's notoriously ambiguous injunction to 'render to God what is God's and to Caesar what is Caesar's' (Mark 12:17) necessarily prompts the questions, 'But what is God's? And what is Caesar's?' Constantinianism, the uniting of the spiritual power of Church and the temporal power of Empire, is a way of answering that question that, in Cochrane's view and Auden's, reduces God to the status of an especially exalted Caesar. It is to make this point that in his 'Christmas oratorio', 'For the Time Being' Auden introduces a great choral hymn to Caesar. Each stanza of the hymn begins with the line 'Great is Caesar: He has conquered Seven Kingdoms', and ends with the affirmation, 'Great is Caesar: God must be with Him' (*CP* 2007, pp. 371–73). Although it is the pre-Christian Romans who make these claims, Auden is warning his Christian readers of the dangers of conflating worldly success with spiritual favour (similar to the 'wicked doctrine' he later detected and denounced in the last lines of 'Spain' [see *CP* 2007, p xxx]).

Such thoughts further suggest that God cares deeply about maintaining the existing social order, which is why in the same poem Auden's Herod, far from being a bloodthirsty tyrant, is a self-described 'liberal' who finds it 'dreary' but necessary to call in the military to eliminate the just-born Messiah: he recognizes (as later Constantinians would not) that the absolute claims of the Christ are, or ought to be, a constant threat to *any* existing social order. Thus, in his review of Niebuhr's *Nature and Destiny of Man*, Auden admits that Christians have often been guilty of 'acceptance of the status quo', but denies that this is an 'orthodox attitude' and insists that it is instead the natural outgrowth of 'Stoic apathy' (*Prose II*, p. 132).

What Auden learned from his reading of Cochrane and his own meditations on these matters is that – in Augustinian terms – the relationship between the City of Man and the City of God is endlessly fraught and historically variable. His 1949 poem 'Memorial for the City' can be seen as an extended meditation on such complexities: its opening lines – 'The eyes of the crow and the eye of the camera open / Onto Homer's world, not ours' – indicate that the necessary discriminations will need to be pursued by an inner eye, a spiritually alert vision. The 'Post-Vergilian City' takes many forms: the 'New City' in the time of Pope Gregory, Martin Luther's 'Sinful City', the 'Rational City' of Mirabeau and the French Revolutionaries, on to the 'abolished City' of the mid-twentieth century. The city supposed to be united under the Constantinian double banner of God and Caesar has collapsed into chaos, and for mere humans, its fulfilment seems far off: 'This is Adam waiting for His City' (*CP* 2007, pp. 589–94).

Ultimately, for Auden, it is not on public triumphs that the City of God can be built, but instead on every citizen's recognition that his or her knowledge is always partial and his or her desires often irreconcilable with the desires of others. This is the theme of 'Vespers', the fifth of the 'Horae Canonicae', which features a 'twilight meeting' between two temperamental opposites, an Arcadian who longs for a restored Eden and a Utopian who strives for a perfected New Jerusalem. They are 'incorrigible each', but can possibly become 'accomplices' if they seek, as Martin Luther might have put it, not a Constantinian Theology of Glory but a politically humble Theology of the Cross: together they may 'remember our victim ... on whose immolation (call him Abel, Remus, whom you will, it is one Sin Offering) arcadias, utopias, our dear old bag of a democracy are alike founded: / For without a cement of blood (it must be human, it must be innocent) no secular wall will safely stand' (pp. 635–37).

I V

Auden seems never to have rejected this political theology – although his interest in it declined – but around a decade after he had been 'bowled over' by Kierkegaard, he came to question the sufficiency of a moral theology based so completely on being 'in the wrong' in relation to God as the *Ganz Andere*. Writing in 1950 for a *Partisan Review* symposium on 'Religion and the Intellectuals', Auden would comment that 'the typical "modern" heresy is ... a Barthian exaggeration of God's transcendence which all too easily becomes an excuse for complacency about one's own sins and about the misfortunes of others' (*Prose III*, p.172). This is surely a self-accusation.

I do not think that Auden ceased to believe that 'against God we are always in the wrong', but instead came to see that relatively little *follows* from that acknowledgment. And as he came to see the limitations of the Kierkegaardian view on this matter, he was led to see the many things that Kierkegaard omitted.[4] In 1955, he would comment:

> Much as I owe Kierkegaard ... I cannot let this occasion pass without commenting on what seems to be his great limitation, a limitation which characterizes Protestantism generally. A planetary visitor might read through the whole of his voluminous works without discovering that human beings are not ghosts but have bodies of flesh and blood. (*Prose III*, p. 579)

It is true, Auden continues, that every person has 'a unique "existential" relation to God, and few since St. Augustine have described this relation more profoundly than Kierkegaard'. But it is also true that 'as a creature composed of matter, as a biological organism, every man, in common with everything else in the universe, is related by necessity to the God who created that universe and saw that it was good'.

In this passage we see the major themes of Auden's later moral theology: the insistence that we live in the realm of natural necessity as well as that of existential choice; the affirmation that 'all good works are done' with the human body; the accompanying recognition that good works are indeed valued by God; the necessity of gratitude for a body that, as part of Creation, is good; the necessity of gratitude for all Creation itself; and the importance of realizing that meaningful human community is best rooted in the humble gratitude of the embodied. And one might also add to the list Auden's increasingly strong sense that ordinary, everyday Catholic religious practice is more deeply connected to these truths than the sophisticated Protestant theology he had imbibed for a decade.

Auden's poems of the 1950s are saturated in these themes. The 'Bucolics' express gratitude for the distinctive features of a variety for landscapes, 'Precious Five' for the virtues of the five senses. The latter poem ends with the exhortation to keep

> That singular command
> I do not understand,
> *Bless what there is for being,*
> Which has to be obeyed, for
> What else am I made for,
> Agreeing or disagreeing?
>   (*CP* 2007, p. 589)

The extensive sequence 'Thanksgiving for a Habitat' – begun in 1958, although not completed until 1964 – gives thanks and praise for each room of his Kirchstetten cottage, linking the rooms to the services they provide to the body, and in its last poem affirms that 'without / the Spirit we die, but life / without the Letter is in the worst of taste' (*CP* 2007, p. 715).

But Auden's deepest exploration of his theology of the body may be found in 'Horae Canonicae', his meditation on the Crucifixion. The sequence begins as 'the kind / Gates of the body fly open', preceding consciousness, will, and memory, if only for an instant, and thereby giving the poet the briefest of reprieves from the day's 'routine of praise and blame': 'Still the day is intact, and I / The Adam sinless in our beginning, / Adam still previous to any act' (*CP* 2007, p.625).

But once the day begins, so do 'acts', and the praise and blame that accompany them – especially the blame, for this day (simultaneously the day of the Crucifixion of Christ, its commemoration on each year's Good Friday, and any and every day) will demand the sacrifice of 'our victim', and will then force us to contemplate our role in that sacrifice. But this no one wishes to do: 'we are not prepared / For silence so sudden and so soon', yet this is what we must face: 'We are left alone with our feat' (p. 632). Given the circumstances, 'It would be best to go home, if we have a home, / In any case good to rest' (p. 634).

And it is during this siesta that the work of healing begins – not through anyone's historical and existential encounter with the Wholly

Other God, but through the ordinary biological work of the body, which is itself another victim of our corrupt acts: 'while we are thus away, our own wronged flesh / May work undisturbed, restoring / The order we try to destroy', as 'At the right moment, essential fluids / Flow to renew exhausted cells' (p. 634). In this account, the condition of having a working body takes precedence – temporal, yes, but also theological, in the economy of God's grace – over any Kierkegaardian or other account of existential situation. Embodiment makes forgiveness and reconciliation possible.

v

In 1968, reflecting on what was then thirty years of reading Kierkegaard, Auden came to this conclusion:

> Given his extraordinary upbringing, it is hardly surprising that Kierkegaard should have become – not intellectually but in his sensibility – a Manichee.... [O]ne does not feel in his writings the sense that, whatever sorrows and sufferings a man may have to endure, it is nevertheless a miraculous blessing to be alive. Like all heretics, conscious or unconscious, he is a monodist, who can hear with particular acuteness one theme in the New Testament – in his case, the theme of suffering and self-sacrifice – but is deaf to its rich polyphony. (*F&A*, p. 191)

In articulating his theology of the body, and in further theological reflections that occupied his last years, Auden sought to correct and counterbalance his earlier 'Barthian exaggeration of God's transcendence'. One of the ways he did this was through an embrace of the spirit of Carnival – a celebratory, communal reversal of Kierkegaard's perpetual and solitary Lent. This embrace appears only sporadically and indirectly in his very late poetry, but is articulated quite fully in an essay he left incomplete at his death, 'Work, Carnival and Prayer'.⁵ The essay bears a debt to Mikhail Bakhtin's *Rabelais and His World*, although Auden dissents from Bakhtin at times; in any event, its chief argument is that Work, Carnival, and Prayer are the three distinctly human realms of action, that each of them is necessary, and that 'a satisfactory human life, individually or collectively, is possible only if proper respect is paid to all three worlds' (*F&A*, p. 472).⁶ Auden believed that 'the hippies' were attempting to recover Carnival, but were doing so at the expense of Work; his own history had been just the opposite, an intensely disciplined focus on his own vocational labours. But that focus leads to an overemphasis on the ways that people differ: 'In the world of Work ... we are not and cannot be equal, only diverse and interdependent'. The realm of Carnival (or Laughter), by contrast, 'is much more closely related to the world of Worship and Prayer ... for both are worlds in which we are all equal'.

So at the end of his life, Auden returns to a theme that had dominated his theology in the first years of adult Christian life – the radical equality of all before God – but now the theme is heard in a very different key. Instead of counselling abasement before the God in relation to whom we are always in the wrong, Auden prefers to see the humour of it all: the intrinsically *comic* character of human embodiment, of the disparity between human aspirations and human achievements, of the gulf that separates our regal self-images from the commonplace acts of our daily lives. Auden admitted that the 'traditional forms' of Carnival did not appeal to him – he did not 'enjoy crowds and loud noises' – but, he affirmed, 'even introverted intellectuals can share the Carnival experience if they are prepared to forget their dignity' (*F&A*, p. 473). This cheerful disavowal of dignity is the last clearly sounded note of Auden's theology.

NOTES

1 See *LA*, pp. 89–91. There is also a possible fifth event: Auden's experience in June 1933, of feeling benignly 'invaded by a power which, although I consented to it, was irresistible and certainly not mine'. This presumably underlay 'Out on the lawn I lie in bed', written that month, and he judged it 'one of the most crucial' of the 'various factors' that later 'brought me back to the Christian faith in which I had been brought up' (*F&A*, pp. 69–70). He wrote this account in 1964; it is rather odd that in describing his conversion a decade earlier, Auden had made no mention of this 'Vision of Agape'.

2 Søren Kierkegaard, *Either/Or: a Fragment of Life*, tr. Alastair Hannay, (Penguin, 1996), p. 605.

3 Barth did not coin the phrase *Ganz Andere* – that was probably Rudolf Otto – but the phrase attached itself to him.

4 In a 1968 essay subtitled 'Second Thoughts on Kierkegaard' (*F&A*, pp. 182–97), Auden would acknowledge the dangers of overreaction, when reassessing such a formative influence: 'one's first enthusiasm may all too easily turn into an equally exaggerated aversion' (p. 183).

5 Mendelson has called this 'one of [Auden's] most comprehensive and authoritative prose works, rich in contemporary detail and historical exegesis' (*LA*, p. 497); it has never been published, but will appear in the final volume of prose in the *Complete Works*. I am very much in his debt for the comments in this section.

6 This quotation (from a 1970 book review) borrows, somewhat incongruously, from the unpublished essay just mentioned.

CHAPTER XVII

Auden in History

Susannah Young-ah Gottlieb

One of the earliest pronouncements about historiography is also among the most famous: 'Poetry is something more philosophic and of graver import than history, since its statements are of the nature rather of universals, whereas those of history are singulars' (Aristotle, 1451b: McKeon, p. 1464). In a review article from 1955, Auden does not so much dispute Aristotle's apothegm as change the terms in which historiography is evaluated with respect to poetry on the one hand, and the sciences on the other: 'The historical discipline is the most difficult of all, since it lacks the demonstrable certainty of the natural sciences and at the same time cannot enjoy the luxury of the arts which are frankly subjective' (*Prose III*, p. 599). Written in 1955, this statement represents a summation of Auden's decades-long reflection on the nature of history, the role of the poet in history, and the proper procedures for the historian. In reviews and poems of the period, Auden showed a renewed interest in the problem of responsible historiography. Assessing Camus' idea of writerly *engagement*, which he finds dubious, and concerned with the legacy Orwell had left the Anglo-American intellectual community, Auden seeks to develop an idea of history that is free of ideological tendencies, but does not pretend to be neutral with respect to questions of justice. Auden is attracted not to the grand theories of Spengler and Toynbee, which had sparked widespread debate in the 1920s and then again in the 1950s, but to Cochrane, de Rougemont, and Rosenstock-Huessy, each of whom has similarly – albeit less well-known – grand theories of Western history. None of the historians who attract *his* attention, however, posits the kind of necessary chain of events common among, for example, both Marxist theoreticians and anti-Marxist proponents of political and economic 'development'. Auden's reflection on the difficulty of history is occasioned by the publication of the second volume of Ernest Jones's biography of Freud, which he reviews under the title 'The History of an Historian' (*Prose III*, p. 596). This title might be surprising to those who associate Freud with either the scientist, who discovers laws of nature, or the writer, who reinvents myths. For Auden, however, Freud joins the company of those historians he admires because he is, like all good historians, caught in an intractable bind: he must discover laws that he knows are not laws of the kind that scientists discover or legislators make.

Auden understands the historian's discipline as follows: 'In assessing the importance of his data, all historians are governed by the same general principle that the importance of an historical event is in proportion to its causal effect on subsequent historical events which includes its influence on later interpretations of the past' (*Prose III*, p. 598). Historical events are causally related to one another; but because the interpretation of an event can itself be an event, the terms *earlier* and *later* acquire a degree of thickness, in which the later event (the interpretation) can be understood as the cause of the earlier one, because its significance derives from its interpretation. Furthermore, the category of cause must be detached from that of necessity: 'but, in history to say that A causes B does not mean that if A occurs then B has to occur but only that A provides B with a motive for occurring' (*Prose III*, p. 598). Auden thus indicates why he would treat Freud as a historian: his decision to abandon his early speculations about brain mechanics required that he conceive of his data as irreducible to quantifiable occurrences; he recognized that interpretations and reinterpretations of an event are themselves events; and he replaced the category of cause by that of (unconscious) motive. The 'science' that Freud thus invented fulfils the difficult task of history by distinguishing itself from the free inventions of poetry and the law-governed disciplines of science.

The discipline of history encounters a further difficulty, however, which Freud cannot surmount and Jones does not even recognize: the acceptance of a historical narrative is a matter of subjective inclination. The absence of causal determinism is reflected in the non-compulsory character of its results:

> while in the natural sciences, controversies are short lived, for either one side is proved to be right or both sides are proved to be wrong, in the realm of the historical, be it what is normally called history, or psychoanalysis, or theology etc., controversy and schism are perpetual. This does not mean, of course, that everybody is equally right, but that in deciding between two sides, one has to make a qualitative judgment. (p. 599)

Auden presents the disputes between Freud and his erstwhile disciples as paradigmatic cases of disagreement among historians, in which a judgment of taste is inescapable: 'his work feels or "smells" right to me, and

… theirs does not' (*Prose III*, p. 599). Not only are historical disputes as irresolvable as religious heresies, but there is always the possibility of disputing what counts as history. As Auden emphasizes in the 'Interlude' to *Homage to Clio* entitled 'Dichtung und Wahrheit', altering Ranke's famous line about the task of the historian, autobiography is as much a form of history as biography or military historiography: '*Who am I?* (Was ist denn eigentlich mit mir geschehen?) Several answers are plausible, but there can no more be one definitive answer than there can be one definitive history of the Thirty-Years War' (*HtC*, p. 44; *CP* 2007, p. 656). One can be called a 'good historian' as long as one is careful with data, determined to discover laws by which they are governed, aware that an interpretation is itself a possible datum, and cognizant that the laws in question are not equivalent to natural laws.

The last criterion is decisive, for it expresses the difficulty of history in general. There is no identifiable point where 'motive' parts ways with 'cause'. As historians become convinced that the motives they have identified propel the events under discussion, they are tempted to confuse them with causes. One historian who, as it were, succumbed to this temptation is Marx, or, at least, orthodox Marxists, who conceive of history in terms of necessary stages of development. Despite Auden's interest in, and respect for, Marx, whom he often pairs with Freud (*Prose I*, p. 48 and *EA*, p. 375) and sometimes with Kierkegaard (*Prose II*, p. 214), Marxist historiography is highly problematic. The point is not that the author of *Capital* is wrong; instead, 'Marx seems to me correct in his view that physical conditions and the forms of economic production have dictated the forms of communities' (*EA*, p. 373). But as Auden writes in a review of Edmund Wilson's *To the Finland Station*, a history of Marxist historiography, this view is irreducibly subjective, amounting to a 'wager': 'All human activities are dependent upon making presuppositions which cannot be proved but are acts of faith, and are regarded as absolute, i.e., as being binding whether they lead to worldly success or failure' (*Prose II*, p. 89).

Auden does not so much criticize Marxist historiography as largely ignore it. He is similarly dismissive of academic historiography, especially in the form of social science. More to his taste is Charles Cochrane's *Christianity and Classical Culture*, which is concerned with the same events as Gibbons' *Decline and Fall of the Roman Empire* but which Cochrane interprets in a very different way. For him, as for Gibbon, the decline of Rome is hastened by the advent of Christianity, but Cochrane sees the reason for this decline in a fundamental failure of classical culture as a whole, which never established 'any intelligible connection between the natural affective bonds and the life of justice' (*F&A*, p. 35). The final part of Cochrane's study is devoted to Augustine, who, instead of making Christianity into a substitute for ancient philosophy, seeks to show 'that the Christian faith can make sense of man's private and social experience, and that classical philosophy cannot' (*F&A*, p. 35). Auden's review describes and expands on Cochrane's exposition of Augustine's theory of love as a corrective toward his – and our – age: 'Our period is not so unlike the age of Augustine', Auden concludes, 'the planned society, caesarisms of thugs or bureaucrats, paideia, scientia, religious persecution, are all with us. Nor is there even lacking the possibility of a new Constantinism' (*F&A*, p. 39), in which Christianity would again be elevated to a state philosophy. Cochrane identifies a law of cultural decline, which can be transferred to other periods: promoting a view of life that overlooks the phenomenon of love, does not dampen decline but hastens it. Auden's attraction to Freud becomes even clearer from this perspective: for the inventor of psychoanalysis, like Augustine, is concerned with nothing so much as the history of love.

And this is also true of Auden. It is no surprise that he took an interest in Denis de Rougemont's *Love in the Western World*, which was published at the beginning of the Second World War and offered a univocal explanation for the disastrous course of European history: romantic love, which first supplemented and then replaced the Church, is ultimately suicidal, as demonstrated by the myth of Tristan and Isolde. The erotic object is everything, the lover nothing, and when the object turns out to be nothing as well, the nihilism inherent in romantic love arrives at its catastrophic dénouement, requiring another kind of love altogether. Auden's review of *Love in the Western World* sympathetically describes its contents while unobtrusively including Auden's 'only criticism' of de Rougemont's 'profound and brilliant study': 'I find his definition of Eros a little vague' (*Prose II*, p. 139). What is introduced as a minor quibble launches a profound critique in which Auden disputes the notion that Eros is distinguished from Agape as evil is opposed to goodness. For Auden, whose reflections freely draw on Kierkegaard's writings, the relation of Eros and Agape is thoroughly 'dialectical': 'The task of human Eros' – 'human' because Eros is a phenomenon of life in general – 'is how to actualize the possible by a series of decisions in which one future possibility is grasped by the present, and the rest thereby rendered impossible' (*Prose II*, p. 139). Despite Auden's appreciation of *Love in the Western World*, his review leaves no doubt that it is flawed history. It is not as though de Rougemont is dishonest about dates; but he is careless with regard to the fundamental datum at issue: the erotic dimension of love.

Love in the Western World shares at least one trait with another histori-cal study to which Auden was drawn, Eugen Rosenstock-Huessy's *Out of Revolution*: both de Rougemont and Rosenstock-Huessy locate the source of the contemporary European crisis – *Out of Revolution* appeared in 1938 and Auden first encountered it around 1940 – in a seemingly minor inno-vation of the medieval period. In the chapter of *The Dyer's Hand* entitled 'The Poet and the City', Auden reflects on the occupation of the writer and humorously describes his response to strangers when they ask him his profession: 'The most satisfactory answer I have discovered, satisfac-tory because it withers curiosity, is to say *Medieval Historian*' (*DH*, p. 74). There is a degree of truth in this ruse, for Auden was attracted to the field of medieval history in an almost systematic fashion: Cochrane describes the crisis of classical culture from which its medieval counterpart emerges; de Rougemont identifies the medieval innovation of romantic love as the origin of the contemporary crisis; and Rosenstock-Huessy identifies the introduction of All Souls Day as the actual birthday of 'the Occident', to which the subtitle of *Out of Revolution* refers: 'Autobiography of Western Man'. Working his way back from the Russian Revolution, through the French Revolution, to the German Reformation and the Italian Renaissance, Rosenstock-Huessy finally arrives at the origin of the European revolutionary spirit in the year 1000, when All Souls' Day supplemented and thus replaced All Saints' Day: we are not all saints, but we are all souls, and in anticipation of our death, according to Rosenstock-Huessy, we gain our past as well as our future, and we do so as a unified yet dispersed collection of individual pasts and futures.

A remark Auden includes in his verse commentary on the sonnet sequence in *Journey to a War* (written before he had read any of the his-torians under consideration here), indicates the source of his attraction to their work: 'This is the epoch of the Third Great Disappointment' (*JtW*, p. 292; *Prose I*, p. 692): the first is the collapse of classical culture, the sec-ond is the demise of Christianity in its classical form, and the third is the crisis of modernity. *Out of Revolution* can be read as an elaboration of this schema, for a moment of disappointment is an integral element of revolu-tion in general. Nowhere does Auden discuss this work at length, and in the brief preface he wrote in 1971 for a collection of Rosenstock-Huessy's writings, he is notably reticent about the style of Rosenstock-Huessy's thought, which he admits is 'a bit hard to take'; but Auden places *Out of Revolution* alongside Hannah Arendt's *Human Condition* as works of social-political thought with which he felt a particularly strong affinity.[1] And it is not difficult to see why *Out of Revolution* appealed to him, for it fulfils the conditions of good history: it is concerned with nothing so much as determining the 'law' that governs revolution in general; it recognizes that revolutions always change the concept of revolution, so that every revolution reinterprets previous ones; and above all, it abstains from the discourse of necessitation. Thus, the book moves backward, beginning with the October Revolution and culminating in All Souls Day. Given this unusual historiographical procedure, it is impossible for a reader to imagine that prior events are supposed to be understood as causes rather than motives of later events. 'Homage to Clio' (*HtC*, pp. 3–6; *CP* 2007, pp. 610–13), as the poem that begins the volume of the same name, presents itself as a summary of Auden's engagement with history and historiography. The title is traversed by a subtle tension. As one of the original muses, Clio became associated with history in late antiquity, probably in response to her name, which derives from *kleiō* ('to acclaim', 'to make famous'). In Auden's poem, however, she is not the proverbial 'muse of history'. First she is called the 'Muse of the unique / Historical fact' and then again 'Muse of Time'. She thus becomes a historical muse in a sense other than the one with which she has been identified: her role changes over time. At no point, however, does she have anything to do with either acclaim or fame. As Auden emphasizes when he first names her, Clio is silent. The primary action of the poet, 'homage', therefore reinforces the historical tension embodied in her name, for the poet acclaims a muse who herself refuses to speak. Auden further intensifies the contrast between the poet's acclamation and Clio's silence by concluding his homage with Clio's own lack of praise: 'I dare not ask you if you bless the poets, / For you do not look as if you ever read them / Nor can I see a reason why you should'.

Clio, then, can be seen but not heard. Both the metrical and thematic patterns of the poem are derived from this break in the perceptual field. Perhaps adapting the third Asclepeiadean strophe as revived by Horace – but modified beyond any assured recognition of its classical origin – Auden composes 'Homage to Clio' in the syllabic metre he associates most definitively with his own contemporary, Marianne Moore. His twenty-three quatrains alternate between lines of eleven and nine syllables with remarkable consistency. As he notes in a discussion of Moore's prosodic practice, English readers tend not to hear syllabic verse, attuned as they are to accents, and Auden exploits this tendency by employing what he calls 'the fullest elision', that is, 'always eliding between contiguous vowels or through *h* (*Prose III*, p. 650). Metrical pattern thus diverges from its audible expression: in the second stanza, for example, 'any hour' counts as two syllables, although heard as three. Even in its smallest units, there emerges a difference between the temporal measure that structures the poem and the time of its audible expression. Auden's decision to use only internal rhyme, rather than end-rhymes tending to produce 'more static and logical' effects (*Prose III*, p. 649), reinforces this divergence, so the resulting metrical pattern remains silent.

Clio's silence stands in contrast to the vociferous noises of nature, which dominate the opening stanzas of the poem, culminating in the array of sound words that frame the sixth stanza – from the earthquake's 'roar' through the 'whispers of streams', to the rhyme-stop, 'loud sound', that Auden suspends in the enjambment of the line and qualifies in the sound chiasm of the next, 'Not a din'. At this precise point, Auden introduces a caesura that reflects back on his own position, while naming Clio as the counterpoint to natural volubility: 'but we, at haphazard / And unseasonably, are brought face to face / By ones, Clio, with your silence'. The 'we' that encounters Clio in her silence is not, as Auden stresses, a collective subject, and her silence is not apprehended aurally but, instead, experienced only as singular encounters between individuals. There's no preparation for the encounter with Clio, hence it is 'haphazard'. When it happens, we are removed from the raucous frivolity of nature, whose battles, described in the opening stanzas, are of no consequence, for 'they all win'. In contrast to the poet whose attention is drawn toward a book, the animals around him live solely 'by observation'. But in contrast to the seasonality of creaturely activity, the poet's meditations are conducted 'unseasonably'. Auden here alludes to Nietzsche's *Thoughts out of Season*, which includes his famous essay 'On the Use and Abuse of History for Life'.[2] The openings of Nietzsche's essay and Auden's poem are almost mirror images of each other. Whereas the latter presents the animals as observant, the former begins by calling on its readers to 'observe the herd which is grazing beside you' (Nietzsche, p. 1). Nietzsche emphasizes the silence of the happy animal: 'A man demands of the beast: "why do you not talk about your happiness and only gaze at me?" The beast wants to answer, too, and say, "That comes about because I always immediately forget what I wanted to say". But by then the beast has already forgotten this reply and remains silent' (Nietzsche, p. 1). Whereas Auden rejects the indifference of the observant creatures who escape the pain of memory – 'to chirp like a tearless bird ... unthinkable' – Nietzsche finds that observation of creaturely life incites unhappiness among human beings:

'A leaf is continuously released from the roll of time, falls out, flutters away – and suddenly flutters back again into the man's lap. For the man says, "I remember", and envies the beast, which immediately forgets and sees each moment really perish' (Nietzsche, pp. 1–2). The German word, *Blatt*, here translated as 'leaf', also means 'page', and the book read by the poet in 'Homage to Clio' is even more differentiated from the ever-observant creatures than he is himself (with his 'unsatisfactory smell'): 'To observation / My book is dead'. Thus does a *Blatt* instigate the poet's untimely reflections. The point of Nietzsche's *Thoughts out of Season* is to show that 'historical sense' is only a highly qualified value. Auden does not envy the unhistorical existence of animals. The poet's paradoxical pronouncement, 'I was glad I could be unhappy', corresponds to his unqualified homage – the word derives from *homo* and emphasizes the quality of humanity – to Clio.

Auden does not, however, wholly disagree with Nietzsche. The principal aim of Nietzsche's essay lies in showing that monumental history freezes the past, making it impossible to create a future. 'Homage to Clio' is as hostile to monumentalism as 'The Uses and Abuses of History for Life', presenting it in the image of granite, which can represent natural forces but not Clio's frailty: 'How shall I describe you? They / Can be represented in granite'. Clio's silence is matched by a similar resistance to visualization. She cannot be captured in an image that would outlast the moment of her appearance and therefore remains unnoticeable when she appears: 'what icon / Have the arts for you, who look like any / Girl one has not noticed and show no special / Affinity with a beast?' This question corresponds to a statement Auden makes in a section of *The Dyer's Hand* entitled 'Two Bestiaries', the first part of which is an amusing critique of D. H. Lawrence, whose ability to represent animals is directly proportional to his inability to live in human and therefore historical society: 'Man is a history-making creature who can neither repeat his past nor leave it behind; at every moment he adds to and thereby modifies everything that had previously happened to him. Hence the difficulty of finding a single image which can stand as an adequate symbol for man's kind of existence' (*DH*, p. 278). Auden's other 'bestiary' is that of Marianne Moore, who is as delicate in her use of animal images as she is in her deployment of the syllabic line. 'Two Bestiaries' concludes with a reflection on Moore's poem, 'The Pangolin'. Emphasizing that it was written during the Second World War, Auden quotes only two of its lines – 'in fighting, mechanicked / like the pangolin' – and concludes with a paradoxical 'moral' that summarizes the uselessness of animal imagery for poets who want to find an emblem of history: 'men ought to be gentle-natured like pangolins but, if they were, they would cease to look like pangolins, and the pangolin could not be an emblem' (*DH*, p. 305).

Even at the point where the poet finally identifies Clio with a human figure – one that in its attitudes and acts recalls the Virgin Mary – he includes a note of hesitant self-reflection: 'I have seen / Your photo, I think, in the papers, nursing / a baby or mourning a corpse'. The world of animals, including the creaturely dimension of humanity, is subject to the forces of Aphrodite and Artemis, one of whom stands for eros, the other thanatos. Freedom from the cyclical movement of these two realms does not imply, however, that there are no constraints. Auden uses a simile in order to emphasize that Clio generates an obligation. Historical uniqueness may escape visual icons as well as sonic renderings; but those who understand themselves as bound to the uniqueness of historical existence are like the 'music' that recalls all of the nine daughters of Mnemosyne: 'Lives that obey you move like music, / Becoming now what they only can be once, / Making of silence decisive sound'.

Because each note in music is motivated by previous ones, never caused by them, historical existence is comparable to musical development. Auden's emphasis on the significance of historical interpretation – each new event can prompt the revaluation of previous ones – emerges as a structuring element of his poem. The last simile in the poem, 'Move like music', thus contrasts with its first one: 'to chirp like a cheerless bird'. The birds are not romantic nightingales that make natural music; instead, they emit a 'tribal outcry'. Recognition of the difference between the two comparisons solicits a retrospective reinterpretation of the opening stanzas in which the animals are seen to engage in warfare. In these highly metaphorical stanzas Auden does not turn to epic simile (discussed at length in his essay on Moore's bestiary); far from being emblematic of historical existence, animals are incomparable to anything human – except when human beings conform to the cyclicality that governs both the generations of animals and the movements of mechanisms: 'round and round like the Laxey Wheel'. The time of historical existence cannot be measured according to the circular movements of a clock or calendar but is, instead, given only when it is found: 'it sounds / Easy, but one must find the time, Clio'. Alluding to the idea of *kairos* as opposed to *chronos*, Auden is also altering the sense of easiness with which he first introduces Clio: after one is brought 'face to face' with her silence, 'Nothing is easy'. The disease or malaise of historical existence that Nietzsche captures and Auden glosses is not, as the opening stanzas suggest, the presence of memory traces but, instead, the absence of 'the time', understood not only as Christological *kairos* but also as the 'haphazard' moment when one could have done something out of season, that is, voluntary and non-constraining.

The final stanzas of 'Homage to Clio' not only invite a retrospective reinterpretation of its opening; they also solicit a similar reinterpretation of Auden's earlier poetic reflections on history, especially his 1937 poem 'Spain'.[3] One of the poems in the volume entitled *Homage to Clio* is called 'T the Great', where the once terrifying name of Tamburlaine is reduced to a preposterous anagram: 'II Down – A NUBILE TRAM' (*CP*, p. 599). A more serious wordplay appears in 'Homage to Clio' itself, for the title of the poem pays homage to George Orwell's description of the Spanish Civil War in his *Homage to Catalonia* from 1938. Apart from the poem 'Spain', written to raise money for medical aid, Auden had been otherwise reluctant to describe his experiences there: 'I did not wish to talk about Spain when I returned', he said many years later, 'because I was upset by many things I saw or heard about. Some of them were described better than I could ever have done by George Orwell, in *Homage to Catalonia*' (quoted Carpenter, p. 215). Orwell, for his part, disliked Auden from a distance (they had never met) and wrote a scathing review of 'Spain', first in 1938 and then more expansively in 'Inside the Whale' (1940). While praising the poem as 'one of the few decent things that have been written about the Spanish war', he objected to the line, 'The conscious acceptance of guilt in the necessary murder'; its last phrase, he asserted, 'could only be written by a person to whom murder is at most a word'.[4] Auden thought that Orwell misunderstood him but was troubled enough by the phrase to change it for *Another Time*. He excluded the poem from his *Collected Poems* and in the foreword to the 1966 collection repudiated its final lines: 'I once wrote: "History to the defeated / May say alas but cannot help nor pardon". To say this is to equate goodness with success. It would have been bad enough if I had ever held this wicked doctrine, but that I should have stated it simply because it sounded to me rhetorically effective is quite inexcusable' (*CP* 2007, p. xxx).

Auden's disavowal of these lines sets the scene for 'Homage to Clio'. The final stanza of 'Spain' asserts a condition, the opposite of that with which the later poem opens: 'the animals will not look. / We are left alone with our day, and the time is short' (*AT*, p. 96; *EA*, p. 212). In 'Homage to Clio', the animals are keenly observant; we are singular but not solitary, and the time is always there to be found. Most importantly, the poem both elaborates and retracts the phrase 'necessary murder' by expanding it. In a certain sense, Auden explains what he meant without making the explanation into an excuse: 'Muse of Time, but for whose merciful silence / Only the first step would count and that / Would always be murder'. This oddly hyperbolic pronouncement discloses the horror inherent in the 'Laxey Wheel', and by extension, the confusion of historical time with its natural and mechanical counterparts. If motive converges with cause, then everything that follows from each 'step' is necessary, including 'the necessary murder'. The opposite of 'necessary murder' is forgiveness, which always begins anew and is freely given. In 'Spain' history does not pardon. In 'Homage to Clio' the poet asks of Clio that she 'forgive our noises'. The last word not only refers to the outcries of the animals and rumblings of 'The Stammerer' and his compatriots but also the 'youthful noise' Auden associates with the rhetoric of 'Spain'. In the act of forgiveness, the past is not forgotten; but remembrance does not require a 'one-eye-for-one' recompense and is therefore free – again, not free to make up what happened but free to understand events as chances for 'face to face' encounters. The poet thus adds a further appeal to Clio, which corresponds with his praise of Freud as an historian: 'And teach us our recollections'.

According to the scenario Nietzsche proposes at the beginning of his essay on history, a 'leaf' of memory flits by, making us unhappy in our historical existence. Auden changes the leaf to a book, which must be interpreted. The distinction between motive and cause derives from the interpretable character of memory that expresses itself in the active word *recollection*: if the past were crystallized into a leaf that somehow remains in the present, then the nexus of cause and effect would be unbreakable. It is for this reason that the poet ultimately identifies Clio with the 'Muse of Time'. At stake in the final stanzas of 'Homage to Clio' is the temporal structure as a whole. Thus, obedience to Clio is music-like observation of time – not ideological compliance with supposed laws of historical development. As he writes in his review of Camus' *The Rebel*, 'since history is something man *makes*, it is meaningless to talk of *obeying* it' (*Prose III*, p. 501). Clio is asked to 'teach us our recollections' so that these recollections are understood to be teachable in the first place, that is, we learn that the backward perspective of memory, which interprets past events as causes, tends to forget the fact that each action could have been otherwise. To the extent that we can learn from our recollections, the past is not a closed book, but open, like the one the poet holds in his hands. The word *recollection* contains the word *collection*, and may be read as the volumes of collected poetry through which Auden 're-collects', 'forgives', and 'throws away' his earlier poems. In the section of *The Viking Book of Aphorisms* devoted to 'History', Auden quotes a much later Nietzsche: 'By seeking after origins, one becomes a crab. The historian looks backwards; eventually he also *believes* backwards' (Faber, 238; *Twilight of the Idols*, § 24). The final appeal to Clio can be understood accordingly: make me a historian but keep me from this dreadful 'eventually'.

NOTES

1 See Auden, 'Thinking What We are Doing', p. 72.
2 The titles of the Nietzsche texts are drawn from the translations that were widely circulated at the time; full details are given in the Further Reading for this chapter, at the end of the volume. Auden would have known that the essay is better translated as 'The Use and Disadvantage of History for Life'.
3 For a discussion of 'Homage to Clio' that compares it with 'Spain', see Smith 1985, pp. 171–73; full details in Further Reading.
4 George Orwell, *All Art Is Propaganda* (Harcourt, 2008), pp. 125–26.

(i) Creative Contexts

CHAPTER XVIII

The Body

Edward Mendelson

Auden's poems try to understand the human body as it is, not as a sign of something else, not as something to be idolized for its innocence or energy, not as something to be transcended or escaped, and never as something to be valued or devalued for any reasons that the human mind projects on it. For Auden, the body, and the human scale of the body, was the measure of all things. Its rhythms provided him with the raw materials of his metres and cadences. It provided a vision of connectedness and relationship among persons who would otherwise be separate. When he wrote and thought in the language of theology, he insisted that the immortality of the disembodied soul had never been a Christian doctrine, but that the final resurrection of the body, which he understood – 'whatever else is asserted by [that] doctrine' (*F&A*, p. 68) – as an assertion of the sacred importance of the body, a central element of the incarnational Christianity to which he had committed his beliefs. The body was at the heart of Auden's literary, ethical, and theological understanding of the world.

Auden was unique among major twentieth-century writers in the sanity and depth of his sense of the body and its significance. W. B. Yeats typically perceived the body either through the visionary simplifications of myth – for example, when he dreamed of Maud Gonne's 'Ledaean body' – or through the physical senses that were either fascinated or appalled by the body's gross reality – for example, when he noted, with inexact physiological detail, that 'Love has pitched his mansion in / The place of excrement'.[1] James Joyce increasingly perceived the body in mythical terms that dissolved individual flesh into the vast movements of water and earth. D. H. Lawrence imagined the body as the locus of mystical forces that radiated or converged on the solar plexus. T. S. Eliot, until old age, was repelled by the body's smells and textures, by its inevitable trajectory toward 'dung and death'. Without any literary tradition to help him find his way, Auden taught himself to value the body without idealizing it, to recognize it simultaneously in its inherent innocence and its adaptability as an accomplice in the criminal actions of the human will. His sense of the value of the body pervades not only the vocabulary, images, and arguments of his poems, but also their fertile variety of metre and rhythm.

Before he began writing poetry at the age of thirteen, Auden learned from his parents an approach to the physical world that was simultaneously realistic and symbolic. His father was a physician and professor of public health with wide interests in archaeology and mythology; his mother had trained but never practised as a nurse. In his father's library, Auden found treatises on physiology and psychology that treated the body as an organism to be understood empirically, not as a source of mystery or shame. Auden's family were Anglo-Catholic, members of the most ritualistic wing of the Anglican Communion, and his boyhood experience as an incense bearer in the communion service seems to have given him a lifelong conviction of the sacred importance of the physical world of the senses.

Throughout his career, Auden thought seriously about the relation between the instinctive body and the voluntary will, between bodily needs that were the same in everyone and deliberate choices that were different in everyone. But he placed these themes at the centre of his work only in the latter half of his career, starting in 1947 when he was forty years old. In his earlier years, his poems alluded to the body and asserted its autonomy, but seldom focused on it. In 1928, when he was twenty years old, one of his poems referred in passing to 'The body warm but not / By choice' (*CP* 2007, p. 12). Then, in 1933, he first began to write about his own body in the seriously comic style that he used throughout his later work. In the first stanza of 'A Summer Night' ('Out on the lawn I lie in bed' (*CP* 2007, p. 117)), he looks outward to two elements of the physical world: 'My feet / Point to the rising moon'.

These lines are a compressed statement of Auden's sense that his own body is both an aspect of himself and an aspect of a physical world that is distinct from his mind and will. Later in the same poem, the moon looks down indifferently on all the things that human beings value; throughout Auden's later poetry, the body is indifferent to the things that the mind desires. In his deepest meditations on the body's indifference, for example in the poem 'Memorial for the City' (*CP* 2007, p. 589), he treats the body's indifference to the projects of the will as, among other things, a source of hope. In deliberate opposition to a widespread tendency in Christian thought to treat the body as inherently fallen, Auden treats it as a promise of salvation. The epigraph to 'Memorial for the City' is a quotation from the medieval mystic Julian of Norwich about the moment when the soul receives the senses of the body: 'In the self-same point that our soul is made sensual, in the self-same point is the City of God ordained to him without beginning'.[2]

One of Auden's recurring themes in the 1930s was the contrast between the determined, instinctive world of nature and the contingent, voluntary world of the human will. The body was part of the natural world; but the will was a relatively recent innovation in evolutionary time. 'Our Hunting Fathers' (*CP* 2007, p. 122), written in 1934, begins by pointing toward the 'finished features' of the animal world – 'finished' because thought and experience cannot change features that were shaped entirely by the instinctive, evolutionary force that Auden, in his early work, frequently called 'Love', meaning something like the Freudian Eros, the life-instinct that opposed the death instinct, Thanatos. That same force of Eros, in human beings, by nature makes choices; it does not follow instinct. It can 'think no thought but ours'; it does what we choose to do.

Auden enlarged on this theme in 'Spain' (1937; *SP* 2007, p. 54), where the same evolutionary force, now called 'the life', gave social organization to the non-human world, gave the sponge its 'city state', gave the shark and tiger their 'vast military empires', and gave the robin its 'plucky canton', so called because it is peaceful and compact like a Swiss province. But in human beings, the same force is 'whatever you do … your choice, your decision'. But two years later, when he wrote 'September 1, 1939' (*SP* 2007, p. 95), Auden denied everything he wrote before or after about the voluntary quality of human emotion. In lines that he later dropped from the poem – before dropping the whole poem from his collected works – he wrote:

> Hunger allows no choice
> To the citizen or the police;
> We must love one another or die.

Auden used the semicolon where standard usage requires a colon; the first two lines explain the third, and all three lines amount to a statement of biological necessity. Love, like hunger, is an appetite that must be satisfied or the human organism must die.[3] This ignored Auden's deep conviction that the body's sexual appetite was a biological necessity that could be one of the means by which the whole person expresses a voluntary choice to love or not to love. In 'First Things First' (*CP* 2007, p. 581), a poem written in 1956, he reaffirmed this conviction: 'Thousands have lived without love, not one without water'.

From 1940, when Auden returned to the Anglican church, until around 1947, Auden's religion was an intensely private version of Protestantism that focused almost entirely on the will and treated the flesh in an indirect way, as something with a symbolic significance rather than a significance of its own. In 'The Sea and the Mirror: A Commentary on Shakespeare's *The Tempest*' (1944), Caliban is the voice of the inarticulate flesh, and Auden devised an elaborate intellectual *jeu d'esprit* in order to give Caliban a voice. Because the flesh has no voice of its own, it must borrow someone else's voice, which is inevitably artificial; and so Auden gave Caliban the diction of the most artificial voice he knew, the style of the later novels of Henry James. The effect was to give the flesh a voice that least expressed its nature.

In his next long poem, *The Age of Anxiety* (1947), he treated the body in a more or less similar way. The four characters in the poem experience a shared vision of 'prehistoric happiness', a vision that, 'by human beings, can only be imagined in terms of a landscape bearing a symbolic resemblance to the human body' (*CP* 2007, p. 482). The section of the poem that portrays this vision, 'The Seven Stages', imagines a maternal body on a scale so vast that none of the characters are aware of it as a body. By the time he finished *The Age of Anxiety*, Auden was dissatisfied with his own treatment of this theme. He began to turn away from his isolating Protestant perspective on the world toward a more Catholic and communal one and he took practical steps, not merely intellectual ones, in a new direction. In the summer of 1948, he travelled to Italy and stayed in Ischia, where he summered again for the next ten years.

One of the first products of his Italian journey was the poem 'In Praise of Limestone' (*CP* 2007, p. 538), which he began in England on the way to Italy in 1948, and finished in Ischia. He described it to friends as a celebration of the English limestone landscape that he loved as a child, and which he had now discovered had many resemblances to the limestone landscape of Italy. What he did not say, but which is obvious in the poem itself, is that the poem is an allegory about the sacred importance of the human body. It is a 'region / Of short distances and definite places', where a 'secret system of caves and conduits' lies below the 'rounded slopes' of the surface. It is among other things a womb, a place 'connected / To the big busy world by a tunnel, with a certain / Seedy appeal'.[4]

The poem presents itself as a meditation on an Italian landscape that has been shaped by human beings in ways that preserve a human scale.

That landscape, the poem says, is not a place of great historical change, nor is it the kind of place tyrants want to modify, nor the place where solitary saints go for refuge. The peaceful quiet of the limestone landscape is not 'the historical calm of a site / Where something was settled once and for all'. But it is precisely in its lack of historical significance that it has its real significance. 'History' in Auden's later work is the realm in which human beings made individual choices; the body is entirely unconcerned with history or individuality. The last part of the poem affirms that the body has 'a worldly duty which in spite of itself / It does not neglect': merely by existing, merely by reminding human beings of that part of themselves that they share with everyone, that is not the product of their choices or their will. It 'calls into question / All [that] the Great Powers assume; it disturbs our rights'.

The closing lines make the theological point toward which the whole poem has moved. Our 'Common Prayer' is to escape the shared condition of the body and be uniquely ourselves; our greatest comfort, the poem says, is music, 'which can be made anywhere, is invisible, / and does not spell' – everything that the body is not. And we are right to wish to transcend the body 'in so far as we have to look forward to death as a fact'. If death is a mere fact, then the body has no sacred significance. 'But if / Sins can be forgiven, if bodies rise from the dead' – the two promises of Christianity – then the body is crucial to both those promises. Auden's closing image of 'a faultless love / Or the life to come' is emphatically not a vision of heavenly glory, but one of bodily ordinariness: 'what I hear is the murmur / Of underground streams, what I see is a limestone landscape'.

A year later in 1949, Auden wrote his most extensive meditation on the body's relation to history, the four-part poem 'Memorial for the City' (*CP* 2007, p. 589). The third part portrays both the shared city and each individual psyche divided by the arbitrary divisions, by the literal barbed wire that separates two villages or two trees, or the inner divisions that separate everyone's will from everyone's flesh. 'Behind the mirror' – that is, behind that which divides each psyche from itself – the body, 'our Image', is the same. It has 'No age, no sex, no memory, no creed no name', because it is aware of none of those things. It has erotic impulses, but no awareness of sexual identity any more than it has any awareness of its past or any beliefs. Auden noted elsewhere that, in all languages, the first and second person pronouns have no gender; 'I' and 'you', to the extent that they are unique persons, not members of any category, are unsexed. In Auden's thought, the body, too, has no gender, even though it typically has feminine attributes.

Auden rarely used a common word in an idiosyncratic sense, but he did so with the body. In this poem, the body is 'our Image'; in his later poem 'Nones' (*CP* 2007, p. 632), the body is 'our Double'. He asks in 'Memorial for the City' whether 'our Image' is 'our friend' – does it share the purposes of the will? The poem answers its own question: 'No; that is our hope; that we weep and It does not grieve'. It is because the body has no interest in the divisions and distinctions that the will insists on that we can hope to recover from those distinctions. The last section of the poem is the body's own riddling statement of its own nature and its own purposes: 'It was I who suggested his theft to Prometheus ...' (the body needs warmth, so Prometheus stole fire); 'To me the Saviour permitted His Fifth Word from the cross; to be a stumbling-block to the stoics ...' (Christ on the cross said 'I thirst', affirming that the God-man does not disdain his flesh); 'I rode with Galahad on his Quest for the San Graal; without understanding I kept his vow ...' (the body could not imagine why Galahad should choose to be chaste, but was the part of himself that refrained from sex). The body states many more such riddles before concluding:

As for Metropolis, that too-great city; her delusions are not mine. Her speeches impress me little, her statistics less; to all who dwell on the public side of her mirrors, resentments and no peace. At the place of my passion her photographers are gathered together; but I shall rise again to see her judged. (*CP* 2007, p. 594)

What the city values – public speeches, statistical ways of thinking, resentments that arise from comparing one's own status with someone else's – hold no interest for the body. But the body, in these lines, is no longer in conflict with the will, because in Auden's understanding of what it means to be a person, someone who can authentically say 'I', who has unique personal commitments, and who values other unique persons, is equally indifferent to public as opposed to personal speech, to statistics, and to any sense of self based on comparisons with anyone else.

In the late 1940s and early 1950s Auden worked for seven years on an ambitious sequence of Good Friday poems, 'Horae Canonicae' (*CP* 2007, p. 625). This was an encyclopedic work that traced in parallel the events of a single day, of an individual lifetime, of the rise and fall of a city, and of the cosmic history from creation to apocalypse; the action of the poem occurs simultaneously anywhere in the contemporary world, in the Mediterranean village where Auden wrote most of the poems, in a large city like New York, and in ancient Jerusalem. The central poem of the seven-poem sequence, 'Nones', focuses most closely on the body and its unconscious, saving powers. After the crucifixion, after the crowd has dissolved into individual persons, everyone is alone. In a guilty interlude of sleep, we dream of 'our Double' – the body – which pays no attention to us. And we sleep so that the body can undo the damage done by every individual will against its own body and others', so 'while we are thus away, our own wronged flesh / May work undisturbed, restoring / The order we try to destroy':

> valves close
> And open exactly, glands secrete,
> Vessels contract and expand
> At the right moment, essential fluids
> Flow to renew exhausted cells,
> Not knowing quite what has happened, but awed
> By death like all the creatures …

At the end of an earlier stanza, the poem describes our solitude in these lines: 'The hangman has gone to wash, the soldiers to eat: / We are left alone with our feat'. Auden confirmed (in conversation with me in 1971) that the last word of these two lines was a deliberate pun. The body has no concern with serious dignity, so it is suitably described in a pun; and the fact that we are alone with our body is what makes possible the body's restorative work.

In 1958, Auden stopped summering in Italy and began summering in a house he had bought in rural Austria. He wrote a poem 'Good-bye to the Mezzogiorno' (*CP* 2007, p. 640) in which he contrasted his own northern model of life lived inwardly in the mind to the Mediterranean model of life lived outwardly in the flesh, and acknowledged that he could only be a visitor, not a native, in the more southern world: 'between those who mean by life a / *Bildungsroman* and those to whom living / Means to-be-visible-now, there yawns a gulf / Embraces cannot bridge'. His vision of the body became darker. He focused more sharply on the body's complicity with the will, rather than on its refusals of the will. He had already alluded to that complicity in 1949 in 'Prime' (*CP* 2007, p. 625), the first poem in 'Horae Canonicae', where the body is 'No honest equal, but my accomplice now, / My assassin to be'. From this period on, the mutual antagonism of accomplices became a recurring subject. In 'You' (*CP* 2007, p. 721), a riddling address to his body written in 1960, he anticipated the changing of its character from the current 'pleasanter side'. For they both know 'A day will come / When you grow savage / And hurt me badly':

> Totally stupid?
> Would that you were:
> But, no, you plague me
> With tastes I was fool enough
> Once to believe in.
> Bah!, blockhead:
> I know where you learned them.

At the end of the poem, he affirms his sense (which may or may not be accurate) that he is personally responsible for his flesh: 'Why am I certain, / Whatever your faults are, / The fault is mine'.

Auden's whole manner of thought was dialectical: having explored one aspect of a question, he soon afterward explored an antithetically opposite aspect of it. After writing about his body in the dark mood of 'You', he countered that poem with a comic vision of the same matters. In 'On the Circuit' (*CP* 2007, p. 728), his 1963 poem about the lecture and reading tour that he made each year in order to pay his bills, he anatomizes the contradictory feelings of Spirit and Flesh while alluding to 'our' feelings which combine Spirit, Flesh, and his whole person:

> Spirit is willing to repeat
> Without a qualm the same old talk,
> But Flesh is homesick for our snug
> Apartment in New York.

In the last years of his life, Auden wrote about the body in ways that combined a visionary sense of its glory with an unillusioned sense of its decay. One of the greatest of his late poems, 'River Profile' (*CP* 2007, p. 806), written in 1966, describes the life of the body from conception through death to a promise of resurrection, but does so in rapid stanzas that emphasize the brevity of the body's life. The poem's epigraph is from an aphorism by the German romantic poet Novalis: 'Our body is a moulded river'. Each of the poem's dozen Horatian stanzas records a stage in bodily life, imagined as a stage in the progress of a river from a mountain storm to its dissolution in a delta. The initiating storm is a sexual act: 'thundering / head-on collisions of cloud and rock in an / up-thrust, crevasse-and-avalanche, troll country'. In another bodily pun, the river emerges 'below the melt-line'. Then it grows to an anonymous stream, reaches a 'size to be named', rushes through spiral courses, becomes slow and turbid as it flows through a metropolis, then, at last, approaches 'the tidal mark where it puts off majesty' as it 'wearies' to a 'final'

> act of surrender, effacement, atonement
> in a huge amorphous aggregate no cuddled
> attractive child ever dreams of, non-country ...

In the background of these lines is W. B. Yeats' 'Among School Children'. Toward the end of his poem, Yeats asks himself whether a youthful mother, could she see her infant child aged sixty or more, would think her son a 'compensation for the pang of his birth'; the poem then concludes in a vision of images seen by the inner eye, 'Presences / That passion, piety or affection knows' (*Yeats*, p. 325). Auden's conclusion is visionary in an entirely different way. He sees in the ordinary physical fact – a drop of dew – an image of the resurrection of the body, of the unimaginable moment when the 'unlovely monster' of the flesh will achieve its final transformation, 'image of death as // A spherical dew-drop of life':

> Unlovely
> monsters, our tales believe, can be translated
> too, even as water, the selfless mother
> of all especials.

Auden's last extended study of the body was 'Talking to Myself' (*CP* 2007, p. 871), a poem written in 1971, two years before his death. It tells the same story told in 'River Profile', but specifically about himself and his own body, rather than parabolically about all selves and all bodies. Like the dew-drop born from the 'mother / of all especials', his own body 'Arrived / among that unending cascade of creatures spewed / from Nature's maw'. The criminal conspiracy of body and mind now takes the form of the partnership of a drug dealer and his customer. If 'You', the body, are 'short-winded / as cigarette-addicts are, I was the pusher / who got You hooked'. Their relation is not merely criminal, however, but also – for the first time in Auden's work – a marriage: 'Our marriage is a drama', he asserts, but unlike a 'stage-play', where the unspoken is un-thought, 'in our theatre / all that I cannot syllable You will pronounce / in acts whose *raison-d'être* escapes me'.

As in 'In Praise of Limestone' the body is an image of something greater than itself: 'You can serve me as my emblem for the Cosmos'. And, as in 'Memorial for the City' and 'Nones', the body's refusal to co-operate with the choices of the will is again a source of hope, but in a very different way:

> I'm scared of our divorce: I've seen some horrid ones.
> Remember: when *Le Bon Dieu* says to You Leave him!,
> please, please, for His sake and mine, pay no attention
> to my piteous Don'ts, but bugger off quickly.

The body that in his earlier poems healed wounds and restored order now, at the end of Auden's life, offers hope of a quick and painless separation.

NOTES

1 'Crazy Jane Talks with the Bishop', *Yeats's Poems*, ed. Jeffares, Macmillan, London 1989, p. 375. Henceforth abbreviated *Yeats* in the text.
2 Auden seems to have derived his quotation from Charles Williams' *The Descent of the Dove* (1939); Auden attributes the quotation to 'Juliana of Norwich', adding a feminine suffix to Julian's name either because he misremembered it or because he wanted to identify her as a woman.
3 The only surviving typescript (in the Berg Collection, New York Public Library) has a comma after the second line.
4 The body is usually feminine in Auden's poetry, even when it is his own, and even in poems prompted by the sexual life of two men. In his 1937 poem, 'Lullaby' (*CP* 157) the two lovers lie in post-coital contentment on the 'tolerant enchanted slope' of Venus – metaphorically on the *mons veneris*.

CHAPTER XIX

The Cinema

Keith Williams

The films of Gracie Fields may be 'more valuable to the social historian than the poems of W. H. Auden',[1] but Auden's encounter with the movies is nonetheless highly revealing about a moment with profound and ongoing consequences. Response to the cinematic imaginary is a defining characteristic of the writing of his time, epitomizing how traditional cultural hierarchies came to be increasingly questioned or creatively breached.[2] In 1934, according to Paul Rotha, 18,000,000 Britons saw films each week, generating £40,000,000 in revenue; whereas in 1936, the BBC's first regular TV service reached only 20,000 sets in Greater London.[3] In this pre-war era, then, commercial newsreels mediated Baudrillard's 'hyperreality' ('the real's hallucinatory resemblance to itself')[4] to the widest audiences, which documentary, although favoured by intellectuals, rarely reached. Arthur Marwick argues that, statistically, popular features tell us more about the political unconscious of the time, 'the unvoiced assumptions' of people who watched them.[5] Frequent cinemagoers were typically young, working-class, urban, and female (the opposite demographic to prominent poets); nonetheless, intermediality between 1930s writing and cinema is symptomatic of changes in relations between 'Literature' and popular forms. Studies of Auden and film have tended – perhaps understandably, given his practical involvement – to concentrate on documentarism.[6] His writings, however, indicate critical and creative interests in a wider spectrum of genres and audiences. Moreover, Auden didn't approach film in isolation, but through its interconnections with other media as an ideological matrix, reflecting Charles Madge's notion of a 'twisted skein'.[7]

A whole complex of cinematic motifs and susceptibilities, that would animate but also increasingly trouble Leftist writers, already figures in 'Consider this and in our time' (1930). Its famous topical imperative has the immediacy and virtual presentness of cinematic visualisation in aerial perspective, 'As the hawk sees it or the helmeted airman'; the noted 'air-mindedness' of 1930s culture is indivisible from 'film-mindedness'. Fliers or mountaineers were modernity's perfect heroes and the medium's ideal subjects for showcasing dramatic camera angles, breath-taking perspectives, and vicarious thrills, but also for harnessing the political imagination. Auden's poem exercises an idealized 'mobilized virtual gaze', which Ann Friedberg considers characteristic of cinematized modern sensibility.[8] This mimics organic vision yet enhances it as only technology can, zooming down into pinpoint close-up:

> The clouds rift suddenly – look there
> At cigarette-end smouldering on a border
> At the first garden party of the year.
>
> (*EA*, p. 46)

Not only would this schismatic border become the key motif in writing of the 1930s, Auden's incendiary cigarette, discarded by oblivious socialites yet clearly visible to us, warns against its potential as a flashpoint between competing states and ideologies. All the poem's changes of perspective and angle, its pannings and zooms, construct modernity as an interconnected visual space, but one which the cinematic principle of montage fractures at the very point of intelligibility. This makes it a highly provisional solution to the contemporary politico-aesthetic crisis; but for Auden and those following his lead, the attempt to discern order and meaning in a world disrupted by recent global conflict and current economic collapse had to confront new media.

Just as movies were most critically refracted in Leftist texts, so they had the most dynamic influence of all media on 1930s literary form, especially because writers like Auden felt cinematic techniques might modernize their own medium and enhance the force of its message. In the course of attacking capitalist media, many developed their own types of montage. Louis MacNeice accounted for Auden's observational alertness to the contemporary scene by linking it with the camera's – 'He admires the cinema's unrivalled capacity for rapportage' – but also acknowledged that Auden derived this method from Modernist forebears. T. S. Eliot 'cuts quickly ... by juxtaposing shots of the contemporary world with shots ... hoarded and selected from his world of books or culture'.[9] Stephen Spender recalled the Auden group's particular enthusiasm for the montage form of early Soviet movies, because they had 'all those qualities we found most exciting' in modernist art, like *The Waste Land*, but also 'conveyed a message of hope' countering Eliot's pessimism about the modern condition.[10] Pre-Stalinist Soviet films – by Eisenstein, Dovzhenko,

Ekk, Pudovkin, and Vertov – saturate writings by Auden and his coterie, combining the appeal of formal innovation and political soundness.[11] However, the promulgation of 'Socialist Realism', the Soviet Union's formally conservative cultural policy from 1934, and simultaneous reaction against 'degenerate art' in Nazi Germany cut off the supply of such films. Moreover, ironic symmetry between the two regimes and their operating methods gave British Leftists like Auden increasing pause for thought about the fit between their artistic and ideological commitments.

One shortcoming, Valentine Cunningham has suggested, was that cinematic-aerial perspective could lose sight of common humanity, in offering panoptic fictions of 'historical knowledge and certainty' where the privileged position of camera-eyed airman merged with sovietized Marxist. In fact, the commanding view from the dialectical airship (as Arthur Koestler conceived it)[12] was prominent in both totalitarianisms as they contested the cinematic imaginary. German flying films culminated in Leni Riefenstahl's *Triumph des Willens* (1935), with Hitler descending as a Wagnerian saviour-god: in its opening sequence, 'clouds rift', revealing views of Earth from the Junkers trimotor bringing the *Führer* to *Nürnberg Parteitag*. By 'Spain' (1937), Auden's cinematic-aerial perspective displays the dialectic of thesis and antithesis – presented as a continuous montage of contrasting scenes between historical past and urgent reality of present 'struggle'. 'Spain', however, questions the inexorable 'scientific' logic of Marxist synthesis, by leaving its visions of the future contingent on individual existential and ethical choice: whether or not to commit to action in the Civil War.

Cinematic effects of other kinds were also integral to Auden's critique of bourgeois domesticity and its self-deceptions. Ominous images in 'As I walked Out One Evening' (1937) of glaciers knocking in cupboards and deserts sighing in beds may evoke the striking superimpositions in location and dimensional relativity, in which film specializes. Similarly, Auden slips between brittle surfaces of social ritual to the fears beneath by visual matching reminiscent of the transitions of surrealist cinema, as 'the crack in the teacup opens / A lane to the land of the dead' (*EA*, p. 228). Newsreels, too, extended sensory awareness beyond the body's immediate limits, creating a virtual perception of events elsewhere happening collectively. In Auden's work, collisions between topical representation of public crises and the world of individual experience and private emotion prompted increasingly sceptical perspectives, challenging the status of mediated reality. Interaction between these disparate modes of knowledge and existence became a particular ethical preoccupation. 'Easily, my

dear, ...' (1934) contains a 'newsreel' verse juxtaposing hyperreal events
with personal life, while cleverly suggesting the enlarging effect of diagonal movement on screen:

> Ten thousand of the desperate marching by
> Five feet, six feet, seven feet high:
> Hitler and Mussolini in their wooing poses
> Churchill acknowledging the voters' greeting
> Roosevelt at the microphone, Van der Lubbe laughing
> And our first meeting.   (*EA*, p. 153)

Auden saw how news media filtered facts into public consciousness.
International coverage, for instance, sometimes seemed a continuation
of war by other means, enacted between photogenic airmen or climb-
ers: in summer 1936, a British attempt on Nanda Devi was jingoisti-
cally reported in newsreels. Consequently, the expedition in the topical
Auden/Isherwood drama of that year, *The Ascent of F6*, is spun into a
similarly Lippmanesque 'media fiction',[13] sublimating the Depression
public's desires and discontents. A whole ideology is invested in the race
against Ostnian rivals, as their 'typical' member of the public dimly
grasps: 'You see? The foreigner everywhere, / Competing in trade, competing in sport, / Competing in science and abstract thought: / And
we just sit down and let them take/ The prizes! There's more than a
mountain at stake' (*Plays*, p. 332). Others followed Auden's cue in using
cinema to epitomize connections and contradictions between public and private existence. Publicization of a round-the-world air-race
in John Sommerfield's cinematic novel *May Day* (also 1936) is likewise
exposed as mediated wish-fulfilment, a mass distraction from industrial re-organization. Most famously, Day Lewis's 'Newsreel' (1938) was
constructed in topical montage, with subversive commentary excavat-
ing the emotional subtext of screen-reporting in the audience's deepest
anxieties and desires.

Auden and Isherwood reflected writers' increasing sense that national
media did not afford access to a wider reality, so much as construct
mutually exclusive and antagonistic versions of it. Thus their play *On the
Frontier* (1938) appropriately adapts cinema's 'split-screen' effect for simultaneous action: the border dividing the Ostnia/Westland set is dominated
by portraits of the Leader on one side, the King on the other – staging
the paradox that modern communications shrank geographical distances
while expanding ideological ones. Wireless sets beneath relay complemen-
tary half-accounts of the same terrorist bombing into respective national
'homes', each blaming the other. As Cunningham puts it, the play shows

mediated words and images fatally interlocked in 'the same warmongering direction' (Cunningham 1988, p. 290).

Some British writers saw popular features as narcotic wish-fulfilment, paralleling the Frankfurt School's developing critique of 'mass culture'. Typically, Aldous Huxley's 'Dreamland' argued this picture palace 'implied a whole social programme, a complete theory of art', substituting cinema for religion as 'opium of the people'. As in *Brave New World* (1932), Hollywood represented 'Fordisation' of images, its cult of riches, glamour, and success furnishing 'imaginary compensations' for 'poverty and social insignificance'.[14] Huxley's cue was followed by British Marxists, epitomized by Christopher Caudwell's *Illusion and Reality* (1937), diagnosing popular film as pseudo-culture of commodity-production. Popular cinema appears similarly condemned in poems such as Auden's 'A Communist to Others' (1932), whose 'Brothers', released from toil in 'office, shop and factory', find themselves 'By cops directed to the fug / Of talkie-houses for a drug' (*EA*, p. 120).

The addictive habits of film-goers are also noted in 'Here on the cropped grass of the narrow ridge' (1933), which features 'Gaumont theatres / Where Fancy plays on hunger to produce / The noble robber, ideal of boys' – alluding to modernized Robin Hood fantasies (*EA*, p 142). Similarly, *The Dog Beneath the Skin*'s Chorus redirects attention from 'cinemas blazing with bulbs: bowers of bliss / Where thousands are holding hands', to 'Look left' at the Depression romcoms distracted them from: 'locked sheds, wharves by water' (*Plays*, p. 218). More zanily, the Chorus also names movie idols, playing against type, as coded signs of an international capitalist plot to con the public:

> If Wallace Beery
> Should act a fairy
> And Chaplin, the Wandering Jew;
> The reason is
> Just simply this:
> They're in the racket too!
>
> (*Plays*, p. 211)

According to Walter Benjamin, the star system substituted for the living individual's unique aura of 'personality, the phoney spell of a commodity'.[15] Industrialized charisma is objectified by Auden and Isherwood as a (hetero)sexual fetish: glamorous star 'Miss Lou Vipond' is played by 'a shop-window dummy', burlesquing fantasies of vicarious desire. As she bestows her favours, the nonentity-hero exclaims in delighted disbelief, 'Goodness knows what she can see in a chap like me!' (*Plays*, pp. 271, 268).

Nevertheless, Auden's position was more complex and nuanced, less doctrinaire about popular pleasures. MacNeice pointed out that, ironically, bourgeois socialization prevented intellectuals from admitting they too were 'merely a bit of the crowd': high-minded contempt while flourishing radical credentials came uncomfortably close to conventional snobbery.[16] Squaring the circle of popular form with radical content was the period's leading cultural conundrum (epitomized by H. G. Wells's notion of the cinematic 'broadbrow', mediating between 'high' and 'low').[17] In fact, with MacNeice, Auden summarized his regard for the potential of homegrown features, in this respect, in *Letters from Iceland* (1938). Mocking false sentiment and avoidance of 'controversy' (largely because of the British Board of Film Censors' stringent taboos), they saluted artistry, where due, and sympathized with *emigré* and native-born film-makers' frustrations:

> We hope one honest conviction may at last be found
> For Alexander Korda and the Balcon boys
> And the Stavisky Scandal in pictures and sound
> We leave to Alfred Hitchcock with sincerest praise
> Of *Sabotage.*
> To Berthold Viertel just the script
> For which he's waited all his passionate days.
> (*Prose* I, p. 366)

Auden's topical criticisms of the media sometimes drew on popular forms for their satiric edge. His reportage with Isherwood, *Journey to a War* (1939), features a newsreader reminiscent of a recent cartoon animation (who could have inspired Orwell's porcine propagandist 'Squealer' in *Animal Farm* (1945)): 'He resembles the most optimistic of Walt Disney's Three Little Pigs. The word "defeat" has no place in his mouth. Every Japanese advance is a Chinese strategic withdrawal' (*Prose I*, p. 515). In 'Letter to Lord Byron II', '[T]he little mickey with the hidden grudge' represents the Everyman of the time, the anonymous individual struggling with the tyrannies of mass modernity and his own complexes. He is a composite of Chaplin's 'Charlie', Strube's 'little man' *Daily Express* cartoon strip and Disney's animated mouse (*Prose I*, p. 213).

Another aspect of Auden's engagement with cinema involved his own contribution, and his thoughts on the practical problems of creating verse for cinema itself are encapsulated in a 'reported lecture' to the North London Film Society. Here he considered the intricacies of matching or counter-pointing the multiple connotations of words ('auras of meaning') to the concreteness and specificity of film's images and the space-time rhythms of its formal techniques. There are also indications he was abreast of debates and experiments concerning possible cinematic equivalents to Modernist 'stream of consciousness' or interior monologue, initiated by the famous meeting between Joyce and Eisenstein in 1929 (see 'Poetry and Film' (1936), *Plays*, pp. 511–13). Unlike Isherwood, who scripted features such as Viertel's *Little Friend* (1934) (experience later fictionalized in *Prater Violet*), Auden never learnt the craft of the screenplay in the commercial industry. Documentary, however, was a minority category of film relished by many writers for combining homegrown social realism with imported Soviet montage cutting. It seemed to offer creative participation in a more genuinely collective art, revealing what John Grierson called 'the essentially cooperative or mass nature of society' (quoted Cunningham 1988, p. 329), although some found its progressive potential studiously limited in practice. Grierson's model was dependent on an establishment economic base, through Government and industry sponsorship of the Empire Marketing Board (EMB), and the General Post Office (GPO) Film Units he set up. As a radical alternative, independent actuality films rarely had funds, technical equipment, and distribution access to achieve equivalent production standards or reach even the limited audiences of the EMB or GPO. Auden's verse commentaries are rare examples of documentary involvements reaching relatively wide publics (at least compared to his verse titles for the London Film Society screening of Vertov's *Three Songs of Lenin*), while also addressing similar concerns as his poetry.

Most famously, the GPO's *Night Mail* (1936; dir. Basil Wright and Harry Watt) cross-sections the communications of modern Britain, using the rail-post infrastructure to bring together everyone, however 'far apart in space or the social complex', in Storm Jameson's influential definition of documentary.[18] Messages are exchanged between banks and customers, relations and lovers, from every corner of these islands and abroad. Auden's verses nonetheless strove to imply the social inequalities inscribed within the material of literacy itself ('Clever stupid, short and long, / The typed and the printed and the spelt all wrong'). They ride the film's visual poetry of technology and democratic civics, but also problematize it at this intricate, 'micro-political' level (*Plays*, pp. 422–33). Auden's model was widely imitated, as in Graham Greene's 1937 commentary inaugurating the Empire Air Mail, *The Future's in the Air*.

Auden also wrote end commentary for Rotha's *The Way to the Sea* (1937), combining subjects beloved of Leftists in Soviet modernization films: railways and electrification. Again, Auden's language (coordinating with Benjamin Britten's score) mapped the sociological landscape along the London to Portsmouth line. The film concludes with imagery of mass beach pleasures recalling 'August for the people and their favourite islands' (1935), overshadowed by battleships on the eve of war. Although Auden only wrote sections of *The Londoners* (dir. John Taylor, 1939) for the Realist Film Unit, it typified the Modernist tendency to create collective heroes out of metropolises themselves, as in the 'city symphony' genre epitomized by Walther Ruttmann's *Berlin* (1927). Publicizing fifty years of metropolitan government, it contrasted sprawling *laissez-faire* slums with modernized infrastructure, social housing, and public health, using visionary images reminiscent of Auden's exhortation to 'look shining at / New styles of architecture, a change of heart' (*EA*, p. 36). Not only did the film proleptically model the welfare state, it was festooned with Audenesque motifs of popular pastimes, Bauhaus-style polyclinics and cavorting *Sonnenkinder*.

Nevertheless, mismatch between documentary's conciliatory principles and literary radicalism was too strained for the GPO's 1935 project *Negroes*. Auden's verses subverted Grierson's brief – converting image of Empire into Commonwealth of Nations – by exhuming 'acts of injustice' buried in its foundations of conquest and slavery. The film was not completed until 1938 (as *God's Chillun*) and may never have been screened publicly. As Christopher Innes notes, however, its semi-choric format at least pointed the way to Auden's libretti, which produced a truer synergy between collaboration and creative autonomy (*CCWHA*, pp. 91–92). In-joking about his units' achievements in *Letters from Iceland* – 'And here's a shot for the chief – epic: the *Drifters* tradition' (*Prose I*, p. 346) – expressed Auden's scepticism about documentary's 'creative interpretation of actuality' (as Grierson defined his own method).[19] A sequence of 'rushes' ends:

> Well. That's the lot.
> As you see, no crisis, no continuity.
> Only heroic cutting could save it.
> Perhaps MacNaughten might do it
> Or Legge.   (ibid., p. 349)

Auden reviewed Rotha's *Documentary Film* in 1936, criticizing the movement's distrust of 'subjectivism' and 'fiction', and its lack of mass appeal. The implication had been, he suggested, that:

'The private life is unimportant. We must abandon the story and report facts, i.e. we must show you people at their daily work, show you how modern industry is organised, show you what people do for their living, not what they feel'.

But the private life and the emotions are facts like any others, and one cannot understand the public life of action without them.

Not only did Auden feel documentarism excluded vital connections between a public world of collective action and private motivations and experience, but also its puritanical division between 'reality' and 'entertainment' left unsquared the circle of aesthetic form and popular reach: though producing films with excellent qualities, to ordinary moviegoers they 'were finally and fatally dull' (*EA*, pp. 354–55). Moreover, documentary units did not engage in burning topics so much as promote policy and commerce; so *Letters from Iceland* mischievously willed a hot potato to the GPO – 'a film on Sex' – and to Grierson himself 'something really big / To sell' (*Prose I*, p. 365). Because 'truth rarely has advertisement value', Auden doubted that documentary's paymasters would ever be disinterested enough to sponsor 'an exact picture of the human life within their enormous buildings' (*EA*, pp. 355–56).

Auden's work demonstrates how the contentious subjectivity of bearing camera-eyed witness, as much as its objectivism, became increasingly foregrounded in texts of the 1930s. In the mid-1920s, following Brian Howard's interest in the technologism of Weimar *Neue Sachlichkeit* ('New Objectivity'), British writers saw the camera as setting new standards for observational accuracy. Isherwood typified this tendency and almost certainly knew *Kino Glaz* ('*Cinema Eye*') of 1924 and other Vertov films; but he also typified increasing suspicions about privileged epistemological neutrality and related fallacies of 1930s 'camera consciousness', as Feigel puts it.[20] His own editorial 'fixings' of fact, epitomized by *Goodbye to Berlin* (1939), acknowledged that the camera-eyed witness is ineluctably part of the reality he reports, albeit often expressed in displaced form: demonstrating the ultimate ethical fallacy of detachment. Conversely, Isherwood relished film's double-edged potential for inadvertent psychoanalytic, as well as socio-economic, revelations. Nevertheless, Auden's coterie came to view experience through a film-minded 'mobilized virtual gaze'; but if early Auden provided a template for visual self-awareness, like Isherwood's cinematized form, this became more qualified. 'Easily, my dear, …' (1934) begins casually leafing through a photo-sequence of the day's events; by 1937 in *Letters from Iceland*, Auden was posing as both cameraman and editor:

> Let me pretend that I'm the impersonal eye of the camera
> Sent out by God to shoot on location.
> And we'll look at the rushes together.   (*Prose I*, p.346)

But neutral visualization is then problematized by quoting painter William Coldstream's belief that artists are more rightly 'both perceiver and teller, the spy and gossip' (ibid., p. 346). Auden reviews impressions like 'raw' footage, complete with fuzzy shots, pans, cuts, random close-ups and adventitious details, but also foregrounds the messy contingency and questionable associations documentary diegesis edits out. This epitomizes the critical tension between multi-levelled poetic performance and strictly emulated film technique; he finally makes explicit differences implied all along, admitting one form cannot literally be imported into the other: 'The novelist has one way of stating experience, / The film director another / These are our versions – each man to his medium' (*Prose I*, p. 350). In fact, 'I Am Not a Camera' (1969) would be Auden's final conclusion about cinematized style, in the eponymous poem disputing Isherwood's famous analogy (*CP* 2007, p. 841).

Auden and Isherwood feared propaganda might make film a particularly repressive medium during hostilities. In *Journey to a War*, they witnessed a patriotic melodrama that might soon become the norm in British features too: 'We both wondered how long it would be before we were applauding similar trash, only a shade more sophisticated, at all the London cinemas' (*Prose I*, p. 593). Looking back, on the eve of the Second World War, Auden pondered what 'huge imago made / A psychopathic god' (*EA*, p. 245), alluding simultaneously to the psychoanalytic term for unconscious representations of authority figures, but also to the 'cult of personality', which literally magnified mass hysteria and aggression through images of 'superhuman' leaders. Conversely, he raised critical consciousness of these phoney public faces megalomaniac politicians projected, and their potential for charismatic virtual 'presence' and emotionally charged 'parasocial' relationships. *Journey to a War* reported Chiang Kai-shek as unlike 'the cloaked, poker-stiff figure of the newsreels'; however, they witnessed him instantly morphing into this familiar persona at the next photo-opportunity (*Prose I*, p. 524). Similarly, *On the Frontier*'s Leader 'plays very stiffly, like a newsreel photograph of himself' ('Notes on the Characters', *Plays*, p. 359). In Fritz Lang's *Das Testament des Dr Mabuse* (1933), banned by the Nazis, the master criminal's 'living' presence is unmasked as mere recording, so the Leader is similarly exposed: 'Why he isn't a man at all! He's a gramophone!' Such inauthentic simulacra cast doubt on politicians in general and the veracity of their causes. *Westland*'s Leader is a virtual imago for transference and sublimation, purging and ennobling 'by proxy' as 'our national martyr' (*Plays*, p. 371).

Despite Auden's departure for neutral America in 1939 and disillusionment with the force and ethics of camera-eyed style, the migration of writers into both feature and documentary forms of cinema accelerated dramatically. His involvement left an active legacy, in their engagement with the industry's sponsors and regulators (principally the Crown Film Unit and Ministry of Information); but also, sometimes in unexpected ways, in the quality of their products. James Agee, a most astute U.S. critic of British war films, recognized this, especially in ex-documentarist Alberto Cavalcanti's *Went the Day Well?* (1942). Loosely based on Greene's 'The Lieutenant Died Last', it was transformed by a writing team into something recognisably Audenesque, that embodied his forebodings about Britain's unresolved internal contradictions and complexes. Nazi parachutists in British uniforms, directed by a collaborationist squire, take over an idyllic village but encounter savage resistance: the 'Deep England' setting, familiar from propaganda, signifies patriotic values topographically, but also, like many pre-war Auden texts, questions them. Whereas the film is tinged with proto-*Invasion of the Body Snatchers* paranoia, it also graphically reveals the capacity for violence in ordinary civilians (especially women) faced with the ultimate ethical choice of defending their community from a ruthless enemy, ambiguously both without and within. The film's reception at home was deeply controversial as 'the wild card, the joker in the British war-time cinema pack'[21]; but Agee regarded it as defamiliarizing polite civic structures, opening up, in symbolic microcosm, Britain's potential for appeasement, with corruption and class war lurking beneath. For him it had the 'sinister, freezing beauty of an Auden prophecy come true'.[22]

NOTES

1 Jeffrey Richards and Anthony Aldgate, *Best of British: Cinema and Society 1930–1970* (Blackwell, 1983), p. 4.
2 See Kristin Bluemel, (ed.) *Intermodernism: Literary Culture in Mid-Twentieth-Century Britain* (Edinburgh University Press, 2009); Lara Feigel *Literature, Cinema and Politics 1930–1945: Reading Between the Frames* (Edinburgh University Press, 2010).
3 See Paul Rotha, *Documentary Film* (Faber, 1935; 3rd edn., 1952), pp. 52–57.
4 See Jean Baudrillard, *Selected Writings*, ed. M. Poster (Polity, 1988), pp. 145–47.
5 Arthur Marwick, *Class, Image and Reality in Britain, France and the USA since 1930* (Collins, 1980), p. 22.
6 See, for example, Marsha Bryant, *Auden and Documentary in the 1930s* (University of Virginia Press, 1997).

7 Charles Madge, 'Press, Radio and Social Consciousness', in Cecil Day Lewis (ed.) *The Mind in Chains: Socialism and the Cultural Revolution* (Frederick Muller, 1937), pp. 147–63 (147–49).

8 See Anne Friedberg, *Window Shopping: Cinema and the Postmodern* (University of California Press, 1993), pp. 2–3.

9 Louis MacNeice, *Modern Poetry* (Oxford University Press, 1938), pp. 86 and 166.

10 Stephen Spender, *World Within World: the Autobiography of Stephen Spender* (1951; repr. Hamish Hamilton, 1964), pp. 132–33.

11 For numerous examples, see (among others), Williams, Keith, *British Writers and the Media, 1930–45* (Macmillan, 1996) and Feigel (see note 2 in this chapter).

12 Koestler admitted a journey by airship over the Soviet Union conditioned the propagandism of his resulting reportage *Von Weissen Nächten und Roten Tagen* (1933) (see *Arrow in the Blue: The First Volume of an Autobiography* (Hutchinson, 1952; repr. 1983), pp. 388–91).

13 See Walter Lippmann, *Public Opinion* (Allen Lane, 1929), pp. 14–19.

14 'Readers and Writers' in Aldous Huxley, *The Olive Tree and Other Essays* (London: Chatto and Windus, 1936; repr. 1947), pp. 1–45 (39–40).

15 'The Work of Art in the Age of Mechanical Reproduction' (1936), Walter Benjamin, *Illuminations,* ed. Hannah Arendt (Fontana, 1973), pp. 217–52 (231).

16 'In Defence of Vulgarity' (December 1937 BBC talk), in MacNeice, *Selected Prose*, pp. 43, 45.

17 See H. G. Wells, introduction to *The King Who Was a King: The Book of a Film* (Ernest Benn, 1929), p. 22.

18 See Storm Jameson, 'Documents', *Fact,* no. 4 (July 1937), pp. 9–18 (17–18).

19 See his 'The Documentary Producer', *Cinema Quarterly,* vol. 2, no.1 (1933), p. 8.

20 See Feigel (note 2 in this chapter), especially pp. 122–23.

21 See Penelope Houston, *Went the Day Well?* (London: BFI, 1992, pp. 35–36).

22 *Nation* (15 July 1944), repr. in *Agee on Film,* 2 vols., vol. II, *Reviews and Comments by James Agee* (Peter Owen, 1963), p. 104.

CHAPTER XX

1930s British Drama

Steve Nicholson

When the Group Theatre staged Auden's *The Dance of Death* alongside *Sweeney Agonistes* at the Westminster Theatre in October 1935, the programme contained a series of radical proposals by Auden under the title 'I WANT THE THEATRE TO BE' (see *Plays*, pp. 497–98).[1] Together, they reflected an impatience with current practice, and some were prescient of future innovations. His declaration that 'DRAMA IS NOT SUITED TO THE ANALYSIS OF CHARACTER, WHICH IS THE PROVINCE OF THE NOVEL' rejects the Stanislavskian slavishness of much serious drama, and his suggestion that an audience 'OUGHT TO KNOW WHAT IS GOING TO HAPPEN NEXT' nods to a Brechtian theory hardly recognized in Britain until the mid-1950s; the insistence that 'DRAMA BEGAN AS THE ACT OF THE WHOLE COMMUNITY' and that 'IDEALLY THERE WOULD BE NO SPECTATORS' pre-echoes Augusto Boal's invention of the 'spect-actor' which has informed much community and political theatre practice of the last thirty years, and the assertion that drama is 'ESSENTIALLY AN ART OF THE BODY', and that 'THE BASIS OF ACTING IS ACROBATICS, DANCING, AND ALL FORMS OF PHYSICAL SKILL', anticipates the onslaught on verbal, representational and intellect-based performance launched in the name of 'physical theatre' four decades later; even the veneration of music hall and pantomime – 'most living drama of to-day' at *Plays* p. 497 – as models for imitation and appropriation chimes with the later approach of practitioners such as Joan Littlewood and John McGrath.

But, while it ran counter to dominant mainstream conventions of the time, Auden's vision was not entirely without connections to other pioneering practices already surfacing, and some venues – notably, though not only, private clubs – gave audiences the chance to encounter more experimental approaches to performance occurring outside Britain. If many critics and audiences would instinctively have rejected the sort of cultural avant-garde Auden proposed, he was not without influence. In 1936, W. A. Darlington, the *Daily Telegraph* theatre reviewer, described Auden's aspirations as 'ridiculous nonsense'. But he was more positive about the actual practice: 'Auden's bite is a good deal better than his bark', he wrote, and the production he witnessed of *The Dog Beneath the Skin* 'proved that cock-eyed theory need not preclude sound practice'.[2] Later, Darlington – in many respects a traditionalist in his theatrical tastes – praised Auden and Isherwood as 'men of real literary gifts who are trying experiments in the theatre and are not content to play the more lucrative game of giving the public what it understands'.[3] Debate which polarized art and accessibility, the highbrow and the lowbrow, the political and the escapist ran through the decade.

Another key component of Auden's manifesto was a rejection of theatre's fascination with superficial representations of the real and the ordinary, as though anything else is beyond comprehension. 'THE DEVELOPMENT OF THE FILM HAS DEPRIVED DRAMA OF ANY EXCUSE FOR BEING DOCUMENTARY', he wrote, and called instead for theatre texts whose language would voice 'THE SAME COMPRESSED, SIGNIFICANT, AND UNDOCUMENTARY CHARACTER, AS DRAMATIC MOVEMENT'. In its broadest sense, Auden is calling for a theatre which is poetic rather than literal; one which licenses metaphor, rhetoric, and an imagined world. He was not the first writer to do so. In an essay written in 1928 and entitled 'Why Poets Write Plays', the verse dramatist Gordon Bottomley had lamented the fact that while it was 'poets who invented the Theatre', current fashions meant that they were now effectively excluded from it:

Theatre has in the last fifty years come to be looked upon as a mirror of our own daily life, a place where we can see people dressed like ourselves and behaving like ourselves, and hear them speaking like ourselves.

Most plays, said Bottomley, were contrived 'to produce an effect of things happening just as they do in real life', and were measured and judged in relation to their success in achieving this. 'And yet', he insisted, 'most of the supremely great plays that mankind has produced ... do not attempt to produce an effect of reality'; instead, characters 'speak to each other in a way in which men and women have never spoken to each other in real life'; that is, he explains, 'they talk unmitigated poetry'.[4]

Bottomley's attempt to reclaim the theatre for poets appeared in the programme for the Cambridge Festival Theatre production of Georg Kaiser's *From Morn to Midnight* – an expressionist play and genre which eschewed any attempt to mirror the surface of the everyday. It was a not untypical play to find in the repertoire of the Festival Theatre, which, in the hands of Terence Gray in the late 1920s and early 1930s, was reso-lutely – almost perversely – determined to set itself against the theatrical establishment. Gray defined the venue as an 'Art Theatre', in opposition to the ubiquitous 'Trade Theatre', a fundamentally capitalist enterprise designed to generate profits for investors by providing 'a barely respectable resort for after-dinner diversion'.[5] Unembarrassed by charges of elitism, Gray's programme sought to confront his audiences with ground-break-ing playwrights from abroad – among them Kaiser, O'Neill, Pirandello, and Benavante. He might not have endorsed all aspects of Auden's call to arms – it is hard to imagine Gray celebrating popular forms of entertain-ment – but there were important areas of overlap. Thus, Gray devotes three chapters of his book on theatre to an attack on 'The Tyranny of Words',[6] while on a practical level he appointed the choreographer and ballet dancer Ninette de Valois to work in rehearsal with his acting com-pany. For Gray too, dance – defined as 'all forms of studied movement' – was more fundamental to performance than text:

For the human soul has no other medium so potent for the expression of emo-tion, nor any medium so natural. … The human body is a man's natural means of self-expression … his instinctive and immediate means of expressing the emo-tions which arise within him … the human body rather than the intellectualised spoken word is the medium that is most essential for dramatic art.[7]

He believed that the primary obstacle holding back the development of theatre as an art-form was that 'the new type of dramatist – the dance-dramatist – has yet to appear'.[8] Had he not abandoned the theatre in 1932 and gone to live abroad, Gray might have acknowledged the significance of Rupert Doone and the Group Theatre, for which Auden wrote.

'The theatre was not invented for the purpose of mirroring our daily life', wrote Bottomley.[9] But playwrights were handicapped by the refusal or inability of most critics to discuss their work in other terms. The catch-all label of 'expressionist' was lazily applied to anything which challenged dominant conventions, and reviews too often focused on extracting the narrative, irrespective of the form which mediated it. This emphasis is fre-quently visible in the readers' reports written in the Lord Chamberlain's Office as part of the censorship process to which all new plays were sub-jected. For example, Velona Pilcher's *The Searcher*, staged at the start of the decade, was probably the most original and striking anti-war play of its time.[10] While grounded in the playwright's real-life experiences around the battlefields of Europe in 1918, it employed a range of poetic registers and devices, incorporating sections from instruction manuals and official documents as well as heightened verse and recurring patterns and rhythms. The staging reflected this approach, as the audience is invited to watch the action not objectively but through the distorted and 'tortured vision' of a woman driven insane by the horrors of war. 'From the opening curtain to the closing curtain, all things seen, spoken and staged shall appear to us as they appear to the Searcher, whose vision we accept for this hour'.[11] So choruses of identical, giggling nurses and flabby doctors cheer when told that the next day's battle will create 2,000 new wounded soldiers, and are seen partying in their gas masks around the beds of the dying. The Censorship could only respond as though such images were intended as a literal representation of actuality, describing the depiction of the medical profession as 'ugly and unjust', and therefore inappropriate to present, while the Lord Chamberlain himself described the play as 'the work of a lunatic'.[12]

At the other end of the decade, the *Observer*, in its review of *On the Frontier*, took Auden and Isherwood to task for expressing their ideas 'in the form most likely to deter the general public'. Such an approach, the review suggested, inevitably left the play in a political ghetto:

For preaching to the converted their mixture of realism and fantasy, of choral comment and of Left Wing wise-crackery, has been proved, by previous work in other conventicles, a satisfactory method. But surely our dramatists want to reach the people who would be going to the Globe theatre in any case and not merely on Sunday nights and for that purpose a straightforward realistic play, of which *On the Frontier* has some excellent elements, would be really effective because it would avoid the atmosphere of pretentiousness so tiresome to the average playgoer and so dear to our anti-realists. In this case the singing of choruses (in such a manner as completely to obscure the words) to music which made one fear to be removed to hospital suffering from Percussion, is simply a hindrance. A few of the elect may deem it marvellous, but the average bourgeois playgoer, whose darkness Messrs. Auden and Isherwood must wish to enlighten, will only want the players to cut the cackle...

For the *Observer*, 'the best thing in the play is the realistic psychological study of Westland's dictator', and the power of this element 'makes it the more sad that the whole theatrical effect should have to be subjected to and spoiled by the anti-realistic elements'.[13]

Like Velona Pilcher, and anyone else seeking to use the stage to reflect on international political issues, the Group Theatre – and Auden – also had their difficulties with the Lord Chamberlain. Some critics would later claim that 'Dramatists ignored the war'.[14] This is by no means true, but such an assertion fails to acknowledge one of the primary reasons why it might have seemed to be the case. As early as February 1934, the Lord Chamberlain refused to allow an anti-Nazi play to be performed:

I have no wish to deter people from showing up the brutality of the Nazi regime, but this can perfectly well be done in books and novels, and even published plays, but not by plays acted on the English stage.[15]

And although loopholes existed, this rule was maintained for the next five and a half years. No appraisal of theatre in the 1930s can therefore fail to acknowledge the role of official censorship in determining what audiences could see and playwrights could write – even if that role is not always visible because it is expressed partly through absence – what the playwright and theatre critic Hubert Griffith called 'the unborn children' – the plays that were never written.[16]

In 1935, the Lord Chamberlain's Reader described *The Dog Beneath the Skin* as an 'obvious attack on Germany'. He warned that 'Many people will object to the whole play as Communist propaganda', but recommended that 'it cannot wisely be banned on that score'. The Office consulted Lord David Cecil, the former Eton and Oxford literary biographer, who cautioned that a total refusal would 'go against the opinion and sentiment of the vast majority of responsible and sober intellectuals – at any rate of my own and younger generations'. Cecil recommended that, given the reputation of the play's authors, 'it would be a grave mistake of policy' to reject it:

Mr Auden is one of the most considered of our younger authors – and though personally I must admit I do not care much for his work, I think it original, sincere and talented, intended neither to shock or to court notoriety but genuinely to express his literary and other views. Nor is he an eccentric, not taken seriously: he has a large party of admirers among reputable and sober critics. For this reason I should hesitate very much before completely banning his work.

Not for the first or last time, the Censorship chose a more subtle strategy, referred to internally as the 'Death of a thousand cuts', in which a lengthy list was compiled of lines and images which could not be approved: 'I dare say if the Lord Chamberlain requires all these excisions the author will withdraw the play', noted the Reader; 'It would not be a great loss'.[17]

Three years later, the same authors' *On the Frontier* divided opinion within the Lord Chamberlain's Office. The script, submitted soon after Chamberlain's signing of the Munich agreement, was read first by

Geoffrey Dearmer, himself a published poet and someone who appreciated the literary credentials of the play's authors. 'To forbid this would be to subscribe to fascist ideology', he warned his superiors, and he forcefully expressed his view that to criticise and attack the European dictatorships was 'the right, and duty, of modern English poets'. His superior at St James's Palace saw things differently: 'I agree that the totalitarian principle is one which is abhorrent to the normal Englishman', he wrote, 'but I disagree that it is the duty of modern Poets to attack this principle'. And he added, tellingly, that 'At such a time as this the best interests of the country are served by avoiding any unnecessary exasperation to the leaders of the German people'. The play was ultimately approved on the grounds that it was sufficiently oblique in its approach to pass muster. But the attention given to specific details is revealing: all references to 'the Leader' were cut, and although the substitution of 'Guidanto' – the Esperanto equivalent – was allowed, a written endorsement stipulated that 'the word "the" in front of "Guidanto" … should be omitted'.[18]

The need for such careful control of the theatre reflects the fact that despite the growth of the film industry, it was a medium still seen as likely to agitate debate and spread ideas – not least, political ones. Several broadly left-wing theatre movements emerged during the 1930s, and their work and approaches embodied recurring arguments over which styles and genres should best be employed in order to maximise impact. The didactic direct-address and often heavy-handed propaganda largely favoured by the Workers Theatre Movement (WTM), which dated back to the mid-1920s, began to be discredited after the British representatives at an International Olympiad in Moscow in 1933 were exposed to strong criticism from other international delegates for their one-dimensional approach and lack of technique. An editorial published in the WTM Bulletin soon afterwards which asked 'What Have We Gained From the Olympiad?' reaffirmed that 'the most effective method' for working-class audiences and performers remained 'the open-platform method', but the movement's self-styled Central Committee was ready to initiate a second front by simultaneously encouraging a 'left play-producing society'.[19]

Inviting submissions to a play-writing competition in 1935, *Left Review* recommended that 'the drama of a Socialist theatre necessarily evokes new themes which may lend themselves to presentation in the old form but more probably will develop new theatrical forms for themselves'.[20] Writing in the same journal and from the same political perspective,

Barbara Nixon heralded the Group Theatre for their 'courage to experiment boldly in novel theatrical forms'. However, she cautioned against concentrating too much on aesthetics, and was adamant that the company's work would 'only be of real value if it combines an equal excellence of content'. More specifically, she warned that 'If the Group Theatre remains exclusively a society interested in art and form only for the art or form's sake, it will remain ineffectual, and only obtain an audience which although exclusive and intelligent will be very small'.[21] As John Allen also acknowledged: 'The problem which faces the dramatist who wants to express Socialist ideas in his plays, is the form into which he should cast his plays to give them a popular basis'.[22] Allen had been a founder member of Group Theatre, working both as an actor and an administrator, but disenchanted by its failure to speak to the working class, he left in 1936 and became a leading director and organiser within the much more overtly political Unity Theatre, an organization which had strong links with the British Communist Party. Writing a year after his defection in celebration of Unity's production of Herbert Hodge's political cartoon *Where's that Bomb*, Allen drew a direct comparison:

I can think of no two writers whose work is more dissimilar than these two. Auden's is introverted and twisted, Hodge's extravert and robust, Auden's exclusive, a thing of a class, Hodge's popular, a thing of the people.[23]

For Allen, the direct involvement of the working class in the process of making as well as viewing culture was itself a political act – almost irrespective of content:

Capitalism has appropriated 'culture' to such an extent, that the right, or even the possibility of self-expression has become the exclusive property of the middle and upper classes. The fact of a man being obliged to work for eight or more hours a day at some back-breaking job at a factory bench is an argument that he has more rather than less need to express himself in what spare time he has, than the listless intellectual who can live all day with Beethoven quartets and Auden poems.[24]

The difference was not just between individual playwrights, but between the two companies and what each represented. Allen himself had appeared in the original production of *The Dog Beneath the Skin*, but by 1937 he was attacking the Merseyside branch of Unity for reviving it, and contemptuously dismissing Auden as the 'author of a dissatisfied bourgeoisie ... speaking another language ... writing for another class ... with sentiments which have little interest for the fighting spirit of the militant working classes'.[25]

Despite this, Unity's work embodied some of the principles of Auden's manifesto. He had championed, at least in theory, the breaking of the absolute divide between stage and auditorium: 'IDEALLY THERE WOULD BE NO SPECTATORS. IN PRACTICE EVERY MEMBER OF THE AUDIENCE SHOULD FEEL LIKE AN UNDERSTUDY'. Unity remained determinedly non-professional, with its working-class actors – and occasionally authors – drawn directly from its audience; in several productions, the use of actors planted in the audience to respond to action on stage and encourage 'real' audience members to do likewise also blurred the distinction. Although the training Unity offered through its summer schools tended to emphasise Stanislavsky's approach as the basis for acting, it did present the first British performance of a play by Bertolt Brecht, and introduced several new theatrical forms to the British stage – including Living Newspapers, Political Pantomimes, and Mass Declamations – which hardly depended on the analysis of character Auden had derided. *Busmen* juxtaposed verbatim material from parliamentary speeches and committees with short realistic scenes, slide projections, amplified narration through 'the Voice of the Living Newspaper', and a ballet representing the imposed 'speed-up' on buses. *Crisis*, another documentary drama, opened on the night Chamberlain flew to Munich for negotiations, and was updated on a daily basis, with new material given to actors as they arrived from work to perform that evening.[26]

Unity's Political Pantomimes translated contemporary issues into a popular and entertaining form. In *Babes in the Wood*, Austria and Czechoslovakia were the babes, Hitler and Mussolini the robbers, and Chamberlain the wicked uncle; and while the musical comedy and doggerel verse could be seen as tending to trivialize its subject, the combination of popular form with political message proved popular. Satire was a primary weapon, as when the Fairy Godmother figure – Lady Wishfulfilment – proposes to the audience that the best way to respond to problems is to ignore them:

> If your job doesn't give contentment,
> If you are rather poorly paid
> Don't complain or show resentment
> Call on little me for aid ...
> What's the use of facing facts,
> The horrid things they aren't much fun
> Why worry about this life's bad acts
> There's a fairy life for everyone.

The main object of satire is not the individual, but instead the media and its role in promoting naivety and ignorance:

> I'm a source of inspiration
> To the optimistic press
> I write nearly all the leaders
> You read each day in our free press
> No matter what happens I always say
> There's not going to be any war today.

Unity's work was generally defined more by its commitment to accessibility than to an aesthetic avant-garde. However, a form which stands in some contrast to this is the mass declamation, a long, choral poem. Unity presented several declamations by Jack Lindsay – sometimes on a theatre bill alongside one act plays, and sometimes in outside venues such as Trafalgar Square. *On Guard for Spain*, *Who are the English*, and *Salute the Soviet Union* were linguistically and structurally quite complex, and a world away from the rhyming couplets of many other Unity scripts. Lines were divided between individual voices, different choruses, and the whole company, and the verse was staged with carefully composed groupings and stylized movement, and, when indoors, with orchestrated lighting and sound scores.

FULL CHORUS:	Who, Who, Who are the English?
LEADER:	who are the English
	according to the definition
	of the ruling class?
	All you that went forth,
	lured by great sounding names
	which glittered like bubbles of crystal
	in your eyes
	till they burst and you burst with them,
	(intonation of voices, bursting bombs, etc.)
1 MAN'S VOICE:	shot to shreds
	from one end of the shuddering earth to the other end,
2 MAN'S VOICE:	shot that the merchants pockets
	Might clink and bulge…

John Allen maintained that mass recitations such as this were 'one of the surest ways of re-establishing a connection between poetry and the working classes',[27] while Lindsay himself attacked those who believed that 'Art is esoteric' and 'only to be appreciated by the few'. He was particularly contemptuous of what he saw as misguided attempts by other contemporary poets to engage with contemporary affairs – and may even have had Auden and the Group Theatre partly in his sights:

> We have had verse of late years in England that strove to grasp the political issues. But since it strove to do so in terms of the bourgeois audience, it came to a dead-end; the audience it addressed was in the last resort the types of narrowing, contracting capitalism not the class rising to supplant capitalism … the elegists of bourgeois decay, however witty, must sink with their fading audience unless they can make the leap which will bring them to solidarity with the workers.[28]

Most of the work and ideas discussed in this chapter failed to penetrate the commercial theatre industry during the 1930s, and looking back at the period twenty years from the late 1950s, the theatre critic J. C. Trewin provided a confident summary of what would be remembered from that decade:

> To a drama historian of the future the Thirties will mean such diverse things as the plays of J. B. Priestley, James Bridie, Emlyn Williams … the Coward of *Private Lives* and *Cavalcade* and *Conversation Piece* … "Gordon Daviot" and … Dodie Smith; Shaw's conversations … the last bitter plays of Maugham; the Gielgud classical seasons, the rise of the Old Vic, the flowering of Olivier; the flourish of Drury Lane and its Novello musical plays.[29]

Trewin also cites the early verse dramas of Eliot and the emergence of British ballet, but there is little room in his account for most of the political and aesthetic innovations referred to here, and his evocation leaves out much that needs to be remembered, and which appeared significant at the time. In 1936, The *Sunday Times* described the Group Theatre's production of *The Dog Beneath the Skin* as the sort of production that 'makes one feel unusually hopeful about the theatre'. It went on to make an interesting prediction: 'Perhaps in time to come the contribution of the present age to drama will be seen to be something between revue and musical comedy'. For fear this implied that slightness and frivolity would be the decade's chief bequest to the future, the article went on to remind readers that 'there is no reason why revue should not be put to serious uses, and none why the form of musical comedy should not become the form of musical satire'.[30] That may only be one aspect of the theatrical legacy we can take from the decade, but it remains a potent one.

NOTES

1 The version quoted here follows the notice accompanying the programme for the October 1935 production of *Dance of Death*, in the Production File at the Victoria and Albert Performance Archives. The text in *Plays* does not use capitals, and corrects some mis-readings of Auden's manuscript: these variants are noted within square brackets.

2 *Daily Telegraph*, 31 January 1936. See V&A Theatre and Performance Archive: Production File: *The Dog Beneath the Skin*, January 1936.

3 *Daily Telegraph*, 13 February 1939. See V&A Theatre and Performance Archive: Production File: *On the Frontier*, February 1939.

4 Gordon Bottomley, 'Why Poets Write Plays', *The Festival Theatre Review*, XXIX, 28th January 1928, pp. 4–7.

5 Terence Gray, 'The Theatrical Purveyors Association', *The Festival Theatre Review*, XXIX, 28th January 1928, pp. 8–10.

6 Terence Gray, *Dance Drama: Experiments in the Art of the Theatre* (W. Heffer & Sons Ltd, 1926).

7 Terence Gray, *Dance Drama*, p. 27.

8 Terence Gray, *Dance Drama*, p. 29.

9 Gordon Bottomley, 'Why Poets Write Plays'.

10 First performed at the Grafton Theatre, London, April 1930.

11 Velona Pilcher, *The Searcher* (Doubleday, 1929), Foreword.

12 Lord Chamberlain's Correspondence Files, 1900–1968: 1930/9450: *The Searcher*.

13 The *Observer*, 19 February 1939. See V&A Theatre and Performance Archive: Production File: *On the Frontier*, February 1939.

14 J. C. Trewin, *The Turbulent Thirties* (Macdonald, 1960), p. 127.

15 Letter from the Lord Chamberlain to the Foreign Office, 9 February 1934. See Lord Chamberlain's Correspondence Files, 1900–1968: *Take Heed*: Licence Refused (1934).

16 Hubert Griffith, 'Preface' to Dorothy Knowles, *The Censor, the Drama and the Film 1900–1934* (George Allen & Unwin, 1934), p. 4.

17 Lord Chamberlain's Correspondence Files, 1900–1968: 1935/14254: *The Dog Beneath the Skin*.

18 Lord Chamberlain's Correspondence Files, 1900–1968: 1938/1878: *On the Frontier*.

19 WTM Bulletin No. 5, September/October 1933, p. 1.

20 'Wanted a Play', *Left Review*, I, 7, April 1935, p. 276.

21 Barbara Nixon, 'Theatre Now', *Left Review*, II, 3, December 1935, pp. 105–07.

22 John Allen, 'The Socialist Theatre', *Left Review*, III, 7, August 1937, pp. 417–22.

23 John Allen, 'Theatre', *Fact*, July 1937, p. 37.

24 John Allen, *Notes on Forming Left Theatre Groups*, Left Book Club Theatre Guild, 1937, p. 2.

25 Jerry Dawson, *Left Theatre: Merseyside Unity Theatre: a Documentary Record* (Merseyside Writers, 1985), p. 2.

26 For unpublished Unity Theatre Scripts see 'Unity Theatre Archive, 1935–1994', held at the V&A Theatre and Performance Archive.

27 John Allen, 'Report', *Left News*, August 1937, no. 16, p. 484.

28 Jack Lindsay, 'A Plea for Mass Declamation', *Left Review*, October 1937, III, no. 9, pp. 511–51.

29 Trewin (see note 14) p. 17.

30 *Sunday Times*, 2 February 1936. See V&A Theatre and Performance Archive: Production File: *The Dog Beneath the Skin*, January 1936.

CHAPTER XXI

The Documentary Moment

David Collard

Auden was in his late twenties and scraping together a living as a school-master when he sounded out his Oxford contemporary Basil Wright about a job in the GPO Film Unit. He was immediately signed up by John Grierson to join a full-time team of artists and technicians. Auden's initial contribution, as is well known, was to work with Benjamin Britten on a madrigal for the experimental short *Coal Face*, and later to provide the syncopating end commentary for *Night Mail*, which was both a criti-cal and a commercial success. The tendency ever since has been to regard Auden's time in film as an eccentric footnote to the grand sweep of his lit-erary career, and as a jewel in the crown of the poetically undistinguished documentary movement. The story, however, is more complex than that. Auden was himself an early, outspoken critic of the movement, and the movement in turn, personified by its founder and prime-mover Grierson, was equally ambivalent about the poetic genius employed briefly in its midst.

After a promising start, the first failure of Auden's career with the Unit was *Negroes*, an ambitious attempt, with Britten and director William Coldstream, to present the history of slavery in the West Indies through a fully scored film with a libretto, 'a most elaborate affair' according to Auden. Grierson cancelled the project after two months' work, ostensibly on the grounds that there wasn't enough footage to complete the film and because of the spiralling budget and lack of progress. Grierson may also have had qualms about a subject far beyond the Unit's remit, and one which could jeopardize relations with government paymasters. One can imagine the col-laborators' frustration at the sudden end to their project and, to make mat-ters worse, a roughly edited version of the film would be released in 1938 as *God's Chillun*, with freshly shot linking passages nervously fronted by the West Indies' cricket captain, George Copeland Grant.

That *Coal Face*, *Negroes* and *Night Mail* were collaborations between the greatest poet and composer of their generation should alone make them of exceptional cultural interest; but, for the most part, their work together remains more admired than researched. And as for Britten's many other documentary film scores, which number thirty in all, there has been surprisingly little scholarly engagement.[1]

Auden found the male sodality of the GPO Film Unit congenial, the co-operative and idealistic atmosphere stimulating, and the chance to learn new skills from some prodigiously talented colleagues appealing, but his early commitment soon turned to disaffection and growing hostility towards the movement's principles.

What were the reasons for this disaffection? Despite that gratifying flurry of early success, the setback of *Negroes* made it clear to Auden that a career in film could be every bit as erratic as one in literature. It was also an unwelcome taste of the failure that would dog the remaining months of Auden's time in the Unit.

The next GPO production was *Calendar of the Year* (directed by Evelyn Spice), and Auden, to reduce costs, had to double as production manager and assistant director. The film was over budget and behind schedule and the still-inexperienced Auden must have felt increasingly embattled and beleaguered. Although the job titles were grand enough, the work itself was typically menial and Auden was treated as a general dogsbody by senior colleagues. As Harry Watt, co-director of *Night Mail* recalled: 'To me, at that moment, he was only somebody to run along the railway line with a spare magazine, and if he turned up late – as he was inclined to do – he got the hell bawled out of him'.[2]

A further prompt to Auden's growing dissatisfaction was a minor episode in the troubled *Calendar of the Year* production, when an officious government supervisor refused permission for civil service telephone operators to be filmed in their shirtsleeves. Auden later cited this as a typical (if, on the face of it, rather trivial) example of the frustrations and humiliations attendant on film-making, although it must also reflect his inability to compromise constructively with others. Auden was an efficient and effective collaborator but not necessarily a team player.

Then there was Auden's contribution to *Beside the Seaside*. This twenty-three-minute promotional film, virtually unknown today, was directed by Marion Grierson (John Grierson's youngest sister) for the independent Strand Film Company on a commission from the Trade and Industrial Association of Great Britain. Released in December 1935, it aimed to promote the charms of British coastal resorts to visitors from overseas.

In the print held by the National Film and Television Archive, Auden is credited for a 'Section of Commentary', and that unconventional credit conceals another troubled production history. Auden would later claim that the film was never completed.[3] It may be that he was referring to the film as originally conceived, or it could simply be sour grapes. Certainly very little of Auden's original verse commentary (written in November 1935) remains, and this is a loss to film history as part of it is particularly distinguished and (for want of a better word) *poetic*. Readers familiar with Auden's poetry but not his time in documentary may be surprised to learn that the original commentary included the poem beginning: 'Look, stranger, at this island now / The leaping light for your delight discovers' (*EA*, p. 157).

It is tempting to speculate what a director like Humphrey Jennings might have made of these verses. From the airy and luminous opening lines with their Shakespearean cadences, the poem develops into what John Fuller calls 'properly digested Hopkins' (Fuller 1998, p. 152), expressing a sense of rediscovered Englishness, of homecoming. It is a matter of wonder that Marion Grierson chose not to use these verses, which were clearly written with film in mind, using the established rule-of-thumb: 'three syllables to the foot on 35 mm and seven syllables to the foot on 16mm'.[4] All GPO productions were shot on 35 mm, but Strand Film favoured 16 mm. *Beside the Seaside,* with its short, choppy lines, was evidently written for 16 mm stock. The original poem is an intensely visual and auditory piece, expressed in warm and expansive phrasing, the pace and imagery lending itself readily to a film interpretation. It is almost a verbal storyboard, and the opening stanza in particular calls out for an aerial shot of a sunlit coastline, glittering waves and soaring gulls against backlit cumulus clouds, the clipped cadences of a 1930s commentator, Geoffrey Tandy perhaps, briskly enunciating the verse.

When it came to the crunch, however, just two lines of the poem made it into the final commentary, both richly onomatopoeic: 'the swaying sound of the sea' and 'the shingle scrambles after the sucking surf' (*Plays*, p. 429). Without explicit evidence we cannot know for certain whether the decision to drop most of 'Look, stranger' was simply pragmatic, given that it was aimed at prospective overseas travellers to the United Kingdom. *Night Mail* aside, poetic commentaries were deemed inappropriate for documentary productions because they were very difficult to translate and subtitle effectively.

So a poem that was, for whatever reason, deemed dispensable in the documentary film movement was central to Auden's poetic development, and is one among many examples of his skill at co-opting public commissions into a more personal agenda. The complete poem would appear under the title 'Seaside' in the BBC publication *The Listener* on 18 December 1935. The verses were later set to music by Britten in 1937 as *On this Island* (Opus 11, dedicated to Christopher Isherwood) and the first line would of course provide the title for the reputation-forging collection, published in October 1936 by Faber and Faber as *Look, Stranger!*

By the time Auden wrote the verses for *Beside the Seaside* he had become technically proficient, as his confident work on subtitles for the Film Society's October 1935 screening of Dziga Vertov's *Three Songs for Lenin* confirms. We may reasonably infer that Auden was displeased by the rejection of his work, whatever the reason, and this may have contributed to an argument with Basil Wright (dated by Mendelson as happening in either late 1935 or early 1936), which in turn prompted Auden's decision to resign prematurely from the Unit. The argument apparently started with minor squabbles over *Calendar of the Year*'s production details and budget but rapidly escalated into a more serious dispute over the aims and methods of the documentary movement as a whole. Auden would later suggest, in his verse 'Letter to William Coldstream, Esq.', that he was 'suspected, quite rightly, of being disloyal' (*LfI*, p. 222, *Prose I*, p. 345), and wrote what amounted to a professional suicide note in an unsigned review of Paul Rotha's seminal volume *Documentary Film*, printed in *The Listener* on 19 February 1936. It is clear that Auden's nascent repudiation of the movement dates to much earlier in his time at the Unit.

In the Rotha review, Auden undertakes a thorough demolition of the documentary ideal: he dismisses the products of the movement as lacking entertainment value for the ordinary film-goer and being (in a memorably ferocious phrase) 'finally and fatally dull'; he asserts, sacrilegiously for the time, that film itself is 'not the best medium for factual information' and questions the integrity and honesty of film-makers in approaching a subject without sufficient knowledge and understanding (which, he oddly insists, would not happen in the case of a novelist). Finally, he raises the touchy issue of class, asserting: 'It is doubtful whether an artist can ever deal more than superficially ... with characters outside his own class, and most British documentary directors are upper middle' (*Prose I*, pp. 129–30).

Auden is here stuck in the common predicament of the leftish middle-class intellectual, hamstrung between awareness of his own privileged position and a romantic identification with the working class. He raises an issue which, however nonsensical, remains to this day a sticking-point for critics of the movement, namely that it is *necessarily* patronizing for the privileged artist to explore social inequalities and injustice, that any approach to representing the realities of (say) working-class life is *necessarily* compromised by the educational and cultural backgrounds of the film-makers and that even the best intentions are by definition condescending and therefore illegitimate. I don't propose here to consider these issues, merely to note that Auden was among the first to open this can of worms. The review of Rotha's book prompted a withering response from Grierson that probably concealed a deeper and abiding resentment at his protégé's betrayal and defection.[5]

Grierson may still have been thinking of Auden's disloyalty two years later in a peppery review published in a trade paper. It is a swift and efficient debunking of what would emerge decades later in France as Auteur Theory but also, I suggest, contains a swipe at Auden:

Only an idiot will pretend of any film that he has been the 'onlie begetter'. The creative force lies in the unity, and those personal credits which flutter across the opening of a film, though they may comfort the wives and mothers of the individual filmmakers, give no picture of the process. I never saw a poor film happen except that three or four heads were devoted commonly to it, with personal nonsense out. I never saw personal nonsense come in and a film prosper.[6]

Had there been some 'personal nonsense' about credits? Had Auden's work on *Negroes* and *Calendar of the Year* antagonized his boss more than is generally thought? The original 'onlie begetter' was of course another Mr W. H., the anonymous dedicatee of Shakespeare's sonnets, and one wonders if Grierson was here mischievously referring to an ex-employee sharing those initials.

Grierson, nine years older than Auden, was a severe, unyielding, doctrinaire and by most accounts quite humourless man who expected (and usually earned) unquestioning loyalty from his staff. As the movement's founder, as well as producer, chief theorist and critic, he had proprietorial controlling tendencies which may have further encouraged Auden's natural inclination towards dissidence and rebellion. Grierson's Calvinist character and solemn stolidity were at odds with Auden's chronic lack of seriousness and camp sensibility. Grierson made his mark on documentary and his energy, commitment and integrity are beyond doubt. But for the most part, it is not his more serious propagandistic productions which attract and retain our interest today but precisely the more poetic and lyrical efforts he later denounced. When viewing Grierson's more campaigning documentaries (*Housing Problems*, *Enough to Eat* and *The Smoke Menace*), the powerful eighteenth-century Quaker phrase comes to mind: 'Speak Truth to Power'. Surely that is a fundamental if unacknowledged aim of documentary as conceived by Grierson – not only to educate the population as an essential precondition of a liberal democracy, but also to educate the governing classes in their responsibilities. Grierson's genius lay in his ability to generate establishment support for a series of government-sponsored indictments of 'a range of problems: housing, access to health care, sanitation, air pollution, malnutrition and unemployment. The Unit's in-house poet was certainly left-leaning but not, to use a favourite Grierson phrase 'politically *engagé*'.

In a score-settling 1959 lecture at the National Film Theatre in London, Grierson pays generous tribute to his influential forerunners in documentary (Pudovkin, Eisenstein and Flaherty),[7] and praises the directors and cutters involved in the movement, placing particular emphasis on 'working together … as a *team*'. It is notable how very grudgingly he admits that some of the films he produced had 'poetic streaks, or *streak* rather' (diminishing the significance of the poetic or lyrical approach to a single strand). He goes on (without much enthusiasm) to cite Basil Wright and Humphrey Jennings as *poetic* film-makers, not mentioning Auden at all. His lingering distaste for any type of lyrical documentary is palpable ('some *tended* to the poetic') and it is surely significant that his authoritative collection of writings, *Grierson on Documentary* (edited by Forsyth Hardy and published by Faber and Faber in 1946), contains only a single disparaging reference to *Night Mail* and no reference whatever to Auden.

Apart from the Auden link, *Beside the Seaside* does little to support my claim that many of these 1930s films remain fresh, vital, urgent and compelling. Some critics have nevertheless found plenty to admire, praising Marion Grierson for her light touch, wit and invention; but, like other low-budget promotional films of the period, it is largely assembled from library footage, and what's lacking is scene-by-scene coherence or governing perspective.

It is not certain whether Auden ever saw the final version of this film. On 7 February 1936, he delivered a lecture to the North London Film Society at the Tottenham Court Road YMCA under the title 'Poetry and the Film' and a reported version, probably based on Auden's notes, appeared in the short-lived arts magazine *Janus* (*Prose I*, pp. 712–14).

Auden opens by airily contrasting the artists representing the outlook of the rentier class (Cézanne, Proust and Joyce) and the popular art of the masses, the music-hall, now supplanted by the cinema. He then summarizes (as he sees it) the essential qualities of film – the power to concentrate on detail and its continuous forward movement in time (which, he says, limits its effectiveness as a means of communicating ideas). Much of what Auden says is unexceptionable, reflecting much of the contemporary debate around film as propaganda: 'The proper concern of film is the building up of a general impression by means of a particular detail; the analysis of character; and the material that contemporary life offers'. The Janus article continued:

> There are a number of ways poetry can be used in film. The most obvious way is as a general emotional commentary. Mr Auden had just contributed to a publicity film, *By the Sea-side*, [sic] in which poetry had been applied in this way; one of the shots seemed to him to be particularly good in its impact. The scene was the departure of people from the hot and dusty city to a coast. Someone is carrying a tennis racket, and as the net of the racket fills the screen covering all the bustle and heat, the words 'like a cool fish in a grotto' are heard from the sound track. (*Prose I*, p. 714)

As reported, Auden misremembers not only the title of the film but also both the shot itself and the specific line of commentary (which is 'like a *smooth* fish in a grotto'). Or perhaps he correctly recalls an earlier version later abandoned, or simply a discussion with collaborators of a shot which never made it to the final cut. The assumption that any audience would, even unconsciously, register a connection between a verbal reference to fish and a visual depiction of a tennis racket net is surely most unlikely. At best, it might be an in-joke by the (uncredited) editor, something dropped after a Friday evening look at the rushes.

The National Film and Television Archive has only one print of *Beside the Seaside* and in this print the 'fish in a grotto' line can indeed be heard; but it accompanies a shot of camisole knickers and a pair of kitten heel slippers being hastily packed into an overnight bag, likely signifiers of a saucy seaside weekend. How knickers or tennis racket contribute to 'the general emotional commentary' is anyone's guess. Auden was also reported as saying: 'The visual image is a definite one, whereas verbal images are not sharp; they have auras of meaning, ... for this reason highly developed metaphors cannot be included in the film medium' (*Prose I*, p. 713). Whether the unused fish/net conceit would have worked as a metaphor, highly developed or not, is a moot point.

What is of interest, judging from his lecture, is that Auden has clearly been looking closely at Russian montage effects, no doubt at Film Society screenings of Eisenstein and Pudovkin, and developing his own ideas about image and commentary working together or in opposition. He instinctively applies poetic principles to a montage commentary, but what is revealing is that he doesn't appear interested in the high-minded socially ameliorative aims of the documentary movement and the contribution, if any, of poetry to those aims.

I have argued elsewhere that *The Way to the Sea* (Strand Films 1937, directed by Jack Holmes), Auden's final film collaboration with Britten, comes closer to Auden's conception of what a poetic documentary should be (see *AN*, no. 30, June 2008, pp. 8–21). And it is in this strange, unsettling and subversive film that we find an entirely successful (and unmetaphorical) combination of words and image in a beautiful single shot accompanying Auden's lines: 'The consciously beautiful, certain of easy conquests, / The careworn, the unrewarded, the child-like'. Image and commentary work perfectly in unison as figures boarding a ferry simply step into shot, right on cue, overseen by the 'consciously beautiful' crewman: the careworn (an elderly couple), the unrewarded (a very nondescript pair) and finally some children. It is elegant, subtle, unobtrusive and effective. It also matches an earlier shot of passengers shuffling towards their train at Waterloo, which in turn is later echoed in the mechanical movement of bottles passing through some apparatus.

In one respect *Beside the Seaside* is significant, as the original poem marks a shift in Auden's pre-occupation with ideas of borders and frontiers and demarcations which so dominate his poetry of the earlier 1930s. His attention now moves to a sustained investigation of the island. Auden's diagnosis and continuing exploration of cultural and social insularity is a hallmark of his writing after 1935 and this rejected commission could be seen as the most significant poetic turning point since 'Who stands, the crux left of the watershed'. As Mendelson puts it: 'by 1935 Auden knew that he could no longer justify or excuse his national symbols. His real setting was "this island now", not England at all, but the holiday island of his art' (*Early Auden*, p. 339).

Their makers' squabbles now forgotten, these films are gradually acquiring their own aura of meaning. Re-viewing several while preparing this essay, I was again struck by the intense emotional charge underlying the sometimes strident, patrician and didactic tone, a contrast reminiscent of Auden's lovely, balanced *Night Mail* line: 'The cold and official and the heart's outpouring' (*EA*, p. 291). Aside from the intense poignancy evoked in any modern viewer looking at crowds of people who are now in all likelihood dead, many films of this socially and politically unstable period articulate a quiet indignation, a cold fury at the state of things or, at the other end of the spectrum, a clear-sighted optimism, a faith in the future and a belief in the benefits of progress. Our modern default-setting perspective is of course cynical, equipped as we are with the disabling knowledge of how the optimistic 'clever hopes' for a mature liberal democracy would expire in barbarism and misery at the end of that 'low, dishonest decade'. There is a risk that in mocking their naive hopes and ideals we devalue our own.

A week after the Film Society lecture, Auden wrote to his brother John:

I don't think, somehow, I shall go back to the film unit. There's not the faintest chance of making the kind of film I should like, there's no time to do anything else, and the atmosphere is exactly like a public school.[8]

Given Auden's notorious equation of public school with a Fascist state, these were harsh words indeed. And that, for the time being, was that. Auden joined Isherwood in Portugal the following month (where they would work together on *The Ascent of F6*, recycling verses from *Negroes*), then spent the summer of 1936 travelling in Iceland. He would re-engage productively with documentary film-makers over thirty years later, and with remarkable results. But that's another story.

NOTES

1 Two studies of Britten's film scores are: Judith Brimmer: *Enter the Dream-house: Benjamin Britten's involvement in the Documentary Film Movement of the 1930s* (University of Nottingham MA Dissertation, 2002) and Philip Reed: *The Incidental Music of Benjamin Britten: a study and catalogue of his works for film, theatre and radio* (University of East Anglia PhD Thesis, 1987). Marsha Bryant's *Auden and Documentary in the 1930s* is the main scholarly publication on its subject but limits itself to a consideration of *Coal Face* and *Night Mail*. My forthcoming *Auden on Film* will include all Auden's documentary commentaries in full.

2 *Don't Look at the Camera* by Harry Watt (Elek Books, 1974), p. 81.

3 1961 recording of Auden introducing a reading of 'Look, stranger'. Tape in the Yale University Library. See note in *Plays* p. 670.

4 *The Technique of Documentary Film Production*, by W. Hugh Baddeley (Focal Press, 1963), p. 202.

5 'As Auden's apprenticeship matures he may feel less despondent': *World Film News*, April 1936.

6 *World Film News*, March 1938.

7 This lecture appears on the British Film Institute's DVD boxed set *Land of Promise: The British Documentary Movement 1930–1950* (BFIVD756).

8 RSL: *The Royal Society of Literature Review* 2008. Letter dated 24 February 1936.

Thanks to Professor Anne Janowitz (Queen Mary College, London), Jude Brimmer (Britten-Pears Foundation, Aldeburgh), Virginia Ironside, and Edwin Collard for their help, support, and conversation.

CHAPTER XXII

Travel Writing

Tim Youngs

For Auden, 'travelling was a norm'. He visited twenty-seven countries, had 'long-term homes' in five of them, and travelled abroad in forty-one of his forty-nine adult years.[1] During his early life, few of his compatriots would have been so mobile. Travel overseas required wealth and leisure time. The year and a half Auden spent travelling and writing after he left Oxford in the summer of 1928 was enabled by an allowance from his father. For much of that time, he was in Berlin, an experience that 'provided him not only with much of the matter and manner of his poetry, but also with the occasion for rapid intellectual and poetic growth'.[2] In Auden's lifetime, travel grew more affordable and accessible, so that it 'was becoming not so much a rarefied class privilege as a more general condition' (*AN* 24, p. 13). To those who distinguish between travel and tourism, regarding the latter as inferior, that greater mobility leads to a loss. Paul Fussell takes up just such a position in his important but increasingly criticized study of inter-war travel literature: 'Because *travel is hardly possible anymore*, an inquiry into the nature of travel and travel writing between the wars will resemble a threnody, and I'm afraid that a consideration of the tourism that apes it will be like a satire'.[3]

Although Auden's writing and travels extended over half a century, the main focus of the present essay will be on the 1930s, an extraordinarily rich decade for travel writing. Besides Auden's two travel books, *Letters from Iceland* (1937) written with Louis MacNeice and *Journey to a War* (1939) co-authored with Christopher Isherwood, titles that appeared in these years include: Robert Byron's *The Road to Oxiana* (1937), E. E. Cummings' *Eimi* (1933), Peter Fleming's *Brazilian Adventure* (1933), Graham Greene's *Journey without Maps* (1936), D. H. Lawrence's *Etruscan Places* (1932), Wyndham Lewis's *Filibusters in Barbary* (1932), George Orwell's *The Road to Wigan Pier* (1937), J. B. Priestley's *English Journey* (1934), Freya Stark's *The Valleys of the Assassins* (1934), and Evelyn Waugh's *Waugh in Abyssinia* (1936).

Despite John Lucas's sensible warning against 'the folly of trying to define cultural history in terms of decades',[4] certain features of the 1930s pertinent to its travel books may be identified. The inter-war years saw an intense concern with boundaries, in both their literal and figurative senses. Public conflict within and between nations produced an instability that both coincided with and provoked individual insecurities, contributing to a situation in which 'Identities, either of self or other, were no longer stable'.[5] Uncertainty permeates the literature of the period. The instability of the external world is mirrored by doubts about the integrity of the self. Psychology opened a gap between the bodily self in the world and the unconscious drives that impelled or obstructed it. The 'teachings of Freud and Jung', Branson and Heinemann point out, 'were becoming sufficiently widely popularized to form part of the idiom of artists and writers'.[6] In Berlin, Auden met John Layard and became enthusiastic about ideas derived from American psychologist Homer Lane. Auden gives this influence jaunty expression in *Letters from Iceland*: 'I met a chap called Layard and he fed / New doctrines into my receptive head'.[7] Freud's idea that 'it is impossible to overlook the extent to which civilization is built upon a renunciation of instinct',[8] governs Graham Greene's *Journey without Maps* (1936). An account of Greene's journey in West Africa, it has become one of the most prominent of travel books to model itself on the concept of a parallel journey; of movement through a physical landscape that mirrors a journey into oneself. In it, Greene writes:

The method of psycho-analysis is to bring the patient back to the idea which he is repressing; a long journey backwards without maps, catching a clue here and a clue there ... until one has to face the general idea, the pain or the memory. This is what you have feared, Africa may be imagined as saying, you can't avoid it ... so you may as well take a long look.[9]

Greene's text has as an epigraph the second stanza from Auden's 'O Where Are You Going?'.

The stylistic and structural experiments that typify literary travel writing of the time, including Greene's symbolic rejection of maps, may be read as a reaction against the decade's violent efforts to fix people; to label and pin them down. Howard Booth's reading of *The Road to Oxiana* recognizes this:

because the decade in which it was written saw overly-firm and insistent world views, its deliberate use of ambivalence forces the reader to engage with difficulties of interpretation. ... Byron's aim was to question the dominance and univocal deployment of Western and colonialist narratives.[10]

The juxtapositions and commingling that some find a harmful breaking of the unity of the travel book are a formal challenge to the contemporary emphasis on purity. Several travel books of the 1930s indicate that their authors do not possess the only or even the right way of looking at things. This they suggest through their use of irony, parody, and ambiguity; through difficulty of interpretation and through the admission of multiple perspectives. Many of the texts comment on how perception depends on point of view and on the unreliability of general remarks. Auden writes in *Letters from Iceland* that 'what we see depends on who's observing' (*LfI*, p. 211), and he admits to the superficiality of the tourist's impressions: 'At the best he only observes what the inhabitants know already; at the worst he is guilty of glib generalisations based on inadequate and often incorrect data' (*LfI*, p. 213). This he applies to his own three-month visit. Similarly, in his prefatory note to *The Lawless Roads*, Graham Greene advised his readers: 'This is the personal impression of a small part of Mexico at a particular time, the spring of 1938'. Later he asks, 'How to describe a city? Even for an old inhabitant it is impossible: one can present only a simplified plan, taking a house here, a park there as symbols of the whole'.[11] In 1927, D. H. Lawrence had begun his book on the same country by pulling back from the larger scene to the person who produces it:

We talk so grandly, in capital letters, about Morning in Mexico. All it amounts to is one little individual looking at a bit of sky and trees, then looking down at the page of his exercise book.[12]

The passage from which this is extracted directs our gaze from the whole to the part, as though we are looking at a painting or watching a film. Both visual media influence the travel writers of the time. In fact, some, including Lawrence and Lewis, were also painters, and Auden had worked for six months with a film collective before his trip to Iceland.[13] In E. E. Cummings' *Eimi* (1933), a linguistically and stylistically innovative account of the author's journey to the Soviet Union, Cummings admires work by Matisse:

5 gradually distorted heres (flat upon a flatgreen aslope insolently that; or against crudely blue skyflattest this; or andishly among both's neither) splurge; opposite, swiftly reproportioned, if of no world, creatures lymphatically pauseflowing (what neverdancers always-dancing!) reel, droopingly are precise of rhythm perpetually selfinventing the constituents.[14]

'Selfinventing the constituents' is what the most technically inventive and intellectually adventurous travel books of the period do also.

But the innovations that better enabled travel writing to express the modern condition have often gone unappreciated.[15] Jeffrey Hart's dismissal of *Letters from Iceland* as being of no 'distinction whatever' and of *Journey to a War* as 'a book that has nothing of interest to say about China or the war' is representative of a significant strand of critical opinion. Fussell describes both texts as marking the 'decadent stage in the course of the between-the-wars travel book', and complains that in them, 'the narrative is disturbingly discontinuous, interrupted by jokiness, nervousness over what literary mode is appropriate, and self-consciousness about the *travel book* genre itself' (Fussell 1980, pp. 219–20). Such judgements turn into negatives everything that is interesting and remarkable about the works. One of Hart's charges against *Letters from Iceland* is that 'the point of the whole thing is elusive'.[16] But elusiveness is part of the point of it. Edward Mendelson, whose edition of Auden's prose and travel books between 1926 and 1938 is Hart's target ('its interest as literature approaches zero'[17]), has observed that:

On his poetic voyages Auden never reaches the goal for which he sets out. Either his goal is illusory; or it refuses to offer the challenge a traveller needs if he is to change; or, simply, 'he does not want to arrive'. (*Early Auden*, p. 341)

Besides elusiveness and the illusory, Auden was concerned to expose, comment on, and play with the structures of travel writing. In his 'studiedly self-reflexive' *Letters from Iceland*,[18] he addresses the making of the narrative in explicit terms. Probably the most quoted example of this, and one that imitates a popular art practice of the day, is from his address to Lord Byron in which he announces that he will present a *collage* of 'photographs, / Some out of focus, some with wrong exposures, / Press cuttings, gossip, maps, statistics, graphs' (*LfI*, p. 21). In a later chapter, he writes of how, 'In the bus to-day I had a bright idea about this travel book'. He had brought an edition of Byron with him and 'suddenly thought I might write him a chatty letter in light verse about everything I could think of, Europe, literature, myself'. Whereas other letters in the book will speak of Iceland more directly, this letter, which will 'form a central thread', will 'have very little to do with Iceland, but will instead be a description of an effect of travelling in distant places which is *to make one reflect on one's past and one's culture from the outside*' (*LfI*, p. 141, my emphasis).

The fun that Auden has with travel should not, then, be mistaken for a lack of seriousness. That he gave much thought to the relationship between literary form, content and the social context is clear from statements in his travel books and elsewhere. Reviewing Christopher Caudwell's

Illusion and Reality, 'a Marxist book on the aesthetics of poetry', Auden wrote: 'Mr Caudwell goes on to trace the history of English poetry from the Elizabethan period to our own, and to show *the relation between its changes in technique and subject matter and the changes in economic production*' (*Prose I*, p. 386, my emphasis). Auden hailed the importance of Caudwell's study and declared: 'I agree with it' (p. 387). We must view the form of both of Auden's travel books accordingly and see their co-authorship, their mixture of forms and media, their interruptions and juxtapositions not as damaged goods but as serious though witty engagements with their 'frontier-obsessed' (Fussell 1980, p. 33) environment.

Letters from Iceland consists of a preface, Auden's verse letter to Byron interspersed throughout the narrative in five parts, letters to other recipients, an anthology of Icelandic travel addressed to John Betjeman, MacNeice's Eclogue from Iceland, 'Auden and MacNeice: Their Last Will and Testament', an epilogue for Auden by MacNeice, an appendix with charts, and several photographs taken by Auden. As for *Journey to a War*, Mendelson notes that Auden and Isherwood 'worked their diaries into a single travel diary', and that, although all the poems are by Auden, 'The Travel-Diary', which was 'written as a first-person narrative by Isherwood, includes passages reworked by Isherwood from diary entries, articles printed in magazines, and travel narratives that he and Auden wrote during and after their journey' (*Prose I*, pp. 822, 824). In the Preface to *Letters from Iceland*, Auden and MacNeice go beyond attributing the volume to each other and tell us that: 'We must beg those hundreds of anonymous Icelanders, farmers, fishermen, busmen, children, etc., who are the real authors of this book to accept collectively our gratitude' (*LfI*, p. 9).

A further contribution made by Auden and Isherwood to discourses of travel is the undercutting of heroism. They were not unique in this. Helen Carr observes that in the 1920s and 1930s, travel writing had 'become deliberately anti-romantic' and 'anti-heroic'.[19] Robert Byron depicts himself falling at night and finding himself 'lying naked in a bed of snow and excrement, which clove to my body in the frost'.[20] In *Christopher and his Kind* (1977), Isherwood quotes from his first autobiographical volume, *Lions and Shadows* (1938) in which he asserts that attempts at 'the huge northern circuit, the laborious terrible northwest passage' are made by 'the truly weak man, the neurotic hero' who dreads normal life; the 'truly strong man', on the other hand, is 'calm' and 'balanced' and has no need 'to climb the impossible glacier' but can sit 'drinking quietly in the bar'.[21] Isherwood comments that, 'From Christopher's and Wystan's point of view, The Truly Weak Man was represented by Lawrence of Arabia, and hence by their character Michael Ransom in *F.6* (Isherwood 1977, p. 192). This inversion of the dominant ideas of heroism and strong leadership has an urgent political purpose in the decade of Hitler, Mussolini, Franco, and Stalin. In literary terms, the questioning of hero-worship manifests itself in poking fun at others and in self-deprecation. It often involves parody. In Auden, this is itself a result of his travels, as Buell observes: 'One trait that distinguishes the poems written after Berlin is the extensive and wholehearted use of parody and caricature'.[22] Parody depends on a shared consciousness of the original that is parodied and of the structure and expectations of the copy. Imitated and imitator are laid side by side, the incongruity creating humour, but reflection too. In *Journey to a War*, a joke is had at the expense of the authors themselves and of newspaper correspondent and travel writer Peter Fleming:

Laughing and perspiring we scrambled uphill; the Fleming Legend accompanying us like a distorted shadow. Auden and I recited passages from an imaginary travel-book called 'With Fleming to the Front'.[23]

Elsewhere, Isherwood describes himself, Auden, and their servant and interpreter, Chiang, as resembling 'a group of characters in one of Jules Verne's stories about lunatic English explorers' (*JtW*, p. 104).

Related to the rejection of heroism is a questioning of authority, including that of one's own. In the foreword to *Journey to a War*, Auden and Isherwood explain that they were commissioned by their publishers to 'write a travel book about the East' and that they were decided by the outbreak of the Sino-Japanese War in August to go to China, leaving England in January 1938 and returning in July. This, they admit, is their first time east of Suez, and 'We spoke no Chinese, and possessed no special knowledge of Far Eastern affairs'. Almost cheerfully, they confess that:

[W]e cannot vouch for the accuracy of many statements made in this book. Some of our informants may have been unreliable, some merely polite, some deliberately pulling our leg. (*JtW*, p. 13)

Undercutting one's own authority in travel texts may not be new to the twentieth century but it is a characteristic of much (though by no means all) travel writing of the 1930s. In contrast to the assured, incontrovertible pronouncements of travellers during the ages of colonial expansion, there is uncertainty here, covered by humour. 'I am never much good at defending the British Empire, even when drunk', writes Isherwood (*JtW*, p. 175). In his 'Letter to Lord Byron', Auden asks: 'Where is the John Bull of the good old days, / The swaggering bully with the clumsy jest?' and answers his own question thus: 'His meaty neck has long been laid to rest, / His acres of self-confidence for sale; / He passed away at Ypres and Passchendaele' (*LfI*, p. 55). Even figures better known for their ridicule of foreigners derided domestic practices. Evelyn Waugh, for example, condemned the British as 'the more treacherous' of European nations during the partition of Africa,[24] and mocked the use to which travel writing was put after the Italian invasion of Abyssinia:

Everyone with any claims to African experience was cashing in. Travel books whose first editions had long since been remaindered were being reissued in startling wrappers.[25]

Auden was not alone in working in a genre while joking about it.

But the flippant has a deadly context. In a verse letter to Isherwood, Auden writes in *Letters from Iceland* that: 'Europe is absent. This is an island therefore / Unreal' (*LfI*, p. 26). He seems to welcome the distance but then discovers that it is the isolation that is unreal. There are at least seven references in the book to Nazis, the last of which expresses the hope that Erika Mann, whom Auden had married in 1935 so that she could gain a British passport and escape persecution, 'may have her wish / To see the just end of Hitler and his unjust rule' (*LfI*, p. 38). MacNeice writes that:

> We are not changing ground to escape from facts
> But rather to find them. This complex world exacts
> Hard work of simplifying; to get its focus
> You have to stand outside the crowd and caucus.
>
> (*LfI*, p. 33)

Just as Auden's often playful experiments with form invite attention to the structures and conventions of narrating travels, so he is aware that journeying abroad entails reflection on departure points. In the context of the second half of the 1930s, this means the rise of fascism and the threat of war. Stan Smith notices this when he remarks: 'Uncomfortable journeys in search of adventure in remote places lead to unwelcome, necessary revelations which take one back to the heart of one's own distant culture' (Smith 2004, p. 3). For all the humour, there is an ominous urgency; a foreboding of a conflict broader than the one that has already broken out in Spain, news of which breaks out while Auden is in Iceland. 'I'm home to Europe where I may be shot' (*LfI*, p. 212), Auden writes from Iceland. In fact, when *Letters from Iceland* was finished, Auden resolved, in December 1936, to fight with the International Brigade in Spain, although before his arrival the following month he had decided to drive an ambulance instead (see *Early Auden*, pp. 195, 196). Auden's poem *Spain*

(1937) has been described by Smith as, in a sense, 'the most representatively symbolic piece of travel writing of the whole era' (Smith 2004, p. 6). In China, where Auden and Isherwood watch a Chinese war-propaganda film, 'We both wondered how long it would be before we were applauding similar trash, only a shade more sophisticated, at all the London cinemas' (*JtW*, p. 184).

The context of Auden's travel books is a world in which 'the keels of new destroyers / Get laid down somehow though all credit's frozen' (*LfI*, p. 232); one in which:

War is bombing an already disused arsenal, missing it, and killing a few old women.... War is a handful of lost and terrified men in the mountains, shooting at something moving in the undergrowth.... War is untidy, inefficient, obscure, and largely a matter of chance. (*JtW*, p. 202)

It is a world that we should recognize. Through content and technique, Auden's travel books and those of a number of his contemporaries encourage us to look more closely at the disjuncture between proclamation and actuality, between stated values and fact, between surface and depth. 'I want a form that's large enough to swim in', writes Auden in *Letters from Iceland*, 'And talk on any subject that I choose' (*LfI*, p. 21). That impulse to enlarge the form was shared by several of his contemporaries and has scarcely been emulated since.

NOTES

1 See Nicholas Jenkins, 'The Traveling Auden', *AN* 24, July 2004, pp. 7–14.
2 Frederick Buell, *W. H. Auden as a Social Poet* (Cornell University Press, 1973), p. 104.
3 Paul Fussell, *Abroad: British Literary Traveling between the Wars* (Oxford University Press, 1980), p. 37, my emphasis. Hereafter cited as 'Fussell 1980'.
4 John Lucas, *The Radical Twenties* (Five Leaves Press, 1997), p. 211.
5 Helen Carr, 'Modernism and travel (1880–1940)', in Peter Hulme and Tim Youngs, eds., *The Cambridge Companion to Travel Writing* (Cambridge University Press, 2002), pp. 70–86 (quotation at p. 73).
6 Noreen Branson and Margot Heinemann, *Britain in the Nineteen Thirties* (Weidenfeld and Nicolson, 1971), p. 258.
7 W. H. Auden and Louis MacNeice, *Letters from Iceland* (Faber and Faber, 1937), p. 210. Further page references will be given parenthetically, prefaced by *LFI*.
8 Sigmund Freud, 'Civilization and Its Discontents' [1930], in Freud, *Civilization, Society and Religion*, The Penguin Freud Library, vol.12 (Penguin, 1985), pp. 243–340 (quotation at 286–87).
9 Graham Greene, *Journey Without Maps* (William Heinemann, 1936), p. 107.

10 Howard J. Booth, 'Making the Case for Cross-Cultural Exchange: Robert Byron's *The Road to Oxiana*', in Charles Burdett and Derek Duncan, eds., *Cultural Encounters: European Travel Writing in the 1930s* (Berghahn Books, 2002), pp. 159–72, quotation at pp. 163–64.

11 Graham Greene, *The Lawless Roads* [1939] (Penguin Books, 1947), pp. 5, 69.

12 D. H. Lawrence, *Mornings in Mexico* (Martin Secker, 1927), p. 9.

13 See Marsha Bryant, 'Auden and the "Arctic Stare": Documentary as Public Collage in *Letters from Iceland*', *Journal of Modern Literature* vol. XVII, no. 4 (1991), pp. 537–65.

14 E. E. Cummings, *Eimi* (Covici, Friede, 1933), p. 185.

15 I have discussed this in my 'Auden's travel writings' (*CCWHA*, pp. 68–81), and in my 'Travelling Modernists', in Peter Brooker et al., eds., *The Oxford Handbook of Modernisms* (Oxford University Press, 2010), pp. 267–80.

16 Jeffrey Hart, 'How Good was Auden?', *The New Criterion* (February 1997), http://www.newcriterion.com/articles.cfm/howgoodwasauden-hart-3394 accessed 15 March 2010.

17 Hart, 'How Good was Auden?'.

18 Stan Smith, 'Burbank with a Baedeker: Modernism's Grand Tours', *Studies in Travel Writing* vol. 8, no.1 (2004), pp. 1–18, quotation at p. 6. Hereafter cited as 'Smith 2004'.

19 Carr, 'Modernism and travel', p. 82.

20 Robert Byron, *The Road to Oxiana* [1937] (Penguin, 1932), p. 120.

21 Christopher Isherwood, *Christopher and His Kind 1929–1939* (Eyre Methuen, 1977), p. 192. Hereafter cited as 'Isherwood 1977'.

22 Buell, *W. H. Auden*, p. 84.

23 W. H. Auden and Christopher Isherwood, *Journey to a War* (New York: Random House, 1939), p. 214. Further page references will be given parenthetically as *JtW*.

24 Evelyn Waugh, *Waugh in Abyssinia* [1936] (Penguin, 1986), p. 12.

25 Waugh, *Waugh in Abyssinia*, p. 40.

CHAPTER XXIII

Auden and Post-war Opera

Michael Symmons Roberts

It is not hard to see why poets have been drawn to work in opera. It offers a chance to break the silence of the page, to hear your words set to someone else's music (though the poet's own music can be lost in this), and to have those words transfigured by highly trained singers and performed to a hall full of attentive listeners.

For W. H. Auden, whose view of opera was as high as any poet's, the pull of the libretto was even stronger. Since being introduced to the operatic canon in New York by his partner Chester Kallman in 1939, Auden had been a devoted follower of the Metropolitan Opera season, which had given him a love of – among others – Wagner, Verdi and Strauss. By 1940, in his introduction to a Greek literature anthology, he was sure enough of the value of opera to declare that: 'as a period of sustained creative activity in one medium, the seventy-five-odd years of Athenian drama, between the first tragedies of Aeschylus and the last comedy of Aristophanes, are surpassed by the hundred and twenty-five years, between Gluck's *Orpheus* and Verdi's *Othello,* which comprise the golden age of European opera' (quoted *Lib*, pp. xvi-xvii).

As his appreciation of opera deepened in the 1940s, Auden began to see a way forward for himself as a poet. His attempts to write an authentically public poetry in the 1930s had left him with the conviction that poetry 'cannot appear in public without becoming false to itself' (quoted *Lib*, p. xv). But here, in what he called 'the last refuge of the high style' (*SW*, p. 116), it was still possible for a poet – working as a librettist with a great composer – to speak with directness and emotional intensity. As Edward Mendelson points out: 'When Auden renounced as dishonest the grand style he had used in his public poems of the 1930s, he renounced only his use of that style in lyric and personal poetry, not the grand style itself. He still hoped to use it if he could find the proper vehicle' (*Lib*, p. xvi).

Auden was not alone in this view. What makes opera 'elitist' for some (expense, difficulty, artificiality) make it the ultimate art form for others.

246

For those who love it, opera brings together the finest of poetry, drama, music, performance and visual art in the service of the great themes – love, loss, betrayal, sacrifice, honour. But the qualities that make opera so sublime when it works, can bring it down in flames when it doesn't. With such a complex set of collaborative relationships (beginning, but only beginning, with that between librettist and composer), many new operas fail because the elements fall out of balance. And when they do, there is a waiting pack of blood-baying critics ready to defend the canon (as they construe it) by seeing off the interloper.

By the end of the war, Auden had tasted this side of opera too. *Paul Bunyan*, his much-heralded collaboration with the young composer Benjamin Britten, had a mixed reception from audiences and critics in 1941. By 1947, Britten was working with other librettists, and the two were barely on speaking terms. For five intense years, Auden and Britten had produced a small but significant body of work, but *Paul Bunyan*, which promised so much, failed to deliver. It should have had everything. As Mendelson observes, the last time a major English poet and a major English composer had created an opera together was in 1691, when Purcell and Dryden came together to produce *King Arthur* (*Lib*, p. xvii). Now it could happen again, with an English poet at the height of his powers and a young composer already regarded as a nascent genius with a growing audience eager to hear anything new from his pen. The subject seemed fitting too: heroic and mythic, with its own Arthurian echoes. There are many possible reasons why *Bunyan* failed to live up to its promise – ill-served by an unconvincing premiere, too 'English' in its accent and attitude, the lack of a truly shared vision between the collaborative partners – but it sits rather uncomfortably in the body of Auden and Britten's work together. Their partnership produced some wonderful music – mainly in the form of songs and choral works – but when they parted company, Auden and opera still had unfinished business together.

By the time he received a letter from the great Igor Stravinsky in 1947, inviting him to write the libretto for a new opera to be called *The Rake's Progress* and based on William Hogarth's series of eighteenth-century paintings depicting the moral and financial collapse of a rich young man in London, Auden was more than ready to respond. Now fully settled in America, he had taken great strides in his understanding of the possibilities for poetic drama. This came not just through his own dramatic poetry – pieces like the Pulitzer Prize winning *Age of Anxiety* and 'The Sea and the Mirror' – but also through experimental work in radio and film. And all the time his passion for opera was growing. The opportunity to work with an internationally acclaimed major composer (as opposed to the younger Britten) was too good to miss. As Auden wrote to Stravinsky in October 1947: 'I need hardly say that the chance of working with you is the greatest honour of my life'.[1] In the same letter, he set out his oft-repeated conviction that: 'it is the librettist's job to satisfy the composer, not the other way round'.

Auden headed to California, and he and Stravinsky worked together on a structure based on Hogarth's paintings. In ten days during November 1947, at the Stravinsky house off Hollywood's Sunset Boulevard, the two men set out the pattern for a major work. According to Stravinsky's own account (Stravinsky and Craft, 1960):

Primed by coffee and whisky, we began work on the *Rake's Progress*. Starting with a hero, a heroine, and a villain, and deciding that these people should be a tenor, a soprano, and a bass, we proceeded to invent a series of scenes leading up to the final scene in Bedlam that was already fixed in our minds. We followed Hogarth closely at first and until our own story began to assume a different significance. (Stravinsky and Craft 1960, p. 280)

But back in New York, as this project got under way, Auden introduced a significant new twist – he insisted on working in partnership with Chester Kallman. This idea was introduced to Stravinksy in a letter sent in January 1948: 'Herewith Act I. As you will see, I have taken in a collaborator, an old friend of mine in whose talents I have the greatest confidence' (Stravinsky and Craft 1960, p. 284). Uncertain at first about the idea of a new co-librettist, Stravinsky (who had approached Auden at the recommendation of Aldous Huxley) warmed to the idea, and one of the most significant collaborative partnerships in modern opera – Auden and Kallman – was born.

Much has been written about the complex personal relationship between Auden and Kallman. The emotional trajectory of the relationship is well documented. The younger Kallman quickly lost interest in Auden as a lover, and embarked on a series of other relationships. Auden – 'the more loving one' – regarded his relationship with Kallman as a marriage, and initially wore a ring to prove it. What Kallman brought to their professional relationship was a wide knowledge and love of opera (he was, after all, the one who introduced Auden to the operatic canon), and a track record as a poet in his own right, albeit with a lesser reputation than Auden's. In 'Translating Opera Libretti', in *The Dyer's Hand*, Auden sets out the principles of collaborative writing, arguing that the partners in a successful collaboration must 'surrender the selves that they would be if they were writing separately and become one new author;

though, obviously, any given passage must be written by one of them, the censor-critic who decides what will or will not do is this corporate personality' (*DH*, p. 483). This tone of self-denial chimes with a passage in his essay 'Notes on Music and Opera', in which Auden says: 'The verses which the librettist writes are not addressed to the public but are really a private letter to the composer. They have their moment of glory, the moment in which they suggest to him a certain melody; once that is over, they are as expendable as infantry to a Chinese general: they must efface themselves and cease to care what happens to them' (*DH*, p. 473).

Like many poets who work in opera, I have often quoted Auden's words to try to explain the difference between writing poetry and libretti, although I usually miss out the bit about the Chinese general. In essence, Auden is arguing that great opera is founded on an unequal partnership. As with film, where a screenwriter may tell you (not without bitterness) that although the story and characters are created in the script, film is still a director's medium, so it is with opera. Auden believed that opera was essentially a composer's medium. But far from challenging this secondary role (as did one of his heroes, Strauss' librettist Hugo von Hofmannsthal), Auden embraced it. In his essay 'Some Reflections on Music and Opera' (1952), he criticized Hofmannsthal's approach:

Much as I admire Hofmannsthal's libretto for *Der Rosenkavalier*, it is, I think, too near real poetry. The Marschallin's monologue in Act I, for instance, is so full of interesting detail that the voice line is hampered by trying to follow everything. The verses of 'ah non credea' in *La Somnambula*, though of little interest to read, do exactly what they should, suggest to Bellini one of the most beautiful melodies ever written, and then leave him free to write it. (*Prose III*, p. 301)

In the light of this, his decision to forge a buried co-authorship with Chester Kallman becomes more than just a creative one. Although subsequent work on their manuscripts has revealed that Auden and Kallman were – for the most part – pretty even collaborators (splitting the text roughly half and half), they were always reluctant in interviews to break the seal of joint authorship. Auden was particularly impatient with any attempt to minimize the role of Kallman, or to ascribe particular passages to the more famous older poet. Nonetheless, Mendelson is one of several critics who have teased out their individual contributions to the texts: 'The finished libretto displays Kallman's skill at local dramatic effects and his light but sharp-edged exuberance of tone', contrasted with Auden's 'structural intelligence and the anachronistic allegory that he had perfected in his longer poems' (*Lib*, p. xxi).

The purpose of a good libretto is to inspire the music. End of story. The music is primary, but the words come first. The unfortunate flip-side of this self-effacing view of the librettist's role, was that Auden and Kallman found the same opinion held sway in the opera world. Famously, during rehearsals for the premiere of *The Rake's Progress* in Venice in 1951, Stravinsky was given accommodation in a luxury hotel, whilst the librettists were at first given rooms in what Mendelson describes as 'a brothel' (p. xxiii).

If a good libretto is 'a private letter to a composer', then Auden and Kallman received a wonderful reply from Stravinsky. Unlike *Paul Bunyan*, *The Rake's Progress* entered the canon quickly – in spite of the inevitable dissenting critical voices for a new opera – and has held its high reputation. Over the next quarter century, Auden and Kallman produced more co-written libretti, including *Elegy for Young Lovers*, for the composer Hans Werner Henze in 1959–60, a new English version of Mozart's 'Magic Flute' in 1955 and 'Love's Labour's Lost' in 1969, but nothing surpassed *The Rake's Progress*, which remains the only Auden and Kallman libretto to find a lasting place in the hearts and homes of opera lovers.

So if *The Rake's Progress* libretto is the finest work for opera by one of the greatest poets of the twentieth century, working with his closest and most fitting collaborator, then how good is it as poetry? According to Auden's essay 'The World of Opera', published in *Secondary Worlds*, the question is off limits: 'The job of the librettist is to furnish the composer with a plot, character and words: of these, the least important, so far as the audience is concerned, are the words'. He goes on to suggest, as many frustrated librettists have before and since, that in the opera house, the audience 'will be very fortunate if they hear one word in seven' (*SW*, pp. 89–90). Auden's conclusion is that 'the verbal text of an opera is to be judged, not by the literary quality or lack of it which it may have when read, but by its success or failure in exciting the musical imagination of the composer' (*SW*, p. 90). The advent of surtitles in British and American opera houses has eclipsed Auden's pronouncement. Surtitles are now employed not just for translations of texts for Italian, French and German language operas, but for modern English operas. The audience may still only hear one word in seven, but the entire libretto is fed to them, line by line, in towering electronic text above or alongside the stage. Auden, if his writing on opera is taken at face value, might well disapprove of this.

Auden and Kallman's libretti clearly inspired composers – notably Stravinsky and Henze – to great heights, but is he being too self-effacing when he insists on the librettist's secondary role? In 'Notes on Music and

Opera', published in *The Dyer's Hand*, he goes even further. The opera listener, he argues, is not only unaware of the quality of poetry being sung, but even of the words. What the listener hears is simply sung syllables. He supports this view with an account of an experiment conducted by Cambridge psychologist P. E. Vernon, in which a Campion song was performed with the real words replaced by syllabically equivalent nonsense. Depressingly, only 6 per cent of the audience noticed that anything was wrong. Auden, however, doesn't seem at all depressed by this. For him, as soon as the music is written, the libretto has done its job (see *DH*, p. 473).

It would be fair to conclude from these arguments that any opera could readily be translated, without significant loss of quality, as long as the syllabic value of the words was matched. But in the same essay, Auden declared himself 'not generally in favor of the performances of operas in translation' (*DH*, p. 473). He goes on to argue that Wagner or Strauss operas translated into English sound intolerable to his ears, whatever the literary merits of the translation. In fact, the translation could be superior poetry to the original, but still sound intolerable, 'because the new syllables have no apt relation to the pitch and tempo of the notes with which they are associated' (*DH*, p. 473). At first glance, this makes perfect sense, and taps into many contemporary debates on the merits of translation versus accessibility in contemporary opera.

But put together, Auden's fragments and essays on the librettist's role seem at times contradictory and even precious. If opera offered Auden an authentic form of public poetry which he had struggled to achieve in the 1930s, then was he really writing a 'private letter to the composer' when he and Kallman put pen to paper? At the end of Act III of *The Rake's Progress*, the libretto declares that:

> Every wearied body must
> Late or soon return to dust,
> Set the frantic spirit free.
> In this early city we
> Shall not meet again, love, yet
> Never think that I forget.
> God is merciful and just,
> God ordains what ought to be,
> But a father's eyes are wet.
> (*Lib*, p. 91)

So, are we to read this as a private letter to Stravinsky, designed simply to inspire him, and to function merely as a set of syllables thereafter? Are we to read it as text on the page at all? It certainly sounds like a form of public poetry.

And does he claim too much for the primacy of the composer in these collaborations? Stravinsky clearly found Auden a formidable intellect, and accounts of their letters and conversations suggest that Auden was no mere secondary presence in their discussions. There is no doubt that the composer is king in the concert hall and opera house, but in the process of making an opera, most successful collaborations between composers and librettists are complex, open and equal. Even the question of how few words an audience might hear is open to debate, and composers, directors and singers are increasingly aware of their own responsibility (notwithstanding surtitles) to ensure that the libretto is as clear and audible as possible. Auden's stated strong views on poetry in opera do seem to belie the evidence of his working relationships, and the public and poetic qualities of the libretti he produced.

In Alan Bennett's play *The Habit of Art*, there is an imagined meeting in Auden's Oxford rooms between the ageing poet and his former composer-collaborator Benjamin Britten. In fact, the two men became estranged years before the play is set, and there was no rapprochement. In Bennett's play, Britten is about to embark on a major new opera – 'Death in Venice' – and is beset by doubts about it. He has come to visit Auden for encouragement and blessing. The librettist for 'Death in Venice' is Myfanwy Piper, and in Bennett's imagined conversation, Auden tries to persuade Britten to sack Piper and allow him to adapt Thomas Mann's novel. It is a fascinating notion. What would Auden have done with that story, with those characters? But ironically, Myfanwy Piper – who had no reputation as a poet outside her work in opera – is in many ways a perfect example of the model librettist of Auden's essays.

Piper's adaptation of Henry James' *Turn of the Screw* for Britten has secured its place in the operatic canon at least as convincingly as any of Auden's libretti. And as a 'private letter' to the composer, Myfanwy Piper's libretto seems exemplary, giving Britten not just a compelling and mysterious story, but an inspiring kit of parts for different forms of musical expression – nursery rhymes, Latin lessons, folk songs, soliloquies and others. Her text is rich in texture and variety, and inspired Britten to some of his most beautiful and dramatic operatic writing. But set out on the page, the *Turn of the Screw* libretto looks thin. It lives a half-life without the music. By Auden's own definition, perhaps Myfanwy Piper is the ideal librettist. But his own work with Chester Kallman, despite – or perhaps because of – its divergence from his principles of submission and restraint, has given us some of the finest poetry in twentieth century opera.

For Auden, the love affair with opera was a heady and complex one. What he gave to opera were the gifts of a major poet, in harmony – when it worked – with a composer of equal stature. Opera's gifts to Auden included the opening of new imaginative possibilities, which fed back into his own poetry. But perhaps the central gift was a renewal of the happiness and some of the intensity of his relationship with Chester Kallman, which had reached a very low ebb in 1947 when Auden suggested they might collaborate on *The Rake's Progress*. As Richard Davenport-Hines recounts, Auden 'was so keen to be seen publicly as Kallman's partner that, when the latter did not attend a performance, Auden avoided going on stage to receive applause by himself' (RD-H 1995, pp. 254–55).

For a major poet at a turning-point in his life and work, these public/ private letters to composers were a powerful source of creative impetus. His attempts in essays and interviews to explain or codify how a librettist should work – although sometimes at odds with his own practice – demonstrate the high regard he had for this most difficult of forms.

NOTES

1 Robert Craft and Igor Stravinsky, *Stravinsky in Conversation with Robert Craft* (Pelican, 1962), p. 279. Hereafter cited as 'Stravinsky and Craft'.

(ii) Precursors and Contemporaries

CHAPTER XXIV

Earlier English Influences

Chris Jones

In 'A Meaning of Auden' (1975), Geoffrey Grigson recalled his first impressions:

> Looking backwards then, I ask how do we first detect – or rather how do we so often miss – the new writer? The first poem I remember by Auden, never republished, and I have never hunted it out again, seemed to me to have risen out of an 'Englishness' (he was English, after all) until then unexpressed or not isolated in a poem. Auden was reading English; English at Oxford involved him in Old English, which involved him in *Beowulf.* In the poem he saw the blood-trail which had dripped from Grendel after his arm and shoulder had been ripped off by Beowulf. The blood shone, was phosphorescent on the grass – or so I remember the poem (in the *Cherwell* perhaps?). It was as if Auden ... had given imaginative place and 'reality' to something exploited for the Examination Schools, yet rooted in the English origins.
>
> (*Tribute*, pp. 13–14)

'Looking backwards' on Auden then, Grigson finds him, or chooses to remember him, as also looking backwards onto the origins of Englishness, imagined as rooted in the heroic literature of Old English. Grigson associates this sense of Ur-Englishness with Auden's own personal identity, and collocates an origin myth for Auden's literary career with an origin myth for English literary tradition. Such patterns of recognition are attractive and certainly possess substantial explanatory power, although they can also tempt into oversimplification. After all, Auden poems, both lost and surviving, predate this one and his acquaintance with Old English by at least four years. English poems, lost and surviving, predate *Beowulf,* for at least 400 years. And there are of course literary influences at least as important to Auden's sense of Englishness: Shakespeare, Hardy, the language of the King James Authorized Version of the Bible, and of English hymns. Nor is Englishness the sole 'meaning of Auden', this most cosmopolitan of poets, although it may be the defining key to his identity as a poet. Furthermore, because it is sometimes even contested that Old English *is* the origin of English as a language or literary tradition, to see it as such is a choice deliberately made rather than an essential, given fact.

But Grigson is right that Auden is the first English poet to make that choice in the way he does. Whereas a poet such as William Barnes (1801–86) had looked backwards to Old English in his attempts to write an English free of foreign loanwords, in effect winding back the linguistic clock to before the Norman Conquest, Auden's own use of early English is not so conservative. Instead, he was concerned with bringing Old English, originary or otherwise, into the contemporary present, where it had to rub along in the rag-bag mélange of Auden's other eclectic influences, interests, and hobby-horses. This is evident from the opening lines of the same poem that Grigson remembered, published in November 1926 (not in fact in *The Cherwell* but another student magazine, *Oxford Poetry)* under the title 'Thomas Epilogizes':

> Inexorable Rembrandt rays, which stab
> Through clouds as through a rotting factory floor,
> Make chiaroscuro in a day now over,
> And cart-ruts bloody as if Grendel lately
> Had shambled dripping back into his marshes.
> The train runs on, while in the sagging West
> Gasometers heave Brobdingnagian flanks
> Like dragons with their bat-wings furled for sleep.
>
> (*Juv*, p. 146)

So the Old English epic *Beowulf* is exploited for a simile which is provided by the bloody traces of a wounded, but absent monstrous villain (Grendel), and then deployed to parallel a preceding simile drawn from a decaying industrial landscape ('as through a rotting factory floor'), elaborating an image of sunrays, metonymically likened to a pictorial representation of itself by a sixteenth-century Dutch painter; all this is seen from the window of a train moving through an actual industrial landscape, architectural features of which resemble 'dragons' (another of Beowulf's adversaries), whose huge size is indicated by an adjective coined from a fictional land of giants in Jonathan Swift's *Gulliver's Travels*. It is a ghastly mish-mash, written in inventive pastiche of T. S. Eliot, but one can already detect the genuine Audenesque notes in this piece of juvenilia. What is more, it provides a clear indication of the distinctive manner in which Auden would habitually come to deploy early English in his own poetry, especially its first phase of maturity: not, in fact, 'looking backwards', or not *only* looking backwards, but also forwards.

By early English, I mean here those forms of English that predate what linguists call 'Early Modern English' (roughly, the English of Shakespeare). Early, or Medieval, English is usually treated as two separate stages: Old English (or Anglo-Saxon) and Middle English. The former describes that period of the language dating from the migration of the Angles, Saxons, and Jutes from the continent to what is now England (during the fifth century A.D.) and continues until whenever the effects of the Norman Conquest are deemed to make themselves felt on the language; it is now common to speak of Old English lasting into the mid twelfth century, even though 1066 is obviously a catchier date to use as an end point. Middle English describes the period conterminous with Old English and Early Modern, and during which influence from French became much more significant. In Auden's case, it is not always easy to decide whether an influence comes specifically and distinctly from Old rather than Middle English, as certain kinds of models and precedents are common to or look similar in both, as we will consider shortly. Moreover, in Auden's case, there is also an argument for treating Old Norse (sometimes called Old Icelandic) under the rubric of 'Early English'. This may seem surprising, until one considers that Scandinavian was widely spoken in parts of England for long stretches of the early Middle Ages, especially in Auden's home county of Yorkshire, which was part of the Danelaw. Additionally, by the time he came into contact with these medieval languages, there had been a long-established pattern of understanding the early history of English as the result of successive waves of southern Scandinavian speakers arriving in the British Isles and reinvigorating a once common stock with progressively changed dialects. That is to say, Angles, Saxons, and Jutes coming from their ancestral homelands near the foot of the Jutland peninsula brought a first wave of 'southern Scandinavian' in the form of Anglo-Saxon; this was later alloyed with the Old Norse tongue brought by Danish Viking settlers; finally the Normans arrived, who, although much changed by their stay in northern France, had earlier come from the same Scandinavian homelands (hence their name Nor(th)-men). English, according to this model, was a patina of different layers of speech brought by successive Scandinavian communities.

For Auden, there were very personal reasons for investing in the notion of early English being a blend of Scandinavian dialects. He was born in Bootham, York, which is a Norse placename: *búðum*, 'at the market booths' (Carpenter, p. 3). As a child, he was often told by his father George that the family name went back to Auðun skökull, one of the first Norse settlers to colonize Iceland (Carpenter, p. 7), and translations of the Icelandic sagas were favourite reading in Auden's nursery library. Later in life, the poet made two pilgrimage-like trips to Iceland, once in 1936 and again in 1964. Undoubtedly, then, Auden regarded his personal and familial roots as Anglo-Scandinavian. Important as it undoubtedly was to him, his sense of Englishness, therefore, was not entirely straightforward and uncompli-cated, but slightly skewed or queered by this Anglo-Scandinavian bent; he came at Englishness at something of an angle.

Auden explicitly acknowledged the proximity of Old Norse to his own understanding of 'Early English', when he refers to both it and Anglo-Saxon poetry collectively as 'the "barbaric" poetry of the North' in *A Certain World*, and recalls how he was 'immediately fascinated both by its metric and its rhetorical devices, so different from the post-Chauce-rian poetry with which I was familiar'. The same entry goes on to quote Michael Alexander's translation of the Anglo-Saxon poem *Deor*, 'one of my favorites' (*CW*, pp. 22, 23–24). So deep and prolonged was this fas-cination that late in life, and together with the scholar Paul Taylor, he produced a book of translations from Norse, which arguably should be counted among the results of 'earlier English influences'. *Norse Poems* (1981) is really the culmination of an interest in pre-Chaucerian devices which had led Auden to imitate Old Norse poetic effects, as well as those of Old and Middle English, for much of his career. For example, the lyric 'Hushed is the lake of hawks', embedded within the long poem *The Age of Anxiety*, is an attempt to approximate the *drottkvaett* stanza of Old Norse, consisting of lines of three stressed syllables, in which the first of two lines contains both an alliterative pairing and an assonance, while the second line contains an internal rhyme and an alliterative link back to the first line (although the first couplet of Auden's lyric does not achieve this last requirement):

> Hushed is the lake of hawks,
> Bright with our excitement,
> And all the sky of skulls
> Glows with scarlet roses;
> The melter of men and salt
> Admires the drinker of iron;
> Bold banners of meaning
> Blaze o'er our host of days.
>   (*CP* 1991, p. 519; *CP* 2007,
>   pp. 516–17)

This lyric also demonstrates Auden's fascination with the device com-mon to Old Norse and Old English, of 'kenning', that is, an oblique and metaphorical epithet for referring to a subject indirectly; here 'lake of hawks' is a kenning-like reference to the sky, and analogous to the Anglo-Saxon kenning for the sea, *hwælweg* ('whale-path'), as used, for example, in line 63 of *The Seafarer*, a canonical Old English text, which Auden studied. The kenning is a form of mini-riddle: what is it that is a path or road for whales?; a house of bones? (OE *banhus*, the body, home to the soul); a sky candle? (OE *heofoncandel*, the sun); what are 'houses for fishes'? (the seas, from Auden's poem 'The Wanderer', first line 'Doom is dark and deeper than any sea-dingle'). The riddle was also a favourite genre of the Anglo-Saxons, and we should perhaps link Auden's own fondness for abstruse and riddling modes of presentation to the influence of earlier English on his work. An appreciation of 'riddles and all other ways of not calling a spade a spade' was one of the benchmarks by which Auden professed to measure literary judgment in his inaugural lecture as Oxford Professor of Poetry (*DH*, p. 47).

It was at Oxford University that Auden first encountered Old and Middle English, when he changed his studies from biology to English in the summer of 1926. Auden was not excited by the philological approach of some of his teachers at Oxford, and in fact, he only received a third class degree, perhaps because his talents were so out of sympathy with the kind of skills required of him by the examination papers in Medieval English, with their heavy emphasis on historical linguistics.[1] Nevertheless, more than a decade later, Auden could write that (alongside Dante and Pope) the Middle English poet Langland was one of the three greatest influences on his writing (*Prose II*, p. 92). In 1962, Auden placed even more importance on Medieval English, recalling an epiphanic moment while being taught by J. R. R. Tolkien: 'at a certain point he recited, and magnificently, a long passage of *Beowulf*. I was spellbound. This poetry, I knew, was going to be my dish'. In the same lecture he added 'Anglo-Saxon and Middle English poetry have been one of my strongest, most lasting influences' (*DH*, pp. 41–42). It was, we should note, the *sound* of this poetry that first attracted Auden, not its subject matter; a point to be considered in more detail shortly.

Set texts for the Medieval English papers at Oxford included the seventh edition (1894) of Sweet's *Anglo-Saxon Reader* (with Riddles, Charms, Gnomic Verses, *The Battle of Maldon*, *The Seafarer*, *The Wanderer* and *The Dream of the Rood* among the passages nominated for study); Morris and Skeat's *Specimens of Early English* (1898), which included set passages from Layamon's *Brut*, *The Owl and the Nightingale* and *King Horn*); and Sisam's *Fourteenth-Century Verse and Prose* (1921), including excerpts set from *Sir*

Gawain and the Green Knight, *Pearl* and Langland's *Piers Plowman*. In addition, *Beowulf* (in Klaeber's edition) and Chaucer's canon were studied more thoroughly. It has also been established that Auden knew well several other anthologies of Norse, Old English, and Middle English, drawing on them when composing poems such as 'The Wanderer' and *The Orators*.[2]

It is revealing that, from the pantheon of Middle English poets, Auden singled out Langland rather than Chaucer as one of his most significant influences, and is best understood in terms of his attraction to the sounds of early English. Langland wrote in an alliterative, stress-based metre which, in several basic respects, is similar to the verse structures of Old English, but quite different from those of Chaucer and most subsequent English poetry. In the accentual syllabic tradition, which came to predominate in English until the free verse revolutions of the twentieth century, a line of verse consists of a fixed number of syllables arranged in regular patterns of accented and unaccented syllables. Shakespeare's twelfth sonnet, for example, opens with a line of ten syllables, which alternate regularly between unaccented and accented, in an 'off-on' pattern: 'When *I* do *count* the *clock* that *tells* the *time*' (my italics for accented syllables). In stress-based alliterative verse, however, such as existed in Old and some Middle English poetry, not every syllable is counted. Instead, a line of verse would typically consist of four strongly stressed syllables, with a more elastic number of unstressed syllables falling between them; although in 'classical' Old English verse, there seems to have existed slightly more constraint on the number and place of the unstressed syllables than was the case for Middle English poets like Langland. Nevertheless, there was always a good deal more flexibility with regard to syllable count than is the case in later, mainstream English metrical verse. In medieval alliterative English poetry (which rarely rhymed) two or three of the four strongly stressed syllables would alliterate with each other. In Old English there were stricter conventions about these alliterations than in much Middle English; the third strongly stressed syllable always alliterated with the first or the second or both the first and second strongly stressed syllables, but never with the fourth. We can see some of these principles at work in *The Age of Anxiety* (again I have italicised stressed syllables):

> *Lies* and *leth*argies po*lice* the *world*
> In its *periods* of *peace*. What *pain taught*
> (*CP* 1991, p. 461; *CP* 2007, p. 458)

Here the third stressed syllable in each line alliterates with both the first and the second, but not the fourth. In a metrical form like this, it is both allowed and expected that the first stressed syllable of a line ('lies') might be followed by only one unstressed syllable ('and'), while the second might be followed by three ('-ar', '-gies', 'po-'). Similarly the metre allows that one line might begin with stressed syllables, falling to the unstressed (like the first of these two lines), while another might begin with one or more unstressed syllables rising to the stressed syllables (like the second). Finally, medieval alliterative verse also allowed for two stressed syllables to follow one another consecutively in certain metrical patterns.[3] An example here would be 'pain taught', although in fact in 'classical' Old English poetry such a double stress would not normally occur at the end of a line. In mainstream English accentual-syllabic tradition, all these features would be considered as anomalous rather than integral.

What Auden responded to when he heard Tolkien reading aloud was an aural structure; not free, but differently regular from the metrical verse with which he was familiar, and yet still 'natively' English: a prosodic contour according to which unstressed syllables may be treated more freely, because different expectations govern the arrangement and patterning of stressed syllables. As long ago as 1940, the critic Henry Wells had understood that Auden and some of his contemporaries had found a 'new energizing factor for modern verse' in the relative metrical freedoms offered by early English poetry.[4] *The Age of Anxiety* is, in part, the attempt to write out this new/old sound structure on an almost epic scale, adapting patterns from Old and Middle English, as well as Old Norse alliterative verse, to accommodate the changed linguistic features of contemporary English – a fact crucial to understanding Auden's use of the past in a live tradition; he does not attempt to revive and slavishly follow 'rules' for composition in Medieval English, as some critics seem to have mistakenly supposed. Such a project would inevitably fail, because the English language has changed grammatically and syntactically in ways that render the exact replication of medieval metres impossible. As always, Auden is about the words of the dead being 'modified in the guts of the living', as he put it in his elegy for Yeats. In fact, it is these modified early English voices that constitute the main bulwark against the otherwise overwhelming influence of Eliot in Auden's verse. As noted at the beginning of this chapter, early English forms but one ingredient in a modernist pot-pourri of allusions and influences that recalls Eliot in its overall design. But early English is an element not actually present in Eliot's own influence, and so it sounds the most obviously un-Eliotic note in Auden's verse music. The modified patterns of early English voices largely prevent Auden from succumbing to the overpowering cadences of his master.

But Auden's uses of early English are not merely about establishing a formally distinctive voice; they serve political ends, whether those ends are domestic and personal, or public. So 'The Wanderer' deploys Old And Middle English to contemplate a homosexual coming out (although I now hold the view that, rather than 'crossing the threshold of the closet', this poem actually marks a retreat from such an act⁵); *The Orators* makes use of a number of Old English and Old Norse sources in the attempt to map the psychology of a dictator in its 'English Study'; 'Letter to R. H. S. Crossman, Esq.', written against the backdrop of the Spanish Civil War, alludes to *The Battle of Maldon*; *The Age of Anxiety* adapts early English rhythmic patterns to tell of the Second World War. In all these cases, the forms may derive from the Middle Ages, but the matter is modern, just as Grendel's blood was relocated to a modern industrial landscape in 'Thomas Epilogizes'. Auden was no nostalgic archaizer in his use of early English; instead, the different flexibilities for ordering language offered by these early models seem to accord in him with a desire to pattern the apparent chaos of the bleaker or more despair-inducing aspects of contemporary experience. Even at the end of his life and career, as Auden attempts in the late poem 'Nocturne' to contemplate the afterlife, he does so by turning to the sounds and patterns of early English alliterative measures:

> How else shall mannerless minds
> in ignorance imagine
> the Mansion of Gentle Joy
> it is our lot to look for,
> where else weak wills find comfort
> to dare the Dangerous Quest?
> (*CP* 1991, p. 880; *CP* 2007, p. 882)

To the end, looking backwards was for Auden always a way of looking forwards.

NOTES

1 For examples of the questions Auden was set in his final examinations of 1928, see Chris Jones, *Strange Likeness; the Use of Old English in Twentieth-century Poetry* (Oxford University Press, 2006), pp. 70–71.
2 These were: Nora Kershaw, ed. and trans., *Anglo-Saxon and Norse Poems* (Cambridge University Press, 1922); Bruce Dickins, ed. and trans., *Runic and Heroic Poems of the Old Teutonic Peoples* (Cambridge University Press, 1915). Auden also knew Joseph Hall, ed., *Selections from Early Middle English 1130–1250* (Clarendon, 1920), and is also likely, John Fuller suggests, to have used R. K. Gordon, trans., *Anglo-Saxon Poetry* (Dent, 1926).

3 For an introduction to early English alliterative prosody, see Donald Scragg, 'The Nature of Old English Verse', in Malcolm Godden and Michael Lapidge, eds., *The Cambridge Companion to Old English Literature* (Cambridge University Press, 1991), pp. 55–70.

4 Henry Wells, *New Poets from Old: a Study in Literary Genetics* (Columbia University Press, 1940), p. 12.

5 Jones (2006), pp. 89–97 (p. 91). I am grateful to John Fuller for changing my mind on this matter.

CHAPTER XXV

Auden and Shakespeare

Stephen Regan

Shakespeare's Sonnet 121, greatly admired and frequently quoted by Auden, is distinguished by the candour with which it reflects on the troubling discrepancy between self-knowledge and public esteem, and by its unflinching acknowledgement of what it is to be 'vile' and 'bad'. In a startling act of self-disclosure, the sonnet turns from a confessed vulnerability to the judgement of others into a declaration of trust in one's own being: 'No, I am that I am, and they that level / At my abuses reckon up their own'.[1] In its forthright exposure of private dilemmas in the face of public admonishment, and in its acutely sensitive weighing of self-worth against social reputation, the sonnet encapsulates a concern with self-realization and self-representation that was to preoccupy Auden profoundly in both his critical and his creative writings.

If Shakespeare's finely discriminating moral intelligence made him a poet for all times, his dramatization of the ego also made him, for Auden, the most modern of artists. Shakespeare's pervasive interest in self-fulfilment and the political obstacles that might inhibit it seemed to Auden to invite, if ultimately resist, the insights of Freud and Marx, engaging modern readers in the unfathomable mystery of personality and its 'millions of strange shadows'.[2] Shakespeare's sonnets, edited by Auden for the popular Signet Classic Shakespeare Series in 1964, provided the perfect model for a mode of writing that was at once intensely lyrical and highly dramatic. More than any other modern poet, with the possible exception of Robert Frost, Auden recognized the value of the sonnet as a dialogical form in which contending values and ideas could be brought into a highly charged relationship, and in which the play of consciousness was, itself, the ostensible subject. The sonnet appealed to Auden much as the dramatic monologue appealed to T. S. Eliot. It was a form in which the most private thoughts and feelings could acquire artistic impersonality. For this reason, he had little interest in the identities of the young man and the Dark Lady, or even in the homoerotic content of

Shakespeare's sonnets. The mystery and obscurity of the sonnets were, in Auden's estimation, an integral part of their artistic accomplishment and lasting appeal.

The attraction of the sonnet as a space where complicated personal dramas might be worked out in compressed form is evident in Auden's work as early as 1927, but the influence of Shakespeare is most strongly marked in the sequence of twelve love sonnets, a version of which was sent to Christopher Isherwood in 1934. The early sonnets are revealing stylistically in that they show Auden savouring the lyric potential of the Shakespearean sonnet (in such smoothly crafted lines as 'Turn not towards me lest I turn to you'), even while endeavouring to distort and fracture the staple iambic line. Among the rhetorical skills gleaned from Shakespeare's sonnets is the intimate pause effected by a well-placed caesura: 'Turn not towards me, lest I turn to you' (*EA*, p. 146). There is tenderness and devotion in these early sonnets, but fear, jealousy and disappointment prevail, so that like their Shakespearean counterparts they constitute a dramatization of what Auden neatly summed up as 'the anxiety into which the behaviour of another person can throw you'.[3] The anatomy of conflict is conducted on a massive public scale in the ambitious sonnet sequence, 'In Time of War', completed in the autumn of 1938. This time, the voice is stridently Auden's own, and the rhyming couplet is generally eschewed, except in those instances where geography and politics collide with a striking contemporary urgency: 'And maps can really point to places / Where life is evil now: / Nanking; Dachau' (*EA*, p. 257).

As well as instructing Auden in the writing of bitter, brooding sonnets, Shakespeare was to exercise his critical intelligence in a prolific output of essays, lectures and reviews from the late 1930s onwards. Auden immersed himself in a comprehensive reading of Shakespeare's plays after agreeing to conduct a series of lectures and discussion groups on the entire canon at the New School for Social Research in New York in 1946–47. The published lectures, largely reconstructed from student notes, are an entertaining miscellany of scholarly research, amusing digression and brilliant improvisation. As well as offering a lively account of the plays and sonnets, the lectures provide us with a valuable insight into Auden's intellectual and philosophical preoccupations in the 1940s. His enthusiastic interest in genre, psychology and music are given free rein here, and the lectures clearly constitute a foundation for the boldly provocative and idiosyncratic readings of Shakespeare that surface later in *The Dyer's Hand* (1962). Auden's incisiveness and originality as a critic of Shakespeare are evident, too, in the extraordinary critical-creative experiment, 'The Sea and the Mirror', which he modestly described as 'A Commentary on Shakespeare's *The Tempest*' when it first appeared in *For the Time Being* (1944).

'The Sea and the Mirror' is a powerful imaginative synthesis of the existential dilemmas and aesthetic ideals that had preoccupied Auden since his emigration to the United States in 1939 and his renewed embrace of Christianity soon after. If the writings of Søren Kierkegaard, Reinhold Niebuhr and Charles Williams provide some of the intellectual under-pinnings of the poem's sustained reflection on the fundamental question of how best to live, so too does Saint Augustine's *Confessions*. The more immediate and urgent context of the poem, however, is the Second World War and the assault on democracy and political liberalism. Auden's reli-gious and political anxieties converge to produce a dramatic enquiry into what the role of the artist should be in the middle years of the twentieth century. An explanation of why *The Tempest* might have prompted this ambitious reconceptualization of the role of art can be found in Auden's 1947 lecture on Shakespeare's late play, in which he claims that the fail-ure of art to transform humanity 'grieves Prospero greatly'.[4] Briefly cit-ing Prospero's assessment of Caliban as 'A devil, a born devil, on whose nature / Nurture can never stick' (4.1.188–89), he concludes: 'You can hold the mirror up to a person, but you may make him worse'.[5] Already, at this stage, Auden is moving towards the stance that he would adopt in the Prologue to *The Dyer's Hand* (1962), where the role of art and poetry is not one of magical enchantment and transformation, but instead one of disenchantment and disintoxication (see *DH*, p. 27).

The familiar Shakespearean image of the mirror carries with it an insistence on the necessary, if precarious, revelation of truth, while the sea, in its seeming boundlessness, is a reminder of the perilous enterprise of seeking the truth. In *The Tempest*, the sea surrounding the island is that uncertain element that can both destroy and deliver, but in Auden's poem it has more obvious modernist connotations of the unfathom-able gulf between mind and world. Auden's Prospero beautifully articu-lates both Renaissance and modernist viewpoints as he reflects on final things and surrenders words to 'the silent dissolution of the sea'.[6] In some respects, as John Fuller points out, '"The Sea and the Mirror" is not only a commentary on Shakespeare's play but a completion of it' (Fuller 1998, p. 357). In his later Shakespearean criticism in *The Dyer's Hand*, Auden claims that *The Tempest* is 'overpessimistic and manichean' (*DH*, p. 134), a verdict that helps us to understand why 'The Sea and the Mirror' deals so insistently with the body-spirit duality, even to the extent of challenging, complicating and recasting the oppositions and antagonisms inherent in the play.

'The Sea and the Mirror' is at once a critical engagement with the ethical values and artistic ideals of Shakespeare's play, and an imaginative working out of Auden's own aesthetic *credo* in lyric verse and elevated prose. The poem consists of a 'Preface' in which the Stage Manager addresses the critics after a performance of *The Tempest*, followed by three parts or chapters. In chapter 1, Prospero grants Ariel his freedom, while meditating on the unpredictability of life and the inevitability of death; in chapter 2, the Supporting Cast speak 'sotto voce', with each character telling his or her own destiny in a specially contrived verse form; and in chapter 3, Caliban makes a formal address to the audience on the role of art, ironically taking on the civilized manners and rhetorical attributes of that supreme stylist, Henry James. The Stage Manager's speech recalls 'The Circus Animals' Desertion' by W. B. Yeats in its comparison of theatrical and artistic skill with the tricks of the circus performer. The aged, as well as the children, are excited and entertained by the performance, but the preface deftly moves from art to religion, and from the realm of pleasure to the realm of evil, in the biblical image of 'the lion's mouth whose hunger / No metaphors can fill' (*S&M*, p. 4). The poem's consideration of the distance between 'Shall-I and I-Will' is a reminder of the difference between contemplation and action in a world of difficult ethical choices. Beyond art and literature is the Unknown: 'the smiling / Secret which cannot be quoted' (*S&M*, p. 4). Anticipating a major theme in 'The Sea and the Mirror', the 'Preface' proposes, through its allusion to Prospero's famous speech (4.1.155–58), that 'this world of fact we love ... Is unsubstantial stuff'. Even so, the apprehension of the Unknown is conveyed in words that echo some of the most profound insights in Shakespearean tragedy: 'All the rest is silence / On the other side of the wall; / And the silence ripeness, / And the ripeness all'.[7]

In chapter 1 of 'The Sea and the Mirror', which Auden described to Isherwood as 'the Artist to his genius' (*S&M*, p. xx), Prospero bids farewell to Ariel in a dignified speech that both reflects upon the role of art and contemplates the existential journey that lies ahead. In renouncing magic, Prospero opens himself to suffering and accepts reality: 'So at last I can really believe I shall die' (*S&M*, p. 5). There is a lingering stiffness and hauteur in Prospero's manner, but the resounding echo of Shakespeare's

Sonnet 121 suggests that part of Auden's scheme is to depict a moment of profound self-realisation:

> Now, Ariel, I am that I am, your late and lonely master,
> Who knows now what magic is; – the power to enchant
> That comes from disillusion.   (*S&M*, p. 6)

Against the idea of art as magical enchantment, the poem asserts the contrary view of holding up the mirror to the world. In the first of three songs, Prospero entertains the possibility of seeing 'Nature as / In truth she is for ever' (*S&M*, p. 7). The renunciation of power and the acquisition of spiritual insight and self-knowledge are dependent on confession and forgiveness. Prospero admits, 'All by myself I tempted Antonio unto treason', and he acknowledges Caliban as 'my impervious disgrace' (*S&M*, p. 8). The journey towards enlightenment is one that he must take 'Alone and on foot' (*S&M*, p. 10). Auden's presentation of Prospero shows little of the coldness and arrogance of which he later disapproves in *The Dyer's Hand*. Instead, chapter 1 seems to exert a sympathetic identification with Prospero, not least in its touching characterization of the exiled Duke as an ordinary old man, 'Just like other old men, with eyes that water / Easily in the wind, and a head that nods in the sunshine' (*S&M*, p. 11).

If the failure of art to transform humanity 'grieves Prospero greatly',[8] as Auden claims, it is nevertheless the case that Shakespeare's characters, with the exception of Antonio and Caliban, do appear changed by their experiences on the island. To be more precise, what each member of the Supporting Cast articulates in the lyric monologues that constitute chapter 2 is a transformed but nevertheless partial apprehension of their own predicament. The cast appears 'dotted about the deck' of the ship returning to Naples, and each speaker is represented by an appropriate verse form (*S&M*, p. 13). Antonio's caustic sarcasm is brilliantly depicted in intricate *terza rima*, subtly subverting all of the well-established associations of the verse form with love and freedom. As Arthur Kirsch points out, Auden's Antonio is reminiscent of Iago, a specimen of 'the unregenerate will, a demonic outsider' and 'an insistent counterpart to Prospero' (*S&M*, p. xxii). At the end of each lyrical address, including his own, Antonio speaks in a mocking refrain which undermines the hopes and aspirations of Prospero and the cast. His assertion of his own recalcitrant ego is both an ironic, deflationary echo of Sonnet 121 and a declaration of solidarity with Richard III: 'Your need to love shall never know / Me: I am I, Antonio, / By choice myself alone' (*S&M*, p. 14).[9]

Auden handles an impressive repertoire of verse forms with consummate technical skill. Ferdinand declares his innocent love for Miranda in an alexandrine sonnet, while Stephano expresses his sensualist cravings in an alliterative ballade that sounds like downmarket Swinburne: 'Embrace me, belly, like a bride' (*S&M*, p. 15). If Auden's Stephano is a Falstaffian type, his Gonzalo is a moralist akin to Polonius, whose brisk trochaic tetrameter aptly suits his hasty rationalization of events and his easy dismissal of the absurd and the mysterious: 'There was nothing to explain' (*S&M*, p. 17). Adrian and Francisco are permitted only a 'camp couplet' or 'camp lament'[10] on the transience of nature – 'Good little sunbeams must learn to fly, / But it's madly ungay when the goldfish die' – whereas Alonso is given the longest speech of all, consisting of a verse letter to Ferdinand in eight twelve-line stanzas (*S&M*, p. 18). The song of the Master and Boatswain initially sounds like a bawdy sea shanty, but there is a nostalgia and a plangency, worthy of Housman's 'lads', that points to a deeper and more serious preoccupation with the sorrow of love: 'And hearts that we broke long ago / Have long been breaking others' (*S&M*, p. 22).

'Pallid Sebastian' and 'Tense Trinculo' are presented as complicated personalities whose emotional and intellectual development has been hindered by childhood fantasies. Sebastian is associated with a pre-Oedipal inability to distinguish thought from action ('And anything pretended is alive') and a relentless obsession with failure and defeat (*S&M*, pp. 23–25). This negative psychology is aptly conveyed through the intricate and insistent patterns of the sestina. Trinculo, on the other hand, displaces anxiety into laughter. The apparently simple but deeply repressed desires of this 'cold clown' are fittingly conveyed through alternately rhymed quatrains in iambic trimeter (*S&M*, p. 24). The closing lyric is given to Miranda, whose elegant villanelle for Ferdinand seeks to reconcile the fundamental oppositions in the poem, bringing together the mirror of art and the sea of life in its closing couplet: 'My Dear One is mine as mirrors are lonely, / And the high green hill sits always by the sea' (*S&M*, p. 26). At the same time, the fairy-tale imagery of the villanelle and the occasional awkwardness of its eleven-syllable lines suggest a precarious innocence and naivety.

Chapter 3 of 'The Sea and the Mirror' is a virtuoso performance which breaks with the versified speeches of the Supporting Cast and allows Caliban to stand in for Shakespeare and speak direct to a modern readership about ethics, aesthetics and religion. Caliban speaks with wit and eloquence about the roles that he and Ariel assume in the play. The chapter is a brilliant prose disquisition on the value and purpose of art, but as John Fuller points out, its appeal has much to do with 'the admonitory and ventriloquial voice of Caliban, forever confiding, cajoling, comforting and castigating' (Fuller 1998, p. 363). After taking Shakespeare to task for his misleading aphorism about a mirror held up to nature, Caliban enlightens those aspiring writers who might have 'decided on the conjuror's profession' (*S&M*, p. 36). Finally, he contemplates release for himself and Ariel, imagining an English landscape that appears to be based on the North Pennine mining country that Auden knew so well: 'an old horse-tramway winds away westward through suave foothills crowned with stone circles – follow it and by nightfall one would come to a large good-natured waterwheel' (*S&M*, pp. 44–45). The ultimate direction of the chapter, however, is away from nostalgia and towards religious meditation and the acknowledgement of 'that Wholly Other Life' (*S&M*, p. 52). The Postscript has Ariel speak to Caliban of 'What we shall become', with the final exhausted couplet suggesting a unity and a wholeness found only in death: 'One evaporating sigh / ... I' (*S&M*, p. 56).

Auden retained his interest in *The Tempest* as a 'disquieting work', revisiting it in *The Dyer's Hand* (*DH*, p. 128). Here, Ariel continues to exert a fascination as 'the invisible spirit of imagination', but Auden's attitude to Prospero appears to have hardened: 'Prospero's forgiving is more the contemptuous pardon of a man who knows that he has his enemies completely at his mercy than a heartfelt reconciliation' (*DH*, pp. 132, 129). Shakespeare is very much a central interest in *The Dyer's Hand* (the title is taken from Sonnet III, which like Sonnet 121, distinguishes between public reputation ['name'] and personal being ['nature']).[11] The book is often wayward and provocative, but full of astute and learned judgements, as with Auden's instructive account of why comedy is 'not only possible within a Christian society, but capable of a much greater breadth and depth than classical comedy' (*DH*, p. 177). In three essays in particular, 'The Prince's Dog', 'Brothers & Others' and 'The Joker in the Pack', a Marxist-inflected political criticism is tempered with Christian humanism in a mode of enquiry that repeatedly weighs the thirst for power against the appeal of charity. Auden's probing, incisive readings of *Henry IV*, *The Merchant of Venice* and *Othello* are among the finest Shakespearean criticism of the twentieth century.

The essays on Shakespeare are a superb instance of Auden's mature critical style and its diverse registers and tonal shifts. 'The Prince's Dog' is expertly pitched and makes its impact through the appealing rhetorical intimacy and jesting that Auden perfected in his public lectures:

What sort of bad company would one expect to find Prince Hal keeping when the curtain rises on *Henry IV*? Surely, one could expect to see him surrounded by daring, rather sinister juvenile delinquents and beautiful gold-digging whores? But whom do we meet in the Boar's Head? A fat, cowardly tosspot, old enough to be his father, two down-at-heel hangers-on, a slatternly hostess and only one whore, who is not in her earliest youth either; all of them seedy, and, by any worldly standards, including those of the criminal classes, all of them *failures*. (*DH*, p. 183)

The essay is remarkable for the diverse ways in which it seeks to understand 'why Falstaff affects us as he does' (*DH*, p. 198). Auden asks us to imagine what the play would be like without Falstaff and even what the play would look like to Falstaff sitting in the audience. At times, he seems inclined to fold back *Henry IV* into the morality tradition and read the play as a parable in which Falstaff is 'a comic symbol for the supernatural order of Charity', but at its best the essay probes the drunkenness and fatness of Falstaff with great psychological acuity. Recalling the theme of self-revelation in Sonnet 121, Auden observes that 'Falstaff is perfectly willing to tell the world: "I am that I am, a drunken old failure"', while 'Hal cannot jeopardize his career by such careless disclosure but must always assume whatever manner is politic at the moment' (*DH*, p. 206).

Turning from *Henry IV* to *The Merchant of Venice* in 'Brothers & Others', Auden offers a brilliantly succinct account of the contrast between a feudal, land-owning society and an international mercantile society. Both plays, he claims, are structured around incompatibilities: the existence of Falstaff is incompatible with the historical world of political chronicle, while 'the romantic fairy story world of Belmont is incompatible with the historical reality of money-making Venice' (*DH*, p. 221). The essay is notable for its study of how a change in the nature of wealth from landownership to capital radically alters the social conception of time, but the Marxist perspective here is complemented by a Christian humanist account of love and hatred, and by an urgent insistence on the mutual dependency that is vital in a modern capitalist era. The remarkable essay on *Othello*, 'The Joker in the Pack', follows a similar critical trajectory, transporting us from an initial attempt to understand Iago in terms of 'an estrangement from a specific social situation' (*DH*, p. 259) to a modern appraisal of Iago as a Freudian analyst who knows and exploits Othello's repression. The essay astutely claims that Iago 'desires self-destruction as much as he desires the destruction of others' (*DH*, p. 252), but its motivating impulse is the observation that Iago is 'a portrait of a practical joker of a peculiarly appalling kind' (*DH*, p. 253). Once again, Auden brings his appreciation of Sonnet 121 to bear on his analysis of the plays. Comparing Iago's 'I am not what I am' to the 'Divine *I am that I am*', he asserts that Iago's determination 'to make game of others, makes his existence absolutely dependent on theirs; when he is alone, he is a nullity' (*DH*, p. 257). Auden's final analysis is one very much in tune with the insights of Jan Kott's *Shakespeare Our Contemporary* (1964). With a chilling reminder of how human beings can be reduced to the status of things which are 'completely scientifically knowable and completely controllable' through sleep deprivation and lobotomy and other experiments, he shows why Iago is such an 'alarming' figure for a modern audience growing up in the aftermath of the Nazi death camps and during the political surveillance of the Cold War years (*DH*, p. 270).

In the final session of the Shakespeare lectures that Auden gave in New York in 1946–47, he returned to the idea of the playwright 'holding the mirror up to nature', associating this with the 'continual process of simplification' in his work.[12] Although the early sonnets speak ambitiously about 'outlasting time', Shakespeare seems increasingly to suggest, as Theseus does in *A Midsummer Night's Dream*, that 'The best in this kind are but shadows' (5.1.214). Auden finds a refreshing lack of self-importance in Shakespeare: 'To be able to devote one's life to art without forgetting that art is frivolous is a tremendous achievement of personal character. Shakespeare never takes himself too seriously'. In the same lecture, however, he reminds his listeners that 'It is a temptation to everybody to invent their own Shakespeare'.[13] Auden's Shakespeare is a writer who speaks eloquently and urgently to modern readers in ways that prefigure and illuminate their own troubled psychological, religious and political preoccupations. He is also a writer who gives Auden the confidence and authority to disclose himself: 'I am that I am, and they that level / At my abuses reckon up their own'.

NOTES

1 William Shakespeare, *The Sonnets*, ed. W. H. Auden (Signet, 1964), p. 161.
2 Sonnet 53. Ibid., p. 93.
3 W. H. Auden, *Lectures on Shakespeare*, ed. Arthur Kirsch (Faber and Faber, 2000), p. 93.
4 *Lectures on Shakespeare*, p. 306.
5 Ibid., p. 307.
6 W. H. Auden, '*The Sea and the Mirror*', ed. Arthur Kirsch (Princeton University Press, 2003), p. 5. Hereafter cited within the text as '*S&M*'. 'The Sea and the Mirror' is also to be found in *SP* (both editions) and *CP* 2007.
7 These closing lines of the 'Preface' are a conflation of speeches in *Hamlet* (5.2.369) and *King Lear* (5.2.11).
8 *Lectures on Shakespeare*, p. 306.

9 The speech echoes that of Richard III: 'Richard loves Richard; that is, I am I' (5.5.137).

10 These descriptions are Arthur Kirsch's, *S&M*, pp. xxv, 87.

11 *The Sonnets*, p. 151.

12 *Lectures on Shakespeare*, p. 319.

13 Ibid., p. 308.

CHAPTER XXVI

Yeats

Michael O'Neill

For Auden, Yeats is both a version of that mythic personage 'the Adversary' who appears in the early poem 'Taller to-day' and an exemplary figure (*EA*, p. 26). Indeed, 'the Adversary' who 'put too easy questions / On lonely roads' and possesses semi-comic menace gestures, not wholly irreverently, towards the rough beasts, anti-selves, and antithetical others thronging Yeats's work. The rebirth of Yeatsian tropes and concerns in Auden can be disconcerting and even disturbing, and yet it bears witness to a dynamic, living relationship.

Auden is among the stronger poets, to borrow Harold Bloom's language, to feel the need to exorcize the spirit of Yeats. As Stan Smith implies at the start of a perceptive discussion ('Persuasions to Rejoice: Auden's Oedipal Dialogues with W. B. Yeats', *AS II*, pp. 155–63), the younger poet's effort to reject Yeats on the grounds that 'he has become for me a symbol of my own devil of unauthenticity' is a testament to the Irish poet's diabolic power (quoted *AS II*, p. 155); 'poetry for Auden', Smith notes, commenting on Auden's remark, 'is … necessarily of the Devil's party, an equivocal and treacherous mode of utterance perpetually betraying its user' (*AS II*, p. 155). The equivocal treacheries involved in Auden's attempts to make Yeats the scapegoat for poetry's infatuation with 'unauthenticity' – that is, 'false emotions, inflated rhetoric, empty sonorities' (Auden, quoted *AS II*, p. 155) – are often imaginatively productive.

The complications latent in the case mounted by Auden against Yeatsian magic are instructive here. In Yeats's 'utter lack of effort to relate his esthetic Weltanschauung with that of science' (*Prose II*, p. 62), as Auden put it in a 1940 review of his *Last Poems*, Yeats appeared to Auden to embrace an intellectually disreputable cultic view of the art. For what holds sway, especially in Auden's post-1930s work, is the 'counter-truth' – to borrow Yeats's word from 'The Circus Animals' Desertion'[1] – that 'Poetry is not magic. Insofar as poetry, or any other of the arts, can be said to have an ulterior purpose, it is, by telling the truth, to disenchant and disintoxicate' (*DH*, p. 27). In his brilliant counterpointing of the two poets, Richard Ellmann sets this comment against the early Yeats's view that 'The proper metaphor for poetry is magic'.[2] But, true to his fascination with conflict, dialectic, and contraries, Yeats is also a poet who seeks to 'wither into the truth' ('The Coming of Wisdom with Time'), or to cast off an increasingly threadbare 'coat / Covered with embroideries / Out of old mythologies' ('A Coat'). Conversely, the Auden who abjures poetic magic also, as Ellmann notes, 'repeatedly emphasizes that poetry is a rite, surrounded with awe' (Ellmann 1967, p. 124). This poet knows that poetry is not an art for the good, decent moral majority: they may be 'nice', 'Kind and efficient', but 'Have they ever', the poet wonders, 'Wanted so much to see a unicorn, even / A dead one?' ('A Healthy Spot'; *CP* 2007, p. 327). Clearly, the speaker has felt the unicorn-spotting urge and, to this degree, is on the side of the Yeatsian desire for visions, whether of rough beasts or 'golden apples of the sun' ('The Song of Wandering Aengus'). Here and elsewhere, Auden may send up his own impulse to romanticize, to trust in 'the luck of verbal playing', but the sending-up cannot disguise a dislike, in poetry, of 'Plain cooking made still plainer by plain cooks' ('The Truest Poetry is the Most Feigning'; *CP* 2007, p. 617), where the triple use of 'plain' or its cognates makes the point with cheerful brio.

For Auden, as for Yeats, 'Processions that lack high stilts have nothing that catches the eye' ('High Talk'). Audenesque stilts differ from Yeatsian ones; they have access to ironic buttons that can make stilts fold snappily away. But Yeats, too, can undercut his own 'masterful images' ('The Circus Animals' Desertion'). Admittedly, Yeats may mythologize his own de-mythologizing, enchant through evocations of his own disenchantments, and intoxicate through the strong poetic drink of sour disintoxications, as when in 'Meru' he speaks of man as 'Ravening, raging and uprooting that he may come / Into the desolation of reality': the last line, there, enacting a let-down after the expectant verb 'come', but also sounding like a resonant discovery. Yet the lure of this 'desolation' is as strong in his work as is the witchery of Celtic myth. Yeats's poetry involves an unresting remaking of the poetic self. He recycles symbols and lyric plots, but over and over he refashions and refigures. He revises earlier work, most famously 'The Sorrow of Love', a *fin-de-siècle* mythic sigh of a lyric remodelled in the 1920s to assume later Yeats's more Byzantine-gong-like music; leading Louis MacNeice, for one, to regret the transformation: 'The poem is no longer languid', writes MacNeice, 'but it no longer rings true' (MacNeice 1967, p. 71).[3]

Auden is quick to revise earlier poetry, and in his readiness to recast poems and impose near-arbitrary patterns of ends and beginnings on his career he shows that Yeats's practice was not lost on him. Admittedly, for Auden, the motive for revision is less aesthetic than ethical, as when he seeks, notoriously, to limit the damage caused by lines that struck him later as 'dishonest' such as the close of 'Spain'. But his fear of dishonesty and 'unauthenticity' cannot disguise his sense of poetry as a virtuosic contraption that can exceed its own knowingness. One lesson learned from Yeats is the importance of continual development for the significant poetic career. In 'Yeats As An Example' (1948) he praises Yeats as a 'major poet', defined thus: 'the major poet not only attempts to solve new problems, but the problems he attacks are central to the tradition, and the lines along which he attacks them, while they are his own, are not idiosyncratic, but produce results which are available to his successors' (*Prose II*, p. 388). Auden saw aspects of Yeats's beliefs as 'idiosyncratic', and has more than a little sympathy for the 'Public Prosecutor' of 'The Public v. the late Mr. William Butler Yeats', who asks, 'What are we to say of a man whose earliest writings attempted to revive a belief in fairies and whose favourite themes were legends of barbaric heroes with unpronounceable names, work which has been aptly and wittily described as Chaff about Bran?' (*EA*, p. 391). But it was clear to him that 'the problems [Yeats] attacks are central to the tradition' and that his solutions 'produce results which are available to his successors'.

Ellmann sees it as emblematic of fundamental differences that Yeats was drawn to towers and Auden to lead-mines, the Irish poet fascinated by the expansion and control of mind, the English by 'the self's buried workings' (Ellmann 1967, p. 110). But, to adapt Ellmann's title ('Gazebos and Gashouses') and an implicit emphasis of his chapter for my own purposes, Auden's gashouses gather to themselves as much enchantment as do Yeats's gazebos. In many poems of the 1930s, Auden appeared to be a tight-lipped clinician of emotional fevers, diagnosing rather than suffering affective states. This impression can mislead, and calls to mind, if only as a complex parallel, Yeats's wish to write a poem 'maybe as cold / And passionate as the dawn ('The Fisherman'), where the two adjectives behave as though they were near-synonyms, but inflect each other in surprising ways. Auden, too, in ways that suggest a careful reading of Yeats, contrives to write poems in the 1930s and beyond that were simultaneously 'cold' and 'passionate'.

Passion may be withheld in Auden's love poems, and, in fact, a poem such as 'Love by ambition' (*EA*, p. 30) impresses less as a love poem than as a cold-eyed, psychoanalytic, and post-Darwinian investigation of the passion whose presiding rhythmical presence is Laura Riding. But the 'Love' who 'Designs his own unhappiness / Foretells his own death and is faithless' has something in common with the Yeats of poems such as 'The Wild Swans at Coole', telling us of his sore-hearted state in a fashion that is, for the most part, vigilantly latent and self-aware. 'Their hearts have not grown old', for example, tells the reader that the poet's heart *has*, but does so the more successfully for not saying so explicitly. It stands in subtle relation to the earlier assertion, 'And now my heart is sore', a line that seems blatantly emotional, but cunningly refrains from saying whether the soreness is a momentary or abiding state, and prepares us for the later suggestion that the poet's true sorrow is less a sudden pang than a changed and not wholly definable state, even if the former serves as evidence of the latter.

Yeats sponsored not only nuance and qualification in Auden, but also bravura performance. As MacNeice notes, 'Yeats's latter-day trend towards ballad finds a parallel in W. H. Auden and implies a recognition that "light" verse is not the logical contrary of serious verse' (MacNeice 1967, p. 149). In fact, Yeats's balladic endeavours leave their impression on Auden's highly serious experiments with 'light' verse in the 1930s. Poems in 'Words for Music Perhaps' (first published as a sequence in *The Winding Stair* in 1933, although some had appeared in periodicals before this date) license Auden's own brilliant and enigmatic experiments in the genre. The Yeats who writes, 'So never hang your heart upon / A roaring, ranting journeyman. / *Fol de rol, fol de rol*' ('Crazy Jane Reproved'), has more than a little kinship with the Auden of a poem such as 'O who can ever gaze his fill'. Auden concludes one stanza with a refrain that is sympathetic to Yeats's blend of cavalier recklessness and deep disillusion, and yet imbued with a post-Freudian despair that makes the poem both diagnostic and personally despairing:

> *The greater the love, the more false to its object*
> *Not to be born is the best for man*
> *After the kiss comes the impulse to throttle*
> *Break the embraces, dance while you can.*
> (*EA*, p. 205)

That 'impulse to throttle', hard on the heels of the Sophoclean allusion, shows Auden out-Yeatsing Yeats in the suave brutality of its tonal modulation. Yeats alludes to the same Sophoclean sentiment in the concluding stanza of the final lyric in his 'A Man Young and Old' sequence from

The Tower, and it is probable that Auden recalls, yet transforms, that Yeatsian moment in his ballad. Yeats uses ballad to set the energies of the oral tradition against the mechanistic, anti-libidinous strictures of the new Irish Free State; Auden makes the ballad sing jaunty, masked, and quietly terrifying tales about civilisation and its many discontents.

In 1943, Auden expressed the view that Yeats's poems lacked a 'certain inner resonance' (*Prose II*, p. 174). But that is not the sense given by his poetry's interaction with his forebear's work. To read the early poem 'I chose this lean country' (*EA*, p. 439) is to recognize, in its open remodelling of the final section of Yeats's 'The Tower', how Auden's taut style drew immediate sustenance from the older poet's practice. Auden read 'The Tower' in the *Criterion*, in June 1927, and borrows Yeats's use of the first person as well as his deployment of a drumming but complexly controlled trimeter line with vigilant off-rhymes. *Pace* Ellmann, the poets cannot be distinguished on the grounds of 'the talk of love' being 'unifying' in Yeats and enforcing 'a separation' in Auden (Ellmann 1967, p. 104). 'The Tower' ends on a down-beat as it imagines the onset of old age, turning experience into 'a bird's sleepy cry / Among the deepening shades': 'deepening' allows no escape from the poem's shelving towards the only end of age (even if Yeats is able to imagine post-mortal states beyond death). Auden's early poem, which he would revise to make the echoes of Yeats less marked (see *EA*, p. 28), is certainly drawn towards the isolated subjectivity coiled within the use of 'I' in the third section of 'The Tower'. At the same time, this isolated subjectivity seeks to generalize itself: 'I think how everyman / Shall strain and be undone' (*EA*, p. 440). The story of Auden's poetry, so far as the communication of affective states is concerned, has to do with the shifting negotiations between an 'I' which is the more compellingly present for its conspicuous absence (as in this poem's revised version) and a strong wish to speak to and on behalf of an 'everyman'.

In later poems, Auden puts the money of his feelings less on such universalizing than on the capacity of the poet, in whom language dwells and has its being, to initiate and undertake something close to individualist quest. For Auden, poetry's work has a design on its reader, even if that design is to liberate the reader from the designs of others. That purpose expresses itself in different ways in his 1930s poetry, but often implicitly obeys the injunction to 'Make action urgent and its nature clear' (*EA*, p. 157). This does not quite commit itself to a specific programme of 'action', and if in many Auden poems of the period there is a 'clear' sense that 'action' is 'urgent', it coexists with a refusal to preach. 'All I have is a voice / To undo the folded lie' (*EA*, p. 246), he writes in 'September 1, 1939', and the mingled humility and pride in the lines represent Auden's adaptation of a Yeatsian voice audible in vocational declarations, such as: 'These, these remain, but I record what's gone' ('Fallen Majesty'), or the proudly doubt-surrounded commitment of 'I write it out in a verse' ('Easter 1916').

In fact, in his commitment to poetry Yeats embodies a standard of aesthetic value that takes on ethical significance for Auden. In 'Yeats as an Example' (1948) he praises Yeats for having 'transformed a certain kind of poem, the occasional poem, from being either an official performance of impersonal virtuosity or a trivial *vers de société* into a serious reflective poem of at once personal and public interest'. He cites as an example 'In Memory of Major Robert Gregory', commending it as a poem that 'never loses the personal note of a man speaking about his personal friends in a particular setting ... and at the same time the occasion and the characters acquire a symbolic public significance' (*Prose II*, p. 388). The praise might apply with modifications (there is little sense of the dedicatee as a personal friend) to 'In Memory of W. B. Yeats', the poem in which Auden seeks to come to terms most deeply and definitively with a writer whose politics and poetry he was troubled by in different ways (the former for its proto-Fascism, the latter for its temptations to sonorous insincerity), but whose 'gift', as he puts it memorably, 'survived it all'. In making this remark in the poem's second section, Auden sought to make the poem more personal by turning from third-person statement to second-person address in printings after the poem's first appearance. As Edward Mendelson notes, the praise remains troubled, because Auden could never lose the sense that 'in both life and art the gift was not enough'; for Mendelson, it is the reason why 'Auden mistrusted Yeats as an ally even when he defended him' (*LA*, p. 21).

But, as Mendelson makes clear, Auden was as drawn to the 'gift' as much as Yeats was to the entangling manoeuvres and visitations of his anti-self or 'Daimon'. 'In Memory of W. B. Yeats' (*EA*, pp. 241–43) approaches the question of Yeats's 'gift' by degrees. Formally, its three sections show a progression from the unrhymed free verse of the first section to the more iambic and rhymed, though conversational, second section, to the measured and complexly celebratory trochaic quatrains of the third section. The three sections offer, first, a sense of Yeats as divided from his poems and words by the fact of his physical death; second, a dual declaration that poetry (including Yeats's) 'makes nothing happen' but is 'A way of happening'; and third, an implicit defence of Yeats because, despite his reactionary views, he, like Kipling and Claudel, will be pardoned by 'Time' for 'writing well'. The elegy moves towards its close by way of a rhyme crucial to Yeats, between 'voice' and 'rejoice'. Auden requests that the poet 'follow right / To the bottom of the night' and asks: 'With your unconstraining voice / Still persuade us to rejoice'. He sees the older poet as able to 'follow' where his muse led him, namely, on a journey into 'the bottom of the night', almost like an unbelieving mystic.

Stan Smith reads the elegy as establishing Auden's 'claim to supplant Yeats' and offers detailed intertextual evidence for the poem itself as enacting the process by which 'The words of a dead man / Are modified in the guts of the living' (*AS II*, pp. 163, 162). But Smith's Bloomian argument ignores the subtle grace by which Auden allows authority to the words of the 'dead man'. If it is, to pursue an ambiguity highlighted by Smith (*AS II*, p. 158), Yeats who must 'follow right / To the bottom of the night', he is 'following' his destiny; if it is the later poet who must 'follow' Yeats, then that following is indeed a succession, but also a concession. Yeats emerges as the trailblazer. The confrontation with the nocturnal abyss will yield further reason to 'rejoice'. The implication is that Yeats's refusal to 'constrain' his voice has the 'tragic gaiety' which he applauds in his 'Lapis Lazuli'. Auden's rejoicing Yeats is still a rhetorician who must 'persuade us to rejoice', for all the Irish poet's distinction between rhetoric and poetry, and the phrase concedes much to Yeats: it allows his poetry to be 'A way of happening' which it is appropriate for the reader to allow to happen.

Yeats's poetry was a way of happening from which Auden could evolve his own verbal modes of being. 'Summer Night' (as titled on its first publication in *The Listener* in 1934), 'September 1, 1939', and 'The Shield of Achilles' are among the poems that reveal Auden's debt to the Yeats who 'released stanzaic poetry, whether reflective or lyrical, from iambic monotony' (*Prose II*, p. 388). For Auden, the Yeats of poems such as 'Among School Children' or 'The Results of Thought' produced work which offered both 'coherent dignity and music' and 'freedom for the most natural and lucid speech' (*Prose II*, p. 389). Similar praise can be extended to the Auden who notes wryly in 'Summer Night' how he and his friends 'Look up, and with a sigh endure / The tyrannies of love' (*EA*, p. 137), manipulating his rhythms to imitate a balancing act that gives 'love' its due, while recognizing the dire urgencies posed by 'tyrannies' of a more public kind; or who deploys rhyme royal in alternation with a more clipped eight-line stanza in 'The Shield of Achilles' to set modern barbarity and mythic tragedy in sharp juxtaposition and connection; or who, in 'September 1, 1939' alludes in his title to a famous Yeatsian poem

'September 1913' and in his complexly rhyming eleven-line stanza finds from the poem's start 'freedom for the most natural and lucid speech':

> I sit in one of the dives
> On Fifty-Second Street
> Uncertain and afraid
> As the clever hopes expire
> Of a low dishonest decade ...
> (*EA*, p. 245)

All the adjectives, there, have an Audenesque quality of stringent intelligence. But they also show immersion in the Yeats who demonstrates for Auden that 'In lyric writing what matters more than anything else, more than subject-matter or wisdom, is diction' (*Prose II*, p. 63). Part of Yeats's bequest to poets is a diction that can accommodate the seemingly prosaic and inform it with a new power: 'The unfinished man and his pain / Brought face to face with his own clumsiness' in 'A Dialogue of Self and Soul', for example, where the language, from the elision forced between the first two words to the awkwardness enacted in the final phrase, empathizes with the 'pain' of confronting one's 'own clumsiness'. Throughout poems such as 'September 1, 1939' Auden's language is more evidently demotic, but it rehearses in its own way Yeats's interplay between the poet's individual self and the society of which he is a part.

Yeats prompts Auden to judgement, in part, because passing judgement on others and self, often in the form of questions, is a central theme and activity in the Irish poet's work: 'Did that play of mine send out / Certain men the English shot?' he wonders in 'The Man and the Echo', tormented by the thought that poetry (or drama) does or did make things happen. For the poet weighing cultures in his imaginative scales or compiling an anthology of modern poetry and rejecting Wilfred Owen (as Yeats did), judgement is inseparable from the attempt to 'hold in a single thought reality and justice', as he wrote of the 'stylistic arrangements of experience' proffered by his *A Vision*.[4] This systematizing and judging Yeats has fascinating affinities with the Auden who, when 'reading a poem', asks both how this 'verbal contraption' works and 'What kind of guy inhabits this poem?' (*DH*, pp. 50, 51), who incessantly composes antithetical lists (writers as Alices or Mabels, for example), and who, in his semi-comic but deeply serious prose accompaniment to his elegy for Yeats, uses the device of speeches prosecuting and defending the poet to articulate his ambivalence and his tricky, even tricksy, conviction that 'art is a product of history, not a cause' (*EA*, p. 393).

In that piece, Auden distinguishes 'one field in which the poet is a man of action, the field of language', and, for all its deft sophistries, there is no doubting the intensity of his belief that 'The diction of *The Winding Stair* is the diction of a just man, and it is for this reason that just men will always recognise the author as a master' (*EA*, p. 393). The very form of this sentence suggests that Yeats's 'mastery' is proof of his 'just' dealings with language, and the imperious force of the older poet's work registers in the younger man's prose, just as it does in many of Auden's rhetorical variations on Yeatsian manoeuvres. It is as though Auden suspects that Yeats is, indeed, a 'master', whereas he is, at best, a self-aware virtuoso. Not that he has a monopoly on self-awareness. Each poet leavens high artistic accomplishment with doubt, made to face, in Yeats's case, the necessary promptings of 'The foul rag and bone shop of the heart', or, in Auden's, the fact that 'the heart, / As ZOLA said, must always start / The day by swallowing its toad / Of failure and disgust' ('New Year Letter'; *CP* 2007, p. 239). When Auden rises to the heights, as at the end of 'September 1, 1939', he fends off Yeats through an explicit identification with 'Ironic points of light'; but that identification belongs to his prayer that he might 'Show an affirming flame'. Yeats (as read by Auden) assumes that, by virtue of being what it is, his poetry shows such a flame, and his uncomplacent faith inspires Auden to gaze into, or to know he is deliberately not gazing into, 'the bottom of the night' with a new freedom and eloquence, in work composed from the late-1930s onwards.

Both poets seek to affirm, both to test secular rationalism to the limits and beyond. If Auden concludes many poems with prayer or request, Yeats finishes with question or declaration, as when he ends 'A Dialogue of Self and Soul' with an uncompromising assertion: 'We are blest by everything, / Everything we look upon is blest'. There, a chiastic enfolding swaddles reality in the poet's blessing, the more striking for erupting so unexpectedly after the tortuous tracking 'to its source' of 'Every event in action or in thought'. When Auden speaks of blessing, he invokes it as a secular prayer, at the close of 'Lay your sleeping head, my love'; the last stanza prays for the beloved that 'the winds of dawn' will 'Such a day of sweetness show / Eye and knocking heart may bless' (*EA*, p. 207). As always in the drama of influence, there is difference here, but the collocation of 'sweetness' and 'bless' speaks eloquently about Auden's admiration for the diction of a major poem in *The Winding Stair* and serves to remind us of the pervasive, complex reworkings of Yeats that take place throughout the younger poet's work.

NOTES

1 All Yeats's poetry will be cited from *Yeats's Poems*, edited and annotated by A. Norman Jeffares, with an appendix by Warwick Gould (1989; Macmillan, 1991).

2 Richard Ellmann, *Eminent Domain: Yeats among Wilde, Joyce, Pound, Eliot and Auden* (Oxford University Press, 1967), p. 124. Hereafter cited in the text as Ellmann, 1967.

3 Louis MacNeice, *The Poetry of W. B. Yeats*, with a foreword by Richard Ellmann (Faber and Faber, 1967), p. 71. Hereafter cited in the text as 'MacNeice 1967'.

4 Quoted in *The Poems of W. B. Yeats: A Sourcebook*, ed. Michael O'Neill (Routledge, 2004), pp. 28, 27.

CHAPTER XXVII

Eliot

Hugh Haughton

I

Eliot's judgement about Yeats, that he was 'part of the consciousness of an age which cannot be understood without [him]', is equally true of Auden and Eliot himself. For Auden, however, consciousness of the presiding spirit of Eliot was integral to his understanding of his own age, and much of his work involves a subliminal dialogue with his predecessor.

Asked whether he was American or English, Eliot replied 'whichever Mr Auden is, I am not'.[1] Despite their generational and other differences, however, the two poets had much in common. Both took their bearings from both sides of the Atlantic; both their careers were shaped by 'conversion' to orthodox Anglican Christianity; and both moved from publically embracing the aesthetically revolutionary to the culturally conservative. Publishing under their initials rather than their first names, both shared a fascination with poetic form, an interest in reviving poetic drama, a distrust of Romanticism, and a love of Dryden, Herbert, Tennyson, Kipling, Edward Lear, detective stories, hagiography, theology, liturgy, and cross-words. Both rewrote Shakespeare (Eliot in 'Coriolan', Auden in 'The Sea and the Mirror'), composed Christian dramas (*Murder in the Cathedral*, 'For the Time Being'), and relished light verse and the bawdy (Eliot's *Possum's Book of Practical Cats* and Bolo poems, Auden's 'Academic Graffiti' and 'The Platonic Blow'). Both assumed the role of influential public intellectual, while as poets they combined the pedantic and the vernacular, traded in learned allusions, and were committed to tradition as well as modernity, composing a series of esoterically ironic lyrics as well as ambitious sequences that sought to embody the *Zeitgeist*. Eliot, lecturing in Virginia in 1933, said that 'one is what one is, and the damage of a lifetime, and of having been born into an unsettled society, cannot be repaired at the moment of composition'.[2] That sense of cultural 'damage' unites the two poets, who always wrote as poets of civilization rather than the private self. 'Whichever Mr. Auden is, I am not' may have held good in terms of nationality and politics, but not in many other respects.

If, as Edward Mendelson notes, 'Auden's adult career began with a rejection from T. S. Eliot', that negative beginning had positive effects. 'Not more than a few weeks before he received Eliot's rejection', Mendelson continues, Auden wrote 'his first poems in what he would later recognise as his own voice' (*EA*, p. xiii). 'Who stands, the crux left of the watershed', dated August 1927, was the earliest of these. The following January, his poem 'Control of the passes was, he saw, the key' noted that 'The street music seemed gracious now to one / For weeks up in the desert. Woken by water …' (*EA*, p. 25): the desert, the key, the water, even the street music subliminally recall *The Waste Land*, a poem in which the word 'Control' looms large in the final movement. They also, however, suggest the younger poet's control of the passes into a 'new district' of his own. That his sense of a 'watershed' coincided with his submission of the early poems to Eliot in June 1927 and their rejection that autumn, is, as everything was for Auden, symbolic. So, too, was Faber's eventual publication of his first book in 1930, at the outset of what became the Auden decade. He was the first of the new generation Eliot put his firm's money on, a gamble that led subsequently to his publishing all of Auden, Spender, and MacNeice. This meant that 1930s Leftist poetry was largely printed under the strange auspices of the author of *After Strange Gods*. In response, whereas Eliot continued to 'represent' Auden as his publisher, Auden in his poetry and prose sought to represent his own deep but also deeply ambivalent feelings about Eliot as poetic predecessor and intellectual sponsor.

II

In their first letters to each other, Eliot acted as a friendly commentator and adviser on Auden's early verse, while Auden treated his publisher with respectful gratitude, even to the point of asking for advice on which way to vote in the 1933 general election. In his early verse, however, Auden was less uniformly respectful. In his uncollected letter poem, 'Happy New Year' (1932), he cooked up a revue-style tableau of the British cultural scene which offers a fleeting image of Eliot among his post-war London set: 'Unhappy Eliot choosing his words / And D'Arcy's beautiful head at a glance / I noticed building a sanctum for birds' (*EA*, p. 448). Eliot 'choosing his words' is familiar from accounts of his conversation, but Auden's choice of the word 'Unhappy' is the more telling for being free of parodic intent, because Eliot was indeed 'unhappy' during the period before and after the break-up of his marriage in 1933. The poem associates him with the Catholic apologist Father Martin D'Arcy (acknowledged in the foreword to *After Strange Gods*), alongside the Sitwells, Pound, and the aggressively masculine Wyndham Lewis in drag, 'disguised as a maid'. Auden's account of Eliot and the priest building a 'sanctum' (not a 'sanctuary') for 'birds' may suggest those Eliot had evoked in *The Waste Land* (hermit-thrush, in 'What the Thunder said'), *Ash-Wednesday* VI (quail, plover) and 'Marina' (woodthrush).

Eliot crops up again in Book III of Auden's weirdest cultural fantasia, *The Orators*. Here the older poet figures as part of a celebration of Spring that implicitly sets itself against the 'cruellest month' of *The Waste Land*: 'Spring again / In the buds, in the birds, in the bowels, and the grain' (*EA*, p. 104). Again Eliot figures in an ecclesiastical as well as literary context:

> Where is Lewis? Under the sofa.
> Where is Eliot? Dreaming of nuns.
> Their day is over, they shall decorate the Zoo

The speaker of the Ode isn't Auden, of course, but he must have relished that vision of Eliot 'dreaming of nuns' in the controversial political context of 'the Simonites, the Mosleyites and the I.L.P.' (*EA*, p. 105). In the first edition, the relevant line reads 'Where is Moxon?', with the name of Tennyson's publisher discreetly substituted for that of Auden's. Nonetheless, those in the know would have guessed whom Auden had in mind here in his characteristic role as Herald of Obsolescence. In invoking the 'nuns', he was presumably thinking of the 'silent sister veiled in white and blue' and the 'Blessèd sister' invoked by Eliot in *Ash-Wednesday* (IV and VI), whose day could be considered as 'over' too: yesterday was all the past. Rhyming 'dreaming of nuns' with 'guns', Auden sets up an image of Eliot as an obsolete ecclesiastical contemplative in the street-wise political culture of the 1930s.

In 'A Letter to Lord Byron', from *Letters from Iceland* (1937), Auden takes a number of equally ironic pot-shots at his publisher, as part of a running commentary on *Ulysses*, Surrealist exhibitions, Disney, and almost every aspect of the *Zeitgeist*. A propos of Byron, Auden says he had had a 'packet from the critics', including the two Eliots[3]: George had condemned him as a 'vulgar genius', 'But T. S. Eliot, I am sad to find, / Damns you with: "an uninteresting mind"' (*EA*, p. 182). If this mischievously bites the hand that feeds him, Auden rubs it in by dubbing Eliot's judgement 'A statement which I must say I'm ashamed at', while praising Byron's invention of 'A style whose meaning does not need a spanner, / You are the master of the airy manner' (*EA*, p. 183). While intimating Eliot's manner *does* 'need a spanner', he may also be recalling that in *After Strange Gods* Eliot had written that 'You cannot write satire in the line of Pope or the stanza of Byron': a remark which may have helped prompt Auden's 'Letter', which, although written in *rime royale* rather than *ottava rima*, systematically calls up the ghost of the Byronic stanza.[4] Consciously emulating Byron's 'airy manner', the 'Letter' combines social commentary with autobiography:

> A raw provincial, my good taste was tardy,
> And Edward Thomas I as yet preferred;
> I was still listening to Thomas Hardy
> Putting divinity about a bird;
> But Eliot spoke the still unspoken word;
> For gasworks and dried tubers I forsook
> The clock at Grantchester, the English rook.

Auden's account of his literary conversion here gives Eliot near-divine status; however, it also suggests a certain rueful *Schadenfreude*. Opting for Eliot's poetic settings rather than Rupert Brooke's defines a parting of the ways in literary history as well as his own development, rejecting the Georgian moment symbolized by Edward Thomas, Hardy, and Brooke for the modernity of *The Waste Land*. 'Gasworks and dried tubers' offers a brilliant *reductio ad absurdum* of Eliot's imagery, creating a witty ideogram of his compound vision of a modern industrial Britain.

This account of Auden's transfer of allegiances is not unregretful, however, and the iconic 'English rook' stubbornly outlives the 'gasworks' he forsook it for, just as the traditional stanza he employs outlives Eliot's *vers libre*. Auden was bowled over by Eliot's poem when first introduced to it at Oxford, apparently by Tom Driberg in 1926. Although 'Letter to Lord Byron' represents this as a conversion-experience, it does so with an irreverent irony that satirizes the Eliot ethos: 'At the *Criterion*'s verdict I was mute, / ... And through the quad dogmatic words rang clear, / "Good poetry is classic and austere"' (*EA*, p. 195). While recognizing Eliot as the harbinger of modern subject-matter, the lines betray some uneasiness with a version of modernism that brought in its wake Aquinas, classicism, the *Criterion*, and a 'double-breasted suit'. Auden's satirical portrait of the artist as a young Oxonian, shows him aping the dogmatic classicism of his poetic guru. 'Letter to Lord Byron' deploys the 'uninteresting' Byron to out-wit 'classic and austere' Eliot as well as Auden's own earlier selves, and in doing so offers an airier take on the modern world anatomized in *The Waste Land*. Wyndham Lewis had recognized the central satirical component in Eliot's work, but Auden's satirical Camp is a far cry from his melancholy publisher's. Nonetheless, Auden later cites Eliot's productivity amongst reasons to be cheerful ('Eliot has really stretched his eagle wing'). Hesitating between addressing the Byron letter via 'St. Peter or the Infernal Press', Auden says: 'I'll try the Press. World-Culture is its debtor; / It has a list that Faber couldn't better' (*EA*, p. 198). Here Auden's glowing reference to the Faber 'list' pays implicit tribute to Eliot as a publisher, while the allusion to his 'stretched' wing sets up Eliot's poetry as a cause for rejoicing, alongside Spender, Yeats, MacNeice, and Lewis. The 'eagle wing' suggests, of course, the poet of *Ash-Wednesday* who had asked in mock-exhaustion:

> (Why should the agèd eagle stretch its wings?)
> Why should I mourn
> The vanished power of the usual reign?

Eliot's allusive invocation of gifts and scope, wings and power, lies behind Auden's allusion, which insists on the achievement Eliot's poem seems to doubt for itself. Auden's reference to 'the Infernal Press' surely also offers a joking critique of Eliot's 'primer of modern heresy', *After Strange Gods*. Nevertheless, although the young Leftist sets Eliot beside Lewis, 'lonely old Volcano of the Right', he mixes the generations and the political parties in one catholic embrace. This matches Eliot's equally catholic embrace of Auden, MacNeice, and Spender, in a Faber publishing list that after little more than a decade already vied with the Devil's.

Eliot's gift to Auden of *After Strange Gods* was the occasion, in a letter of 1934, of a rare expression of political differences. Auden said he had read the Primer with great interest, but some of Eliot's 'general remarks' had 'rather shocked' him, because 'if put into practice in a political scale' they would 'produce a world in which neither I nor you I think would like to live'.[5] We can assume he was thinking of Eliot's notorious claim about 'free-thinking Jews', later quoted in 'For the Time Being' (1943). There, the narrator comments sardonically that 'the recent restrictions / Upon aliens and free-thinking Jews are beginning / To have a salutary effect on public morale' (*CP* 2007, p. 373).[6] In Eliotic style, Auden's weasel-worded speaker also talks of 'Transmitting an everlasting opportunity / That the Kingdom of Heaven may come, not in the present / And not in our future, but in the Fullness of Time'. Eliot seems to have been unusually forbearing about the ways Auden alluded to him, and this war-time echo of *After Strange Gods* offers a grimly serious retort to it (of a piece with Auden's contemporary essay on Christian anti-Semitism 'Children of Abraham'; *Prose II*, pp. 224–26).

Neither Auden nor Eliot, despite their very different politics, seemed to think of the other as on the 'other side'. Making common cause with Eliot in a letter of 1935, Auden reported that some 'idiot on the wireless' had said that 'the Four Knights' (in *Murder in the Cathedral*) 'talked like the Western Brothers'. This prompted him to suggest he and Eliot should offer a music-hall double-act at the Holborn Empire, as 'a dialogue between a Female Impersonator and Goose'.⁷ The joke recognizes their common interest in popular comic theatre; Auden's interest was evident in *The Dance of Death* (1933), where the Announcer asked 'Do you care for Musical Comedy, Worm's eye view, red lips?' (*Plays*, p. 83), while Eliot's figured in *The Use of Poetry and the Use of Criticism* where he said that 'the poet aspires to the condition of the music-hall comedian'.⁸ In his essay on 'Marie Lloyd' Eliot paid tribute to one of the great popular music-hall entertainers of the age, and something of this carried over into *Sweeney Agonistes* and *Old Possum's Book of Practical Cats*.⁹ The same could be said of Auden in his satirical revues and popular songs of the 1930s. Although at this time Auden was in many ways diametrically opposed to Eliot, explicitly in 'Letter to Lord Byron', and implicitly in his plays and lyrics, he was also in an ongoing 'dialogue' and even 'double-act' with his publisher.

III

In the 1940s, after his transplantation to the land of Eliot's birth, Auden began to reflect on him in prose as well as verse. The great essay on Hardy and 'Literary Transference' (1940) retells the story of his literary conversion: 'In the autumn of 1924 there was a palace revolution after which [Hardy] had to share his kingdom with Edward Thomas, until finally they were both defeated by Eliot at the battle of Oxford in 1926' (*Prose II*, p. 44). Elaborating on this witty political account of literary influence, Auden observed that 'the provincial England of 1907, when I was born, was Tennysonian in outlook; whatever its outlook the England of 1925 when I went up to Oxford was the Waste Land in character. I cannot imagine any other single writer could have carried me through from the one to the other' (*Prose II*, p. 46). As a 'poetical father', Hardy serves as a bridge between Tennyson and Eliot, with *The Waste Land* serving as a symbolic replacement of *The Idylls of the King* (a brilliant insight, given Tennyson and Eliot's shared roots in medieval romance). In the 'Preface to *Oxford Poetry* 1926' (written with Charles Plumb), Auden had written: 'If it is a natural preference to inhabit a room with casements upon Fairyland, one at least of them should open upon the Waste Land' (*Prose I*, p. 3). In a later essay, Auden said Eliot 'had made it possible for English poetry to deal with all the properties of modern city life, and to write poems in which the structure is musical rather than logical' (*Prose II*, p. 388). The notion of a land under a curse permeates early Auden, and these words suggest just how much his musical poetry of 'modern city life' owed to Eliot's.

Auden's view of the modern waste land was changed, as Eliot's was, by his religious conversion. This clearly changed his view of Eliot, too. Edward Mendelson observed that his 'first clear statement of his new beliefs, outside his circle of intimates, was in a letter to T. S. Eliot on 17 December 1940' (*LA*, p. 158). There the momentous announcement appears alongside a list of errata for '*New Year Letter*':

> I think a lot about you and whether you are safe, the more so because thanks to Charles Williams and Kierkegaard, I have come to pretty much the same position as yourself, which I was brought up to anyway (Please don't tell anyone about this).

Eliot had been discreet about his own conversion, before nailing his colours to the mast in *For Lancelot Andrews* (1928). Auden's private acknowledgement to the most famous Christian convert of his time of his own is startlingly oblique: there is no mention of Christ, Christianity, or the Church, no 'Road to Damascus' experience, just an acknowledgement that he has 'come to pretty much the same position'.

Auden's public tribute to Eliot reaches its apogee in an essay on 'Vocation and Society' of 1943, which ended:

> I cannot conclude more fittingly than with the closing lines from the most recent poem of the greatest poet now living, one in whom America and England may both rejoice, one whose personal and professional example are to every other and lesser writer at once an inspiration and a reproach, Mr. T. S. Eliot. (*Prose II*, p. 182)

He goes on to quote from the end of the recently published *Little Gidding*. We can hear the converted Auden, at this critical juncture, aware not only of 'the voice of this Calling' but the call of Eliot's voice as 'an inspiration and reproach'. Initially aesthetically converted by *The Waste Land*, Auden has transferred his allegiance to the devotional author of *Four Quartets*. He may also have hoped that Eliot's enabling 'America and England' to rejoice in his poetry would apply in time to his own case.

Their shared Christianity didn't mean the poets adopted 'the same position' on all fronts. Auden's review of *Notes Towards the Definition of Culture* articulated not only how complicated a figure he recognized Eliot to be, but his own more complicated attitude towards him, revealed in the wariness of its appreciation ('the value of Mr. Eliot's book is not the conclusions he reaches, most of which are debateable, but the questions he raises'). These complications are made apparent in a typically perceptive cartoon parable in *The New Yorker* (23 April 1949):

> Like most important writers Mr. T. S. Eliot is not a single figure but a household. The household has … at least three permanent residents. First, there is the archdeacon, who believes in and practices order, discipline and good manners, social and intellectual, with a thoroughly Anglican distaste for evangelical excess … And no wonder, for the poor gentleman is condemned to be domiciled with a figure of a very different stamp, a violent and passionate old peasant grandmother, who has witnessed murder, pogroms, famine, flood, fire, everything; who has looked into the abyss and, unless restrained, would scream the house down … Last … there is a young boy who likes to play slightly malicious practical jokes. The too earnest guest, who has come to interview the Reverend, is startled and bewildered by finding an apple-pie bed or being handed an explosive cigar. (*Prose III*, p. 97)

Although the review's title, 'Port and Nuts with the Eliots', suggests conventional matrimonial gentility (very unlike Eliot's first marriage), it actually refers to the incorrigibly plural nature of Eliot himself. Like the earlier reference to the 'female impersonator', Auden's Household Eliot includes a female dimension represented by this barely-controllable 'peasant grandmother' threatening social disruption. The 'malicious practical jokes' pick up the joke in the title of *Old Possum's Book of Practical Cats*. But if the Reverend Eliot is compromised by his less dignified relatives, he is also in some sense humanized and redeemed by them.

After Eliot's death, Auden made more explicit what was latent in those 'pogroms' witnessed by the grandmother when he re-invoked the Trinitarian Eliot for an Austrian audience in 1968. Now, Eliot 'consisted, firstly, of the American pre-Jacksonian aristocrat', secondly 'the little boy aged 12, adoring practical jokes such as cushions which fart' and thirdly 'the Yiddish momma who wrote the poems' (see *AS III*, p. 213). In ascribing to Eliot's poems the hysterical Jewish voice he might be thought to have feared, this mischievously returns on the anti-Semitic sentence in *After Strange Gods*. It also catches something of the transnational, shifting, Tiresias-like quality at the heart of the Eliot's work. As Mendelson notes, Auden had already portrayed himself in this guise in the poem

'A Household' and the review's unfamiliar take on the household name of 'T. S. Eliot' is revealing about Auden too. Firstly, the great modernist Auden had come to know so well is translated into Auden's idiosyncratic iconography in a way that dramatizes the contradictions at the heart of his work; secondly, however, it dramatizes the different roles Eliot played in Auden's own symbolic Household as transatlantic twin, poetic father, hysterical mother and religious confessor.

In 1948 Auden returned to Eliot in poetry in 'To T.S. Eliot on His Sixtieth Birthday', an occasional poem relatively free of the Oedipal conflict Stan Smith finds in Auden's elegy for Yeats. Where the elegy for the Irish poet, about whom he harboured intensely ambivalent feelings, provoked Auden's most complex meditation on poetry and modernity, the tribute to Eliot returns upon the Grantchester-like world of an English whodunit (*Nones*, p. 65; CP *2007*, pp. 575–76). In *New Year Letter* Auden had said 'The situation of our time / Surrounds us like a baffling crime' (*NYL*, p. 24; *CP* 2007, p. 203), and in this neat quatrain poem, he draws wittily on the iconography of the detective stories both poets loved. It crosses them, however, with multiple allusions to Eliot's poetic iconography. Referring to 'Blank day after day, the unheard-of drought', Auden says 'it was you / Who, not speechless from shock, but finding the right / Language for thirst and fear, did much to / Prevent a panic': the 'unheard of drought' refers of course to *The Waste Land*. Although he does not explicitly dramatize Eliot as a contemporary Sherlock Holmes, Auden implicitly appeals to the idea of the poet as an Oedipal detective, when he says 'we wait for the Law to take its course'.

In saying Eliot was not 'speechless with shock', Auden implicitly returns to the post-traumatic historical moment of post-war England, where Eliot found the 'right / Language for thirst and fear'. The language for 'thirst and fear' recalls Eliot's poem, with its 'dry stone' and 'no sound of water' and its 'fear in a handful of dust'. The 'library bust' and 'tennis court' conform to the English detective story rather than *The Waste Land*, but the 'bloody corpse' remembers 'the corpse you planted last year in your garden'. Like Auden's poem, Eliot's sequence includes a 'blank' (a card that is 'blank') and a 'key missing' ('We think of the key, each in his prison'). The phrase 'Not speechless' recalls the speaker, back from the Hyacinth garden who says 'I could not / Speak', and the figure later implored to 'Speak to me. Why do you never speak. Speak'. Auden has transformed these various echoes and allusions, translating Eliot's many-voiced, polyglot poem into one of his own dry poetic parables: indeed, a parable about dryness. Choosing his words with care, he once more celebrates the predecessor who 'chooses his words with care'. 'Today' is a key word for Auden (as in 'Taller today, we remember earlier evenings' and 'To-day the struggle' in 'Spain'), and in saying at the close 'We know ... today ... Your sixty years have not been wasted', Auden quietly insists on the public role played by the poet of *The Waste Land* in finding the 'right / Language' for his time. To say Eliot's 60 years have not been 'wasted' recalls and resists, with courteous understatement, the title of *The Waste Land*, as well as the close of 'Burnt Norton' ('Ridiculous the waste sad time / Stretching before and after'). Auden pays tribute to Eliot in a language that is both Eliot's and his own, though without the conflicted intellectual intensity of 'In Memory of W. B. Yeats'.

James Schuyler said that Auden was always 'envious' of Eliot, but when Eliot died, Auden said it was 'hell', confessing: 'To me proof of a man's goodness is his effect upon others. So long as one was in Eliot's presence, one felt it was impossible to do or say anything base'.[10] Auden never wrote at length about Eliot thereafter, even when delivering the first Eliot memorial lectures published as *Secondary Worlds*.[11] At their end, however, he spoke of the 'comfort, in hours of doubt and discouragement' provided by 'the example set, both as a poet and as a human being, by the man in whose memory [the] lectures [were] founded'. Auden's poetry and prose document his complex need to grapple with the legacy of Eliot as a crucial part not only of 'the consciousness of the age' but his own consciousness, and indeed conscience.

NOTES

1 Cited in Eliot's blurb for *For the Time Being*. The comment about Yeats closes the essay on him collected in *On Poetry and Poets*. All Eliot's poetry will be quoted from *The Complete Poems and Plays of T. S. Eliot* (Faber and Faber, 1969).
2 *After Strange Gods*, p. 26.
3 In one of his late *Academic Graffiti*, Auden associates George and T. S. Eliot yet again.
4 *After Strange Gods*, p. 24.
5 Letter of Auden to Eliot of 13.3.34 (cited *LA*, p. 150n.).
6 John Fuller records that Auden told Ansen in 1947 that Eliot had not been annoyed by this reference, which helped make the numbering at Bethlehem more immediate for a modern reader (Fuller 1998, p. 351).
7 Letter to Eliot of 11.06.35.
8 *The Use of Poetry and the Use of Criticism*, p. 32.
9 For Eliot and popular culture, see David Chinitz, *T. S. Eliot and the Cultural Divide* (University of Chicago Press, 2003).

10 *Just the Thing: Selected Letters of James Schuyler*, ed. William Corbett (2004), p. 75; Auden, 'T. S. Eliot, O. M.', *The Listener* (7 January 1965), p. 5.

11 'My only certainty was negative: given his character as a man, and the contemporary critical scene, he would *not* wish me to devote them to his own work'. Instead he would discuss 'questions which were close to his heart, as a poet, as a dramatist, and a twentieth-century Christian' (*SW*, p. 11).

CHAPTER XXVIII

Some Modernists in Early Auden

Gareth Reeves

At the age of thirty, Auden was already being hailed, in the same sentence, as both 'traditional' and 'revolutionary', the juxtaposition gesturing at the multifaceted nature of his genius.[1] This chapter will concentrate on several of the 'revolutionary' literary influences behind his early poems, some of which were arguably no more than passing 'crazes' – to draw on the distinction made by Isherwood between 'influence' and 'craze' in early Auden (*Tribute*, p. 77). One tendency is to periodize these 'revolutionary' aspects, as when John Fuller introduces his indispensable *Commentary*: 'Auden is a poet who after about 1932 began in an almost programmatic way to turn his back on the obscurity and formal freedom and experimentation of modernism. Indeed, he is nowadays sometimes seen as our first post-modernist poet' (Fuller 1998, p. vii). Here 'post-modernist' has its strictly chronological sense. But Rainer Emig thinks of 'post-modernism' as something distinct from, not merely after, modernism, when he finds in the arresting dislocations of Auden's early poetry a post-modernism *avant la lettre*,[2] as also, it appears, does Peter Porter when he writes, 'The riddling locutions, the sense that Auden is taking a scalpel to language itself, which is so marked a quality in his early poetry, can seem almost to make him an anticipator of today's "language poetry"' (*CCWHA*, p. 126). The terminology is unimportant, but these attempts to categorize the early poetry testify to its elusive nature.

According to Isherwood, Auden's undergraduate discovery of *The Waste Land* 'marked a turning-point in his work – for the better, certainly; though the earliest symptoms of Eliot-influence were most alarming. Like a patient who has received an over-powerful inoculation, Auden developed a severe attack of allusions, jargonitis and private jokes' (*Tribute*, p. 76). Although he quickly outgrew the most extreme symptoms of this Eliotosis, marked traces still show in his poetry up to and including *The Orators*. He appears to have taken to heart Eliot's modernist challenge that 'poets in our civilization ... must be *difficult*',[3] and yet one can also sense an anti-modernist need, in Spender's words, to 'somehow connect [the writer's] life again with ... political life and influence it'.[4] Even this early, Auden's poetry, as Michael O'Neill writes, 'sought to negotiate between word and world'.[5] In the early poetry, high modernism's characteristically autotelic preoccupation with epistemology, with how self knows world, struggles with ideological concern over the nature of that world.

That struggle is evident in Auden's dealings with one of his first 'modernist' influences, Laura Riding. Perhaps more a passing craze than enduring influence, she was nevertheless a symptomatically important one, and certainly a more significant presence in the pre-*Orators* poetry than is indicated by Robert Graves's waspish 1955 charge that early on Auden 'borrow[ed]' half-lines and whole lines' from her.[6] In Riding's poetry, modernism's epistemological anxiety makes itself felt in an acute linguistic self-consciousness, which evidently infected Auden's early poetry in the way it 'tak[es] a scalpel to language'. 'And all emotions to expression come', declares his poem 'The strings' excitement, the applauding drum' (*EA*, p. 32), alerting us to the fact that at the heart of much of his early poetry is its awareness of itself as an act of utterance. But self-consciousness stymies, the chief casualty being love: 'Love by ambition / Of definition / Suffers partition' (*EA*, p. 30). The need to find expression frames love in past modes of feeling and perception: 'definition' necessarily entails established ways of thinking; self-awareness destroys the experience even as it is taking place. But the style of the poem 'Love by ambition' inclines towards the ratiocination it would eschew. Like 'Love by ambition', Riding's poem 'The Definition of Love'[7] concerns the dangers of the 'ambition / Of definition'. In both poems, consciousness of love interferes with the experience itself. In fact, Riding's poem could be read as a blueprint for the state of love in Auden's early poetry generally. Barbara Everett's remark about the lover in early Auden being 'an uneasy ghost' who is 'pursued by a past but pursuing a present'[8] could equally well be applied to Riding's poem, which concludes: 'And we remembering forget, / Mistake the future for the past'. Auden seems to have been echoing Riding's 'remembering forget' conundrum in his poem 'To ask the hard question is simple' (*EA*, p. 54–55): 'And forgetting to listen or see / Makes forgetting easy; / Only remembering the method of remembering, / Remembering only in another way': as Edward Mendelson explains, 'the mind ... knows only the fact of its own consciousness' (*Early Auden*, p. 92).

Auden's poetry sounds as though for a short period he was in thrall to a style that did not quite suit, that, in his use, is fascinatingly in danger of not getting beyond style. Riding's poetry is ambitious of definition to a degree that would purge utterance of its variousness so as to attain what in the Preface to her *Selected Poems* she calls 'the general human ideal in speaking'. It eschews language's particularizing and expressive potential; it aspires to the abstract. Her poem 'Death as Death' (*Poems of Riding*, p. 89) is remarkable for its single-minded tracking of thought, and – a quality that would have been immediately apparent to Auden – for its ability to make the reader aware of its language as language even as it unfolds: 'Like nothing – a similarity / Without resemblance' takes the words 'Like nothing' and holds them up for inspection. The poem ends by refusing linguistic compromise: 'the actuality' of death is 'a gift too plain, for which / Gratitude has no language', for the language of poetry involves 'resemblances' and what Riding's Preface calls 'verbal rituals'. But much of Auden's early poetry gets its energy, as well as its elusiveness, largely from precisely such compromise, which makes itself felt in a rich tension between abstraction and image. Behind both his poem 'It was Easter as I walked in the public gardens' (*EA*, pp. 37–40) and Riding's 'The World and I' (*Poems of Riding*, p. 187) is a concern with the approximation between language and experience, self and the world. Riding's poem ends by trying to acquiesce in the approximations of knowledge and language: it is best to be 'sure / … exactly where / Exactly I and exactly the world / Fail to meet by a moment, and a word'. Similar anxieties inform 'It was Easter as I walked', but the first part of this poem comes up against the recognition of a delight in 'An altering speech for altering things, / An emphasis on new names', an attitude which does not recognize that 'general human ideal in speaking' and which indeed gets close, in the words of Riding's Preface, to 'court[ing] sensuosity as if it were the judge of truth'.[9] And frequently in Auden's early poetry, Ridingesque abstraction jostles with the 'sensuosity' of human utterance. Nevertheless the presence of Riding in early Auden highlights that negotiation between word and world which is one of its most arresting qualities, even if at times the effect can be mimicry, even parody.[10]

Auden's way with Riding is characteristic of his way with many of his early influences. It affects any attempt, by himself as well as his reader, to pin the poet down politically, for any commitment, particularly in *The Orators*, gets caught up in linguistic self-consciousness, attitude veering into attitudinizing, the portentous suffering deflation even as it conveys urgency. *The Orators* famously begins by asking us to 'think about England, this country of ours where nobody is well' (*EA*, p. 62), but ends up getting us to think about how the poet is thinking about it, just as Auden did years later in his Foreword to the 1966 reissue: 'My guess to-day is that my unconscious motive in writing it was therapeutic, to exorcize certain tendencies in myself by allowing them to run riot in phantasy'.[11] Disorientation and inner division are at the heart of the work, which deserves Everett's question 'does Auden know that there is no difference between the Airman and the Enemy, or not?'[12] The Airman comes to recognize that the Enemy is himself, and that he must therefore commit suicide: 'The power of the enemy is a function of our resistance, therefore … [t]he only efficient way to destroy it – self-destruction, the sacrifice of all resistance … Conquest can only proceed by absorption of, i.e. infection by, the conquered' (*EA*, p. 93). And *The Orators* is an extended act of stylistic suicide. Stylistically, the poet writes himself out by exaggerating, taking over, and hence taking on, the rhetoric of others. He conquers their voices by absorbing and letting himself be infected by them, in a stylistic 'sacrifice of all resistance', a parodic mélange of modernist, contemporary and earlier sources. The writing is 'therapeutic', exorcizing stylistic symptoms by allowing them to run riot. The wide range of writers and thinkers swallowed and regurgitated by *The Orators* has to be considered in the light of this riotous instability of utterance.

This is the case with Saint-John Perse's *Anabase* of 1924, Eliot's translation of which Auden had recently been reading, and which, with its inscrutable rituals, mysterious leader (the 'Stranger'), nomadic world of unspecified frontier, unexplained destiny, and augured exile, would have immediately appealed to the young Auden. As Fuller remarks, 'much that is oblique, exotic and liturgical' in the first two parts of 'Argument', in *The Orators*, 'seem inspired' by *Anabase* (Fuller 1998, p. 92), a work rather more digested by the poet than is indicated by the phrase 'undigested lumps', which in his 1966 Foreword Auden remembers Eliot to have used to describe the borrowing. *The Orators* borrows the mysteriously prophetic tone while frequently turning it into pastiche and comic grotesquerie. 'A schoolmaster cleanses himself at half-term with a vegetable offering' sounds like a take-off of the sort of activity in *Anabase* practised by the 'Stranger', who 'is offered fresh water / to wash therewith his mouth, his face and his sex', or by the 'widows' who undergo 'purification … among the roses'. *Anabase* begins 'I have built myself' and ends '*Who talks of building?*'[13]; the voice of 'Argument' says in arch archaism, 'I waken with an idea of building' (*EA*, pp. 65, 64). Isherwood commented of Auden's high Anglican upbringing that 'The Anglicanism has evaporated, leaving only the height: he is still [1937] much preoccupied with ritual, in all its forms' (*Tribute*, p. 74). But ritualism tips over into self-parody in the *Anabase* strain of 'Argument'.[14]

Self-parody is also distinctly audible behind Gertrude Stein's presence in *The Orators*. Part III of 'Statement' begins with imitation Stein: 'An old one is beginning to be two new ones. Two new ones are beginning to be two old ones. Two old ones are beginning to be one new one. A new one is beginning to be an old one. Something that has been done, that something is done again by someone. Nothing is being done but something being done again by someone' (*EA*, pp. 70–71). These sentences recall the opening of Stein's *Useful Knowledge*, a source Fuller notes (Fuller 1998, p. 97). They also recall the linguistic and epistemological concerns which interested Auden in Riding's work, and which shadow *The Orators* generally. In fact, it is likely that Auden read about Stein in *A Survey of Modernist Poetry* by Riding and Robert Graves. The book's concluding chapter (in all probability chiefly written by Riding) focuses on Stein as an extreme example of the attempt by 'poetic modernism' to escape history, the outcome being a 'sterilization of words until they are exhausted of history and meaning'. The words of Stein's compositions are 'ideally automatic, creating one another', to produce 'repetition and continuousness and beginning again and again and again', as *A Survey* says, itself breaking into Steinian mode.[15] Stein's project, to strip language of the connotations it has accrued over its history, bears certain similarities to Riding's linguistic preoccupations. Elliott Vanskike argues that the project was part of Stein's search for a way of 'writing that would deny history and static identity'.[16] And Auden's Steinian recollection in *The Orators* is a verbal play on that attempt to break free of inherited and imposed identity which haunts all his early poetry and drama, even if, once again, the recollection characteristically collapses into farce, cocking a snook at a style all too prone to parody.

Other influences behind *The Orators* proved more difficult to exorcize, if only because they had been more thoroughly digested, or were more importunate, or more vital to Auden's development. Hopkins, who was a recent discovery of the literary world and a modernist *avant la lettre* in particular falls into this category. The second Ode (*EA*, pp. 96–98) is written in verse inspired by a mixture of Hopkinsesque sprung rhythm and Anglo-Saxon alliterative form. It celebrates a school rugby victory and Fuller rightly remarks that using the drowned nuns of 'The Wreck of the Deutschland' as a 'model' for the rugby-players is 'bizarre', but it is very much in keeping with the tonal swervings of the poem as a whole. And perhaps Fuller's account, which includes some close comparison with Hopkins, comes across as inappropriate for such a quicksilver performance. For instance, Fuller is right to claim that the Ode 'begins in outrageous parody', pointing out that the first line ('Walk on air do we? And how!') echoes the rhetorical questioning of the poet's heart in stanza 18 of the 'The Wreck' ('Ah, touched in your bower of bone, / Are you!' etc.),[17] but then to maintain that '[o]ddly enough, the idiom is exhilarating rather than deflationary' is expecting the kind of consistency not present in this Ode (Fuller 1998, p. 115). Looking back, Auden testified to the dangers of the overmastering attraction of Hopkins for the young poet: 'Hopkins ought to be kept on a special shelf like a dirty book, and only allowed to readers who won't be ruined by him' (quoted Fuller 1998, p. 5). Eroticism is never far beneath the surface of this Ode, and it frequently erupts in Hopkinsesque verbal extravagance, as in the first stanza's metaphorical medley of high-spiritedness run riot. Is this the poetic equivalent of adolescent exuberance? Or has deliberate overwriting crossed the boundary into bad writing? Is the electrical-cum-physiological landscape comically brilliant or hilariously bad? And it is impossible to tell amongst all the horseplay whether or not the schoolmasterly 'sir' of the tenth stanza is a comic version of Hopkins' godly addressee, especially in the context of this stanza's conflation of revivified cliché and erotic Hopkinsesque distorted rhetoric.

Auden later acknowledged Lawrence's influence, and its fraught potential, when he wrote in his 1966 Foreword: 'And over the whole work looms the shadow of that dangerous figure, D. H. Lawrence the Ideologue'.[18] This is the Lawrence who had declared, in his eccentric, strenuous, and at times outlandish psychoanalytic treatise *Fantasia of the Unconscious*, 'Leaders – this is what mankind is craving for', words which sum up the motive behind *The Orators*. Auden gets much of his thinking and terminology about the fall into knowledge and birth of consciousness from *Fantasia*, which outlines a Freudian matrilineal version of inheritance, personal development, and the process of individuation. Consciousness in the individual comes with the growth of the 'idea of the mother': 'the figure of the mother' gradually develops 'as a *conception* in the child mind' (Lawrence's emphasis). The cause of contemporary unhealthy 'self-consciousness, an intense consciousness', is an unnatural acceleration in this process. A child's sexual drives, aroused too early by the mother's possessiveness, can find no outlet, and '[t]his is how introversion begins'. The lineaments of this argument, and some of its vocabulary, are clearly traceable in *The Orators*' 'Prologue', which anticipates the motherly landscape of 'In Praise of Limestone': 'By landscape reminded once of his mother's figure' (*EA*, p. 61). Auden's hero, unable to take charge of his life and participate in sexual relationships, but nevertheless obsessed by sex and always 'ready to argue' and intellectualize it, is like Lawrence's intro-verted contemporary adolescent whose sensual and spiritual faculties get sundered, and who consequently suffers from 'sex in the head'. But, even as 'Prologue' borrows Lawrence's thought, it undercuts his strenuousness. The lines 'Under the trees the summer bands were playing; / "Dear boy, be brave as these roots", he heard them saying' owe something, but not their suavity, to these sentences from *Fantasia*: 'A huge, plunging, tre-mendous soul. I would like to be a tree for a while. The great lust of roots. Root-lust. And no mind at all'. Auden's 'Dear boy' endearingly deflates *Fantasia*'s egotistic oratory. Those tree-roots tap a dark world in *Fantasia*: 'The true German has something of the sap of trees in his veins even now: and a sort of pristine savageness, like trees, helpless, but most powerful, under all his mentality'.[19]

These Lawrentian echoes raise the issue of *The Orators*' political and ideological leanings. Auden's later disquiet about the political implica-tions of *The Orators*, as expressed in his 1966 Foreword, is in keeping with the Airman's self-division: 'My name on the title-page seems a pseudonym for someone else, someone talented but near the border of sanity, who might well, in a year or two, become a Nazi'.[20] Even so, this older Auden does not quite think himself back into the divided self that generated *The Orators*. Nor could he do so even three months after its publication: 'the result is far too obscure and equivocal. It is meant to be a critique of the fascist outlook, but … I see that it can, most of it, be interpreted as a favourable exposition' (quoted *Early Auden*, p. 104). But the mellifluous-ness of 'Prologue' punctures the stridency of *Fantasia*, indicating that the poet was conscious at some level of Lawrence's incipient Nazism. And what are we to make of the context in which Lawrence appears in the first Ode (*EA*, pp. 94–96) with its comical-heroic idiom? 'The hour in the night when Lawrence died and I came / Round from the morphia': 'Yes, self-regarders' declares this Ode later, and self-regard infects this tonally inscrutable juxtaposition of the poet's wound and Lawrence's death. The same Ode sends up Lawrentian matrilineal obsession with the deliber-ately silly line 'One sniffed at a root to make him dream of a woman'. 'Exorcis[ing] certain tendencies in myself by allowing them to run riot in phantasy' does not come across as 'unconscious' here, even if it is uncontrolled.[21]

In the same vein, the fourth birthday Ode (*EA*, pp. 101–06) offers Lawrentian utopianism in highfalutin doggerel. As Mendelson remarks, this 'imaginary new order will display the primitive fascistic virtues Lawrence demanded in his *Fantasia*' (*Early Auden*, p. 114). This Ode's idea of a hierarchical society, in which 'The few shall be taught who want to understand' and 'Most of the rest shall live upon the land', is a parodic version of *Fantasia*'s imagined society in which 'you must have a higher, responsible, conscious class: and then in varying degrees the lower classes, varying in their degree of consciousness'. Later in *Fantasia*, women are to be prevented from 'reading and becoming self-conscious', a requirement that evidently lies behind Auden's lines 'All of the women and most of the men / Shall work with their hands and not think again'.[22] Smugness overtakes idealism in Auden's utopia, whose citizens shall 'Liv[e] in one place with a satisfied face'. The poet's mockery encompasses self-mockery as he exorcizes the Lawrence within himself. The tonal indirections of *The Orators* imply that he felt apprehensive about the naively retrogressive use to which Lawrence's ideas could be put. He evidently wanted to come to terms with the basic Lawrentian tenet that 'Man fell when he became self-conscious', as he was to write several years later in an essay about Lawrence and education (*Prose I*, p. 414). In that essay, Auden enunciates what *The Orators* seems to have been struggling to articulate: 'the fact that the Fascist countries appear on the surface to be putting [Lawrence's] theories into practice makes their study extremely important to socialists' (*Prose I*, p. 413). In particular, the essay takes issue with the sort of practical application of Lawrence's ideas about learning gestured at in the birthday Ode. One impulse behind the Ode may indeed have been to declare a utopia of manual labour, but its ironically self-satisfied air holds the impulse in check.[23]

This chapter has discussed only a selection of the 'revolutionary' voices present in early Auden. But they all demonstrate that what Isherwood called Auden's 'astonishing adaptability' (*Tribute*, p. 77) was not only a great strength, but also a great challenge: the poet was compelled to rise above the highly skilful and productive imitator, mimic and parodist that he was, to be more than the chameleon artist. What we witness again and again in early Auden is the compulsion to *interrogate* other voices, to locate his own truth and his own often difficult integrity, by taking on those others, especially the many powerful contemporary voices by which he was surrounded.

NOTES

1 'The Reason for This', *New Verse*, Auden Double Number (November 1937), p. 1.
2 Rainer Emig, *W. H. Auden: Towards a Postmodern Poetics* (Palgrave Macmillan, 2000).

3 T. S. Eliot, 'The Metaphysical Poets' (1921), *Selected Prose of T. S. Eliot*, ed. Frank Kermode (Faber and Faber, 1975), p. 65.

4 Stephen Spender, *The Destructive Element: A Study of Modern Writers and Beliefs* (Cape, 1935), p. 19.

5 Michael O'Neill and Gareth Reeves, *Auden, MacNeice, Spender: The Thirties Poetry* (Macmillan, 1992), p. 2.

6 Robert Graves, *The Crowning Privilege* (Cassell, 1955), p. 130.

7 *The Poems of Laura Riding: A New Edition of the 1938 Collection* (Carcanet, 1980), p. 80. Subsequent quotations of Riding's poetry are from this volume.

8 Barbara Everett, *Auden* (Oliver and Boyd, 1964), pp. 24–25.

9 Quotations in this paragraph are from Laura Riding, 'Preface', *Selected Poems: In Five Sets* (Faber and Faber, 1970), pp. 15, 12.

10 The two previous paragraphs draw on Reeves, chapter 1 in *Auden, MacNeice, Spender: The Thirties Poetry*, pp. 17–30.

11 *The Orators: An English Study*, 3rd edn. (Faber and Faber, 1966), p. 8.

12 Everett, *Auden*, p. 31.

13 Quotations are from Saint-John Perse, *Anabasis: A Poem*, with a translation into English by T. S. Eliot (Faber and Faber, 1930).

14 This paragraph draws on Reeves, chapter 4 in *Auden, MacNeice, Spender: The Thirties Poetry*, pp. 89–90.

15 Laura Riding and Robert Graves, *A Survey of Modernist Poetry* (Heinemann, 1927), pp. 277, 287, 286. The concluding chapter differs from the 'word-by-word' collaborative nature of the rest of the book in being 'a revision by both authors ... of an essay separately written ... by one of them' (p. 5).

16 Elliott Vanskike, '"Seeing Everything as Flat": Landscape in Gertrude Stein's *Useful Knowledge* and *The Geographical History of America*', *Texas Studies in Literature and Language*, 35 (1993), p. 151.

17 *The Poems of Gerard Manley Hopkins*, ed. W. H. Gardner and N. H. Mackenzie, 4th edn. (Oxford University Press, 1967), p. 57. Subsequent quotations of Hopkins's poetry are from this volume.

18 *The Orators*, 3rd edn., p. 7.

19 Quotations in this paragraph are from D. H. Lawrence, *Fantasia of the Unconscious* (1923; rpt Secker, 1933), pp. 78, 62, 109, 116, 38, 39.

20 *The Orators*, 3rd edn., p. 7.

21 The two previous paragraphs draw on Reeves, chapter 4 in *Auden, MacNeice, Spender: The Thirties Poetry*, pp. 94–104.

22 *Fantasia of the Unconscious*, pp. 68, 78.

23 This paragraph draws on Reeves, chapter 4 in *Auden, MacNeice, Spender: The Thirties Poetry*, pp. 109–10.

CHAPTER XXIX

Auden in German

Rainer Emig

Auden's interest in Germany, its language and culture, started with children's stories such as Heinrich Hoffmann's *Struwelpeter* and the fairy tales collected by the Brothers Grimm, which, together with *Icelandic Legends*, enjoyed pride of place on the shelves of his nursery. Although Auden never mastered German completely, it is the only foreign language in which he composed poetry.[1] But German also acquired a dubious aura because of the historical events of the first half of the twentieth century, an ambivalence that becomes visible when the 'reservoir of darkness' in Auden's 'New Year Letter' of 1940 speaks its sombre pronouncements on loss, duty, and love in this language (*CP* 2007, p. 226). Whereas other chapters in the present volume discuss Auden's experiences in Berlin and Austria, and the title of the present chapter might misleadingly suggest that it considers translations of Auden's works into German, what is really at stake here is how Auden made his contact with German literature fruitful for his own creative endeavours. This contact was manifold and by far exceeds the literary realm: psychological, philosophical, political, and especially theological treatises by German authors had an impact on Auden's development. This is not astonishing considering the common verdict, here in the words of Alan Bennett in the Introduction to his play on Auden and Benjamin Britten, *The Habit of Art*, that 'Auden was a library in himself' (Bennett 2009, p. vi).

The present essay will restrict itself to the relationship of Auden's works with those of three important, but also significantly different, German authors: Johann Wolfgang von Goethe (1749–1832), Rainer Maria Rilke (1875–1926), and Bertolt Brecht (1898–1956). It will become evident that simplifying concepts, such as that of 'influence', are misguided when it comes to Auden's engagement with their works – and in the case of Brecht also with the writer himself. Wider concepts of intertextuality and creativity will have to be applied.

Goethe represents a pivotal figure in German literature and culture, so much so that the equivalent of the British Council bears the name *Goethe-Institut* to this day. This corresponds to Goethe's career and his desire to become an established national figure. After a period of still quite Romantic *Sturm und Drang*, he accepted a ministerial post at Weimar and managed to become the leading voice of German Classicism and an international figurehead of German intellect. Auden always rejected demands to become an official spokesperson – of British or American culture – most pronouncedly with his removal to the United States in 1939. He, who disliked the Romantics (with the notable exception of Byron) and had already called *Sturm und Drang* adolescent in 'Letter to Lord Byron' of 1936 (*CP* 2007, p. 109), liked the later Goethe's sympathy for controlled styles and philosophically infused sentiments. Goethe's prolific production also provided parallels: like Auden's it encompassed poems, plays, and prose. Goethe's amateur interest in the Natural Sciences, visible in his treatise on colours that Auden jokingly mentions in 'Academic Graffiti' (*CP* 2007, p. 678), also appealed to Auden, whose early fascinations had been mining and technology. In addition, Goethe's frank attitude towards erotic desire (although mainly of the heterosexual variety) and humorous depictions of sexual frustration and failure formed an analogy to Auden's lifelong ironic dissection of the libido. Neither writer subscribed to a body-mind dichotomy that relegated sexuality to a mere undercurrent of an otherwise enlightened rationality. Desire, anxieties, fears, and aggression form part of their concept of the human, and in a wider sense both remain anthropocentric Humanists.

Goethe makes a first appearance via a twisted quotation in a mixture of German and English in 'Letter to Lord Byron': '*Gerettet* not *Gerichtet* be the Law', in which saving rather than judging is advocated (*CP* 2007, p. 85). Two literary travellers, one willing, the other ostracized by British Regency society, are claimed as fellow tourists by a young Auden still uncertain of his role, but already choosing canonical figures as reference points. The Goethe mentioned is the author of *Faust*, a key text in Auden's consideration of responsibility and evil. Contrary to Marlowe's Faustus play, Goethe's does not show evil as metaphysical and supernatural. His fascinating Mephisto is a sophist and a bureaucrat. He does not impress Faust by displays of magic, but by voicing what Faust is thinking anyway, indeed what every enlightened Western intellectual would have thought or felt. Evil thus becomes a personal and a cultural weakness rather than an external force eager to seduce human beings. It is telling that Auden reverses the order of saved and judged to emphasize this.

The last stanza of 'Epithalamion' (1939) continues this theme with the lines 'Goethe ignorant of sin / Placing every human wrong' (*EA*, p. 455). By this time, Auden himself had joined the universe of the Great, not only by making a name for himself in Britain, but also by marrying into the family of Thomas Mann, by this time widely regarded as Goethe's successor in the German-speaking world. But the lines remain curious: do they state that ignoring transcendental evil makes one capable of categorizing injustice correctly? Or do they signal that an elevated status makes it difficult to understand evil properly? This would be much more in accord with the renewed appearance of Goethe's *Faust* in 'New Year Letter' (1941), where references to the play are again used to discuss creativity and evil, and especially in references to Goethe in *The Enchafèd Flood* (1950), where Goethe's Faust and Peer Ibsen's Peer Gynt are compared on the grounds that they cherish society, but ultimately desert it.

Goethe, the Italian traveller, is claimed as a biographical parallel in 'Goodbye to the Mezzogiorno'. Auden had, together with Elizabeth Mayer, translated Goethe's *Italian Journey* (1816–17) into English in 1962. The greatest homage, however, was the adoption of 'Dichtung und Wahrheit', the title of Goethe's major autobiographical prose work, as the title of an extended prose poem in 1959. Rather than simply creating a biographical analogy, however, Auden's treatment of Goethe and autobiography place both in the context of history and intertextuality. Auden refutes simple and singular influences and, in 'Academic Graffiti' (*CP* 2007, pp. 675–85) eventually places Goethe among a crowd of other Western intellectuals whose views are singularly incompatible, if one considers the placement of Marx next to Zwingli and Goethe next to Kant. But the journey motif is still viewed as a positive parallel when, in his Introduction to the translation of Goethe's *Italian Journey*, Auden claims Goethe as another quest-hero, much like he preferred to see himself.

A more critical attitude to Goethe becomes noticeable when the extended discussion of power and Hegelian master-slave relationships in the essay 'Balaam and his Ass' in *The Dyer's Hand* of 1962 regards Goethe's *Faust* as a failure in terms of dramatic structure. By this time, Auden clearly believed himself entitled to evaluate canonical writers such as Goethe and Byron, as he does in the essay 'Genius and Apostle'. Goethe also features as a model in the libretto to Stravinsky's *The Rake's Progress* of 1951, based on the Hogarth illustrations, about which Auden writes in the lecture 'The World of Opera' in *Secondary Worlds* (1968). The idea of ranking Goethe, as well as ranking himself with Goethe, culminates in Auden's memorial poem to Louis MacNeice, 'The Cave of Making', which contains the famous lines 'I should like to become, if possible, / a minor Atlantic Goethe' (*CP* 2007, p. 692). They are multiply ironic: neither is Goethe an Atlantic or trans-Atlantic writer. His context is European. Considering the titanic status that Goethe had held for nearly 200 years by the time these lines were written, a 'minor' version of him is only imaginable as a parody.

Lastly, though, and most importantly, the daring comparison is prefaced by a polite, although remarkably unpoetic statement that chimes with the poem's theme of creativity, authorship, and selfhood. Not only poetry is a process (and only in the best cases a progress): the self-creation of an author is also a process, and its path is littered with the models, inspirations, irritations, and obstacles of a past tradition. Goethe is an inspiration for Auden, but never a fully-fledged model because of the historic and cultural differences between the two writers. At the same time, this enables Auden to avoid a futile Oedipal struggle with a threatening father figure of the kind that Harold Bloom far too generally postulates for all writers. Goethe can, like Byron, become a travelling companion, a partner in debates, and a fellow sufferer from fame. When Goethe thus returns as a repeated reference point in the often short poems of *Epistle to a Godson*, he receives the gentle, but sometimes critical advice of a fellow-poet rather than the adoration of an ardent admirer. 'To Goethe: A Complaint' (*CP* 2007, p. 717), for example, targets Goethe's mixing of nature descriptions with love poetry and complains that this diminishes both.

Rainer Maria Rilke, much closer to Auden historically, is a very different matter. Here the attraction is not so much biographical and intellectual as formal. Although both writers were strongly influenced by Freudian psychoanalysis, their backgrounds could not be more different, if one sees as decisive elements in Rilke's a broken family, a relationship with a dominant maternal older woman, traumatic war experiences, encounters with Modernist artists, and an early death from leukaemia.

What attracted Auden to Rilke's poetry from the late 1930s onwards was its metaphoricity. Auden's early style is radical in its avoidance of poetic cliché. This sometimes goes as far as sacrificing any trace of traditional metaphors on the altar of a clinical style whose forced similes and symbols often approach the ludicrous, even when they describe serious issues and concerns. Rilke, on the other hand, was famous for the ease with which his metaphors connected the concrete and the abstract – without simplifying or beautifying either. In his review 'Rilke in English' of 1939, Auden himself writes: 'One of the constant problems of the poet is how to express abstract ideas in concrete terms' (*Prose I*, p. 25).

Two opposed solutions present themselves: 'While Shakespeare, for example, thought of the non-human world in terms of the human, Rilke thinks of the human in terms of the non-human, of what he calls Things (*Dinge*), a way of thought which, as he himself pointed out, is more characteristic of the child than of the adult' (*Prose I*, p. 25). It is important neither to misread this statement as Auden turning towards a traditional Humanism nor, its contemporary counter-fashion, as an early manifestation of Post-Humanism. It is, instead, evidence of Auden's lifelong attachment to a self-reflexive anthropocentrism, an awareness that one can never leave one's human position behind, no matter which idealist position one desires to occupy. But this position remains one among others (the social dimension) and one within an objective life-world (the objective dimension). Here emerges another link with Goethe, who famously stated in a poem on nature observation entitled 'Epirrhema' (meaning 'afterword'): '*Nichts ist drinnen, nichts ist draußen: / Denn was innen, das ist außen*' ('There is naught within, naught without / whatever is within is also without').[2]

Rilke's stylistic example helps Auden avoid the extremes of sterility and what he himself rejects as 'preaching' (*Prose I*, p. 25), which means expressing abstractions through abstractions and ending up in a hazy nowhere that marries aesthetics and rationality without doing justice to either. Rilke, especially in his *Duino Elegies*, overcomes the dilemma. Tellingly, considering Auden's own predilections, he does so also by using landscape as a metaphor for human personality and concerns. The Eighth Elegy, for example, starts with a plea for a double observation: 'All eyes, the creatures of the World look out / into the open. But our human eyes, / as if turned right around and glaring in, / encircle them; prohibiting their passing'.[3] 'Our gaze is ever turned towards Creation', the poem states, only in order to add, 'we know only the surface of that glass', thus tantalizingly leaving open the possibility of a higher transcendental meaning. Its conclusion, though, merely speaks of 'us' as observers in a landscape who use the last hill to look back to the valley we have crossed and of perpetual good-byes. When Auden tackles temporality, as he famously does in connection with love in 'As I Walked Out One Evening', Rilkean metaphoricity proves immensely useful. 'And the crack in the teacup opens / A lane to the land of the dead' (*CP* 2007, p. 135) read two of the poem's best-known lines. They might be an echo of 'swift as a flaw runs through / a cup' in Rilke's Eighth Elegy, which, after all, is also concerned with love, life, and their transience, before a background of Etruscan burials.

Auden's 'In Praise of Limestone' is a successful example of integrating Rilke's influence that starts out as a formal escape route but quickly develops into a way of connecting the radical techniques of Auden's early works with the increasingly pressing demands of history,[4] politics, philosophy, and theology. All of them thrive on abstractions but have concrete effects for individual and society alike. But Auden's poem abstains from infusing the various landscapes it describes, not even the privileged limestone one, with transcendental possibilities. It is remarkably detailed and concrete in its descriptions of its cherished limestone landscape and precise in linking alternative landscapes with certain personality types. But lines such as 'how permanent is death' or 'I am the solitude that asks and promises nothing; / That is how I shall set you free' (*CP* 2007, pp. 539, 540) are almost cruel in their refusal of metaphoric promises.

Similar observations can be made concerning the Rilkean influences in Auden's mid- and late-career poems. Italian poems such as 'Ischia' counter lines that resemble Rilke's style and his emphasis on observation with drastic Audenesque precision. Thus, 'how gently you train us to see / things and men in perspective' is followed by 'undeneath your uniform light' (*CP* 2007, p. 541). The unpoetic 'uniform' reactivates the authoritarian, indeed military, potential of the verb 'to train' of the earlier verse, and suddenly we are no longer in a sun-drenched timeless Mediterranean, but in post- or already Cold-War Europe.

In Auden's late poem, this technique is refined by removing the brutality of the contrast. In the deliberately mundane settings of 'Thanksgiving for a Habitat' there are echoes of Rilke's subjective object poetics, but the refined imagery of the German writer, which echoes *fin-de-siècle* aestheticism, has been replaced by the post-WWII practicalities of fitted kitchens and bathrooms. A telling image from 'Encomium Balnei', Auden's poem to the bathroom, speaks of 'caracallan acreage / compressed into such square feet' (*CP* 2007, p. 700).

Rilke's poem 'Title Page' in *From a Stormy Night* provides another comparison. It discusses the perception of light and darkness and its relation to human ideas of knowledge and order. It states: 'Do we feign our light? / Has the only real thing for millennia past / Been the night?'[5] While the first two of the quoted stanzas could be Auden's in style and content, the third one, which is also the final one of the poem, is, despite its status as a question, too suggestive to suit Auden's insistence on openness. Auden's late poem 'Thank you Fog' offers his alternative. After praising English fog over New York smog, what the lyrical 'I' experiences here is a return of 'native knowledge' (*CP* 2007, p. 888), not universally valid insights. There is a 'global doom' in the poem, yet it is a specific one brought about by the 1973 Oil Crisis and 'cast' as well as broadcast 'by the Daily Papers'. The 'shapeless silence' outdoors is also not a universal quasi-metaphysical one, but merely the effect of the temporary silence of very specific Wiltshire birds, such as 'the merle and the mavis' (*CP* 2007, p. 889, all).

Perhaps the best implicit summary of Auden's relationship with Rilke's aesthetics is contained in a short poem countering, at an obvious level, the Realism claims made by Christopher Isherwood in a line in his Berlin stories by declaring 'I Am Not a Camera'. 'To call our sight Vision' / implies that, to us, / all objects are subjects' (*CP* 2007, p. 841) declares its first stanza and thereby returns to the initial debate concerning Rilke. While Rilke objectifies human perception and projects subjective states onto objective reality, a practice that parallels Auden's objective and sometimes clinical one, Rilke's tendency of elevating this perception onto the pseudo-transcendental level of a vision runs counter to Auden's cautious approach vis-à-vis truths that are more than 'native knowledge'; that is, local truths determined by specific conditions. Despite Auden's indebtedness to Rilke, he ultimately remains sceptical about the latter's *Schöngeistigkeit*, his belle-lettristic tendency towards aestheticist exquisiteness.

Whereas Goethe represents a European literary myth for Auden, and Rilke a kind of predecessor writing in a different language, Bertolt Brecht is not only a contemporary, but also a personal acquaintance and eventually Auden's artistic collaborator. Auden's first encounter with Brecht took place during Auden's stay in Berlin in 1928 and 1929 when he experienced Brecht's theatre for the first time. Auden watched Brecht and Weil's *The Threepenny Opera*, which had opened in August 1928 (*CCWHA*, p. 84). Its departure from conventional Realism and Naturalism towards a distanced and frequently parabolic style matched Auden's interests, which he put into practice in *Paid on Both Sides* (written in 1928 and published two years later) and *The Dance of Death* (1933) as well as the dramatic collaborations with Christopher Isherwood *The Dog Beneath the Skin* (1935) and *The Ascent of F6* (1936).

What appealed to Auden were Brecht's materialism and his irreverent attitude to established authorities, be they moral, political, or religious. Brecht's refusal to include metaphysical dimensions into his plots and imagery also chimed with Auden's clinical approach. Auden himself admitted that he was 'certainly influenced' by Brecht's plays.[6] There is evidence that the influence was mutual: Brecht, as well as his contemporary Gottfried Benn, also appreciated Auden's poems and saw in them an important aesthetic as well as thematic stepping stones towards what they hoped would become a new form of modern poetry. All in all, the current German vogue for *Neue Sachlichkeit*, New Objectivism, had much to offer to Auden's budding aesthetics.

But there were also limitations to its appeal. Occasional lines in Auden's early poems resemble Brecht's deliberately pruned-down objective vocabulary and straightforward syntax. The opening lines, 'To ask the hard question is simple' (*EA*, p. 54) or 'Hearing of harvests rotting in the valleys' (*EA*, p. 135), respectively from 1930 and 1933, are such examples. 'The Unknown Citizen' of 1939 (*CP* 2007, p. 250), with its parabolic description of the modern person through material possessions and statistical facts, is another case in point. But looking closer and beyond those surface similarities, Auden's love of obscurity combined with his insistence on displaying his erudition make his texts depart noticeably from Brechtian straightforwardness. The 'hard question' of 'The Question' (as subsequently titled) remains tantalizingly unclear and seems to steer in a psychological direction that is alien to Brecht's materialism. The title later applied to the sestina 'Hearing of harvests ...', 'Paysage Moralisé', would have stood out as exotic, because it is too refined, in Brecht's oeuvre.

Auden admired Brecht for his effectiveness and his ability to appeal to a large audience. He certainly also admired the straightforward political convictions evident in Brecht's writings, convictions that were only ever available to Auden in tortured and frequently self-undermining forms; evidenced by his modifications and eventual rejection of 'Spain', but also suggested by *The Orators* of 1932. The occasional poem, Brecht's preferred form, also held a strong appeal for Auden.

Personal relations between the two outstanding writers, both of whom received their share of public interest, were by no means easy. Brecht's solid, but rather confined middle-class background contrasted strongly with Auden's upper-middle-class aspirations. Whereas Brecht's academic career was short-lived, Auden's biography was shaped by his Oxford experiences. Together with Auden's homosexuality, this marked the English writer as a bourgeois decadent in Brecht's books, while Auden came to consider Brecht as narrow-minded and indeed stupid: 'I've got a bit bored with old B. B. A great poet but he could not think' (Carpenter, p. 412). When both became exiles in the United States, though, solidarity was *de rigeur*, in much the same way that Auden supported the politically very different, namely bourgeois-liberal, Thomas Mann by marrying his daughter.

Despite the personal reservations that degraded into bitchy backbiting on both sides, a considerable amount of collaboration took place, largely in the shape of Auden translating Brecht into English. He helped him first with an attempt at a Broadway adaptation of John Webster's *The Duchess of Malfi* in 1943 and 1946, translated songs from *The Caucasian Chalk Circle* (with James and Tanya Stern), Brecht and Weil's *The Seven Deadly Sins* and, most spectacularly, the libretto of the Brecht and Weil opera *The Rise and Fall of the City of Mahagonny*, the latter two with Chester Kallman (see Innes, *CCWHA*, p. 84). *The Seven Deadly Sins* (in its original German title 'The Seven Deadly Sins of the Petit Bourgeoisie') offers many parallels to Auden's *The Dance of Death*. Both appeared in 1933. But Auden's one-act play ends in a rather satirical vein – with Karl Marx making a stage appearance as a *deus ex machina*. In the Mahagonny translation, Auden irons out slang and working-class speech for well-modulated middle-class expressions.[7] That Auden never became completely disaffected with Brecht's works is shown in the work he did in 1964 on a translation of the lyrics of *Mother Courage* for the National Theatre in London, eight years after Brecht's death (Carpenter, p. 412).

Brecht in return praised Auden and Isherwood's plays for 'sections of great poetic beauty'.[8] He did not, however, extol their rigorous thinking, logical argument, and solid political messages. In fact, that would have been hard to do. Ultimately, Brecht's and Auden's understanding of the role of drama and poetry differed. While it would be wrong to accuse Brecht of an anti-aesthetic attitude to writing, his eye was always on the effectiveness of conveying a message. This is true even for more personal poems in his vast oeuvre. In Auden's case, straightforwardness was increasingly identified with hollowness and intellectual as well as moral dishonesty. A poem like 'The Truest Poetry Is the Most Feigning', with the paradoxical quotation as a title, or the denunciation of successful popular lines as 'some resonant lie' in 'Ode to Terminus' (*CP* 2007, p.809) illustrate this development.

Keeping this in mind, it is plain that the German authors paraded as creative contexts for Auden's development as a writer in the present chapter do not and cannot act as simple influences. Neither of them ever became a model or indeed an addiction to the degree that Auden's early poetry imitated Hopkins's inverted syntax or the imagery of Eliot's *The Waste Land*. Auden viewed them instead as imaginary (and in Brecht's case real) acquaintances, but also as colleagues and competitors. His references and allusions to them signal a creative exchange that can occasionally amount to parody, but more often resembles a civilized and highly productive dialogue.

NOTES

1 See David Constantine, 'The German Auden: Six Early Poems' (*AS I*, pp. 1–15), and Rainer Emig, '"All the Others Translate": W. H. Auden's Poetic Dislocations of Self, Nation, and Culture' in *Translation and Nation: Towards a Cultural Poetics of Englishness*, pp. 167–204. Full details are given in the 'Further Reading' section.

2 Johann Wolfgang von Goethe, *Berliner Ausgabe: Poetische Werke*, ed. Seidel, vol. I, pp. 545–46. Full details are given in the 'Further Reading' section.

3 Rainer Maria Rilke, *Duino Elegies*, trans. Stephen Cohn (Northwestern University Press, 1998), p. 65. The further two quotations from Rilke in this paragraph are at pp. 67 and 69.

4 See my *W. H. Auden: Towards a Postmodern Poetics* (Macmillan, 2000), pp. 80–114.

5 Rainer Maria Rilke, *The Best of Rilke*, trans. Walter Arndt (Dartmouth College Press, 1989), p. 37.

6 Quoted in John Willett, *The Theatre of Bertolt Brecht: A Study from Eight Aspects* (Methuen & Co., 1967), p. 220.

7 See Emig, op. cit., n. 1, pp. 182–84.

8 Quoted in *Brecht on Theatre: The Development of an Aesthetic*, ed. and trans. John Willett (Methuen, 1964), p. 154.

CHAPTER XXX

Auden and Isherwood

James J. Berg and Chris Freeman

I

Auden first met Christopher Isherwood in 1915 when they were boarding at St. Edmund's School, in Surrey. They did not know each other well there, but they met again ten years later, when Auden was at Oxford and Isherwood had left Cambridge. While at university, Isherwood had begun writing a surrealistic fantasy with his friend Edward Upward, based in a place they called Mortmere. This was Isherwood's first collaboration, and for the rest of his life he would turn to Upward for literary approval.

Auden and Isherwood's, however, became one of the truly remarkable literary friendships of the twentieth century. By most accounts, Auden looked up to his friend, whom he saw as an already-established writer, even though Isherwood had not yet published his first novel. Isherwood also introduced Auden to Upward, and Auden, in turn, was influenced by the literary pastiche and strangeness of the Mortmere stories. Katherine Bucknell points out that by creating Mortmere, Upward 'helped to shape that sense of humour – a kind of unleashed boyish hysteria ... which both Auden and Isherwood put to use, notably in *The Orators*, *The Dog Beneath the Skin* and *Lions and Shadows*' (*AS II*, p. 177). In these years, Auden showed many of his poems to Isherwood in early drafts, and Isherwood acted as a mentor and editor to the younger poet.

The twenty-four-year-old Isherwood published his first novel, *All the Conspirators*, in 1928. It was neither commercially nor critically successful. Nevertheless, he had the confidence and respect of his peers. In 1929, showing early signs of frustration with life and expectations in England, Isherwood followed Auden to Berlin, first to visit and later to stay, encouraged by the sexual availability of foreign, working-class boys. This time spent travelling together was an early highlight in their relationship. Recalling a brief visit to Amsterdam with Auden, Isherwood wrote that he and his friend 'were both in the highest spirits. It was such a relief and happiness to be alone with each other'.[1] The two were at that time also sleeping together, at least occasionally. Isherwood disclosed this in *Christopher and His Kind*, but downplayed the relationship: 'they had been going to bed together, unromantically but with much pleasure, for the past ten years, whenever an opportunity offered itself.... They couldn't think of themselves as lovers, yet sex had given friendship an extra dimension' (Isherwood 1976, p. 264). For Auden, the feelings seem to have been stronger.

Auden's first book, *Poems* (1930), published by Eliot at Faber and Faber, was well received, justifying a second edition in 1933. Isherwood's second novel, *The Memorial* (1932), published the same year as Auden's second book, *The Orators*, was more popular than his first and was praised by E. M. Forster, whom Isherwood admired. Auden's acclaimed collection *Look, Stranger!* came out in 1936, and the following year was awarded the Gold Medal for Poetry by George VI. 'By 1937, Auden had become the most famous writer of his generation', as Isherwood acknowledged later (see his 'Postscript' in Tribute, p. 78).

Their literary collaboration began casually, when they read each other's work. In 'Some Notes on Auden's Early Poetry' (1937) Isherwood wrote that Auden 'hated polishing and making corrections. If I didn't like a poem, he threw it away and wrote another. If I liked one line, he would keep it and work it into a new poem. In this way, whole poems were constructed which were simply anthologies of my favourite lines' (*Tribute*, p. 75). Nearly forty years later, he offered a new perspective on their creative relationship (resembling that between Pound and Eliot): 'Auden's apparent passivity was an aspect of his creative strength. A powerfully fertile imagination often finds it amusing to subject itself to somebody else's commands' (Isherwood,Tribute, p. 78). For his part, Auden credited Isherwood for the political awareness of their group. In his birthday poem for Isherwood, 'August for the people' (1935), Auden asks: 'So in this hour of crisis and dismay, / What better than your strict and adult pen / Can warn us ...?' (*EA*, p. 157). In these accounts, self-deprecation and self-promotion are operating at the same time; and it is worth noting that for these two writers 'self-promotion' means promoting himself and his friend. As Auden wrote in his 1929 Berlin journal, 'That is what friendship is. Fellow conspiracy'.[2]

They began collaborating on stage plays, which drew on their different talents and strengths: Isherwood, a life-long theatre and film fan, provided the structure and the narrative while Auden provided the poetry in speeches and song. Their first collaboration happened almost by accident in Berlin in 1929 when Auden was working on a play about a reformatory, which became 'The Enemies of a Bishop'. As Parker points out, this partnership provided benefits to both writers. For Isherwood, it recalled his youthful work with Upward, and for Auden, it was 'the marriage of true minds'. In Isherwood, Auden had found the ideal writing partner. He later claimed, 'In my own case, collaboration has brought me greater erotic joy – as distinct from sexual pleasure – than any sexual relation I have had' (quoted Parker 2004, p. 176). Their play was not a success, rejected for publication and not performed. Nevertheless, the two began another project, again instigated by Auden, which became their first produced play, *The Dog Beneath the Skin* (1935).

Two years later, when they were working on *The Ascent of F6*, Auden joined Isherwood in Portugal. It was 'the first time for several years' that the two were together for more than a few days (Carpenter, p. 192). According to Isherwood, Auden, writing quickly, produced nearly finished drafts; Isherwood, working on dialogue, was much slower and required more revisions. An additional dimension of their difference would become important later: 'Wystan writing indoors with the curtains drawn; Christopher writing out in the garden, with his shirt off in the sunshine' (Isherwood 1976, p. 239).

The Auden-Isherwood plays are essentially parables, according to Christopher Innes, with Auden being the more 'parabolic' writer and Isherwood the more 'realist' (*CCWHA*, p. 90). Their final play together, *On the Frontier* (1938), is more overtly political in nature, consistent with the evolution of both men's work in this decade. Although they seemed to think of the plays as side projects, these collaborations mirror developments in their individual work, as for example in Auden's poem 'Spain' and Isherwood's Berlin novels. The plays illustrate their artistic response and political engagement with the world around them. At the same time, their doubts about the efficacy of literature in the face of political reality surfaced in *On the Frontier*, which 'explicitly dismisses humanistic poetry as a way of changing the situation' (*CCWHA*, p. 90). As Innes argues, World War II marked 'a complete break with the ethos and literary modes of the 1930s': notably, the Group Theatre closed after a revival of *F6* starring Alec Guinness, marking 'the end of symbolic Expressionism on the British stage' (*CCWHA*, p. 90).

During the period of their collaboration, they rarely lived in the same place. Auden was working as a school teacher and writing. He had married Erika Mann in 1935, at Isherwood's suggestion, enabling her escape from Nazi Germany (he dedicated *Look, Stranger!* to her); he travelled to Iceland with Louis MacNeice. Early in 1937 he went to Spain to help the Republican cause; while there, Auden 'was shocked at the demolition, despoiling and enforced closure of the churches in Barcelona', which, according to Richard Davenport-Hines, 'began a process of thought that led to his reversion to Christianity' (RD-H 1995, pp. 168–69). Meanwhile, Isherwood was living in Berlin and travelling around the continent with his boyfriend, Heinz Neddermeyer. The young German, in flight from conscription in the Nazi army, was refused entry into England in 1934. Auden was witness to Heinz's expulsion by an immigration official whom he described as a 'little rat' who 'understood the whole situation at a glance – because he's *one of us*' (Isherwood 1976, p. 162). This was an enormous blow to Isherwood, a rejection of his personal life by the government of England. As a response to this, Isherwood 'symbolically rejected [his mother's] England', which he continued to see as the land of 'the Others' (Isherwood 1976, p. 172).

II

The period from January 1938 to August 1939 was a key time for Auden and Isherwood, personally and professionally. Now in their early thirties, they were literary celebrities in London. As such, they were commissioned by Auden's publishers – Faber and Faber in England and Random House in the United States – to write a book together about the East, which meant, to their delight, months of travel, including a return trip through the United States. This journey would change their lives.

On 19 January 1938, they left for China. In Hong Kong, they were welcomed by the British ambassador, Archibald Clark Kerr, who knew Auden's poetry and was a fan of Isherwood's *Sally Bowles* (Parker 2004, p. 375). Auden, who had been in Spain the previous year, had already seen the confusion of war; for Isherwood, this was a new, revelatory experience. Isherwood's plan was to be the observer contributing a prose narrative, while Auden 'would write about the war parabolically to provide a theory of human violence' (RD-H 1995, p. 170). *Journey to a War* (1939) illustrates the same modernist assemblage they had used in their plays. Their refusal to position themselves as objective reporters was seen as their being 'too preoccupied with their own psychological plight to be anything but helplessly lost in the struggle of modern China' (*Daily Worker*, quoted Parker 2004, p. 409). Isherwood understood that the book had 'so annoyed the Left, because it was messy, personal, sentimental, and confused, like myself' (quoted Parker 2004, p. 445). Again, the Auden-Isherwood collaboration produced a distinctly modernist work.

Returning from Asia they spent a short time in New York City. They were welcomed by George Davis, literary editor of two influential American magazines, who had been holding their royalties for some American publications. He also introduced them to a few handsome young men. To both Auden and Isherwood, New York seemed 'immensely exciting, an outlier of Europe vitalized by America' (Carpenter, p. 240) – perhaps it could be their new Berlin. Back in London, Isherwood and Auden responded slightly differently to fame. Isherwood was 'good at self-exposure; he knew all the tricks of modesty and never boasted except in private' (Isherwood 1976, p. 332). Auden, on the other hand, claimed to find literary life in England 'particularly stultifying' (Carpenter, p. 243). He complained that 'in the literary world in England, you have to know who's married to whom, and who's slept with whom and who hasn't. It's a tiny jungle' (RD-H 1995, p. 179). Talk of a return to the United States had begun while they were in New York. Conveniently, a special visa granted them in Shanghai would make it easy for them to enter the country again.

There is some disagreement about whether a return visit was meant to be permanent or just the next of their voyages away from England. Davenport-Hines, for example, claims they both intended the trip 'to be their emigration to the United States. It was the culmination of so many of Auden's ideas since his journey to Iceland' (RD-H 1995, p. 179). In a letter he wrote but did not send to Cyril Connolly in 1944, Isherwood said that 'our coming to America (or maybe I had better not speak for Wystan; this shall be purely personal) was an altogether irresponsible act, prompted by circumstances – like our trip to China, and my wanderings about Europe after 1933. When the war broke out in 1939, it was a fifty-fifty chance what I'd do.... I delayed, because that is always easiest'.[3] It is notable that Isherwood speaks only for himself here, which suggests that he and Auden had different motivations and different plans for what seemed the same journey. In *Christopher and His Kind*, Isherwood describes the casual nature of their leaving: 'He and Wystan exchanged grins, schoolboy grins which took them back to the earliest days of their friendship. "Well", said Christopher, "we're off again". "Goody", said Wystan' (Isherwood 1976, p. 332). Alan Jacobs points out, however, the move 'represented for Auden a means of distancing himself from the expectations British intellectual culture had for him'.[4]

The transatlantic voyage gave them an opportunity to contemplate their future: according to Isherwood, this was the first time they had been alone together in several months. Their extended conversations during the crossing led them to reject the leftist political stances they had adopted publicly throughout the 1930s. No longer 'repeating slogans created for them by others', the two men agreed that 'they wanted to stop.... Their agreement made them happy. Now, more than ever, they were allied. Yet their positions were quite different' (Isherwood 1976, p. 333). In Isherwood's case, the more personal decision that he was a pacifist left him emotionally unsettled.

Auden took to New York. Shortly after their arrival, he met and fell in love with a young aspiring poet, Chester Kallman. Despite the fact that he was already a well-regarded poet and in demand socially, Auden made time to write and 'flourishes exceedingly', as Isherwood observed: 'Never has he written so much' (quoted Parker 2004, p. 428). Again, Isherwood felt differently. He found the dark, gloomy winter insufferable, and, unlike Auden, the personal and professional reputation he enjoyed in London had not followed him. Although *Journey to a War* and *Goodbye to Berlin* were both published in the United States that year, his novel did not sell as well as he had hoped, making it necessary for him to find another way to earn a living. In April, a discontented Isherwood wrote to Forster: 'It's really not New York's fault, but mine, that I've got so little out of being here, except the feeling of pure despair, values dissolving, everything uncertain'.[5] Isherwood headed for Los Angeles to visit his friend, Gerald Heard, the noted philosopher and science writer, with whom he wanted to discuss his own growing commitment to pacifism; he hoped Heard could introduce him to Aldous Huxley, who had also written about pacifism. Huxley helped Isherwood find work in Hollywood; he also introduced him to Swami Prabhavananda, who would become a central figure in his life. Auden and Kallman visited in the summer of 1939, but they thoroughly disliked Los Angeles. According to Don Bachardy, Isherwood's partner later in life, 'Chris was all sunshine and warmth. Wystan liked the dark and the cold'.[6]

When war broke out in September 1939, each considered the possibility of returning to England. Isherwood wrote to Forster at the end of the month: 'What shall I do? Stay here for the present. I am half an American citizen, anyway.... Wystan is in New York. Whatever we do will probably be together' (Zeikowitz 2008, p. 88). Rumblings in the British press about English writers in the United States began in the summer of 1939 and continued. Auden wrote to his brother in June 1940: 'I dont (*sic*) see the point of writing in a cottage waiting for the parachutists ... all that we can do, who are spared the horrors, is to be happy and not pretend out of a sense of guilt that we are not, to study as hard as we can, and keep our feeble little lamps burning in the big wind' (RD-H 1995, p. 207). Infuriated over what he saw as petty and misguided criticism, Forster came to the defense of his friends, stating in a letter to the *Spectator* (5 July 1940) that the attacks raise 'the uneasy feeling that there must be something else behind them, namely, unconscious envy'. He went on to say, 'There is a further objection to this undignified nagging: it diverts public attention from certain Englishmen who really are a danger to the country'.[7] As Richard Canning has suggested, much of the criticism was 'certainly informed by jingoism, homophobia and philistinism'. [8] Nonetheless, as reviews of works by and about the two writers continue to show, those attitudes toward Auden and Isherwood persist in England.

III

Crucial differences in the two writers' personalities can be seen in the geographical choices they made that turned out to be life-changing. Isherwood was becoming committed to life in Southern California; Auden preferred to base himself in New York. The two saw each other frequently, by the standards of those days before inexpensive air travel. Isherwood occasionally visited the East Coast, and Auden often stayed with Isherwood whenever he was on a lecture tour that included California. What they might have thought of as a temporary living situation, however, became permanent as the years went by.

From all indications, it seems that Auden minded their separation more than Isherwood did. Nearly every letter sent by Auden ended with a plea for Isherwood to visit, whether in New York, Austria, or England. Isherwood recognized Auden's devotion to him but did not return it fully. He also believed that Auden wanted him to be 'properly domestic', and that Auden 'had been in love with Christopher'.[9] Throughout their relationship, Auden seems to have been 'the more loving one'; Isherwood, apparently, was never in love with Auden. Looking back on their final year in London, Isherwood recalled boasting of his sexual conquests: 'Auden, particularly, disliked my attitude; it hurt him because he was really fond of me' (Isherwood 1996, p. 3). This fondness haunted Auden and coloured their relationship, especially in the 1940s and 1950s, when Auden's partnership with Kallman was at its most problematic and when Isherwood realized that, in Bachardy, he had met the love of his life. After Auden's death, Isherwood wrote to Spender, 'We were so close to each other when we were young, and then America parted us – it's very strange to realize this, but it did. We never got together for long enough after that' (quoted Parker 2004, p. 780). Auden very much wanted a relationship that mirrored a traditional marriage; his life with Kallman was therefore ultimately unsatisfactory, even though it was long-lasting, because Kallman had no interest in conventional monogamy. Having spent time with both Kallman and Auden, together and separately over a period of about two decades, Bachardy believes that Auden never gave up his love of Isherwood: 'I think there would never have been a Chester if Chris had fulfilled Wystan's hopes. I think Wystan would have been perfectly happy to have settled down with Chris'.[10]

The contrasts between the writers was, of course, much more than a romantic difference. Auden was an intellectual, as is evident in his erudite writing from this period. In a 1940 letter to Stephen Spender, Auden, influenced by Carl Jung, described his 'dominant faculties as intellect and intuition, [and his] weak ones feeling and sensation' (*AS I*, p. 72); Isherwood by contrast was a sensualist. They often saw themselves this way, and once joked that 'poems are written with the head for the heart. Novels are written with the heart for the head' (*AS I*, p. 71). The post-war relationship between Auden and Isherwood was also complicated by their increasing devotion to different religions. Auden began attending Anglican services almost as soon as he arrived in New York. Isherwood became more and more committed to Vedanta, the philosophical branch of Hinduism. His personal life was in some turmoil in the early 1940s. As he engaged more deeply, he lived for some time in the enclave of the Vedanta Society of Southern California and considered becoming a monk, but was unwilling or unable to renounce his sexual life. Professionally, he had nearly stopped writing. As early as the summer of 1939, writing to Forster from Los Angeles, Isherwood expressed anxiety over his lack of productivity – and praised Auden: 'Wystan's work is getting better and better – classic, really' (Zeikowitz 2008, 84). His first American novel, *Prater Violet,* was not published until 1946. On occasion, the more orthodox Auden saw Vedanta as 'heathen mumbo-jumbo'.[11] However, as he wrote to Spender: 'You mustnt [sic] judge [Christopher] by rumours or even anything he writes to you, because in what is a period of re-organisation for him, he cant [sic] express himself properly ..., but deep down, I have a firm conviction that we are not apart but all engaged on the same thing' (*AS I*, p. 80, sic). Agreeing with this assessment much later, Spender argued that 'Auden's and Isherwood's attitudes toward religion had a good deal in common. They both used religion as an external discipline modifying their behaviour in their lives … they both give a feeling of having a "special relationship" with God'.[12]

A final attempt at an Auden-Isherwood collaboration, during the American years, shows how their lives had diverged by the 1960s. They talked off and on, in person and through letters, for years about using Isherwood's Berlin material to write a musical. The final attempt seems to have been when they were both in London in 1961. Isherwood was there to support Bachardy's first one-man show at the Redfern gallery; Auden and Kallman were in London for the premiere of their opera *Elegy for Young Lovers* at Glyndebourne. Auden brought Kallman in on their project, to Isherwood's chagrin: 'He is no use', he noted in his diary.[13] Isherwood's heart was not in the project: 'We've had another of these futile talks about the musical. I simply do not see one.… It is a sheer waste of time talking about it' (Isherwood 2010, p. 82); to his relief, Auden's and Kallman's departure for Austria felt like a tacit abandonment of the idea (Isherwood 2010, p. 85). Clearly, given the astonishing success of Kander and Ebb's *Cabaret* at the end of the decade, there was a musical to be found in this material; however, Isherwood's and Auden's sympathies had shifted, finally, to their new partners.

In designating a loosely affiliated group of writers from the 1930s ('the Auden generation'), scholar Samuel Hynes established critical dogma and Auden was recognized as the pinnacle of his contemporaries. Among those of secondary importance were Isherwood, Spender, and a few others, notably Connolly and Cecil Day-Lewis. As we ourselves have suggested, the post-war dominance of New Critical scholarship devalued Isherwood's work.[14] Because of the highly autobiographical nature of most of Isherwood, formalist analysis had little to say about him, whereas this school of criticism was highly beneficial to poetry such as Auden's, which received much critical attention. Additionally, certain prejudices have had a detrimental effect on Isherwood's reputation: the general suspicion about California and his devotion to Hinduism have been a lingering problem. Significantly, too, it was easier to identify the homosexual elements of his fiction, especially the later, American work, than to fault Auden's work for that particular sin. For decades, readers have assumed that the 'sleeping head' in 'Lullaby' is a woman's. Numerous overtly homophobic reviews of Isherwood's masterpiece, *A Single Man* (1964), attest to the critical opposition to the important themes in his American writings.

But with the emergence of queer theory and gay studies, it has become more possible to evaluate Isherwood's work across his entire lifespan. In the past twenty years, the predominance of memoir as a form has contributed to a resurgence of interest in him. Furthermore, the publication of his voluminous diaries adds to our understanding of his life and makes possible greater appreciation of his work. Much of the material in these volumes also sheds important positive light on Auden's life and work. Perhaps it is now possible to see Auden and Isherwood as the peers that they were when they arrived in New York in January 1939.

NOTES

1 Christopher Isherwood, *Christopher and His Kind* (University of Minnesota Press, 2001), p. 10. First published in USA, 1976; hereafter cited in the text as 'Isherwood, 1976'.
2 Quoted in Peter Parker, *Isherwood: A Life* (Picador, 2004), p. 176. Hereafter cited as 'Parker 2004'.
3 Christopher Isherwood, *Diaries, Vol. I, 1939–1960*, ed. Katherine Bucknell (HarperCollins, 1996), p. 365. Hereafter cited as 'Isherwood 1996'.
4 Alan Jacobs, *What Became of Wystan? Change and Continuity in Auden's Poetry* (University of Arkansas Press, 1998), p. iv.
5 *Letters between Forster and Isherwood on Homosexuality and Literature*, ed. Richard Zeikowitz (Palgrave Macmillan, 2008), p. 88. Hereafter cited as 'Zeikowitz 2008'.
6 Interview between Don Bachardy and the authors, 6 December 2009.
7 Quoted in P. N. Furbank, *E. M. Forster: a Life* (Oxford University Press, 1979), Vol. 2, p. 238.
8 Richard Canning, *Brief Lives: E. M. Forster* (Hesperus Press, 2009), p. 88.
9 Christopher Isherwood, *Lost Years: A Memoir, 1945–1951*, ed. Katherine Bucknell (HarperCollins, 2000), p. 93n.
10 Interview, see note 6 in this chapter.
11 Christopher Isherwood, *My Guru and His Disciple* (Farrar, Strauss and Giroux, 1980), p. 204.
12 Stephen Spender, 'Isyyvoo's Conversion'. *New York Review of Books*, 27.13: 14 August 1980.
13 *Diaries, Volume 2. The Sixties.* ed. Katherine Bucknell (HarperCollins, 2010), p. 77. Hereafter cited as 'Isherwood 2010'.
14 See Berg, James J. and Chris Freeman, eds. *The Isherwood Century: Essays on the Life and Work of Christopher Isherwood* (University of Wisconsin Press, 2000), pp. 4–5.

PART V

The 'Most Professional' Poet

CHAPTER XXXI

Auden in Prose

Sean O'Brien

Auden wrote an immense quantity of prose, some of which has still to be gathered for the complete edition of his work, which has now, with the publication of Volume IV, reached the years 1956–62. The range is wide in subject matter and in form: it extends from book reviews to essays, collections of essays (*The Dyer's Hand*) and lectures (*Secondary Worlds*), the critical monograph *The Enchafèd Flood* and a commonplace book, *A Certain World*. The outlets for this work were likewise numerous and varied. Auden was not alone in noticing that a poet can make a better living from journalism than from his art, but his response to this state of affairs was to get on with his work as both a poet and a prose writer. He is not, for example, recognizable in the figure of Orwell's book reviewer, still in his dressing gown at noon, glaring at a pile of books he has not read, as the deadline nears.[1]

Despite his comments on the matter, in the many book reviews that Auden himself wrote, there is little sign that this work is being done mainly out of a sense of duty to his bank manager: on the contrary, he seems to be absorbed by whatever is set before him, and he creates the cumulative sense that all the reading and reviewing, drawing on literature, science, philosophy, history, theology, music and anything else that catches his interest (the range of 'a minor atlantic Goethe'), are being absorbed into a larger project – one which might finally be called simply *Auden*. The effect is of an extremely civilized industry. Although he warned of the danger to the poet of the 'too exclusively literary a life' created by secondary activities such as journalism, translation and teaching (*DH*, p. 77), it is not clear that any alternative was conceivable for him.

A remarkable proportion of the journalism bears re-reading, partly of course because Auden worked in a time when 'higher journalism' meant what its name implied: a serious, engaged response to the material under consideration, rather than the recycling of received ideas and accounts of literature focused on personalities. It was an adult activity rather than a branch of fashion and publicity; but in the sphere of paid employment, Auden was by no means a snob. That America was 'so large, / so friendly, and so rich' (*CP* 2007, p. 730) created many more and better paid opportunities than Britain could afford. As well as in *The Nation*, *The New Republic* and *Partisan Review*, he wrote for fashionable commercial magazines such as *Mademoiselle* and *Vogue*. The article written for *Vogue* with Christopher Isherwood in 1939, 'Young British Writers – on the Way Up' (*Prose II*, pp. 21–24), a survey of novelists (all of them male), perhaps exhibits a certain constraint, but its authors are not slumming.

A writing life that involving a good deal of journalism and reviewing is by its nature a continuous improvisation. It would therefore appear unsuited to a strategic approach; but Auden's preoccupations – such as the nature and task of the individual, and the relationship of the written world to the lived one – are frequent presences. He is usually at some level writing about what concerns him, and of course his prose would be of less interest to us were it simply an act of unaffiliated professionalism. In Auden's case, the one-thing-after-another life of the reviewer is also being lived by someone whose imagination is much given to systems and explanations: the first is enriched and given point by the second, while forbidding completion of the second's encompassing project. If final authority is perpetually deferred by openness to change, Auden might at one time have ascribed this to an unconscious but deliberate frustration of one wish by another; perhaps later he would have considered the desire for complete knowledge to be sacrilegious.

'Nature, Poetry and History' (1950; *Prose III*, pp. 226–33) appeared in *Thought*, a journal produced at Fordham, the Jesuit University in New York. The first of three essays, it shows Auden at his most ostensibly systematic, in the guise of philosopher and theologian, turning his attention to aesthetics. This is one of several discussions in which he distinguishes between the crowd, which can only be counted; the society, 'a system which loves itself'; and the community, made up of those able to love something other than themselves. The context of these groupings is both natural (seasonal, cyclical) and historical (composed of unique events which provoke other events). Poetry's task is to foster the natural against the mere contingency of the historical. As to poetry, 'The subject matter of the poet is a crowd of occasions of feeling in the past. He accepts this crowd as real and attempts to transform it into a community, i.e. to give it a possible instead of a chimerical existence'. Poetry, then, has a moral task above all, and its beauty is the embodiment of that task.

It is not hard to see why this Augustinian interpretation appeared in a Catholic magazine. One reads the essay with admiration but also, perhaps with what might seem inappropriate amusement, because while it is clearly necessary for Auden to undertake this summing-up and the several other related formulations he wrote, at some level it is difficult to believe that he actually means it. It is too *clear*. It seems to arrive on the page without effort, like a report on work carried out elsewhere. (The God of Auden might have to be imagined making clear, careful lists, with the Commandments as an early example.) Leavis's well-known disapproval of Auden, recorded in the 1950 Afterword to *New Bearings in English Poetry*, was in part directed at the poet's 'air of knowing one's way around'.[2] The underlying accusation seems to be one of inauthenticity, of not necessarily meaning one thing anymore than another. We do not have to share Leavis's prejudices in order to feel that matters are not entirely as Auden makes them appear. This may have something to do with Auden's schoolmasterly clarity: the essay may be more a lesson for us than an act of faith for its author, for whom it is a symbolic rather than an effective deed, a ritual of appeasement. When we read the essays and poems of Eliot, the other great Anglophone religious poet of the twentieth century, it is clear that whatever wisdom the author has gained through the effort of faith is both essential to him and in need of constant refreshment in the face of its own frailty. Faith has a cost: it entails suffering through (self-)knowledge. Eliot's famous proposal that the poet seeks an escape from personality is contradicted by the poems, which are saturated with particular agonies and dilemmas, while paradoxically it is Auden, whose poetic personality is so pronounced and idiosyncratic, whose work reads as in some important sense impersonal, or even perhaps not quite human, as though going through the motions. It is not that Auden did not suffer and struggle; but the written result can read as a superb impersonation rather than the real thing, just as Auden himself can appear a brilliant parody of a certain class of Englishman at a particular time, or even a parody of the basic assembly of factors that we believe adds up to a person 'who can, now and again, truthfully say I' (*SW*, p. 120). This is not to say that Auden's writing is untruthful, but it might be said that while Auden did not write novels (and wrote an admiring, envious sonnet, 'The Novelist'), he nonetheless produced a good deal of prose fiction, which taken as a whole amounts to a developing myth of Reason.

The myth has some resemblances to a game, in that without rules it ceases to have meaning and thus cannot be played: a parlour game must abide by its own rules, as must a detective story. In his greatly admiring review of Tolkien's *The Fellowship of the Ring* (*Encounter*, November 1954; *Prose III*, pp. 491–94), Auden points out two very minor problems of plausibility: the fact that the large families of prolific Hobbits have not outgrown the incurious enclave of the Shire, and the anomaly of a lake formed by the damming of a river but with no escape for the continually arriving water (*Prose III*, p. 492). This will make some readers, or players, throw up their hands in exasperation. Isn't he missing the point? Auden's literalism reminds us that he was born in Yorkshire, where the great ritual of cricket (the greatest game, and yet more than a game) provokes the minutest theological niceties of interpretation and precedent and is treated as indisputably 'real'. His cavils about Tolkien, though, are linked to praise. He argues that the power of Tolkien's Heroic Quest, undertaken by an ordinary representative of his tribe, rather than an aristocrat, lies in our knowing the effect failure would have on the lives of all the creatures of Middle Earth, which is not the case with medieval Quests:

[O]ne is sometimes tempted to ask the knightly hero – 'Is your trip necessary?' Even in the quest for the San Graal, success or failure is only of importance to those who undertake it. One cannot altogether escape the suspicion that, in relation to such knights, the word 'vocation' is a high-faluting term for a game which gentlemen with private means are free to play while the real work of the real world is done by 'villains'. (*Prose III*, p. 493)

Clearly some games are more real than others, although it might be objected that Auden is measuring Arthurian Romance against criteria more suited to tragedy (while doubts about the claims to 'vocation' might also be raised in connection with poetry itself). What Auden also tries to do in his prose writings, as in his poems, is to make his idiosyncrasy, even his eccentricity, normative, as though the task of the prose is to do administratively what the poems do imaginatively. If Auden's early poems had been merely representative of a contemporary climate of feeling, rather than being animated by an alluring strangeness, he would not have achieved such significant and *representative* status. The systematizing administrative tendency does of course also find its way into the poems: it is perhaps the cause of Randall Jarrell's famous denunciation of Auden in his essay 'Changes of Attitude and Rhetoric in the Poetry of W. H. Auden', where he adduces certain stylistic habits as evidence of the corruption of imagination by intellect (and we may interpret intellect as administration).[3] At the close of 'In Praise of Limestone', Auden claims to 'know nothing' of the afterlife, but elsewhere he indicates a supreme familiarity with and competence in whatever he encounters. He might write about humility at times (as in 'The More Loving One') but his personality rarely shows it. In a speech cut from *The Habit of Art*, Alan Bennett suggests how this extends itself into life, when Benjamin Britten laments:

Wystan, you see, could never admit that I'd thought of anything first. 'Oh yes,' he'd say. As if I was just reminding him of something he'd thought of earlier. You could never tell Wystan anything, just remind him of it. [4]

Auden warns against too literary a life, but his own world is imperially literary, and whatever beliefs he holds are part of and must take their place in the whole endeavour – subdued, as it were, to the maker's hand. He operates as if with a series of filters, so that the actual always sounds like him, while the imaginary sounds as if it must be true for the same reason. This is emphatically the case when in *The Enchafèd Flood* he concludes a discussion of the futile, phantasmal nature of the public, as distinct from people, by explaining: 'although it has struck many readers as unjust, Coleridge was imaginatively correct in allowing all the companions of the Ancient Mariner to die ... they are an irresponsible crowd and since, as such, they can take no part in the Mariner's personal repentance, they must die to be got out of the way' (*Prose III*, p. 23). The schoolboy ruthlessness of that closing phrase draws attention to itself, not because Auden has forgotten that he is discussing a work of literature, but in order to ask how seriously the reader is prepared to take the work in question; that is, whether sentimentality, which is utterly foreign to Auden, will displace seriousness.

In a typically provocative remark in *The Dyer's Hand* he observes:

A society which was really like a good poem, embodying the aesthetic virtues of beauty, order, economy and subordination of detail to the whole, would be a nightmare of horror, for, given the historical reality of actual men, such a society could only come into being through selective breeding, extermination of the physically and mentally unfit, absolute obedience to its Director, and a large slave class kept out of sight in cellars. (*DH*, p. 85)

This is startling, funny, knowing and outrageous in its matter-of-factness, but how seriously are we to take it? Auden's point is inseparable from its tone, its gestures, and its appearance of speaking to the like-minded while laying down clear guidance to those who are not yet, and may never be, of their company. In short, the point is inseparable from the performance, because, perhaps more interestingly, the performance is the point. We know that the work of art is not a democracy, because it requires a strict hierarchy in the service of an interest whose identity may well, in the nature of things, not be entirely made known by, or even be knowable to, its maker, who is after all another of its servants. Auden is using a poetic device here, taking an analogy and treating it as if it were literal: the effect is a glimpse of an allegorical nightmare, something almost Chestertonian, which also has common ground with C. S. Lewis, Tolkien and Charles Williams. As in some of the poems, we have moved from the everyday into terrain where the peremptory laws of the folktale and nightmare are as much to the fore as recognizable mundane reality. And as in Auden's comments on *The Lord of the Rings*, there is a slightly eerie literalism at work. Its effect is a reversal of polarity: the reader who smiles and says 'Yes, but …' is offered a glimpse of a world in which the figurative has become actual.

Auden rarely takes a direct interest in people, but he is quick to populate his writing with appropriate characters, for example in the cited passage, which produces a compressed epic in which time has in effect stopped, an earthly hell built partly on foundations offered by Orwell. One effect is to send the reader back to consider what is actually taking place in 'history' poems such as 'Deftly, admiral, cast your fly' and 'The Fall of Rome', which it is tempting to admire for their sheer assurance in the selection and organization of detail; in the light of Auden's poem-as-society they may also seem terrifying in proportion to their apparently neutral calm.

Auden's relatively late lecture, 'Words and the World' (1968), returns to the territory of 'Nature, Poetry and History' to attempt a fresh summary of a subject. Here the argument depends on a distinction between the individual, defined by membership of a species, and a person, who is a unique being, exercising free will. Looking for a perfect congruence between theology and poetry, Auden is as locally brilliant and beguiling as ever, but the essay produces an instructive contradiction. He quotes St Augustine: 'God who made us without our help will not save us without our consent' (*SW*, p. 129), he later remarks: 'if one responds to a poem at all, the response is conscious and voluntary' (*SW*, p. 130). We see the logic Auden is pursuing, but we cannot accept it, because the voluntary element in a response to poetry takes only partial account of the way poetry works. It is interesting that Auden has just been describing the 'deadly … use of words as Black Magic' (*SW*, p. 128), characterized by the reduction of words to mere repetitive sounds with which audiences can be trained to respond to the will of, for example, religious demagoguery (he paints a prophetic picture of a now familiar synthesis of capitalism and televangelism). Unstated here is an anxiety about the irrational element in the appeal of poetry itself, the capacity, as Eliot put it, to communicate before it is understood, operating at pre- and sub-conscious levels of memory and association. The decision to read a poem may be voluntary (though in educational settings the reading of poems is necessarily partly prescribed), but the poem's workings are not governed by that fact. Auden is in danger of throwing the poem out with the Black Magic.

His view is also unhistorical, neglecting the Hebraic, Classical and Catholic influences which have shaped poetry and European languages in general. Such year zero theo-poetics appear more likely than not to emerge from a powerful awareness of the less biddable forces in play in the sphere of poetry, and the 'logic' and literalism of Auden's argument seem to function as a form of appeasement in reverse: let me alone with these barren notions; I claim so little. In this sense 'Words and the World', like much of Auden's prose, is fiction in the service of a myth of Reason in which no poet, Auden included, can finally believe. It is part of the drama of flight from the daemonic. As he wrote in 'Matthew Arnold', 'His gift knew what he was – a dark, disordered city' (*EA*, p. 241). Auden's 'voluntary' acts of language are subverted by his own gift, revealing what he was loth to admit but which, on the whole, is not 'better hid'.

Auden was fortunate in that his eminence and the inherent interest of virtually everything he put on paper meant that people would read the work of his left hand in the first place because he was its author, whatever the ostensible subject under review. Luckily, his writing was not the platform for the display of 'personality' in the way which is now widespread, for while Auden's literary personality is everywhere apparent, it is always *for* something more than itself. It is hard nowadays to name a single author who can demonstrate the same breadth of competence or wield the same authority as Auden in his time, or who can make serious matters look like the natural occupation of the intelligent general reader. Auden was of course *sui generis*, but the world has changed, and the subjects at the centre of his concerns, religion, history, philosophy, music and (most of all) poetry, have undergone developments of their own. More than that, in some probably unquantifiable way, they no longer occupy the same securely central place in contemporary discourse. Many of those who in earlier generations would have felt some obligation to attend to such matters no longer feel it, and in any case no longer have the confidence to engage without the aid of a screen of simplification. Auden himself, at some point in the last twenty years, has ceased to read as a contemporary. His ideas about poetry and about religion are never very far from each other; indeed, the proximity of these subjects seems to cause Auden a good deal of anxiety. His statement that 'Poetry is not magic. Insofar as poetry, or any of the other arts, can be said to have an ulterior purpose, it is, by telling the truth, to disenchant and disintoxicate', (*DH*, 27) shows a convert's fear that the Devil may have copyrighted the best tunes, leaving to virtue only the tedium of the hymnal. As religious belief becomes not only impossible but inconceivable for many people who would form Auden's natural contemporary constituency of readers, it would be a serious loss if it also became impossible to grasp how much his religious thought is bound up with his apprehension of the sometimes ungovernable power of poetic language.

NOTES

1 George Orwell, 'Confessions of a Book Reviewer', in *The Collected Essays, Journalism and Letters of George Orwell*, vol. IV, *In Front of Your Nose*, ed. Sonia Orwell and Ian Angus (Secker and Warburg, 1968), pp.181–184.
2 F. R. Leavis, *New Bearings in English Poetry* (Pelican, 1972), p. 167.
3 Randall Jarrell, 'Changes of Attitude and Rhetoric in Auden's Poetry', *The Third Book of Criticism* (Faber and Faber, 1975), pp. 115–50.
4 Alan Bennett, *The Habit of Art* (Faber and Faber, 2009), p. ix.

CHAPTER XXXII

Auden and Little Magazines

Andrew Thacker

I

An analysis of publication in 'little magazines' can be illuminating for at least four reasons.[1] First, as indicating those magazines a writer considers to be important, illustrating perceptions of contemporary cultural value: seen in Auden's case in his early work for *The Criterion*. Second, the work of a particular writer can sometimes give shape and definition to a periodical, as with Auden's presence in Geoffrey Grigson's *New Verse* (1933–39) which, as Stan Smith argues, can be described as 'Audenesque' in character.[2] Third, tracing a writer's work in periodicals often throws light on the composition of poems, and on their later revision or rejection from collected volumes; Auden was fond of quoting Valéry's dictum that 'A poem is never finished; it is only abandoned', and a consideration of his work for periodicals greatly illustrates the complex textual history of some key works. Finally, reading Auden's poetry in the original mode of publication arguably means we read different poems, with different meanings to those published in book form, even if the words are identical: for example, the periodical codes of *New Verse* when it published the ballad 'O What is That Sound' in 1934 produce a different text to the version published in *Look Stranger!* or that found in the *Collected Poems*.[3]

II

Auden's earliest periodical publications, from 1926, were in magazines associated with Oxford University. His first appearance in an acknowledged little magazine was the publication of 'Paid on Both Sides' in T. S. Eliot's *The Criterion* in January 1930; for the next four years, Auden contributed twelve more pieces, mainly reviews. Another influential contemporary magazine was F. R. Leavis's *Scrutiny*, begun in 1932, to which Auden contributed six reviews in the first three years of the magazine's life. Both were primarily devoted to cultural criticism, but as the 1930s progressed, they also fostered significant debates on social and political issues. Auden, however, found a more welcome home for his political views in two other outlets not readily fitting the definition of a little magazine: the socialist British weekly, *New Statesman and Nation* (1931–57; started in 1913 as the *New Statesman*), and what might be seen as its American equivalent, *The New Republic* (started 1914), a weekly magazine which took a similarly critical view of capitalism during the 1930s and included Edmund Wilson and Malcolm Cowley on its editorial team. Auden contributed many pieces, both prose and poetry, to these two journals throughout the 1930s and was listed as a 'Contributing Critic' to the *New Republic* in the 1950s. 'September 1, 1939', marking one of the key moments in his career, was first published in *New Republic* in October 1939. Between 1930 and 1940, however, the two magazines to which Auden contributed the most (more than twenty items to each) were *The Listener*, the magazine of the BBC, and Grigson's *New Verse*. Whereas the latter was an archetypal little magazine, dominated by the personality of the editor and subject to the financial insecurities of many such magazines, the former was a more middlebrow and financially stable institution, started in 1929 as a way of educating the new radio audience along the lines established by Lord Reith, the BBC's first director.

During the early part of his career, Auden published only a few pieces in classic modernist magazines (such as John Middleton Murry's *The Adelphi*, James Hunnington Whyte's *The Modern Scot*, *Cambridge Left* and *Left Review*), and nothing in one of the key poetry magazines of the 1930s, Julian Symons's *Twentieth Century Verse* (1937–39) – although according to Stan Smith, the poet was a 'touchstone' for the aims of this magazine.[4] In 1937, along with Michael Roberts, Auden edited an 'English number' of Harriet Monroe's influential Chicago magazine, *Poetry*. Apart from *New Verse*, however, his presence in little magazines in the early part of his career was often outweighed by publication in more mainstream periodicals, presumably for financial rather than ideological reasons: between 1938 and 1939 he appeared first in three well-established American periodicals, *Harper's Bazaar*, the *New Yorker* and the *Saturday Review of Literature*. In the 1930s, he would also publish occasionally in magazines or newspapers with a more defiantly political agenda, such as *The Daily Herald*, the feminist weekly *Time and Tide*, or the American left magazines, *New Masses* and *Partisan Review*.

Two other important little magazines to which Auden contributed in the 1940s were John Lehmann's monthly *Penguin New Writing* (1940–50) and Cyril Connolly's *Horizon* (1940–50), both of which developed the idea of the modernist magazine in new directions after the collapse of journals such as *The Criterion, Twentieth Century Verse* and *New Verse* in 1939. Auden had contributed several key works to *New Writing*, Lehmann's 1930s predecessor to *Penguin New Writing*, such as a group of eight poems that included 'Musée des Beaux Arts' (then titled 'Palais des Beaux Arts') to the Spring 1939 issue, and he continued to offer much good work there. Both *Penguin New Writing* and Connolly's *Horizon* were major successes, considering the wartime circumstances of the Blitz and paper rationing. The work Auden contributed to *Horizon* was of a consistently high standard, including 'In Memory of Sigmund Freud' in March 1940 and 'In Praise of Limestone' in July 1948.

From the late 1940s onwards, his work appears much less in little magazines and more in newspapers such as the *New York Times* and *Observer*, or mainstream quality publications such as *Vogue* or *Harper's*. Unlike many other modern writers, Auden showed little interest in editing a periodical, although he served on the editorial board (with Jacques Barzun and Lionel Trilling) of two highbrow book club magazines, *Griffin* (the magazine of The Readers' Subscription) and *Mid-century* (The Mid-Century Book Club) from 1951 to 1962, and was on the founding editorial board for the magazine of translation, *Delos*, in 1968. Throughout the 1950s and 1960s, he contributed regularly to *Encounter*, the monthly established by Stephen Spender and Irving Kristol in 1953 as a replacement to magazines such as *Horizon* and *Penguin New Writing* (both closed in 1950). Auden ceased to contribute, along with many others, with the revelation in 1967 that the CIA had funded *Encounter* as a propaganda weapon in the Cold War.

III

Auden's appearance in *The Criterion* (January 1930) with the verse drama 'Paid on Both Sides' presaged the publication by Faber and Faber later in the year of his first commercial volume. *The Criterion* tended to publish a select range of new and modernist literature rather than avant-garde work, in keeping with Eliot's growing espousal of 'classicism' in literature; in his original plan for the magazine, Eliot wished to publish little creative work as such and instead make it 'primarily a critical review'.[5] As such, the issue that published 'Paid on Both Sides' contained only one other creative work (a short story by the German, Ernst Wiechert), alongside criticism by Ezra Pound and reviews by Eliot, A. L. Rowse and

Middleton Murry. Eliot's editorial in the January 1930 issue, discussing a prize awarded by five European periodicals to the best short story they have published, indicates *The Criterion*'s strong European focus:

It is not merely a means of bringing to notice new prose writers in five languages....We remark upon it still more as visible evidence of a community of interest, and a desire for co-operation, between literary and general reviews of different nations, which has been growing steadily since 1918, and which is now so much more pronounced than at any time before the war as to be almost a new phenomenon. All of these periodicals, and others, have endeavoured to keep the intellectual blood of Europe circulating throughout the whole of Europe.[6]

At this point Auden had already spent a year in Germany and was beginning to offer a critique of England and Englishness informed by his sense of Europe; and although he never subscribed to Eliot's view of the 'mind of Europe', the cosmopolitan contents of *The Criterion* and its willingness to cross cultural frontiers matched many of his own interests (see Edward Mendelson, 'The European Auden', in *CCWHA*). His first *Criterion* review (of a work of philosophical psychology) is interesting for its focus on the theme of the double:

Dual conceptions, of a higher and lower self, of instinct and reason, are only to [sic] apt to lead to the inhibition rather than the development of desires, to their underground survival in immature forms, the cause of disease, crime, and permanent fatigue. The only duality is that between the whole self at different stages of development – e.g. a man before and after a religious conversion. The old life must die in giving birth to the new. That which desires life to itself, be it individual, habit, or reason, casts itself, like Lucifer, out of heaven.[7]

Though Tony Sharpe has noted Auden's tendency in early reviews in *Scrutiny* and *The Criterion* to mimic the dominant style of the editors of these journals, the interest in a doubled identity that is discussed here was clearly important for Auden.[8]

While Eliot continued to publish Auden's works at Faber, Auden himself stopped contributing to *The Criterion* after 1934; perhaps because of an awareness that his political beliefs would not have found a congenial home in Eliot's magazine (Auden's 'A Communist to Others' appeared in *Twentieth Century* in 1932). However, his early desire to be published in *The Criterion* not only testifies to its status in the cultural landscape, but also to his own wish for acceptance by the person he acknowledged as the key literary figure of the older generation. By 1933, it was time for Auden to move on to a new periodical that aimed, in part, to displace Eliot's model of modernist verse, Grigson's *New Verse*.

IV

New Verse was dominated by Auden and the 'Audenesque', even though Adrian Caesar has shown that statistically its editor, Grigson, contributed more to the magazine.[9] In its final issue, Grigson even suggested that the magazine's whole rationale was based on the poet: '*New Verse* came into existence because of Auden'.[10] He had consulted Auden prior to starting the magazine, in order to elicit his support; Auden was rather understated in his enthusiasm for the project: 'Why do you want to start a poetry review. Is it really as important as all that? I'm glad you like poetry but cant (sic) we take it a little more lightly. . . . If you do start one and want my stuff of course you can have it' (quoted Carpenter, pp. 153–54). By the time *New Verse* published a special issue devoted to Auden in 1937 it was clear that his verse was not treated 'lightly', but was central to the manifesto for the magazine Grigson outlined in the first issue:

Poets in this country and during this period of the victory of the masses, aristocratic and bourgeois as much as proletarian, which have captured the instruments of access to the public and use them to convey their own once timid and silent vulgarity, vulgarizing all the arts, are allowed no longer periodical means of communicating their poems. . . . NEW VERSE, then, has a clear function. When respectable poems (as it believes) are being written and forced to remain in typescript, it can add itself as a publishing agent to those few publishers who bring out . . . a few books of verse. It favours only its time, belonging to no literary or politico-literary cabal. . . . NEW VERSE does not regard itself as a verse supplement to such periodicals as the *Criterion* and *Scrutiny*.[11]

It is interesting to consider *New Verse* as part of the same constellation of little magazines in the early 1930s as *The Criterion* and *Scrutiny*, and although Grigson rejected this comparison, the oppositional stance he often took as editor showed that it was not groundless. His dislike of the 'vulgarity' of the 'masses' would also not have been out of place in the two other magazines. There are, however, key differences. In the first issue of *New Verse* Auden's 'I have a handsome profile', satirizing those from 'a great public school' with 'a little money invested' but inhabiting 'a world that has had its day', has a leftish didacticism that would not have sat happily in Eliot's magazine. It was also one of the poems Auden omitted from his oeuvre, not reprinting it in *Look Stranger* or any subsequent collection. His notion of a 'world that has had its day', however, was one fitting the characteristic tone of 'newness' and modernity that *New Verse* shared with *New Writing* and the significant anthologies edited by Michael Roberts, *New Signatures* (1932) and *New Country* (1933). Grigson was later to contrast those authors who still endorsed an aesthetic of 1900 or the 'limitations of Eliot and Pound' and those, spearheaded by Auden, who were committed to the present day: 'But Auden does live in a new day', he proclaimed.[12]

The dominance of Auden in *New Verse* is most noticeable in the contents of the special double issue devoted to him in November 1937. This only avoids the whiff of hagiography by dint of the tempered critical comments by Edgell Rickword, Stephen Spender and Allen Tate. Even these – Rickword's criticism of Auden's 'emotionally irresponsible statements' or the fact that the 'lyric grace' of his latest poems 'is achieved at the expense of that sensuous consciousness of social change which made his early poems such exciting discoveries'[13] – do not outweigh the endorsements by Christopher Isherwood, Louis MacNeice and others. Grigson's explanation for the issue establishes the tone: 'We salute in Auden ... the first English poet for many years who is a poet all the way round. ... He is traditional, revolutionary, energetic, inquisitive, critical, and intelligent'.[14] The appearance of a photograph of the poet, an autographed facsimile of 'The fruit in which your parents hid you, boy' from the issue 4 of *New Verse* and the checklist of Auden's writings concluding the issue all show how the thirty-year-old poet dominated the character of this little magazine. Even Faber contributed to the celebration with an advertisement of its Auden publications headed with the title, 'Vin Audenaire'.

Auden's original contribution to the special issue was the poem 'Dover', whose concern with borders and the frontiers of England and Englishness captured many of the key issues facing writers in the 'new day' of the 1930s. The soldiers and aeroplanes that populate the poem are a marker of upheavals in 'the new European air' both actual and imminent; its images of 'pilgrims', 'migrants' and travellers capture something of Auden's recent travels to Iceland and Spain and his projected trip to China with Isherwood, as well perhaps as anticipating their departure for America in 1939. 'Dover' was probably composed in August 1937, and represents an interesting example of how consideration of periodical publication can throw light on the compositional history and variants of an author's text. The *New Verse* (*NV*) version was revised by Auden for publication in 1940's *Another Time* (*AT*; as reprinted in *EA*), and then again for the *Collected Shorter Poems* Faber and Faber published in 1966 (*CSP*). Some of the changes are merely stylistic or tighten the prosody; such alterations represent Auden as a poet unable to 'finish' his works, as he later noted in a Foreword to Bloomfield's bibliography of his works:

As Mr. Bloomfield himself has pointed out to me, the chief value of a bibliography to a writer is that it helps to ensure that his finally revised text is recorded as the standard. I am sorry, however, to have to warn him, and anybody else who should be interested, that I have made scores of further revisions in the hope of one day being able to reprint. A critic is entitled, of course, to prefer an earlier version to a later, but some seem to think that an author has no *right* to revise his work. Such an attitude seems to me mad. Most poets, I think, will agree with Valéry's dictum: 'A poem is never finished, only abandoned'. To which I would add: 'Yes, but it must not be abandoned too soon'. In some cases, too, one finds that tinkering is no good and the whole poem must go.[15]

In some cases, however, the 'tinkering' with 'Dover' reveals a concern not just to improve syntax or punctuation but to significantly amend the sense. Two instances will suffice to indicate how meanings of the *New Verse* version of the poem are embedded within the cultural and political context of the periodical. Stanza 3 in *NV* ends as follows: 'Within these breakwaters English is spoken; without / Is the immense improbable atlas'. This is an important image that demonstrates the motif of the border and that of England as an island beyond which lies the great mystery of the rest of the world. There is an edge of criticism here for the English-speaker unable to conceive of the rest of the world except as 'improbable' and 'immense', but also a sense of the traveller's excitement, about to voyage out from the familiar. The poem is simultaneously about both entering and leaving England, celebrating its life and traditions at the same time as offering a critique of them, and this line neatly encapsulates this ambivalence. Similarly, Auden's ambiguous attitude to England here is perfectly in keeping with the tenor of *New Verse* as a magazine: looking to develop English poetry into new regions, it was also sharply critical of the insularity and backwardness of much contemporary English culture.

In *AT*, the poem remains the same, but in his post-war revisions Auden changed the line quite considerably: 'Within these breakwaters English is properly spoken, / Outside an atlas of tongues'. Now the division between inside and outside is, arguably, too strictly policed by means of the notion of a 'proper' English, which opposes the non-English speaking parts of the world. The revision sharpens the trope of the frontier, but loses the nuance of the original line which had captured much better the political unease of the troubled 1930s as well as pointing to Auden's own uncertain sense of where his future lay. A similar feature can be found in the closing lines of the poem. In *NV*, the poem ends:

> The soldier guards the traveller who pays for the soldier.
> Each one prays for himself in the dusk, and neither
> Controls the years. Some are temporary heroes.
> Some of these people are happy.

In *AT*, there are minor changes of syntax and punctuation ('Each one prays in the dusk for himself'), but the sense is quite different in *CSP*:

> The soldier guards the traveller who pays for the soldier,
> Each prays in a similar way for himself, but neither
> Controls the years or the weather. Some may be heroes:
> Not all of us are unhappy.

It is difficult to see what is added to the *CSP* version by the addition of the rather trite image of the human inability to control the weather; we can also note that the ambiguity of the dusk in *NV*, another border trope, is now completely lost. But the most striking change is the final line, which arguably overturns the whole sense of the poem. In the *CSP* version, the poet and reader are now dragged into the debate on happiness by means of the collective 'us', whereas the *NV* version positions Auden as the detached observer of those he sees. The rather downbeat sense in *NV* that only 'some' people are happy disappears in the rather more chipper claim that we are not all unhappy. Again the later changes rid the original version of the ambiguities that made it such a fine poem.

Such changes, I would suggest, represent more than mere 'tinkering', especially if the text is relocated within the context of its original periodical publication. 'Dover' in *New Verse* is a different text to that found in the *Collected Poems*, and the full range of its meanings is best appreciated by reading that text in the pages of the periodical, a move which helps link the beautiful ambiguities of the poem to the unsure cultural and political climate of the 1930s. Returning Auden's texts to periodical places of publication is not just a matter of linking their words to other themes and issues in the magazine, but also makes us aware of how such bibliographical features as size, design and typography of a journal affect the meanings of a text. *New Verse* was a little magazine in size, containing relatively few advertisements (mostly for publishers), and was priced at 6d, which the editor suggested was the 'price of ten Players ... or a bus fare from Piccadilly Circus to Golders Green'.[16] Reading it in this context allies the poem to the 'new day' that Grigson saw around him in the early 1930s, and which was partly an attempt to revivify the little magazine tradition of innovation and experiment in poetry.

Another instance of how a poem generates different meanings when read in its original periodical publication is that of 'A Communist to Others', a text which Auden 'abandoned' after complex 'tinkering' (see *EA*, p. 421). It was first published in the impressive yet short-lived radical monthly magazine of the Promethean Society, *Twentieth Century*

(1931–33). This was devoted to rational discussion of political, religious and educational reform, and published six pieces by Auden, including 'A Communist to Others' in September 1932. Auden's poem fitted the concerns of the magazine: Middleton Murry had written on Communism in the issue for March 1932; the April 1932 copy had Trotsky on 'Communism and World Chaos'. Interestingly, its page layout ran to two columns, making 'A Communist to Others' appear as if in a newspaper: this is quite different, for example, from the single column format with relatively large white spaces of *New Verse*, let alone how it reads within the pages of his *Collected Poems*. The periodical codes, therefore, of *Twentieth Century* indicate a mix of political radicalism and cultural experimentation: it had a large format, with a dark red cover and heavy black type recalling the Vorticist magazine, *Blast*. The poem here strikes a revolutionary tone, one which Auden swiftly sought to disown in subsequent printings.

Much more detailed work remains to be done on the nature of modern periodical publication and also on how these diverse bibliographic environments determined the meanings of the texts they published. There are also still a few Auden poems hidden in the periodicals that do not appear in book form, such as 'Case Histories' from *The Adelphi* (June 1931), which is an interesting poem for shedding light on his early reading of Freud. Many of Auden's 'abandoned' poems read quite differently when viewed in the little magazines rather than within the pages of books: interesting textual variants combine with the overall character of these periodicals to produce distinctive cultural texts. As Auden himself said: 'There are no secret literary sins. By cutting or revising a bad poem in later editions, one may show repentance, but the first is still there; one can never forget or conceal from others that one has committed it' (Bloomfield 1964, p. 8).

NOTES

1 For the issues surrounding the definition of a little magazine see the 'General Introduction', Peter Brooker and Andrew Thacker, (eds.), *The Oxford Critical and Cultural History of Modernist Magazines, Vol.1: Britain and Ireland 1880– 1955* (Oxford University Press, 2009), pp. 11–16.
2 See Stan Smith, 'Poetry Then: Geoffrey Grigson and *New Verse* (1933–9), Julian Symons and *Twentieth Century Verse* (1937–9)' in Brooker and Thacker (eds.), *Modernist Magazines, vol.1*, p. 652.
3 For the notion of 'periodical codes' see Brooker and Thacker, 'General Introduction', pp. 5–9.
4 See Smith, 'Poetry Then', p. 655.
5 Eliot to T. Sturge Moore, 3 April 1922, *The Letters of T. S. Eliot, vol. I: 1898– 1922*, ed. Valerie Eliot (Faber and Faber, 1988), p. 518.

6 Eliot, 'A Commentary', *The Criterion*, 9:35 (January 1930), p. 182.
7 Auden, Review, *The Criterion*, 9:36 (April 1930), p. 569.
8 See Sharpe, 'Auden's Prose' in *CCWHA*; on the double in Auden, see Stan Smith, 'Introduction', *CCWHA*, p. 9.
9 See Adrian Caesar, *Dividing Lines: Poetry, Class and Ideology in the 1930s* (Manchester University Press, 1991), p. 117. See Stan Smith, 'Poetry Then', for a critique of Caesar's views.
10 Grigson, 'Twenty-Seven Sonnets', *New Verse*, 2 NS (May 1939), p. 47.
11 Grigson, 'Why', *New Verse*, no.1 (January 1933), pp. 1–2.
12 Grigson, 'The Reason for This', *New Verse*, 26–27 (November 1937), p. 1.
13 Edgell Rickword, 'Auden and Politics', *New Verse*, 26–27 (November 1937), p. 22.
14 Grigson, 'The Reason for This', *New Verse*, 26–27 (November 1937), p. 1.
15 Auden, 'Foreword' to B. C. Boomfield, *W. H. Auden: A Bibliography The Early Years through 1955* (University Press of Virginia, 1964), p. viii. Hereafter cited as 'Bloomfield 1964'.
16 Grigson, 'Why', p. 2.

CHAPTER XXXIII

Double Take: Auden in Collaboration

Richard Badenhausen

My title both alludes to and plays off of Wayne Koestenbaum's ground-breaking 1989 book on the erotics of male literary collaboration, which he called *Double Talk*. The idea of a doubled Auden hardly needs elucidation, as the manner in which he negotiated a variety of dualisms has been explored from many different angles: he himself even fore-grounded the idea in the title of his first book written wholly in America, *The Double Man* (1941). But this trope has rarely been used in conjunction with Auden's many collaborative relationships; even though I think it helps illuminate what Patrick Query has called Auden's 'almost com-pulsive need to collaborate'.[1]

Interestingly, in Koestenbaum's study, Auden is mentioned only once, in passing. Part of the reason for this is that he doesn't fit into Koestenbaum's thesis that when male authors collaborate 'they rapidly patter to obscure their erotic burden'.[2] In fact, in the case of Auden and Isherwood's work together on a wide variety of projects, there was not only great comfort with the underlying homoerotic tension, but those circumstances actually presented solutions to some artistic problems, as in the case of *Journey to a War*. Unlike the nervous chatter of Eliot and Pound during their famous collaboration on *The Waste Land*, the discourse surrounding Auden's authorial partnerships is generally secure and grounded, although the rela-tionships themselves are not without complications. Auden did not fear any of the negative connotations of Koestenbaum's 'collaborators', those who, during times of war, 'have compromised themselves, have formed new and unhealthy allegiances, and have betrayed trusts' (Koestenbaum, p. 8). If anything, collaboration in Auden's life was enabling and enlarg-ing, and he usually recognized it as such.

I am also evoking the emergence of 'double take' as a term of art from the burgeoning 1930s film industry, describing circumstances in which a director examines a shot and decides to do another take to get it right: a technique Auden would have encountered during his brief experience with documentary film-making. While the phrase now alludes more to an additional glance required to confirm or dispel something that has caused surprise, in both cases it turns on the idea of looking, and then looking again: an activity that always interested Auden. Ever the cool, detached observer of human behaviour, Auden developed and maintained this perspective in part from his early training and life-long interest in the sciences. He wrote in 1936 that the 'artist is the person who stands outside and looks, stands even outside himself and looks at his daydreams.... He is a mixture of spy and gossip' (*Prose I*, p. 164). In this respect, Auden is doubled both as a garrulous social animal and a retiring, solitary individual preoccupied with furtive gazing.

The sheer number and variety of Auden's collaborations is extraordinary. He produced seven libretti with his partner Chester Kallman and translated numerous other existing libretti, song lyrics, and plays with him; their earliest libretto involved collaboration with Igor Stravinsky on *The Rake's Progress*. With Benjamin Britten, who had written music for two of Auden's plays and set a number of his poems to music, Auden partnered on documentary films, on plays and programmes for the radio, and on an opera about Paul Bunyan, although their friendship later cooled. Isherwood produced three major plays with Auden, co-authored a travel book documenting their 1938 trip to China, sketched out a couple of unproduced film treatments, and even co-authored an article for *Vogue* in 1939. Auden had earlier generated another travel book with Louis MacNeice. In addition, he was a key member of the Group Theatre in the 1930s, whose various manifestos and production practices not only extolled the cooperative nature of staging drama but sought intentionally to bring the audience into that collaborative circle. This emphasis on collaborating with many different individuals was also seen in Auden's short stint making documentaries with the General Post Office (GPO) Film Unit (1935–36).

But with Auden, it is worth considering collaboration in broader terms, beyond the simple fact of sharing the writing of a text with another individual. I have in mind his many translations, editing projects, and even interactions with earlier authorial versions of himself. That notorious habit of revising and even rejecting prior work fits in especially nicely with my trope of the double take, for the elder poet periodically reread previously published poetry with a censorious eye during those moments when, as he wrote in one late poem, 'I hold council with Me' ('Aubade', *CP 2007*, p. 884). Auden worked on translations of three different Brecht plays, translated poetry in a variety of different languages, and worked on prose translations of texts like Goethe's *Italian Journey* and former Secretary General of the United Nations Dag Hammarskjöld's journals. In those last two cases, where Auden was working in languages he knew only adequately (German) or not at all (Swedish), he enlisted the assistance of a collaborator to first provide a literal translation, from which he would then create a freer rendering. Instead of operating as a doubled performance in which partners struggled within the relationship to define their roles, collaborations on translations were more rigid exercises in which a source text was reworked a number of times along an assembly line – a process that ended up obscuring those hazy origins.

Throughout his career, Auden served as editor or co-editor on a wide range of projects, including anthologies, editions, special issues, and other collections, like *An Elizabethan Song Book*, produced in 1955 with Kallman and Noah Greenberg, who later collaborated with Auden on a medieval musical called *The Play of Daniel*. Auden enjoyed this sort of editorial work, which provided some useful extra income. Editing also served as both a creative and social act that brought the private into the public realm, just as much of his poetry had done. In one co-edited anthology on Medieval and Renaissance poetry, he stated some 'General Principles' grounded in the position that 'The creation of an anthology involves choice, and choice in turn involves the personalities of the editors. Impersonality is as dull in a book of this sort as it is in human beings' (*Prose III*, p. 103). Many of these projects contained a co-editor not just because collaboration came naturally to Auden, but because these associates provided balance. In the case of *The Oxford Book of Light Verse*, after working hard on the edition in the fall of 1937, Auden dumped the unfinished project into the lap of A. E. Dodds (wife of E. R. Dodds), who ended up having to make wholesale corrections, revisions, and additions, even selecting additional poems.

Not all of Auden's collaborations led to completed work. Sometimes they failed because of financial pressures or the changing interests of the project's participants or backers, but in other cases because of Auden's own hard-headedness. He and Bertolt Brecht, whom he came to dislike intensely, engaged in a somewhat tortured collaboration on a Broadway revival of Webster's *The Duchess of Malfi* from 1944 to 1946; little of their material made it into the final production. In 1963–64, Kallman and Auden wrote lyrics for a stage play based on the story of Don Quixote, but their contributions were not used because of disagreements with the producer (*Lib*, p. 507). At other times, he could be more conciliatory: a contracted collaboration with a scholar of languages on a book about

Tolkien, whose work Auden admired very much, was scrapped after its subject objected (Carpenter, p. 379, n. 1).

Part of the purpose of this exhaustive list is to demonstrate that collaboration in its many facets was not only standard operating procedure for Auden, but in certain cases seemed a fundamental necessity of artistic invention. For him creation was a social practice, a strategy that intentionally rejected Romantic conceptions of solitary authorship, grounded in notions of genius and inspiration. One of his habits, in fact, was to draft a poem and then discuss the manuscript with selected friends like Isherwood who, in *Lions and Shadows*, frames his account of their editorial deliberations in terms of social exchange. While Auden was driven by the desire for a successful visit, Isherwood expressed alarm at the amount of influence he had on the work, able either to condemn a poem to the garbage with one negative comment or to generate a finished poem that was in effect 'a little anthology of my favourite lines'.[3] Part of Auden's anxiety surrounding solitary authorship derived from his reading of modern history, according to which cultural and economic changes in the sixteenth and seventeenth centuries had destroyed older foundations of social community. This resulted in the Romantic poets' withdrawal from the public realm, a disastrous turn inward in which writers became isolated 'in an amorphous society with no real communal ties': 'they turned away from the life of their time to the contemplation of their own emotions and the creation of imaginary worlds' (*Prose I*, p. 433). Auden's own aspirations to be a poet with public relevance, at least through the 1930s, made him more receptive to collaborative arrangements, not only with fellow artists but with readers and playgoers: he was preoccupied with reconnecting the artist to the actual world.

His first important productive collaborations took place with Isherwood; they eventually produced three dramas together, *The Dog Beneath the Skin* (1935), *The Ascent of F6* (1936), and *On the Frontier* (1937–38). Both had fairly well-defined roles within the collaborative relationship, with each responsible for pre-assigned parts. They would then synthesize that material and cooperate on an ending, which always gave them trouble. Michael Sidnell points out that in *The Ascent of F6*, Auden handled the 'more abstract and universal' material whereas Isherwood managed the 'more concrete and satirical' parts, including the secondary characters.[4] While Isherwood once declared that they 'interfered very little with each other's work' (*Plays*, p. 598), he tried to stem Auden's desire to slide into ritual: '[w]hen we collaborate, I have to keep a sharp eye on him – or down flop the characters on their knees' (*Tribute*, p. 74). Auden believed each brought a distinctive aspect to the collaboration, identifying Isherwood as a 'realist writer' and himself as a 'parabolic writer' (*Plays*, p. 555).

Auden had cut his teeth with the Group Theatre, a cooperative whose various manifestos emphasized its collaborative underpinnings: 'It is a community, not a building' (*Plays*, p. 491). Founded in 1932 by the dancer Rupert Doone and others, the Group began working with Auden in 1933. Sharing his left-wing politics, the Group aspired to extreme involvement of the theatre audience, whose members would effectively become collaborators in the dramatic production. This fortified Auden's belief that drama is 'essentially a social art', originating as an expression of the 'whole community', so that in its ideal form 'there would be no spectators ... every member of the audience should feel like an understudy' (*Prose I*, p. 70; *Plays*, p. 497).

Auden sometimes expressed similar collaborative ambitions for the readers of his poetry, when focusing on the indeterminacy that resulted from the 'dialogue between the words of the poem and the response of whoever is listening to them' (*SW*, p. 130). This collaborative reshaping seemed acceptable if the poet was part of the community, but Auden started to worry later in the 1930s that such cooperative unity no longer existed. Fears articulated in his 1937 introduction to *The Oxford Book of Light Verse* were coming to pass: 'the private world is fascinating, but it is exhaustible. Without a secure place in society, without an intimate relation between himself and his audience ... the poet finds it difficult to grow beyond a certain point' (*Prose I*, p. 435). So he began to close down these opportunities for the reader, fearing how a poet's words might be 'modified in the guts of the living'. Following his move to America, Auden grew increasingly concerned by negative aspects of readerly collaboration and the disintegration of community. In one fascinating 1942 review of Louise Bogan's *Poems and New Poems*, he argued that because this deterioration resulted in a 'crowd of lost beings united only negatively in virtue of the things that they severally fear', one must then take responsibility for 'one's individual self-development'; a damaging effect was that the poet could not depend on any external help in his own self-development and thus must take over 'the task of directing his life by his own deliberate intention' (*Prose II*, p. 154). Such a fear can partly help explain the attraction of collaboration for Auden and also the ambivalence about doubled creation that occasionally surfaced.

Such uncertainties also contributed to his notorious revisions of his poetry. In this, Auden literally enacted the practice of the double take by gazing at a text and then – having experienced surprise, revulsion, and even anger at what he had previously written – proclaiming that such sentiments of an earlier self were either dishonest or no longer applied. Mendelson characterizes the habit in the following fashion: his revisions were 'imposed on the work of the young poet by an older and uncomprehending editor who happened to bear the same name'.[5] In detailing the implications of some of the better-known cases, Mendelson scrutinizes Auden's anxiety that his earlier feelings and positions were being latched onto by an approving and ultimately uncontrollable public; the fact that such adulation tended to converge around rhetorically powerful moments in the poetry only made matters worse. The potential demagoguery imbedded in a line like 'We must love one another or die' so alarmed the older Auden that he simply chose to erase that expression of an earlier poetic self. Here collaboration acts negatively, with a more powerful individual operating from a privileged position turning his back on a partner and closing down rather than enlarging the possibilities of art.

Such anxieties are nowhere in evidence in two of Auden's most delightful collaborations. *Letters from Iceland* (1937) and *Journey to a War* (1939) reflect an uncertainty about the value of the projects that turns on the question of whether tourists can ever really *know* their destinations, for many impediments prohibit the foreign observer from achieving 'any real intimacy with his material' (*Prose I*, p. 336). And yet, Auden is entirely comfortable with that uncertainty: there is a sense of play about these travel books as well as a self-consciousness about their artificiality, and collaboration necessarily highlights both features. The architectonics of the Iceland volume, in particular – constructed around epistolary communications – implicitly value the social, collaborative nature of that form. That arrangement encouraged Auden to be more inclusive towards his subjects, a development Marsha Bryant investigates by connecting Auden's work on documentaries for the GPO film unit to his subsequent photographs in *Letters from Iceland*. She examines how Auden attempts to address his dissatisfaction with the manner in which the documentary camera diminished its working-class subjects – reinforcing social divisions between the privileged observer and dispossessed observed – by decentring the locus of power in *Letters*, through two devices that popularize modernist strategies of fragmentation: 'exposing the observer and dislocating the viewer'. In this respect, Auden's habit of collaboration conditioned him to approach his subject from a less authoritative position, what Bryant calls a 'more plural ... engagement', and seek its assistance during the construction of meaning.[6]

In another interesting reading of this travel literature, Douglas Kerr sees the collaboration between Isherwood and Auden on *Journey to a War* enacting a debate about their respective positions of ideological and authorial certainty. Kerr juxtaposes Isherwood's insecurity about their material – his 'disorientation' towards Asia and his inability to fix or even find a story in his prose section of the text – with Auden's confidence about placing the Sino-Japanese war within a larger historical narrative in his sonnet sequence.[7] The different forms in which each worked – Auden did most of the poetry and Isherwood the prose – allowed for multiple perspectives, but more importantly permitted different levels of conviction regarding the material: the poetic voice can boom with authority of singular vision, but the prose perspective is typically more diffuse. Isherwood seems compelled to speak as 'We' instead of 'I' through much of the account, which underscores the struggles of the single writer trying to negotiate the tensions between articulating his own perspective and acknowledging the pressures of his travel-partner-cum-collaborator.

Such struggles were present in many of Auden's collaborative arrangements and he periodically thought quite intentionally about the suppression of his own authoritarian impulses within those relationships. In one reply to 'arrogant and stupid reviewers' trying to identify individual voices in co-authored works, Auden explained that partners in literary collaborations 'must surrender the selves they would be if they were writing separately and become one new author; though, obviously, any given passage must be written by one of them, the censor-critic who decides what will or will not do is the corporate personality' (*DH*, p. 483). Auden's career as an anthologist helped pay the bills, but it also allowed him to exercise control over a variety of literary projects while still benefitting from the assistance of a collaborator. For example, the intentionally provocative two-volume edition of poetry for schoolchildren, *The Poet's Tongue* (1935), co-edited with John Garrett, elided the baggage of authorial reputation and historical context by arranging the poems alphabetically by first line and anonymously (though authors are identified in the table of contents and indexes). The introduction allowed Auden to flex his polemical muscles by taking on narrow, conventional conceptions of literature, announcing at the outset that the best definition of poetry is 'memorable speech', thus expanding the canon to include artistic expressions concerned not just with 'the major experiences of life' and 'the eternal verities' but with everyday matters (*Prose I*, pp. 105–06). 'Poetry', he declares, 'is no better and no worse than human nature; it is profound and shallow, sophisticated and naïve, dull and witty, bawdy and chaste in turn' (*Prose I*, pp. 106–07). After staking out this theoretical ground, Auden returns to the writer's dependence on a collaborative relationship with the larger community that helps facilitate artistic production: 'a universal art can only be the product of a community united in sympathy, sense of worth, and aspiration' (*Prose I*, p. 107).

Auden's edition of *The Oxford Book of Light Verse* (1938) continued his attempts to stretch the canon by establishing the relevance of verse that did not fall under the dual umbrellas of serious or difficult poetry. His involvement with that collection partly resulted from a conversation with Charles Williams in which Auden criticized Yeats's recent *Oxford Book of Modern Verse*; later described as 'the most deplorable volume ever issued' by the Press (*Prose II*, p. 3). Auden's introduction to *The Oxford Book of Light Verse*, also preoccupied with the breakdown of community, historicizes light poetry within periods in which 'social and ideological upheavals' did not threaten the unity of particular societies, arguing that all poetry up until the Elizabethans possessed this quality of lightness (*Prose I*, p. 432). His inclusion of a significant amount of American material signalled Auden's iconoclastic streak but also, perhaps, his impending turn towards that culture, reflecting his sense that the frontier ethos of America's previous one hundred years had enabled the production of a folk-poetry reminiscent of 'similar productions of pre-industrial Europe' (*Prose I*, p. 436).

When contacted by Oxford to inquire whether he would like to bring out a new edition of the anthology, shortly before his death, Auden asked Edward Mendelson if he would be willing to collaborate, for with such projects, Auden wrote, 'two heads [are] better than one' (*Prose I*, p. 711). Auden had repeatedly benefitted from such assistance in similar editorial projects, like the five-volume *Poets of the English Language* (1950), co-edited with Norman Holmes Pearson. While Pearson made some of the initial choices for *Poets of the English Language* before consulting with Auden, the poet penned fairly extensive introductions for each volume that not only contextualized the verse within his learned, if highly particularized, view of literary history and culture, but were also selling points in marketing the collection. For Auden, the project had great 'personal value', and he hoped readers would share his own refreshed 'sense of the involvement of the present with the past' and 'understanding of the importance of an awareness of tradition' (*Prose III*, p. 153).

Compiling anthologies appealed to the educator in him and satisfied a strain of didacticism that he never seemed able to shake. He had definite ideas about what students should be reading and how that material should be presented; the introductions to his edited collections often adopt the tone of a lecturer leading his audience by the hand. He had a similar opportunity to shape the public's reception of what it was reading through his collaboration with Jacques Barzun and Lionel Trilling for just less than a dozen years (1951–62) at the Readers' Subscription and Mid-Century book clubs, which allowed them to select titles and position chosen texts in a very specific manner in introductions that appeared in the club magazines. According to Barzun, the social component of the selection process was a key feature of the collaboration: 'We behaved like friends talking over what to recommend to other friends' (xiii). He engaged in a similarly extended editorship for Yale University Press, from 1947 through 1959, when he chose, edited, and introduced an annual selection for The Yale Series of Younger Poets, a series that, under Auden's guidance, published volumes from poets like Adrienne Rich, W. S. Merwin, John Ashbery, James Wright, and John Hollander. While Auden did not enjoy penning introductions to the volumes, he did put significant time and effort into helping these young poets, in many cases composing multiple letters offering suggestions to writers whose work he selected and sometimes to those he did not: even as editor, he recognized the rich possibilities of art as a collaborative, social practice.

Such social practice might, he saw, connect with sexual practice. In his unpublished Berlin journal of 1964, words from Shakespeare's sonnet 116 prompt Auden's reflection about the power of collaboration in his own life:

The marriage of true minds. Between two collaborators, whatever their sex, age, or appearance, there is always an erotic bond. Queers, to whom normal marriage and parenthood are forbidden, are fools if they do not deliberately look for tasks which require collaboration, and the right person with whom to collaborate – again, the sex does not matter. In my own case, collaboration has brought me greater erotic joy – as distinct from sexual pleasure – than any sexual relation I have had. (Quoted *LA*, pp. 470–71)

In this interrogation of Greek notions of *eros*, Auden locates in successful collaborative relationships a higher, transcendent experience beyond sex. Whereas in Koestenbaum's reading there exists a tension constructed around the same-sexed nature of such partnerships, for Auden that status represents an opportunity because an institution like marriage is closed off to him. Additionally, a male lover can generate creative activity simply through his inspirational presence, acting as an 'onlie begetter', to cite Shakespeare's dedication in his sonnets, a phrase Auden co-opted for an unpublished poem addressed to a fellow student he desired at Oxford (Carpenter, p. 68).

Isherwood believed that the sex he and Auden occasionally shared 'had given friendship an extra dimension'[8]; this created both challenges and opportunities when working on *Journey to a War*. Bryant's inspired reading of that text demonstrates how two gay men who initially lacked the authority to document a foreign war solved the problem of negotiating 'competing models of masculinity and mediating signs of European colonialism' by in effect *performing* masculinity and establishing 'theatricality as a norm'. This reorientation allowed Isherwood and Auden to 'stage their self-representation in ways that camp traditional masculinity while maintaining their pose as documentary men' (Bryant, pp. 129, 148). In this case, collaboration provided a key solution to working through problems associated with genre and power by enabling the staging of the discourse *about* these issues. But this performance also takes place somewhat covertly, doubled under the conventions of travel writing and documentary reporting, which fit right in with Auden's habit of often suppressing or eliding homosexual themes in his love poetry, closeting this identity through rhetorical manoeuvres.

One of Auden's most important and prolonged collaborations took place with Chester Kallman; starting in the late 1940s, it formed the 'extra dimension' in a relationship by then no longer sexual. After their successful partnership on *The Rake's Progress*, they co-wrote six more libretti. In one co-signed reply to an unfavourable review of *The Magic Flute*, they made a special point of objecting to the reviewer's minimizing of Kallman's role, arguing that their alliance resulted in a 'wider range of expression than either could have achieved by himself' (*Lib*, p. 644). James Fenton portrays the relationship a little less idealistically, in terms that emphasize Auden's somewhat authoritarian nature: 'Chester was to Wystan like an impossible child ... Wystan was to Chester like an impossible parent ... *this* was the destructive force that he had to avoid'.[9] While theirs may have reminded others of the relationship between an obsessive, controlling Prospero and a lawless, childish Caliban, Auden viewed Kallman as both a full partner and privileged audience to his own doubled performance, inscribing his copy of *The Double Man* with the dedication, 'To Chester who knows both halves' (Carpenter, p. 309). Auden's collaborations thus are also doubled, sometimes looking different from the outside than from within.

The Double Man also contains an epigraph from Montaigne's essay 'Of Glory': 'We are, I know not how, double in ourselves, so that what we believe we disbelieve, and cannot rid ourselves of what we condemn' (*DM*, p. 3). This volume and its epigraph announce Auden explicitly as doubled in many of the ways this essay has explored, but also juxtapose 'We' and 'I' in a way that highlights a recurrent tension in Auden's collaborative arrangements. Working with others provided both emotional and practical benefits, especially during those moments when Auden recalled that '[a]loneness is man's real condition' (*DM*, p. 69; *CP* 2007, p. 237). While collaboration helped stem this isolation, Auden acknowledged in a series of aphoristic riffs about psychology and Freud that the 'real "life-wish" is the desire for separation, from family, from one's literary predecessors' (*EA*, p. 299). At times, that drive to disengage surfaces in his collaborative relationships as an authoritarian impulse. As he aged, his increasing fondness for aphorism demonstrated that the 'two-way creative traffic' of his early career eventually devolved into a one-way street, with the autocratic poet firmly in control. Ironically, Auden had, throughout his life, recognized with horror the historical response of political authoritarianism to circumstances that required cooperation and sympathy. Although he periodically tried to fight such impulses, Auden also understood they might be necessary to produce compelling literature. As he explains in 'The Poet and the City', a really good poem essentially requires 'absolute obedience to its Director, and a large slave class kept out of sight in cellars' (*DH*, p. 85). This just happens not to be a very humane way to construct a society, which of course is Auden's point. The challenge, therefore, became reconciling the need for obedience with the desire for collaboration, all without hurting the art.

NOTES

1 Patrick Query, 'Crooked Europe: The Verse Drama of W. H. Auden (and Company)'. *Modern Drama* 51 (2008), pp. 579–604; at p. 586.
2 Wayne Koestenbaum, *Double Talk: The Erotics of Male Literary Collaboration* (Routledge, 1989), p. 3. Hereafter cited in the text as 'Koestenbaum'.
3 Christopher Isherwood, *Lions and Shadows: An Education in the Twenties*, (1947) repr. (Pegasus, 1969), p. 191.
4 Michael Sidnell, *Dances of Death: The Group Theatre of London in the Thirties* (Faber and Faber, 1984), p. 195.
5 Edward Mendelson, 'The Two Audens and the Claims of History', in *Representing Modernist Texts: Editing as Interpretation*, ed. George Bornstein (University of Michigan Press, 1991), pp. 157–70 (p. 164).
6 Marsha Bryant, *Auden and Documentary in the 1930s* (University of Virginia Press, 1997), pp. 77, 98. Hereafter cited in the text as 'Bryant'.

7 Douglas Kerr, 'Disorientations: Auden and Isherwood's China', *Literature and History* 5.2 (1996), pp. 53–67; at pp. 64, 58.
8 Christopher Isherwood, *Christopher and His Kind 1929–1939* (Farrar Straus Giroux, 1976), p. 264.
9 James Fenton, Introduction to Thekla Clark, *Wystan and Chester: A Personal Memoir of W. H. Auden and Chester Kallman* (Faber and Faber 1995), pp. x–xi.

CHAPTER XXXIV

Auden and Prosody

Sean O'Brien

If in matters of prosody there are observers and believers, then Auden was of the latter party. To him the forms – line, stanza, metre and sound effects – figure as more than themselves, as they also did for a decisively unmodern poet, Walter de la Mare, of whom Auden wrote in 1939: 'He is perhaps the only poet who has used the anthology as a definite creative form. I remember very well the appearance of *Come Hither*, a collection which, more than any book I have read before or since, taught me what poetry is' (*Prose II*, p. 37).

De la Mare's 1923 anthology includes Hardy and Edward Thomas, the first poets to matter to Auden, but the book, which reaches back to Chaucer and beyond, is dominated by narrative and song-form, ballads and lyrics, a sense of the proverbial, and a resolutely pre-industrial view of a largely English and clearly Christian though superstitious world. A curious young person reading *Come Hither* would be in little doubt that prosody was almost the whole of poetry: in order to have anything at all, you had to have a tune. It remains a remarkable book.

A trainspotter's approach to prosody, by which the critic notes chrono-logically the make and formation of the poem's rolling stock, provides information rather than knowledge and may fall into the category of true-but-not-interesting-in-itself: in any event, space forbids it here. But it is hard to avoid the sense that W. H. Auden himself was, like De la Mare, in part a collector of forms for their own sakes as well as for the particular utility of alliteration, ballad, cabaret song, canzone, Skeltonics, sonnet, villanelle, iambic or syllabic metre, and the rest. To use his phrase from 'Making, Knowing and Judging', Auden was able to conceive the poem as 'a verbal contraption' (*DH*, p. 50). Lists and taxonomies appealed to him strongly, and he was certainly a spotter of engines and other machinery. Writing about Hardy, his first poetic love, 'a passion...which no subse-quent refinement or sophistication of...taste can ever entirely destroy', he recorded that until March, 1922, when 'I decided to become a poet', he had been 'the sole autocratic inhabitant of a dream country of lead mines, narrow-gauge tramways, and overshot waterwheels' (*Prose II*, pp. 43, 42). The urge to collect and categorize is often particularly strong in child-hood, especially in male children, and Auden retained much of the child's outlook – imperious, decided, possessive, fearful, secretive, and supersti-tious. Collecting combines the creation and discovery of order; it may also function as a tribute offered to appease the gods.

Auden argues elsewhere that 'one is not free to create *any* order one chooses. The order realized must, in fact, be already latent in the chaos, so that successful creation is a process of discovery' (*Prose II*, p. 125). In this sense, there are no accidents in the succession of forms and metres in which Auden wrote, but there may be a difference between the declared conscious intention and what actually seems to be taking place: Auden progressively civilizes himself, to the point where he speaks for the city he has previously opposed, but prosodically speaking, the old gods are still influential, and whatever drives prosody retains ultimate power.

Auden begins his introduction to *A Choice of de la Mare's Verse* with a discussion of the parable with which de la Mare introduces *Come Hither*.[1] In de la Mare's story, the curious boy Simon is invited into the house at Thrae by Miss Taroone to pursue his education in the panoramic library-cum-gallery of the mysterious traveller, Mr Nahum, before set-ting out on his own adventures. Auden extrapolates from this strange and beguiling tale, rich in de la Mare's incomparable landscape writing, our twofold desire: for the poem to be a beautiful, durable object (the work of Ariel), and for the poem to tell what may be the painful truth (the work of Prospero) – categories like those he describes elsewhere as Escape Art and Parable Art. This clarifying division is characteristic of Auden's criti-cism and essays (the list as a form of order), but its writ does not actually run as far as de la Mare's story or, much of the time, Auden's own poems. In both spheres, Ariel and Prospero operate inseparably, music modified by wisdom, wisdom by music. The artificial division may be necessary to enable the poet-critic to speak of what normally speaks him. But it also misleadingly appears to support the widespread view that poetry is a means of decorating the commonplace.

John Fuller's *W. H. Auden: a Commentary* lists forty-eight entries under Poetic Form in the index (the list may not be exhaustive). Perhaps the number is not huge – Auden asserts that no English poet, not even Browning, 'employed so many and so complicated stanza forms' as Hardy (*Prose II*, p. 47) but the diversity is striking – as is the imaginative unity sustained through all the formal variety, a unity deriving to a considerable degree from a recognition that Auden claimed to have arrived at through Hardy's poems: 'To see the individual life related not only to the local social life of its time, but to the whole of human history, life on the earth, the stars, gives one both humility and self-confidence. From this perspective the difference between the individual and society is … slight' (*Prose II*, pp. 46–47). Auden also notes that the sensitive novice can learn much from Hardy 'about the influence of form on content' (*Prose II*, p. 48) – including, we might infer, that their separation is necessary for discussion but not finally real: for as it is 'above', from the unified panoramic view Auden ascribes to Hardy, so it is 'below', in the sphere of imaginative practicality, where the poet learns from Hardy 'how to make words fit into a complicated structure' (*Prose II*, p. 48).

Auden's descriptions of poetry and other imaginative writing can be summary exercises in Reason – see, for example *The Enchafèd Flood* (*Prose III*, pp. 1–91) – but Reason is in the service of a religious disposition, which sees it as part of Creation, and his poems themselves exhibit a balancing sense of verbal and musical powers. In his book on the fundamentals of prosody, describing the intensified, ritualized attention produced by its organization into lines, Alfred Corn writes: 'poetry has never fully disengaged itself from its associations with shamanism; the poet, like the shaman, has mastered certain techniques – rhythmic, performative, imagistic, metaphoric – that summon the unconscious part of the mind, so that, in this dreamlike state between waking and sleeping, we may discover more about our thoughts and feelings than we would otherwise be able to do'.[2] Even at his most seemingly rational-analytical, Auden is also serving a shamanic function, and the strongest truth-claims may in fact emerge from this necessarily occluded sphere. 'Oh where are you going?' (*EA*, p. 110) is one of the most memorable and least self-explanatory of the early poems:

> 'O where are you going?' said reader to rider,
> 'That valley is fatal where furnaces burn,
> Yonder's the midden whose odours will madden,
> That gap is the grave where the tall return.'
>
> * * *
>
> 'Out of this house' – said rider to reader;
> 'Yours never will' – said farer to fearer;
> 'They're looking for you' – said hearer to horror,
> As he left them there, as he left them there.

Fuller provides a convincing psychosexual decoding of this 1931 poem (as he also does for 'Control of the Passes') but such analysis cannot help but seem reductive, because it must neglect the dramatizing function of the poem's prosody – a ballad form subjected to heavy alliteration and other internal echoes, with simultaneous recurrence and variation of form and phrasing producing the effect of both repetition and instability, most notably in the final stanza, which both abandons the interrogative (change of form apparently indicating resolution) and refuses to answer the questions. The critic may read the poem as a disguise and seek to unmask its wearer, but poetically the disguise is the outcome, the *event*. The *event* of the poem, in which prosody is dominant, shows paraphraseable meaning overwhelmed by crisis (something which reaches an extreme development in Auden's disciple James Fenton's poems 'A Vacant Possession', 'Nest of Vampires' and 'A Staffordshire Murderer'). Even in ostensibly less elaborately composed work from the early period, Auden is inclined to submit the poem to the judgment of prosody, as at the close of part IV of '1929', where love

> Needs death, death of the grain, our death,
> Death of the old gang; would leave them
> In sullen valley where is made no friend,
> The old gang to be forgotten in the spring,
> The hard bitch and the riding-master,
> Stiff underground; deep in clear lake
> The lolling bridegroom, beautiful, there.
>
> (*EA*, p. 40)

No matter how precisely analysis traces the sources of the poem in Auden's experience and his vast, wide-ranging reading, the poem itself survives (indeed, it ignores) interpretation. Through parallelism, and by marrying scripture and psychology in an erotic rite of invocation, it lives its own life somewhere between sense and music. It persuades the reader that its oddities – the familiar omission of articles (but in this case not all of them), the stranding of 'there' at the close of the poem – are not mere devices deployed by an author requiring our attention. They are instead signs of an imaginative necessity, manifested in music, which the poem seeks both to identify and to propitiate, so that prose sense is consumed by music – an aspiration which Auden's ruthless reassignment of passages in the early work serves to confirm rather than deny. Auden may be talking about the world, but it is a world known in prosodic form, a mode of knowledge and experience whose relationship to prose is unapologetically other and privileged. When Alan Pryce-Jones, reviewing *The Orators*, described it as exhibiting 'an imagination without a mind',[3] he was referring distrustfully to the daemonic character of early Auden. It is not so much that the character of Auden's prosody is different from those of most other poets as that it operates with greater invocatory intensity.

Discussing Eliot's *The Family Reunion*, and disagreeing with Eliot's analysis of some of its metrical effects, Auden remarks: 'prosody is to poets what laying a fire is to married couples, a matter on which no one is right but oneself' (*Prose III*, p. 258). Prosodic authority, then, is to be sought in practice: Auden's prosody may satisfy, or observe, certain rules, but these rules operate in individual poems written from specific preoccupations and obligations. If this is a truism, it is magnified and made strange by Auden's imperious idiosyncrasy. And it remains true for his work in syllabics, where the theoretically empty vessel of syllabic form is placed at the service of an urbane voice whose inclination is at once expansive and epigrammatic: see 'Ischia' and 'Ode to Gaea'. He remains alert to the fact that as Corn puts it, 'most readers expect lineation to have a basis in sound' (Corn, p. 135).

In his 'unwritten poem' 'Dichtung and Wahrheit' (1958) Auden makes another seemingly unimpeachable statement: that his first demand of any poem he'd written is that 'it be genuine, recognizable, like my handwriting, as having been written, for better or worse, by me' (*CP* 2007, p. 647). 'Dichtung and Wahrheit' itself is devoted to identifying the ways in which the statement 'I love you' may or may not be true in a poem. Although Auden, operating here in the guise of critic and prose writer, is at pains to present himself as a creature of reason, there is often, in Auden's prose as well as his poems, a strongly ritualistic element. In 'Dichtung and Wahrheit' the discussion of identity has an air of prestidigitation, like the object lesson provided by a favourite schoolmaster who knows that as yet his pupils can understand only part of the material.

While Auden may at times seek to disenchant us with one hand, he is often to be found enforcing the spell with the other, in which he holds a conductor's baton. The composer's art, he states admiringly in the sonnet 'The Composer' (December 1938), is 'pure contraption'. Applied to what he termed the 'transitive' art of language, the effect of his poetic music is at times uncanny (see 'Now the leaves are falling fast', 'As I walked out one evening', or 'Deftly, admiral, cast your fly'). This can be true, and instructive, even when there may seem to be a marked inequality in intensity between imaginative-emotional content and musical form, as is increasingly the case in the post-1945 work. In 'The Managers' (June 1948; *CP* 2007, pp. 601–03) some familiar Auden material – the mechanisms of the state, the innocence of non-human creatures, the nightmarish ordinariness of time passing and history accruing – receives, not its finest treatment (see 'The Fall of Rome', written the year before) but a memorable one nevertheless. Fuller comments: 'The poem drifts forward on its Skaldic rhyming with an extemporising air which none the less accumulates an analytical concern' (Fuller 1998, p. 417). A slightly different formulation might be that Auden is composing a kind of tone-poem to bureaucracy ('L'Après-Midi d'un Fonctionnaire', perhaps), where the lightly-buried rhymes (such as them / resemble; saint / painter) are the equivalent of an end-of-era chromaticism, although the era shows no sign of ending, because it is Hell in administrative form. The Hell in question is one that someone of Auden's class, the dutifully administrative-professional, might well have come to inhabit.

'Nursery Rhyme' (*CP* 2007, pp. 331–32), written, like 'The Fall of Rome', in January 1947, is discussed by Fuller immediately before 'The Managers' ('Their learned kings sat down to chat with frogs; / That was before the Battle of the Bogs. / *The key that opens is the key that rusts*'). Describing the poem's Portuguese *cantiga* form, Fuller declares it 'simply an exercise in cheerfully sinister nonsense', suggests a debt to Graves, and concludes quite reasonably that 'explication is fairly pointless' (Fuller 1998, p. 416). But even in this modest example with its schoolboy humour and self-parody, the kind of work Richard Hoggart perhaps had in mind when he described Auden as seeming at times like 'someone amusing himself cleverly at the piano',[4] form is a means of invocation, or initiation, a tribal reminder, a shadowing forth of mysteries not to be directly spoken of. This is terrain where Auden and Louis MacNeice, another lover of refrains and of 'dark saying', meet up. 'Saying' is an equal partner in that phrase: used as a noun, it retains the force of a verb; it is not the same as 'what is said'; and this too implies the element of *event* which prosody serves and produces.

In *Varieties of Parable*, MacNeice cites the *OED* definition of parable: 'any saying or narration in which something is expressed in terms of something else' and 'Also any kind of enigmatical or dark saying'.[5] These are two rather different propositions: the first suggests a kind of mechanical equivalence; the second provides no such reassurance. As time goes on, Auden might be viewed as trying to move his operations from the latter into the former, so that language becomes a pretext. Fortunately, his success is limited because the second approach has been embedded in his imagination from a very early stage. In a late poem, 'Sports Page', MacNeice concludes, 'all our games [are] funeral games',[6] and it is tempting to suggest that for Auden all our (best) rhymes are nursery rhymes, in that they exhibit a completeness and exercise a compulsion which are disproportionate to their rational content. These very characteristics can lend even Auden's most routine utterances a persuasive disquiet, as though he is trespassing beyond the margins of respectable doctrine.

Auden could confidently assume that readers would recognize his work as his: it is as recognizable as that of Yeats. But its (strange) prosodic authority and at times its authoritarianism, can seem so ample as to make the poems anonymous, like translations of what we might imagine to be the writings of history itself: the poet's 'personality' retires from the stage, in the service of a larger purpose. In a 'public' poem such as 'The Shield of Achilles' this is to be expected. In the realm of intimacy it may be more problematic. A. Alvarez, in *The Shaping Spirit*, complains that Auden never wrote a successful personal love poem, and he cited 'Lullaby' ('Lay your sleeping head', January 1937) as a damning example: 'there is a kind of vague, generalized feeling to the verse, as though Auden were writing a love poem to someone he had never been properly introduced to'.[7] But whereas Alvarez may have correctly identified a limitation in the poem if it is viewed as personal lyric, he may also have missed a larger point. 'Lullaby', while unmistakeably the work of Auden, is a dramatic utterance whose authority is situated between the personal and the universal, so that the degree to which the addressee and the speaker are present *in propria persona* is of less moment than their representative status under the attention of the 'involuntary powers' and 'every human love' (*EA*, p. 207). The privilege and plight of the lovers are both 'real' and transcendent, and it is the poem's prosody which authorizes this view. Fuller comments that 'the delicately hinted rhymes, the harmony between the musical line and the extended statements, and the careful epithets: all these reinforce the poem's gravity' (Fuller 1998, p. 264). The poem resembles a betrothal speech from a masque: Fuller mentions Oberon's closing remarks in *A Midsummer Night's Dream*; the masque in *The Tempest* provides another point of comparison. What gives the poem its uncanny atmosphere is the combination of the orchestration described by Fuller, the whole effect of which is impersonal, with the presence of the first person singular. Viewed in one light, the poem might seem a heresy in its assumption of power; although, as Auden observes in 'Dichtung and Wahrheit', 'Speech ... lacks the Indicative Mood. All its statements are in the subjunctive' (*CP* 2007, p. 648), which is literally the case at several points in 'Lullaby' (although these subjunctives are of course also invocations). In comparison with 'Lullaby', the more personal approach of the later 'The More Loving One' (September 1957) sounds defeated rather than affirmative.

Time, burner-away of 'individual beauty', is as much Auden's subject as any poet's: 'you cannot conquer time' (*EA*, p. 228), a truth enforced by the very indifference to time of the animal kingdom: 'Altogether elsewhere, vast / Herds of reindeer move across / Miles and miles of golden moss, / Silently and very fast' (*CP* 2007, p. 331), making a regular and instinctive journey untroubled by the anxiety about ends and purposes which afflict the human experience of time. As Philip Larkin wrote, 'Truly, though our element is time / We are not suited to the long perspectives / Open at each instant of our lives'.[8] But as we know, the aspiration of poetry is to overcome time's corrosive power. One of Auden's most haunting poems, perhaps the finest example of his dramatic music, Miranda's song 'My Dear One is mine as mirrors are lonely' (*CP* 2007, pp. 421–22), from *The Sea and the Mirror*, deploys prosody in a particularly significant way. It invokes an innocence for which time has not yet properly begun, one able to remember a time before Time. At the same time, it helps us to understand that when we have entered adult, mortal time we use ritual, order, and pattern to evoke the world before Time and after and outside it. In this case the speaker, Miranda, believes that in the words of an earlier Auden villanelle, '(t)he vision seriously intends to stay' (*CP* 2007, p. 312). Discussing 'If I could tell you' (October 1940), Alfred Corn notes: that 'in the best villanelles we experience the poem as a developing or unfolding argument or plot; repetitions do not occur mechanically but in fact expand and deepen as they appear in fresh contexts' (Corn, p. 115). Applied to 'My dear one is lonely as mirrors are lonely', this entirely reasonable description may seem slightly misleading, for the play of the poem operates in two seemingly contrary directions. One is 'developing or unfolding' (the reader's unillusioned perspective, perhaps); in the other, the virtue of innocence is sustained and upheld (again, presumably, with the reader's consent). We will struggle to *locate* either position in the poem, and it may be better to think of them as being simultaneously produced to begin with by the contrast between the lyric momentum essayed in the first refrain, and the (perhaps childlike) monosyllabic hesitations of the verse in the second line before the third line (the second refrain) assumes a more decisive shape:

> \- / / - / - / - - / -
> My Dear One is mine as mirrors are lonely,
> \- - / - / - / - - / /
> As the poor and sad are real to the good king
> \- - / / / - / - - - /
> And the high green hill sits always by the sea.

There may be differences of interpretation: 'My' in line 1 and 'sits' in line 3 might each arguably carry a stress, for instance, although this would disrupt the pattern of five stresses – if such it is. But the authority of the (hendeca-)syllabic verse seems to emerge from a music which may be audible to Miranda, but not to us. Instead, it reaches us like a rumour, something there-and-not-there, like the 'thousand twangling instruments' described by Caliban.

Miranda's villanelle opens with an echo of cadence from the carol 'Lullay my liking, my dear heart, my sweeting', about a maiden who 'lulled a little child, a sweete lording', the Christ-child. Auden's poem provides no lexical warrant for this similarity, but once the resemblance of sound-shape is acknowledged, it influences and complicates the reading of the text, so that the mirror becomes one of prophecy as well as recognition.

Prosody, we see, is the poem's element, rather than its adornment: the poem is a drama, a prosodic event, a musical tide on which speaker and reader are carried forwards. The poem reaches beyond the word spoken and towards the word sung, and thus towards the resulting variety of pitch and the idealizing of language and voice that would, for example, enable the alliteration of the opening line to move towards a condition of pure utterance, the Word unfallen in the fallen world. Time may have to be suffered, but the prosodic imagination is capable of granting us a sense of time suspended even though it goes implacably about its fatal work:

> He kissed me awake, and no one was sorry;
> The sun shone on sails, eyes, pebbles, anything,
> And the high green hill sits always by the sea.

> So to remember our changing garden, we
> Are linked as children in a circle dancing:
> My Dear One is mine as mirrors are lonely,
> And the high green hill sits always by the sea.

In the closing quatrain, lines 1 and 2 both shed the crowding fifth stress found in the mid-lines of previous stanzas; as a result, they seem more decided, more complete, and provide a signal, of a kind familiar from listening to music, that the end is almost upon us. It is perhaps for this reason, and not only because of repetition, that the closing double refrain seems emptier and more formal than its component lines do when placed singly in the earlier stanzas. Their completeness here is shadowed and made cold by a sense of inevitable falling-away. The value of innocence, it would seem, resides partly in our ability to see the limitations which create and dignify it – but this is too dry a way of expressing the matter. Here, and in many other places, Auden's prosodic power persuades the reader and listener that at its best his is not poetry *about*, but poetry *in* and *of* its subject, or as Auden put it, 'language as experience'.[9]

NOTES

1 W. H. Auden, ed., Walter de la Mare, *A Choice of de la Mare's Verse* (Faber and Faber, 1963).
2 Alfred Corn, *The Poem's Heartbeat: A Manual of Prosody* (Copper Canyon Press, 2008), p. 6. Hereafter cited in the text as 'Corn'.
3 *The London Mercury*, XXVI, May 1932, p. 171.
4 Hoggart, Richard, ed., *W. H. Auden: A Selection* (Hutchinson, 1961), p. 41.
5 Louis MacNeice, *Varieties of Parable* (Faber and Faber, 1965), p. 2.
6 Louis MacNeice, *Collected Poems*, ed. Peter McDonald (Faber and Faber, 2007), p. 597.
7 A. Alvarez, *The Shaping Spirit: Studies in Modern English and American Poets* (Chatto and Windus, 1958), p. 90.
8 Philip Larkin, 'Reference Back', in *Collected Poems*, ed. Anthony Thwaite (Faber and Faber, 2003), p. 111.
9 *A Choice of de la Mare's Verse*, Introduction, p. 18.

CHAPTER XXXV

Auden's Forms

Seamus Perry

The first impression, Barbara Everett said in her fine, early book on Auden, is 'abundance and variety'[1]: his task as a poet never lay in struggling with the medium but rather – as Clive James suggested – in managing his immense facility. The challenge of fulfilling the demands made by so many diverse poetic forms was a perpetual stimulus, but he remained savingly aware of the risks (to art and to morals) that might come from placing the wrong sort of emphasis on 'form'. And like most of Auden's most telling warinesses, this one was especially keen, because it arose from risks he knew that he had run himself.

The idea of poetry as a highly specialized kind of game, a display of immense proficiency with its own formal demands and absorbing 'aesthetic-technical problems', recurs ostentatiously in many of Auden's best-known critical utterances.[2] One lasting gratitude he owed to his first master Hardy was his 'metrical variety, his fondness for complicated stanza forms', which represented 'an invaluable training in the craft of making'; and the honour due to W. P. Ker, whose essays Auden had come across by a happy chance in Blackwell's, lay in the 'fascination with prosody' that he managed to instil (*DH*, pp. 38, 42): 'Hardy taught me stanza forms', Auden told Alan Ansen, 'but Ker really made me aware of the perpetual availability of metrical forms' (Ansen, pp. 42–43). Ker was an approximation to that ideal critic fondly imagined by Auden, among whose qualifying credentials was counted a liking for '[c]omplicated verse forms of great technical difficulty, such as Englyns, Drott-Kvaetts, Sestinas, even if their content is trivial' (*DH*, p. 47): such an unusual critic would be a professional version of the 'dream reader' Auden elsewhere invented, who 'keeps a look-out for curious prosodic fauna like bacchics and choriambs'.[3] 'Auden liked to boast that he had now written a poem in every known metre', says Carpenter, writing of the later years when Saintsbury's *History of English Prosody* was firmly established as a sacred text (Carpenter, p. 419): 'he would explain verse forms to me', Stravinsky remembered, 'and almost as quickly as he could write, compose examples … he was even eloquent on such matters'.[4]

Formal demands served a creative purpose by cultivating opportunities for accidence, on the importance of which Auden is always interesting. 'Those who confine themselves to free verse because they imagine that strict forms must of necessity lead to dishonesty, do not understand the nature of art, how little the conscious artist can do and what large and mysterious beauties are the gift of language, tradition, and pure accident' (*Prose II*, p. 48); or, as he put it a little more effusively: 'Blessed be all metrical rules that forbid automatic responses, | force us to have second thoughts, free from the fetters of Self' (*CP* 2007, p. 857). Auden approved of the thought as he found it expressed by Valéry: 'If a man's imagination is stimulated by artificial and arbitrary rules, he is a poet' – for 'a poet is someone to whom arbitrary difficulties suggest ideas' (*Prose III*, pp. 556, 594). 'I can't understand – strictly from a hedonistic point of view – how one can enjoy writing with no form at all. If one plays a game, one needs rules, otherwise there is no fun'[5]: such remarks are both playful and imply a conception of artistry at large as itself a kind of play-activity, an interest no less absorbing for appearing so wholly occupied with trivia – rather like the 'good form' of decorum and social rules that Auden came semi-jokily to fetishize in later life. One's response to such talk can veer between admiration at so winning a lack of pretension and weariness at so intent an air of inconsequentiality: there is, at times, the slightly dismal spectacle of an immensely well-stocked and superbly reflective mind marshalling itself to defend 'fundamental frivolity'.[6] 'Each year brings new problems of Form and Content', Auden wrote in a late 'Short' (*CP* 2007, p. 716), but the 'problems' in question feel more like brain-teasers than an intolerable wrestle with words and meanings. 'It is the glory of poetry that the lack of a single word can ruin everything, that the poet cannot continue until he discovers a word, say, in two syllables, containing P or F, synonymous with *breaking-up*, yet not too uncommon' (*Prose III*, p. 594): that really does contrive to make the whole business sound close-cousin to the crossword. 'Auden is very much a new type of aesthete', as John Bayley noted in 1957, 'who sees art not as religion but as a game to be played with as skilful and individual a touch as possible'[7]; and the oddly Wildean tang to all this sometimes becomes audible, as when Auden reportedly praised *The Importance of Being Earnest* for being 'about nothing at all', unlike *Lady Windermere's Fan*, which committed the blunder of having 'some social reference' (Ansen, p. 63).

But Auden is sometimes drawn to make weightier and more numinous claims for 'form', contemplating in the abstract idea of poetic form a type of perfection. Insofar as a poem is 'a beautiful object', he writes at one point, it is 'a verbal Garden of Eden which, by its formal perfection, keeps alive in us the hope that there exists a state of joy without evil or suffering which it can and should be our destiny to attain' (*F&A*, p. 385). That puts a lot of religious freight on 'formal perfection'; and Auden's frequently-offered analogy between poetic form and political or social organization is not much less momentous. 'The subject matter of poetry is comprised of a crowd of recollected occasions of feeling', which 'the poet attempts to transform into a community by embodying it in verbal society'. So the reader of a good poem becomes for a moment, and in an admittedly circumscribed way, no less than an inhabitant of the Good Place – 'Every good poem is very nearly a Utopia', as he memorably puts it in 'The Virgin and the Dynamo' (*DH*, pp. 67, 71). He was obviously stirred by the thought of such extraordinary correspondences, but they cut a consistently curious figure because the claims they make for form are at once enormous and yet intent on passing themselves off as trifles. While invoking tropes of perfection, Auden insists that the analogies are just that, and that taking them for anything more would be a very grave mistake indeed: 'Beauty … is not Goodness but its formal analogue' (*Prose III*, p. 557). The writings about music often turn upon this doubled sort of thinking: music offers the purest case of what 'Death's Echo' calls *a formal order, | The dance's pattern* (*CP* 2007, p. 154). The forms of music can, as Auden says in 'New Year Letter', gather its listeners into a kind of ideal society: 'a *civitas* of sound / Where nothing but assent was found' (*CP* 2007, p. 198). But music's formal version of goodness is doubly 'formal', because while it is a weighty matter of form it is at the same time merely a matter of form (and not of substance), like a formal opposition registered at a committee meeting: 'Listen! Even the dinner waltz in / Its formal way is a voice that assaults / International wrong' ('Music is International', p. 340). 'In its formal way' adroitly has things both ways there, at once staking a special aesthetic claim for the 'formal' while gracefully deflecting any imputations of *real* importance.

'The subject of a poem is a peg to hang the poetry on', Auden oracularly informed Stephen Spender when they were both undergraduates.[8] It is an early example of the habit, shrewdly diagnosed by Edward Mendelson, of 'exaggerating his aestheticism in a futile attempt to annoy the serious-minded' (*LA*, p. 370). Aestheticism can be its own kind of seriousness, and the young Auden's version was probably a sensationalized

version of Eliot, who had written in *The Sacred Wood* of great verse as a
'vehicle' for 'intense art-emotions'[9]; but the broad conception of poetic
form as something magically autonomous could trace its origins back
to the idealism of Schiller and Coleridge and others, and Eliot was not
alone in his attraction to a revivified version of Romantic aesthetics (even
if he didn't think of it in those terms). Jacob Epstein's enthusiasm for
'form, not the *form of anything*', say, like Clive Bell's charismatic notion of
'significant form', drew on much the same repertoire of ideas as Schiller,
who praised the 'truly successful work of art' in which 'the content should
effect nothing, the form everything'[10]; and Herbert Read in *Form in
Modern Poetry* and other works was busy bringing Coleridge's old doctrine of 'organic form' up to date.[11] Auden was certainly not immune to
this epochal interest; but nor did he simply subscribe. In fact, in common with many of his contemporaries, he viewed assertions of formal
autonomy with acute misgiving; and when in a subsequent book Read
praised the poetry of Shelley as 'not influenced by anything outside the
poet's own consciousness', Auden was ready to object: 'I cannot believe ...
that any artist can be good who is not more than a bit of a reporting journalist' (*Prose I*, p. 132). A pure art, like a '"pure" music' would lack 'any
analogy to any human experience' (*Prose III*, p. 195), and, like his early
champion and sympathetic critic Geoffrey Grigson, Auden instinctively
regarded artistic abstraction as 'too much "art itself"'.[12] He positively preferred painters who seemed 'literary', like Van Gogh, whose works refuted
a purist claim that 'the value of a painting can only be assessed by comparison with other paintings' (*F&A*, p. 297). Van Gogh exemplified a
quite distinct sort of genius, one which Auden had early venerated, in an
unusually exuberant review, as 'intensity of attention or, less pompously,
love' (*Prose I*, p. 43): 'No attitude could be more thoroughly opposed to
critical claims ... for the formal autonomy of art', as Mendelson rightly
says (*Early Auden*, p. 163). The rules of art might at times appear to possess some autonomous and wholly self-justifying pleasure of their own;
but, in truth, even 'formal and elevated styles of poetry are more conditioned by the spoken tongue, the language really used by the men of that
country, than by anything else' (*DH*, p. 356). The strong Wordsworthian
echo there nicely marks a point of divergence between Auden's instincts
and, say, Valéry's refined emphasis on 'the arbitrariness of poetic formal
restrictions' (*Prose III*, p. 594). 'The absolutely pure work of art ... doesn't
exist', was a truth Auden had been drawn to enunciate since the early
1930s (*Prose I*, p. 21). 'All art is based on gossip', he told the nation in a

BBC talk in 1937, 'that is to say, on observing and telling'; and the very best gossip of all is the work of someone who can embellish his tale with 'a wealth of circumstantial detail' (*Prose I*, p. 428).

Poetry, Auden once suggested, was 'the clear expression of mixed feelings' (*NYL*, p. 119); and the best of his thinking about poetry is the product of mixed feelings too – a mix of attitudes that come together, in some of his most characteristic utterances, as a having-it-both-ways, an articulation of the charm of form along with the insistent claim of that which precedes or eludes form, 'a world / Antecedent to our knowing' ('In Due Season': *CP* 2007, p. 801). De Quincey once said that everything might be grasped either by its aesthetic or its moral handle[13]; and many of Auden's formulations continue to inhabit that thoroughly Romantic dualism: enunciations of the pleasures of formal play repeatedly encounter their more worldly counter-principle. So, he may say that poetry is 'a game of knowledge', but at the same time it apparently does some real work: 'a bringing to consciousness, by naming them, of emotions and their hidden relationships' (*Prose II*, p. 345). As, similarly, for Valéry 'a poem ought to be a festival of the intellect'; but then there comes a counter-movement in the sentence – 'that is, a game, but a solemn, ordered, significant game' (*F&A*, p. 363); and a 'significant game', like 'significant form', comes close to being what Louis MacNeice thought Clive Bell's famous tag was: 'a contradiction in terms'.[14] Auden sets out these formative divisions in brilliantly schematic ways in several places, as the work respectively of 'The Novelist' and 'The Composer' (in his two sonnets with those names); or of Ariel (who produces 'a timeless world of pure play') and Prospero (who tell us 'what life is really like'; *DH*, p. 338).

When Auden writes about 'the poet' he is sometimes referring to the total contradictory and hybrid creature, and sometimes to the unrepentant aesthete within. When, for example, he asserts that 'in poetry, all facts and beliefs cease to be true or false and become interesting possibilities' (*DH*, p. 19), it is the work of the irresponsible Poet within the poet that he describes. As the 'actual writer', Auden allowed his own poetry no such latitude, rejecting famous poems for their dishonesty – a matter of expressing, 'no matter how well, feelings and beliefs which its author never felt or entertained' (*CP* 2007, pp. xxix–xxx). To have done so was to have committed the serious misdemeanour of Yeats: 'For Yeats the question was not "Are fairies real?" or "Is the doctrine of the phases of the moon true?" but "Can such ideas organize good poetry?"' (*Prose II*, p. 174). But for Auden, 'nothing is lovely, / Not even in poetry, which is

not the case' ('Plains': *CP* 2007, p. 565). The successful achievements of
form in themselves should raise a question in the wary reader about the
sincerity of what the poem seems to be saying: 'its formal nature cannot
but convey a certain scepticism about its conclusions': 'formally, it would
make no difference' if the lines ran 'Thirty days hath September, | August,
May, and December' (*DH*, p. 26). Ariel the Poet has happily fulfilled his
formal contract, even though Prospero the Historian knows the result has
turned out to be nonsense. The effect is akin to the phenomenon of wit-
tingly comic rhyme, which Auden writes about beautifully in *The Dyer's
Hand*: in a comic rhyme it is 'as if the words, on the basis of their auditory
friendship, had taken charge of the situation, as if, instead of an event
requiring words to describe it, words had the power to create an event'
(*DH*, p. 380). The prophetic pretensions of Romanticism, convinced that
poetry can make things happen, involve a failure to get that crucial joke:
'It's as if one said, "It will rain tomorrow". Perhaps as it happens, it does,
but one only said it because it rhymed with sorrow'.[15]

Mixed feelings about the authority of form are central to Auden's literary thinking both within his verse and outside it; and they find one
articulation in his complex response to Henry James. To Spender's criticisms of *Another Time* Auden responded robustly, conceding his limitations while at the same time claiming for himself some distinguished
company: 'I can only develop along the abstract systematic formalist
line (like Henry James & Valery)' (quoted *AS I*, p. 75). The talismanic
term 'form' appears perhaps most notably in James's preface to *The Tragic
Muse*, where he had famously deplored the 'large loose baggy monsters'
of nineteenth century fiction: 'There is life and life, and as waste is only
life sacrificed and thereby prevented from "counting", I delight in a
deep-breathing economy and an organic form'.[16] James had George Eliot
particularly in view, in whose *Middlemarch* he saw all the handiwork of
the historian and (as it were) precious little of the poet: 'If we write novels so, how shall we write History?' *Middlemarch* possesses 'a fullness of
detail which the reader often finds irritating', says James, nominating the
feature of the novel that many find admirable.[17] So, appropriately, it is
George Eliot who best expresses what goes wrong when form exercises
despotism over the 'detail' it seeks to organize: 'the form itself becomes
the object and material of emotion, and is sought after, amplified and
elaborated by discrimination of its elements till at last by the abuse of its
refinement it preoccupies the room of emotional thinking; and poetry,
from being the fullest expression of the human soul, is starved into an
ingenious pattern-work'.[18]

A devout admiration for the 'disciplinary image' of Jamesian refinement lay behind Auden's graveside tribute:

> With what an innocence your hand submitted
> To those formal rules that help a child to play,
>   While your heart, fastidious as
> A delicate nun, remained true to the rare noblesse
> Of your lucid gift, and, for its love, ignored the
>   Resentful muttering Mass…
> ('At the Grave of Henry James'; *CP* 2007, p. 309)

That is rapt and persuasive in its way; but it has the good and slightly solemn manners that typify Auden's moments of credal formalism. Mendelson is very winning about the poem: 'His poetic prayer to James for artistic purity has the characteristic windiness of his attempts to write what he could not make himself believe' (*LA*, p. 165); and indeed, elements of self-dissent are detectable in the misjudged prop of the nun and that affected snootiness toward the masses. For Auden intuitively responded to George Eliot's wisdom too, and recognized that an overpowering commitment to the demands of form may represent as much the failure of 'intensity of attention' as it does the victory of aesthetic control: 'while all of us in this room can be entranced by the exquisite formal beauty of James's construction', he said in an address of 1946, 'we need not forget that the price which had to be paid for this particular enchantment is high and that it would be a pity if all novelists were expected to pay it' (*Prose II*, p. 298).

Such remarks set an idea of formal purity against an inclusive awareness of 'detail'; or, the other way round, a principle of proliferation and abundance against a counter-principle of restraint. An awareness of some such division in creative energies is a shaping presence from the early writings, if roughly, as in the preface co-written with C. Day Lewis to *Oxford Poetry 1927*, which describes 'a struggle to reconcile the notion of Pure Art (…) with those exigencies which its conditions of existence as a product of a human mind and culture must involve, where the one cannot be ignored nor the other enslaved' (*Prose I*, p. 4; the material omitted quotes Jacques Maritain). 'A good poet can be recognized by his tense awareness of both chaos and order, the arbitrary and the necessary, the fact and the pattern', Auden writes years later: 'while observing facts, it is necessary to inhibit the pattern-making function, and while making the pattern it is necessary to inhibit observation of further facts' (*Prose II*, pp. 125, 122–23).[19] The Poet within the poet would like to be a despot, but the 'actual writer' has a saving regard for the 'formless' plurality that the Poet comes to organize (*DH*, p. 85). The political analogy of which Auden is so fond casts these opposing tendencies as the difficulties of a statesman: 'the poetry, i.e. the verbal society, is coercive upon the feelings it is being asked to embody', while, from the other end of the historical process, '[t]he crowd of feelings, i.e. the potential community, are passively resistant to all claims of the poetry to embody them which they do not recognize as just' (*Prose III*, pp. 163, 164).

In such statements – as when he writes of 'a dialectical struggle between the events the poet wishes to embody and the verbal system' (*Prose III*, p. 552) and so on – Auden displays all his generalizing and abstract virtuosity; but the knowledge that these remarks seek to rationalize is the much more instinctive one of his own experience as an 'actual writer'. James's disputable description of *Middlemarch* as 'a treasure-house of detail, but … an indifferent whole' happens to hit the mark with Auden rather well: '"a loosely-cohering amalgam of brilliant, idiosyncratic details," might be the best brief description of a poem by Auden', writes Barbara Everett (Everett, p. 3). It is perhaps not praise that Auden would have accepted without hesitation: in his full Jamesian mode – as when criticizing the 'swamp of the Accidental' in Joyce – he might have regarded such looseness and local efflorescence as symptoms of 'literary decadence'. And yet you can quickly see the justice of Everett's sympathetic account, and at both ends of the great career:

> A choice was killed by each childish illness,
> The boiling tears amid the hot-house plants,
> The rigid promise fractured in the garden,
>   And the long aunts.
>   ('A Bride in the '30s': *CP* 2007, p. 130)

> Leaf-fall. A lane. A rogue,
> driving to visit
> someone who still trusts him.
>   ('Marginalia': *CP* 2007, p. 798)

This is poetry marvellously alert to what Auden calls '[e]ach diverse form' ('Legend': *CP* 2007, p. 73). Such passages exemplify Bayley's description of the Auden detail: 'though they are introduced for different reasons and in different tones – ironic, lyrical, allegoric – they all exist startlingly clear of their contexts' (Bayley, p. 138), as though they were breaking out into an unexpected and irresponsible sort of freedom – escaping the formal demands of their occasion and proliferating into an unmotivated excess of particularity, implying an unwritten novel that lurks behind the lines. And a kindred exercise of imaginative latitude might be seen to operate on a finer scale too – rhythmically, for example, Auden was a connoisseur of lines that stumble away from their formal requirements:

> And down by the brimming river
> I heard a lover sing
> Under an arch of the railway:
> "Love has no ending."
> ('As I walked out one evening':
> *CP* 2007, p. 134)

With the gawky, mildly ludicrous tilt towards its rhyme on an unstressed syllable, the closing line here also barely rises to an 'ending'. The expectations of a formal pattern imply a miniaturized sense of destiny, and the doomy early verse was often preoccupied by fatedness as a global and self-conscious theme: Auden was naturally pleased to find in the sestina a verse form that 'beats', in Empson's words, 'however rich its orchestration, with a wailing and immovable monotony, for ever upon the same doors in vain'.[20] But in other poems, the rhymes of Auden's line-endings open a thought of escape, even if that escape often emerges as a very mixed blessing indeed, a loose end that insinuates unattachedness:

> Will it come like a change in the weather?
> Will its greeting be courteous or rough?
> Will it alter my life altogether?
> O tell me the truth about love.
> (*CP* 2007, p. 145)

Auden's admiration for Wilfred Owen paid off in a life-long mastery of unclenched endings that evade their lot. To take a later example, there are the beautifully managed near-rhymes that bring to an open-ended close a poem which is all about the possibility of finding out your own route, picking your way with care through an unplanned and uncertain but meaningful universe:

> The Old Man leaves his Road to those
> Who love it no less since it lost purpose,
>
> Who never ask what History is up to,
> So cannot act as if they knew:
>
> Assuming a freedom its Powers deny,
> Denying its Powers, they pass freely.
> ('The Old Man's Road':
> *CP* 2007, p. 606)

The verse intuitively inhabits, and acoustically enacts in its unrhyming rhymes, the whole imaginative space of necessity and freedom that Auden's prose sets out with such assiduous abstraction.

Auden's verse remains perpetually self-conscious about the limitations of the merely formal accomplishment, and delights in throwing away a fine effect for a more honest kind of utterance – 'Just reeling off their names is ever so comfy' ('Lakes': *CP* 2007, p. 562); but it remains gratefully alert, too, to the consolation of form. In 'The Shield of Achilles', a devastating, chastened re-write of Keats's 'Grecian Urn', the short-line stanzas describe the art-world that might have been, and the long-line stanzas the world without art, a wasteland of purposelessness and unthinking ruin:

> That girls are raped, that two boys knife a third,
> Were axioms to him, who'd never heard
> Of any world where promises were kept,
> Or one could weep because another wept.
>
> (*CP* 2007, p. 596)

But the poetry, at least, hears itself keep a promise, managing with such unflashy resourcefulness an unlikely rhyme on '-ept'. The poem finely exemplifies the way that Auden was drawn to imagining, simultaneously, both the value of form and the limitations of form; and his deep fascination for *The Tempest* was the regard of one master of this complicated, doubled art for another. '*The Tempest* is full of music of all kinds, yet it is not one of the plays in which, in a symbolic sense, harmony and concord finally triumphs over dissonant disorder', he wrote (*DH*, p. 526). Rather more emphatically, though, he told Alan Ansen that it was the play that Shakespeare had 'really left in a mess' (Ansen, p. 58); but the 'mess' was itself a kind of achievement, won by a recognition of the limits of 'form' that Auden warmly endorsed and explored at length in 'The Sea and the Mirror'. The play discharges the duties of its comic pattern, but in a self-consciously imperfect way: 'both the repentance of the guilty and the pardon of the injured seem more formal than real' (*DH*, p. 128); but while disempowered from doing 'anything really important', nevertheless the play evidently does something very important indeed: 'let the lips make formal contrition / for whatever is going to happen' ('The Dark Years'; *CP* 2007, p. 282).

NOTES

1 Barbara Everett, *Auden* (Oliver and Boyd, 1964), p. 3. Hereafter cited in the text as 'Everett'.

2 The phrase comes from Auden's contribution to a symposium on his poem 'A Change of Air', *Kenyon Review* 26 (1964), pp. 204–08.

3 Ibid., p. 208.

4 Igor Stravinsky and Robert Craft, *Memories and Commentaries* (Faber and Faber, 1960), p. 154.

5 Quoted in Charles Osborne, *W. H. Auden: The Life of a Poet* (Methuen, 1980), p. 329.

6 From a letter, quoted in Arthur Kirsch, *Auden and Christianity* (Yale University Press, 2005), p. 67.

7 John Bayley, *The Romantic Survival: A Study in Poetic Evolution* (Constable, 1957), p. 169. Hereafter cited in the text as 'Bayley'.

8 *World within World: The Autobiography of Stephen Spender* (Hamish Hamilton, 1951), p. 59.

9 T. S. Eliot, *The Sacred Wood* (Methuen, 1920; 2nd ed., 1928), p. 87.

10 Ezra Pound, *Gaudier-Brzeska: A Memoir* (New Directions, 1970), p. 98; Clive Bell, *Art* (Chatto and Windus, 1914), p. 8; Friedrich Schiller, *On the Aesthetic Education of Man: in a Series of Letters*, ed. and trans. Elizabeth M. Wilkinson and L. A. Willoughby (Oxford University Press, 1967), p. 155. See Angela Leighton, *On Form: Poetry, Aestheticism, and the Legacy of a Word* (Oxford University Press, 2007), p. 14.

11 Herbert Read, *Form in Modern Poetry* (Sheed and Ward, 1932; 1948), p. 9.

12 Frances Spalding, *John Piper, Myfanwy Piper: Lives in Art* (Oxford University Press, 2009), p. 70.

13 *The Works of Thomas De Quincey*, ed. Grevel Lindop et al. (Manchester University Press, 2000–2003), vol. vi, p. 114.

14 Louis MacNeice, *Modern Poetry: A Personal Essay* (Oxford University Press, 1938; 1968), p. 59.

15 Howard Griffin, *Conversations with Auden*, ed. Donald Allen (Gray Fox, 1981), p. 21.

16 *Theory of Fiction: Henry James*, ed. James E. Miller, Jr. (University of Nebraska Press, 1972), p. 262.

17 Ibid., p. 154.

18 George Eliot, *Selected Essays, Poems and Other Writings*, ed. A. S. Byatt and Nicholas Warren (Penguin, 1990), p. 235.

19 See also Auden's remarks on the 'rivalry', in song, 'between the desire for pattern and the desire for personal utterance ... disclosed by the difference between instrumental and vocal music' (*DH*, p. 505).

20 William Empson, *Seven Types of Ambiguity* (Chatto and Windus, 1930; 3rd. edn., 1953), p. 36. See also Fuller 1998, pp. 154–55.

Guide to Further Reading

Sources already referenced in the list of Abbreviations are generally not repeated here, except for the citation of specific content. Thus, the critical studies by John Fuller and Edward Mendelson, widely regarded as indispensable, are referenced there but not here.
The abbreviations are used, where appropriate, in what follows.

AUDEN'S NORTHERLINESS

Bucknell, Katherine (ed.), 'Phantasy and Reality in Poetry (1971)', *AS III*, pp. 139–206 [consists of her introduction, Auden's lecture, her appendix 'Auden's Nursery Library'].
Bucknell, Katherine (ed.), *Juvenilia* [informative annotation of some north-related poems].
Myers, Alan, and Robert Forsythe, *W. H. Auden: Pennine Poet*, North Pennines Heritage Trust, 1999.
Sharpe, Tony, '"The North, My World": W. H. Auden's Pennine Ways', in Katharine Cockin (ed.), *The Literary North*, Palgrave (2012), pp. 107–24.
'Paysage Moralisé: W.H. Auden and Maps', *AN* 29, December 2007, pp. 5–12.

TWO CITIES: BERLIN AND NEW YORK

Bozorth, Richard R., *Auden's Games of Knowledge: Poetry and the Meanings of Homosexuality*. Columbia University Press, 2001.
Chauncey, George, *Gay New York: Gender, Urban Culture, and the Making of the Gay Male World, 1890–1940*, Basic Books, 1995.
Page, Norman, *Auden and Isherwood: The Berlin Years*, Palgrave Macmillan, 2000.
Roberts, Beth, 'W. H. Auden and the Jews', *Journal of Modern Literature* **28**. 3 Spring 2005, pp. 87–108.
Scott, William B., and Peter M. Rutkoff, *New York Modern: The Arts and the City*, Johns Hopkins University Press, 2001.
Sharpe, Tony, *W. H. Auden*, Routledge, 2007.
Smith, Stan, *W. H. Auden*, Basil Blackwell, 1985.

Tippins, Sherill, *February House: The Story of W. H. Auden, Carson McCullers, Jane and Paul Bowles, Benjamin Britten, and Gypsy Rose Lee, Under One Roof in Brooklyn*, Mariner Books, 2006.
Weitz, Eric D., *Weimar Germany: Promise and Tragedy*. Princeton University Press, 2007.

IDEAS ABOUT ENGLAND

Deane, Patrick, 'Auden's England', *CCWHA*, pp. 25–38.
Jenkins, Nicholas, *The Island: W. H. Auden and the Regeneration of England* (forthcoming from Harvard University Press and Faber and Faber).
Smith, Stan, *W. H. Auden*, Basil Blackwell, 1985.

IDEAS OF AMERICA

Auden, W. H., 'Whitman and Arnold', *P II*, pp. 11–13.
  'Opera on an American Legend', *P II*, pp. 129–31.
  'AMERICANA', *DH*, pp. 309–68.
Jenkins, Nicholas, 'Auden in America', *CCWHA*, pp. 39–54.

AT HOME IN ITALY AND AUSTRIA

Brodsky, Joseph, 'To Please a Shadow', in *Less Than One: Selected Essays*, Penguin, 1987.
Mendelson, Edward, 'The European Auden', *CCWHA*, pp. 55–67.
Musulin, Stella, 'Auden in Kirchstetten', *AS III*, pp. 207–33.
See also relevant passages in Carpenter and RD-H 1995.

AUDEN AND THE CLASS SYSTEM

Caesar, Adrian, *Dividing Lines: Poetry, Class and ideology in the 1930s*, Manchester University Press, 1991.
Williams, Raymond, *Culture and Society 1780–1950*, Penguin, 1979.

THE CHURCH OF ENGLAND: AUDEN'S ANGLICANISM

Bridgen, John, 'My Meeting with Dr John and Sheila Auden', *AN* **25**, January 2005, pp. 7–18.
Hillier, Bevis, *John Betjeman: New Fame, New Love*, John Murray, 2002.
Kirsch, Arthur, *Auden and Christianity*, Yale University Press, 2005.
MacCulloch, Diarmaid, *A History of Christianity*, Allen Lane, 2009.
Mendelson, Edward, 'Auden and God', *New York Review of Books*, **6** December 2007, pp. 70–74.
Sharpe, Tony, 'Final Beliefs: Stevens and Auden', *Literature and Theology*, **25**: 1, March 2011, pp. 64–78.

Sykes, S. W., *The Integrity of Anglicanism*, Mowbrays, 1978.

BRITISH HOMOSEXUALITY, 1920–1939

Bozorth, Richard R., 'Auden: love, sexuality, desire', *CCWHA*, pp. 175–77.
Woods, Gregory, *Articulate Flesh: Male Homo-eroticism and Modern Poetry*, Yale University Press, 1987.
A History of Gay Literature: The Male Tradition, Yale University Press, 1998.

AMERICAN HOMOSEXUALITY, 1939–1972

Bozorth, Richard R., *Auden's Games of Knowledge: Poetry and the Meanings of Homosexuality*, Columbia University Press, 2001.
Caserio, Robert, 'Auden's New Citizenship', *Raritan* **17**, 1997, pp. 90–103.
Farnan, Dorothy J., *Auden In Love*, Simon and Schuster, 1984.
Kaiser, Charles, *The Gay Metropolis, 1940–1996*, Houghton Mifflin, 1997.
Newton, Esther, *Cherry Grove, Fire Island: Sixty Years in America's First Gay and Lesbian Town*, Beacon, 1993.
Norse, Harold, *Memoirs of a Bastard Angel*, Morrow, 1989.

AUDEN AMONG WOMEN

Farnan, Dorothy J., *Auden In Love*, Simon and Schuster, 1984.
Fuller, John, 'Pleasing Ma: the poetry of W. H. Auden', Kenneth Allott Memorial Lecture no. 9, *Liverpool Classical Monthly 20, 1995.*
Montefiore, Janet, *Men and Women Writers of the 1930s: The Dangerous Flood of History*, Routledge, 1996.

AUDEN AND THE AMERICAN LITERARY WORLD

Cowley, Malcolm, *The Flower and the Leaf: A Contemporary Record of American Writing Since 1941*, Viking, 1985.
Wasley, Aidan, *The Age of Auden: Postwar Poetry and the American Scene*, Princeton University Press, 2011.

COMMUNISM AND FASCISM IN 1920S AND 1930S BRITAIN

Collini, Stefan, *Absent Minds: Intellectuals in Britain*, Oxford University Press, 2007.
Griffiths, Richard, *Fellow Travellers of the Right: British Enthusiasts for Nazi Germany, 1933–39*, Oxford University Press, 1983.
Linehan, Thomas, *British Fascism, 1918–39: Parties, Ideology and Culture*, Manchester University Press, 2000.
Overy, Richard, *The Morbid Age: Britain Between the Wars*, Allen Lane, 2009.

Pugh, M., *Hurrah for the Blackshirts: Fascists and Fascism in Britain between the Wars*, Jonathan Cape, 2005.
Taylor, D. J., *Bright Young People: The Rise and Fall of a Generation, 1918–40*, Chatto & Windus, 2007.
Worley, Matthew, *Oswald Mosley and the New Party*, Palgrave, 2010.

AUDEN AND WARS

Auden, W. H., 'W. H. Auden Speaks of Poetry and Total War', *P II*, pp. 152–53.
Bolton, Jonathan, '"Lucid Song": The Poetry of the Second World War', *The Edinburgh Companion to Twentieth-century British and American War Literature*, eds. Adam Piette and Mark Rawlinson, Edinburgh University Press, 2012.
Deer, Patrick, *Culture in Camouflage: War, Empire, and Modern British Literature*, Oxford University Press, 2009.
Kendall, Tim, *Modern English War Poetry*, Oxford University Press, 2006.
Sharpe, Tony, *W. H. Auden*, Routledge, 2007.
Smith, Stan, *W. H. Auden*, Basil Blackwell, 1985.
Stern, James, 'The Indispensable Presence', *Tribute*, pp. 123–27.

AUDEN & FREUD: THE PSYCHOANALYTIC TEXT

Auden, W. H., 'Psychology and Art To-day', *EA*, pp. 332–42.
'Sigmund Freud', *P III*, pp. 340–44.
'The Greatness of Freud', *P III*, pp. 385–88.
Rank, Otto, *Das Trauma der Geburt und seine Bedeutung für die Psychoanalyse*, Verlag, 1924; English translation, *The Trauma of Birth*, Kegan Paul, Trench, Trubner, 1929; repr. Dover, 1993.

AUDEN'S THEOLOGY

Fremantle, Anne, 'Reality and Religion', *Tribute*, pp. 79–92.
Kierkegaard, Søren, *Either/Or: a Fragment of Life*, trans. Alastair Hannay, Penguin, 1992.
Papers and Journals: A Selection, trans. Alastair Hannay, Penguin, 1996.
Poole, Roger, 'The unknown Kierkegaard: Twentieth-century receptions', *The Cambridge Companion to Kierkegaard*, ed. Alastair Hannay and Gordon D. Marino, Cambridge University Press, 1998, pp. 48–75.

AUDEN IN HISTORY

Arendt, Hannah, *The Human Condition*, University of Chicago Press, 1958.
Aristotle, *The Basic Works of Aristotle*, trans. Richard McKeon, Random House, 1966.

Auden, W. H., 'Thinking What We are Doing', *Encounter* **12**: 6, June, 1959, pp. 72–76.

Camus, Albert, *The Rebel: An Essay on Man in Revolt*, trans. Anthony Bower, Knopf, 1954.

Cochrane, Charles Norris, *Christianity and Classical Culture: A Study of Thought and Action from Augustus to Augustine*, Clarendon Press, 1940.

de Rougemont, Denis, *Love in the Western World*, Harcourt Brace and Co., 1940.

Kierkegaard, Søren, *Either/Or, A Fragment of Life*, trans. David Swenson and Lilian Swenson, Princeton University Press, 1944.

Fear and Trembling, Sickness unto Death, trans. Walter Lowrie, Princeton University Press, 1941.

Nietzsche, Friedrich, *Thoughts out of Season*, trans. A. M. Ludovici and Adrian Collins, Allen and Unwin, 1937.

The Twilight of the Idols, The Antichrist; Notes to Zarathustra, and Eternal Recurrence, trans. A. M. Ludovici, Allen and Unwin, 1927.

Orwell, George, *Homage to Catalonia*, Secker & Warburg, 1938.

All Art Is Propaganda, Harcourt, 2008.

Rosenstock-Huessy, Eugen, *Out of Revolution: Autobiography of Western Man*, Berg, 1993.

Wilson, Edmund, *To the Finland Station: A Study in the Writing and Acting of History*, Harcourt, Brace and Company, 1940.

THE CINEMA

Bluemel, Kristin (ed.), *Intermodernism: Literary Culture in Mid-Twentieth-Century Britain*, Edinburgh University Press, 2009.

Bryant, Marsha, *Auden and Documentary in the 1930s*, University of Virginia Press, 1997.

Feigel, Lara, *Literature, Cinema and Politics 1930–1945: Reading Between the Frames*, Edinburgh University Press, 2010.

Marwick, Arthur, *Class, Image and Reality in Britain, France and the USA since 1930*, Collins, 1980.

Richards, Jeffrey, and Anthony Aldgate, *Best of British: Cinema and Society 1930–1970*, Blackwell, 1983.

Williams, Keith, *British Writers and the Media, 1930–45*, Macmillan, 1996.

1930S BRITISH DRAMA

Innes, Christopher, 'Auden's plays and dramatic writings: theatre film and opera', *CCWHA*, pp. 82–95.

Query, Patrick, 'Crooked Europe: The Verse Drama of W. H. Auden (and Company)', *Modern Drama* **51**, 2008, pp. 579–604.

Sidnell, Michael, *Dances of Death: The Group Theatre of London in the Thirties*, Faber and Faber, 1984.

THE DOCUMENTARY MOMENT

Anthony, Scott, *Night Mail*, British Film Institute, 2007.

Bryant, Marsha, *Auden and Documentary in the 1930s*, University of Virginia Press, 1997.

Mitchell, Donald, *Britten and Auden in the Thirties: the year 1936*, Faber and Faber, 1981.

TRAVEL WRITING

Branson, Noreen, and Margot Heinemann, *Britain in the Nineteen Thirties*, Weidenfeld and Nicolson, 1971.

Bryant, Marsha, 'Auden and the "Arctic Stare": Documentary as Public Collage in *Letters from Iceland*', *Journal of Modern Literature*, XVII: **4**, 1991, pp. 537–65.

Buell, Frederick, *W. H. Auden as a Social Poet*, Cornell University Press, 1973.

Burdett, Charles, and Derek Duncan, eds. *Cultural Encounters: European Travel Writing in the 1930s*, Berghahn Books, 2002.

Carr, Helen, 'Modernism and travel (1880–1940)', in *The Cambridge Companion to Travel Writing*, eds. Peter Hulme and Tim Youngs, Cambridge University Press, 2002.

Fussell, Paul, *Abroad: British Literary Traveling between the Wars*, Oxford University Press, 1980.

Jenkins, Nicholas, 'The Traveling Auden', *AN* **24**, July 2004, pp. 7–14.

Stan Smith, 'Burbank with a Baedeker: Modernism's Grand Tours', *Studies in Travel Writing*, **8**: 1 (2004), pp. 1–18.

Youngs, Tim, 'Auden's travel writings', *CCWHA*, pp. 68–81.

'Travelling Modernists', in *The Oxford Handbook of Modernisms*, ed. Peter Brooker et al., Oxford University Press, 2010, pp. 267–81.

'Following the progress of the mountain mission: the critique of heroism and nationalism in Auden and Isherwood's *The Ascent of F6*', in *Mountains Figured and Disfigured in the English-Speaking World*, ed. Françoise Besson, Cambridge Scholars Press, 2010.

AUDEN AND POST-WAR OPERA

Auden, W. H., 'Opera Addict', *Prose II*, pp. 400–02.

'Some Reflections on Music and Opera', *Prose III*, pp. 296–302.

'Reflections on *The Magic Flute*', *Prose III*, pp. 604–08.

'HOMAGE TO IGOR STRAVINSKY', *DH*, pp. 465–527.

EARLIER ENGLISH INFLUENCES

Bloomfield, Morton, '"Doom is Dark and Deeper than any Sea-Dingle": W. H. Auden and Sawles Warde', *Modern Language Notes*, **63**, 1948, pp. 548–52.

Howe, Nicholas, 'Praise and Lament: The Afterlife of Old English Poetry in Auden, Hill and Gunn', in *Words and Works: Studies in Medieval English*

Language and Literature in Honour of Fred C. Robinson, ed. Peter S. Baker and Nicholas Howe, University of Toronto Press, 1998, pp. 293–310.

Jones, Chris, 'W. H. Auden and "The 'Barbaric' Poetry of the North": Unchaining One's Daimon', *Review of English Studies*, **53**, 2002, pp. 167–85.

'"One Can Emend a Mutilated Text": Auden's The Orators and the Old English Exeter Book', *TEXT*, **15**, 2002, pp. 261–75.

Strange Likeness: the use of Old English in twentieth-century Poetry, Oxford University Press, 2006.

O'Donoghue, Heather, 'Owed to Both Sides: W. H. Auden's Double Debt to the Literature of the North', in *Anglo-Saxon Culture and the Modern Imagination*, ed. David Clark and Nicholas Perkins, D. S. Brewer, 2010, pp. 51–69.

Phelpstead, Carl, 'Auden and the Inklings: An Alliterative Revival', *Journal of English and Germanic Philology*, **103**, 2004, pp. 433–57.

Salus, Per H., 'Englishing the Edda', *Comparative Criticism, A Yearbook*, ed. Elinor Shaffer, Cambridge University Press, 1979, pp. 141–52.

Toswell, M. J., 'Auden and Anglo-Saxon', *Medieval English Studies Newsletter*, **37** 1997, pp. 21–28.

AUDEN AND SHAKESPEARE

Boly, John R., *Reading Auden: The Returns of Caliban*, Cornell University Press, 1991. *Corcoran, Neil, Shakespeare and the Modern Poet*, Cambridge University Press, 2010.

Fenton, James, 'Auden's Shakespeare', *New York Review of Books*, **23** March 2000, pp. 24–29.

Kermode, Frank, 'Maximum Assistance from Good Cooking, Good Clothes, Good Drink' [Review of *Lectures on Shakespeare*, by W. H. Auden, ed. Arthur Kirsch], *London Review of Books*, 22 February 2001, pp. 10–11.

Kirsch, Arthur, 'Auden's Faith and his Response to Shakespeare', *Literary Imagination*, 2004, pp. 96–111.

Reeves, Gareth, 'Auden and Religion', *CCWHA*, pp. 188–99.

Snyder, Susan, 'Auden, Shakespeare, and the Defence of Poetry', *Shakespeare Survey* 1983, pp. 29–37.

YEATS

Ellmann, Richard, *Eminent Domain: Yeats among Wilde, Joyce, Pound, Eliot and Auden*, Oxford University Press, 1967.

MacNeice, Louis, *The Poetry of W. B. Yeats*, with a foreword by Richard Ellmann, Faber and Faber, 1967.

O'Neill, Michael, ed., *The Poems of W. B. Yeats: A Sourcebook*, Routledge, 2004.

Smith, Stan, 'Persuasions to Rejoice: Auden's Oedipal Dialogues with W. B. Yeats', *AS II*, pp. 155–63.

Yeats, W. B., *Yeats's Poems*, ed. and annotated A. Norman Jeffares, with an Appendix by Warwick Gould, (1989) Macmillan, 1991.

ELIOT

MacKinnon, Lachlan, *Eliot, Auden, Lowell: Aspects of the Baudelairean Inheritance*, Macmillan, 1983.
McDiarmid, Lucy, *Saving Civilization: Yeats, Eliot and Auden between the Wars*, Cambridge University Press, 1984.

SOME MODERNISTS IN EARLY AUDEN

Emig, Rainer, *W. H. Auden: Towards a Postmodern Poetics*, Palgrave Macmillan, 2000.
Everett, Barbara, *Auden*, Oliver and Boyd, 1964.
Graves, Robert, *The Crowning Privilege*, Cassell, 1955.
Lawrence, D. H., *Fantasia of the Unconscious* (1923) rpt London: Secker, 1933.
O'Neill, Michael, and Gareth Reeves, *Auden, MacNeice, Spender: The Thirties Poetry*, Macmillan, 1992.
Riding, Laura, *The Poems of Laura Riding: A New Edition of the 1938 Collection*, Carcanet, 1980.
   'Preface', *Selected Poems: In Five Sets*, Faber, 1970 and Robert Graves, *A Survey of Modernist Poetry*, Heinemann, 1927.
Saint-John Perse, Anabasis: A Poem, with a translation into English by T. S. Eliot, Faber and Faber, 1930.
Spender, Stephen, *The Destructive Element: A Study of Modern Writers and Beliefs*, Cape, 1935.

AUDEN IN GERMAN

Bloom, Robert, 'The Humanization of Auden's Early Style', *PMLA* **83**:2, 1968, pp. 443–54.
Brecht, Bertolt, *Brecht on Theatre: The Development of an Aesthetic*, ed. and trans. John Willett, Methuen, 1964.
Constantine, David, 'The German Auden: Six Early Poems', *AS I*, pp. 1–15.
Emig, Rainer, *W. H. Auden: Towards a Postmodern Poetics*, Macmillan, 1999.
   '"All the Others Translate": W. H. Auden's Poetic Dislocations of Self, Nation, and Culture', in *Translation and Nation: Towards a Cultural Poetics of Englishness*, eds. Roger Ellis and Liz Oakley-Brown, Multilingual Matters, 2001, pp. 167–204.
Goethe, Johann Wolfgang von, *Berliner Ausgabe: Poetische Werke*, ed. Siegfried Seidel, 16 vols. 1965–78, Vol. 1, Verlag Innes, Christopher, 'Auden's Plays and Dramatic Writings: Theatre, Film and Opera', *CCWHA*, pp. 82–95.
Rilke, Rainer Maria, *Duino Elegies*, trans. Stephen Cohn, Northwestern University Press, 1998.
The Best of Rilke, trans. Walter Arndt, Dartmouth College Press, 1989.
Thomson, Peter, and Glendyr Sachs, *The Cambridge Companion to Brecht*, Cambridge University Press, 1994.

Valgemae, Mardi, 'Auden's Collaboration with Isherwood on *The Dog beneath the Skin*', *The Huntington Library Quarterly* **31**:4, 1968, pp. 373–83.

Waidson, H. M., 'Auden and German Literature', *The Modern Language Review* **70**:2, 1975, pp. 347–65.

Willett, John, *The Theatre of Bertolt Brecht: A Study from Eight Aspects*, Methuen, 1959.

Womack, James, 'Auden's Goethe', *Essays in Criticism* **58**, 2008, pp. 333–54.

AUDEN AND ISHERWOOD

Berg, James J., and Chris Freeman, eds. *The Isherwood Century: Essays on the Life and Work of Christopher Isherwood*, University of Wisconsin Press, 2000.

Canning, Richard, *Brief Lives: E.M. Forster*, Hesperus Press, 2009.

Innes, Christopher, 'Auden's plays and dramatic writings: theatre, film, and opera', *CCWHA*, pp. 82–95.

Isherwood, Christopher, *Christopher and His Kind*, University of Minnesota Press, 2001 (1976).

My Guru and His Disciple, Farrar, Straus, and Giroux, 1980.

Diaries, Volume 1, 1939–1960, ed. Katherine Bucknell, HarperCollins, 1996.

Diaries, Volume 2, The Sixties, ed. Katherine Bucknell, HarperCollins, 2010.

Lost Years: A Memoir, 1945–1951, ed. Katherine Bucknell, HarperCollins, 2000.

Lions and Shadows: an Education in the Twenties, New Directions, 1947 (1938).

'Some Notes on the Early Poetry of W. H. Auden', 'Postscript to "Some Notes on the Early Poetry of W. H. Auden"', *Tribute*, pp. 74–79.

Isherwood, Christopher, and Edward Upward, *The Mortmere Stories*, Enitharmon Press, 1994.

Parker, Peter, *Isherwood: A Life*, Picador, 2004.

Spender, Stephen, 'Isyyvoo's Conversion', *New York Review of Books*, 27.13, 14, August 1980.

Zeikowitz, Richard, ed. *Letters Between Forster and Isherwood on Homosexuality and Literature*, Palgrave Macmillan, 2008.

AUDEN IN PROSE

Sharpe, Tony, 'Auden's Prose', *CCWHA*, pp. 110–22.

See also Edward Mendelson's introductions to the individual volumes of Prose published in the Collected Works.

AUDEN AND LITTLE MAGAZINES

Brooker, Peter, and Andrew Thacker, (eds.), *The Oxford Critical and Cultural History of Modernist Magazines, Vol.1: Britain and Ireland 1880–1955*, Oxford University Press, 2009.

Caesar, Adrian, *Dividing Lines: Poetry, Class and Ideology in the 1930s*, Manchester University Press, 1991.

Smith, Stan, 'Poetry Then: Geoffrey Grigson and *New Verse* (1933–9), Julian Symons and *Twentieth Century Verse* (1937–9)' in Brooker and Thacker (eds.), *Modernist Magazines vol. I.*

DOUBLE TAKE: AUDEN IN COLLABORATION

Barzun, Jacques, 'Foreword: Three Men and a Book', in *A Company of Readers: Uncollected Writings of W. H. Auden, Jacques Barzun, and Lionel Trilling from The Readers' Subscription and Mid-Century Book Clubs*, ed. Arthur Krystal, The Free Press, 2001, pp. ix–xvii.
Bryant, Marsha, *Auden and Documentary in the 1930s*, University of Virginia Press, 1997.
Fenton, James, Introduction to *Wystan and Chester: A Personal Memoir of W. H. Auden and Chester Kallman* by Thekla Clark, Faber and Faber, 1995, pp. ix–xii.
Isherwood, Christopher, *Christopher and His Kind 1929–1939*, Farrar Straus Giroux, 1976.
    Lions and Shadows: An Education in the Twenties (1947), Pegasus, 1969.
Kerr, Douglas, 'Disorientations: Auden and Isherwood's China', *Literature and History* **5**.2, 1996, pp. 53–67.
Koestenbaum, Wayne, *Double Talk: The Erotics of Male Literary Collaboration*, Routledge, 1989.
Mendelson, Edward, 'The Two Audens and the Claims of History', *Representing Modernist Texts: Editing as Interpretation*, ed. George Bornstein, University of Michigan Press, 1991, pp. 157–70.
Query, Patrick, 'Crooked Europe: The Verse Drama of W. H. Auden (and Company)', *Modern Drama* **51**, 2008, pp. 579–604.
Sidnell, Michael, *Dances of Death: The Group Theatre of London in the Thirties*, Faber and Faber, 1984.

AUDEN AND PROSODY

Auden W. H., ed., de la Mare, Walter, *A Choice of de la Mare's Verse*, Faber, 1963.
Corn, Alfred, *The Poem's Heartbeat: A Manual of Prosody*, Copper Canyon Press, 2008.
MacNeice, Louis, *Varieties of Parable*, Faber and Faber, 1965.

AUDEN'S FORMS

Bayley, John, *The Romantic Survival: A Study in Poetic Evolution* Constable, 1957.
Everett, Barbara, *Auden*, Oliver and Boyd, 1964.
Leighton, Angela, *On Form: Poetry, Aestheticism, and the Legacy of a Word*, Oxford University Press, 2007.
Read, Herbert, *Form in Modern Poetry*, Sheed and Ward, 1932; 1948.

Index

Acton, Harold, 91
'The Acts of John', 86
The Adelphi, 338, 345
Agee, James, 215
Alexander, Michael, 260
Allen, Bill, 147
Allen, John, 223, 225
Alston Moor, 15, 16
Alvarez, A. A., 365
Amsterdam, 316
Anders als die Andern, 103
Anglo-Saxon Reader (Sweet), 261
Ansen, Alan, 83, 91, 103, 121, 295n, 369, 378
Arendt, Hannah, 107, 126
Aristotle, 181
Arnold, Matthew, 49
Ashbery, John, 124, 355
Astor, Lady Nancy, 146
Atlantic, 125
Auden, Constance, 69, 107
Auden, George, 151, 259
Auden, John, 15, 45, 84, 86, 236
Auden's writings
    '1929', 299, 362
    'A Bride in the '30s', 376
    A Certain World, 19, 77, 87, 260, 329
    A Choice of de la Mare's Verse, 360
    'A Communist to Others', 39, 73, 209, 340, 344, 345
    'A Healthy Spot', 277
    'A Household', 113, 294
    'A Literary Transference', 291
    'A Summer Night', 3, 44, 74, 79, 134, 180, 196, 282
    'A Walk After Dark', 54
    About the House, 86
    'Academic Graffiti', 286, 307, 308
    'Address for a Prize Day', 26, 70
    'Amor Loci', 19, 21, 22
    Another Time, 29, 128, 154, 190, 342, 374
    'As I Walked Out One Evening', 52, 129, 207, 310, 363, 377

'As It Seemed to Us', 14
'At the Grave of Henry James', 75, 131, 375
'Atlantis', 50, 130
'Aubade', 348
'Auden and MacNeice: Their Last Will and Testament', 83, 241
'August for the people and their favourite islands', 41, 43, 212, 317
'Balaam and his Ass', 308
Berlin journals (unpublished), 24, 26, 317, 355
'Brothers and Others', 272, 273
'Bucolics', 59, 64, 77, 178
'California', 52
'Case Histories', 345
'Christmas 1940', 63
'Commentary', 155, 157, 185
'Consider this and in our time', 2, 38, 153, 205–6
'Control of the passes was, he saw, the key' ('The Secret Agent'), 16, 20, 287, 361
'Dame Kind', 108
'Deftly, admiral, cast your fly', 334, 363
'Dichtung und Wahrheit', 183, 308, 363, 365
'Dover', 342–4
'Easily, my dear,…', 207–8, 213
Elegy for Young Lovers, 250, 324
'Encomium Balnei', 311
'England: Six Unexpected Days', 19
'Epilogue' (*Look, Stranger!*), 43, 73
'Epilogue' (*The Orators*), 238, 361
Epistle to a Godson, 309
'Epithalamion', 308
'Few and Simple', 103
'First Things First', 197–8
'For the Time Being', 75, 86, 102, 175, 286
For the Time Being, 268, 290
'From the very first coming down…' ('The Letter'), 16
'Genius and Apostle', 308
'Get there if you can…', 37
'Good-bye to the Mezzogiorno', 62, 201, 308

391

Auden's writings (*cont.*)
'Happy New Year', 287–8
'Hearing of harvests rotting in the valleys',
  44, 313
'Heavy Date', 30
'Here on the cropped grass of the narrow
  ridge…', 73, 209
'Homage to Clio', 113, 115–16, 186–92
Homage to Clio, 183
'Horae Canonicae', 59, 76, 176, 178, 200, 201
'I Am Not a Camera', 214, 312
'I chose this lean country', 280
'I have a handsome profile', 73
'I Like It Hot', 14
'In Due Season', 373
'In Memory of Ernst Toller', 53
'In Memory of Sigmund Freud', 5, 6, 29,
  129, 339
'In Memory of W. B. Yeats', 4–6, 29, 47–8,
  49, 52, 55, 99, 123, 125, 129, 151, 157, 168,
  169, 263, 281–2
'In Praise of Limestone', 21, 22, 59, 85, 87,
  104–6, 107, 108, 113, 115, 198–9, 203, 302,
  311, 332, 339
'In Schrafft's', 111
'In Search of Dracula', 17
'In Sickness and in Health', 102, 172–3
'In Time of War', 53, 99, 155–7, 267
'In Transit', 58
'Introduction' (to Shakespeare's Sonnets),
  74, 90
'Ischia', 56, 60–2, 311, 363
'It was Easter as I walked in the public
  gardens'. *See* '1929'
'Josef Weinheber', 64–5
'Journal of an Airman', 71
Journey to a War, 44, 155, 185, 210, 214, 237,
  240, 241, 242, 319, 321, 347, 352, 353, 356
'Lady Weeping at the Crossroads', 107
'Lakes', 378
'Law, say the gardeners', 129
'Lay your sleeping head, my love', 284,
  324, 365
'Lead's the Best', 15
'Leap Before You Look', 102
'Letter' (Christmas Day, 1941: to Chester
  Kallman), 86, 112
'Letter to Lord Byron', 13, 14, 18, 40, 43, 69,
  71, 77, 210, 240, 241, 242, 288, 289, 290,
  291, 307
'Letter to R. H. S. Crossman, Esq.', 264
'Letter to William Coldstream, Esq.', 231
Letters from Iceland, 22, 42, 210, 212,
  213, 237–8, 240, 241, 243, 244,
  288, 352

Look, Stranger!, 20, 43–4, 73, 95, 231, 317,
  318, 337
'Look, stranger, at this island now', 230–3
'Love by ambition', 26, 278–9, 298
'Lullaby', 8
'Making, Knowing and Judging', 161, 319
'Marginalia', 376
'Matthew Arnold', 335
'Memorial for the City', 28, 59, 158, 176,
  196–7, 199, 200, 203
'Miss Gee', 26, 111
'Moon Landing', 108, 116
'Musée des Beaux Arts', 48, 169, 339
'Music Is International', 371
'My Dear One is mine as mirrors are lonely',
  271, 366–7
'Nature, Poetry and History', 330, 334
'New Year Letter', 6, 19, 20–1, 28, 31, 32, 45,
  47, 49, 51, 53, 69, 80–1, 87, 107, 112, 114,
  128, 129, 131, 133, 151, 153, 157, 284, 294,
  306, 308, 371
New Year Letter, 31, 292
'Nocturne', 264
'Nones', 200, 201, 203
Nones, 294
'Not in Baedeker', 22
'Notes on Music and Opera', 249, 250–1
'Now the leaves are falling fast', 363
'Nursery Rhyme', 364
'O what is that sound…', 337
'O who can ever gaze his fill' 42, 279
'O who can ever praise enough', 42
'Ode to Gaea', 112, 115, 363
'Ode to Terminus', 314
'On the Circuit', 120, 202
On the Frontier, 42, 108, 208, 214, 220,
  221–2, 318, 350
On This Island, 118
'Our Hunting Fathers…', 44, 81, 197
'Out on the lawn I lie in bed', 3, 44, 74, 79,
  180, 196, 282
'Paid on Both Sides', 16, 19, 25, 107, 108–9,
  118, 312, 337, 339
Paul Bunyan, 30, 53, 247, 250, 348
'PaysageMoralisé', 44, 313
'Petition', 162–9
'Phantasy and Reality in Poetry', 21
'Plains', 108, 112, 373–4
'Pleasure Island', 103–4, 105
'Poetry and Film', 210–11, 233–4
'Poetry and Total War', 150
Poets of the English Language, 354
'Port and Nuts with the Eliots', 293
'Precious Five', 178
'Preface to *Oxford Poetry*, 1926', 292

'Preface to *Oxford Poetry*, 1927', 375
'Prologue' (*Look, Stranger!*), 43
'Prologue' (*The Orators*), 110, 302–3
'Prologue at Sixty', 6, 14
'Psychology and Art To-day', 160
'Refugee Blues', 5, 28, 157
'Rilke in English', 309
'River Profile', 202–3
'Rookhope, (Weardale, Summer 1922)', 15, 19
'Seaside', 231
Secondary Worlds, 295, 308, 329
'September 1, 1939', 7, 8, 28, 29–30, 32, 99,
    100, 101–2, 103, 135–6, 149, 151, 158, 197,
    281, 284, 338
'Sext', 76
'Shorts', 2–3, 370
'Sir, No Man's Enemy…' ('Petition'), 6, 7,
    26, 161–9
'Spain'; 'Spain, 1937', 4, 7, 49, 152, 153–4, 190,
    197, 278, 313
'Squares and Oblongs', 112
'Sue', 111
'T the Great', 190
'Talking to Myself', 203–4
'Thank You, Fog', 311–12
'Thanksgiving for a Habitat', 63–4, 311
The Age of Anxiety, 33, 40, 53–4, 102, 157, 198,
    247, 260, 262–3, 264
'The American Scene', 50
The Ascent of F6, 41, 109–10, 152, 208, 318, 350
The Bassarids, 108
'The Cave of Making', 64, 65, 76, 131, 308–9
'The Common Life', 2
'The Composer', 363, 373
The Dance of Death, 42–3, 217, 291, 312, 314
'The Dark Valley', 110
'The Dark Years', 378
The Dog beneath the Skin, 17, 18, 40–1, 109,
    209, 218, 223, 226, 312, 316, 318, 350
The Double Man, 28, 80, 356
The Dyer's Hand, 8, 16, 132, 185, 248, 251, 267,
    268, 272, 308, 329, 333, 374
The Enchafèd Flood, 308, 329, 333, 361
'The Enemies of a Bishop', 318
'The Fall of Rome', 58, 334, 364
'The fruit in which your parents hid you,
    boy', 342
'The Group Movement and the Middle
    Classes', 39–40
'The History of an Historian', 181–2
'The Horatians', 63
'The Liberal Fascist', 39
'The Managers', 77, 363, 364
'The Model', 111
'The More Loving One', 332, 365

'The Novelist', 331, 373
'The Old Man's Road', 377
The Orators, 35, 36, 39, 44, 70–1, 95, 110, 114,
    142, 152, 153, 264, 288, 297, 299–304, 316,
    317, 362
The Oxford Book of Light Verse, 251, 354
'The Platonic Blow', 122, 286
'The Poet and the City', 133, 185, 357
The Poet's Tongue, 2, 353
'The Prince's Dog', 272–3
'The Prolific and the Devourer', 152
'The Prophets', 20, 21, 22, 102
'The Public vs. the late Mr. William Butler
    Yeats', 6
The Rake's Progress, 121, 247, 250, 251, 253,
    308, 356
'The Sea and the Mirror', 198, 247, 268–72,
    286
'The Shield of Achilles', 7, 76, 113, 136–7,
    282, 365, 378
'The Sphinx', 53
'The strings' excitement, the applauding
    drum', 25
'The Truest Poetry Is the Most Feigning'
    277, 314
'The Unknown Citizen', 313
The Viking Book of Aphorisms, 191–2
'The Virgin and the Dynamo', 371
'The Wanderer', 37, 41, 261, 262, 264
'The Witnesses', 37
'The World of Opera', 250, 308
'Thomas Epilogizes', 53, 258
'Time Will say Nothing', 102
'To ask the hard question is simple', 298, 313
'To Goethe: A Complaint', 309
'To T. S. Eliot on His Sixtieth Birthday',
    294–5
'Turn not towards me, lest I turn to you',
    267
'Two Bestiaries', 188–9
'Under Which Lyre', 8, 77, 119–20
US (Auden's poems to accompany which
    film), 54–5
'Vespers', 176–7
'Victor' 111
'Vocation and Society', 292
'Voltaire at Ferney', 119
'We Too Had Known Golden Hours', 76
'Whitman and Arnold', 49
'Whitsunday in Kirchstetten', 86–7
'Who stands, the crux left of the
    watershed' ('The Watershed'), 15, 18,
    19, 44, 72, 287
'Woods', 76
'Words and the World', 334–5

Auden's writings (*cont.*)
    'Work, Carnival and Prayer' (unpublished),
        179–80
    'Yeats as an Example', 75, 278
    'You', 201–2
    'Young British Writers – on the Way
        Up', 330

Babes in the Wood, 224
Bachardy, Don, 321, 322, 323
Bakhtin, Mikhail, 179
Baldwin, Stanley, 36, 39, 43, 156
Barcelona, 24, 79, 152, 319
Barnard College, 119
Barnes, Ernest, 82
Barnes, William, 258
Barth, Karl, 81, 173
Barzun, Jacques, 125, 339, 355
The Battle of Maldon, 261, 264
Baudrillard, Jean, 205
Bayley, John, 370, 376
BBC, 231, 338, 373
Beaton, Cecil, 91
Beaverbrook, Lord, 71
Bell, Clive, 372
Benda, Julien, 131
Benn, Gottfried, 312
Bennett, Alan, 306, 333
    The Habit of Art, 306, 333
Bennington College, 119, 125
Beowulf, 257, 258, 261, 262
Berlin, 24–8, 38, 73, 89
Berlin, Isaiah, 59
Berryman, John, 118
Beside the Seaside, 229–30, 231, 233, 234, 235
Betjeman, John, 56, 82–3, 84, 95, 126, 241
Bevan, Aneurin, 146
Birmingham, 13, 24, 41, 82
Bishop, Elizabeth, 118
Black Country, 18
Blake, William, 81
Blast, 345
Bloom, Harold, 309
Bloomfield, Barry, 342
Bogan, Louise, 57, 118
Bollingen Prize, 123
Bolshevik Revolution, 145
The Book of Common Prayer, 87, 170
Booth, Howard, 238
Boothby, Bob, 146
Bottomley, Gordon, 218, 219
Bowles, Paul, 30, 119
Bozorth, Richard, 16
Branson, Noreen, 238
Brecht, Bertholt, 25, 224, 306, 312–14, 348, 349

Brentford, 17
British Fascisti, 143–4
British Union of Fascists (BUF), 144
Britten, Benjamin, 30, 73, 119, 228, 231, 235,
    247, 248, 252, 306, 333, 348
Brodsky, Joseph, 65, 127
Brooke, Jocelyn, 93
Brooke, Rupert, 289
Brussels, 84
Brut, 261
Bryant, Marsha, 7, 352, 356
Bryn Mawr, 119
Buchman, Frank, 40
Bucknell, Katherine, 8, 316
Burrow, Trigant, 20
Busmen, 224
Byron, George Gordon, Lord, 100, 126, 240,
    288, 307, 308, 309
Byron, Robert, 241
    The Road to Oxiana, 237, 238

Cabaret, 324
Calendar of the Year, 229, 231, 232
California, 32, 248, 322, 323, 324
Callan, Edward, 23
Calvin, John, 172
Cambridge Festival Theatre, 218
Cambridge Left, 338
Cambridge University, 69, 90, 93, 251, 316
Campbell, Roy, 96–7
Camus, Albert, 29, 181, 191
Canning, Richard, 322
Carpenter, Edward, 96
Carr, Helen, 241
Caserio, Robert, 102
Cashwell, 15, 16
Caudwell, Christopher, 240–1
Cavafy, C. P., 126
Cavalcanti, Alberto, 215
Cecil, Lord David, 221
Chamberlain, Neville, 224
Chandler, Raymond, 134
Chaplin, Charley, 210
Chaucer, Geoffrey, 262, 359
Chelsea, 89, 141
Cherwell, 257, 258
Chesterton, G. K., 82, 84
Chicago Sun, 150
China, 44, 74, 152, 157, 242, 244, 319, 342, 348
Christ Church, 13, 70, 94
Churchill, Winston, 41
CIA (Central Intelligence Agency), 339
Clark, Dorothy, 141
Clark, Eleanor, 57
Clark, Thekla, 107

Claudel, Paul, 5, 151, 282
Coal Face, 228, 229
Cochrane, Charles Norris, 174, 175, 176, 181, 183–4, 185
Coldstream, William, 228
Colenso, Bishop, 162
Coleridge, Samuel Taylor, 333, 372
Collini, Stefan, 148
Columbia University, 30, 120, 121
Common Sense, 125
Commonweal, 125
The Communist Manifesto, 41
Connolly, Cyril, 16, 17, 320, 324
Constantine (Emperor), 81
Corn, Alfred, 361, 363, 366
Coward, Noel, 92
Cowley, Malcolm, 118, 338
CPGB (Communist Party of Great Britain), 39, 142, 143
Craft, Robert, 60
Creeley, Robert, 123
Crisis, 224
The Criterion, 16, 280, 289, 337, 339, 340, 341
Cross Fell, 15
Cummings, E. E. (*Eimi*), 237, 239
Cunard, Nancy, 96
Cunningham, Valentine, 207, 208–9

Daily Express, 210
Daily Herald, 36, 338
Daily Telegraph, 218
Dante Alighieri, 261
Darlington, W. A., 218
Darwin, Charles, 163
Davenport-Hines, Richard, 30, 73, 253, 319
Davidson, Michael, 94
Davis, George, 30, 320
de la Mare, Walter, 359, 360
Deane, Patrick, 129
Dearmer, Geoffrey, 222
Delos, 339
Diaghilev, Sergei, 101
Dickey, William, 124
Disney, Walt, 40, 288
Dizzy's (bar), 29, 99–100
Dodds, E. A., 80, 84, 107, 349
Dodds, E. R. 4, 20, 79, 80, 152, 349
Don Giovanni, 126
Donne, John, 163, 166
Dovzhenko, Aleksandr, 206
Downs School, 74
The Dream of the Rood, 261
Drew, Elizabeth, 59
Driberg, Tom, 289
Dryden, John, 247, 286

Eberhart, Richard, 119
Eckersley, Peter, 141
Eden (river), 45
Egypt, 152
Eisenhower, President, 158
Eisenstein, Sergei, 206, 211, 233
Eliot, George, 288, 374
Eliot, T. S., 2, 5, 31, 33, 80, 82, 84, 93, 118, 123, 126, 195, 286–95, 297, 300, 317, 331, 334, 339, 340, 347, 372
  After Strange Gods, 287, 288, 289, 290, 293
  'Burnt Norton', 5, 295
  Little Gidding, 292
  Notes Towards the Definition of Culture, 293
  The Waste Land, 53, 92, 206, 287, 288, 289, 290, 291, 292, 294, 295, 297, 314, 347
Ellmann, Richard, 277, 278, 280
Emerson, Ralph Waldo, 130
Empson, William, 377
Encounter, 125, 332, 339
The English Hymnal, 84
Epstein, Jacob, 372
Everett, Barbara, 1, 3, 128, 298, 369, 376

Faber and Faber, 231, 233, 290, 317, 319, 339, 340, 342
Farnan, Dorothy, 104
Fenton, James, 356, 362
Fields, Gracie, 205
Firbank, Ronald, 91, 92
Fire Island, 15, 30, 60, 103, 104, 105
Fisher, M. F. K., 126
Fitzgerald, Robert, 124
Fleming, Peter, 237, 242
  Brazilian Adventure 237
Fordham University, 330
Forio, 56, 60, 122
Forster, E. M., 26, 317, 321, 322, 323
Fourteenth-Century Verse and Prose (Sisam), 261
Franco, Francisco, 48, 242
Fremantle, Anne, 170
Freud, Sigmund, 24, 25, 26, 58, 74, 81, 94, 99, 105, 129, 148, 160–9, 181, 182, 183, 184, 191, 197, 238, 266, 273, 279, 302, 309, 345, 357
Friedberg, Ann, 206
Frost, Robert, 8, 266
Fuck You, A Magazine of the Arts, 122
Fuller, John, 25, 59, 64, 113, 115, 117, 230, 268, 271–2, 297, 300, 301, 360, 361, 364, 365
Fussell, Paul, 237, 240

Gallipoli, 151
Garrett, John, 2, 353

The General Strike, 42, 146
Gibbon, Edward, 183
Gibson, Wilfrid, 17
Ginsberg, Allen, 104, 121, 122
God's Chillun, 212, 229
Goethe, Johann Wolfgang von, 32, 63, 113,
    130–1, 306, 307–9, 310, 329, 349
    Faust, 307–8
    Italian Journey, 131, 308, 349
Gollancz, Victor, 95
Gonne, Maud, 195
Gorer, Geoffrey, 77
GPO Film Unit, 211, 228, 348
Grant, George Copeland, 229
Graves, Robert, 98, 126, 298, 301, 364
Gray, Terence, 219
Great War, 15, 38, 141, 145, 147, 148, 151, 153
Greene, Graham, 39, 142, 211, 215, 237,
    238, 239
    Journey without Maps, 237, 238
Greenberg, Noah, 349
Gregory, (Pope), 176
Gresham's School, 70
Grierson, John, 211, 212, 213, 228, 232–3, 236
Grierson, Marion, 229, 230, 233
Griffin, 339
Griffin, Merv, 126
Grigson, Geoffrey, 7, 21, 257, 258, 337, 338, 340,
    341–2, 344, 372
Groddeck, Georg, 26, 161
Group Theatre, 217, 219, 220, 223, 226, 318,
    348, 351
The Guardian, 7
Guild of Episcopal Studies, 84
Guinness, Alec, 318

Hacker, Marilyn, 121
Hall, Radclyffe, 90
Hammarskjöld, Dag, 126, 349
Hamsun, Knut, 116
Hardy, Forsyth, 233
Hardy, Thomas, 8, 17, 48, 153, 257, 289, 291, 359,
    360, 361, 369
Harper's Bazaar, 125, 338
Hart, Jeffrey, 240
Harvard, 119, 124
Hayden, Robert, 120
Heard, Gerald, 321
Hecht, Anthony, 122, 125
Heidegger, Martin, 46, 58
Helensburgh, 35
Hemingway, Ernest, 19
Henze, Hans Werner, 250
Herbert, George, 286
The Highway, 41

Hitler, Adolf, 35, 36, 40, 45, 48, 135, 136, 141, 152,
    157, 171, 207, 224, 242
Hodge, Alan, 89
Hodge, Herbert, 223
Hoffman, Daniel, 124
Hoffmann, Heinrich (Struwelpeter), 306
Hofmannsthal, Hugo von, 249
Hogarth, William, 248, 308
Hoggart, Richard, 364
Hollander, John, 121, 124, 355
Hong Kong, 319
Hopkins, Gerard Manley, 163, 166, 230, 301–2
Horace, Quintus Flaccus, 63, 186
Horizon, 339
Horrabin, Frank, 141
House and Garden, 125
Housman, A. E., 75, 271
Howard, Brian, 91, 93
Howard, Richard, 121, 122, 125
Huxley, Aldous, 141, 147, 246, 321
Hyde Park, 143
'The Hymn of Jesus', 86
Hynes, Samuel, 324

Iceland, 14, 17, 21, 74, 236, 239, 240, 243, 259,
    260, 319, 342
India, 45, 158
Ischia, 30, 56, 59, 60, 61, 62, 104, 105, 122,
    123, 198
Isherwood, Christopher, 13, 16, 17, 19, 29, 47, 48,
    51, 53, 54, 75, 79, 90, 95, 97, 109, 129, 152,
    155, 157, 170, 171, 208, 209, 210, 211, 213,
    214, 218, 220, 231, 236, 237, 241, 242, 244,
    267, 269, 297, 300, 304, 312, 314, 316–25,
    330, 342, 347, 348, 350–1, 353, 356
    Goodbye to Berlin, 213, 321
Isle of Wight, 17

Jaffé, Rhoda, 107
James, Clive, 369
James, Henry, 33, 198, 252, 269, 374
    The American Scene, 50, 126
Jarrell, Randall, 118, 128, 130, 332
Jarrow Crusade, 143
Jenkins, Nicholas, 4, 18, 20, 129
Jennings, Humphrey, 230, 233
Johns Hopkins, 119
Johnson, Wendell, 59
Jones, Ernest, 182
Joyce, James, 195, 211, 234, 376
Jung, C. G., 167, 323
Junior League Magazine, 125

Kafka, Franz, 33
Kaiser, Georg, 218, 219

Kai-Shek, Chang, 214
Kallman, Chester, 20, 22, 29, 30, 63, 86, 99,
      102, 103, 104, 105, 108, 111–12, 113, 171, 246,
      248, 249, 250, 251, 252, 253, 314, 321, 322,
      323, 324, 348, 349, 356
Kant, Immanuel, 308
Keats, John, 48, 164, 378
Kendall, Tim, 154
Kenyon Review, 125
Ker, W. P., 369
Kerouac, Jack, 121
Kerr, Archibald Clark, 319
Kerr, Douglas, 353
Kierkegaard, Søren, 58, 80, 81, 99, 126, 171–2,
      173, 177, 179, 183, 184, 268, 292
King Edward VIII, 42
King Horn, 261
King James Bible, 257
Kino Glaz, 213
Kinsella, Thomas, 56
Kipling, Rudyard, 5, 151, 282, 286
Kirchstetten, 54, 56, 59, 63–4, 65, 88, 178
Kirsch, Arthur, 270
Koch, Kenneth, 124
Koestenbaum, Wayne, 347
Koestler, Arthur, 207
Kott, Jan, 274
Kuomintang, 142

Labouchère, Henry, 90–1
Labour Party, 36, 38, 39, 141, 143, 144, 145
Lake District, 13, 17
Lane, Homer, 25, 161, 298
Lang, Fritz, 214
Langland, John, 261, 262
Larkin, Philip, 31, 126, 366
Lawrence, D. H., 26, 39, 44, 74, 76, 81, 94, 147,
      153, 164, 188, 195, 237, 239, 302–4
      Etruscan Places, 237
      Fantasia of the Unconscious, 302–3
Lawrence, Jon, 142
Lawrence, T. E., 44, 152, 153, 241
Layamon, 261
Layard, John, 25, 26, 27, 161, 238
Leavis, F. R., 36, 331, 337
Lee, Gypsy Rose, 30, 119
Left Review, 222, 238
Leger, Alexis ('St. John Perse'), 59, 300
      Anabase, 300
Lehman, John, 338
Lenin, Vladimir Ilyich, 36, 40, 44, 81, 94, 147,
      148
Lewis, C. S., 334
Lewis, Wyndham, 141, 146, 237, 239, 288, 290
      Filibusters in Barbary, 237

Liddell Hart, Basil, 44
Lindsay, Jack, 225
The Listener, 231, 282
Lit, Ladislav, 56
Littlewood, Joan, 217
London, 3, 16, 17, 18, 24, 89, 205, 212, 233, 247,
      287, 314, 319, 320, 321, 322, 324
London Film Society, 210, 211, 233
The Londoners, 212
Lord Chamberlain, 220, 221
Los Angeles, 321, 323
Lowell, Robert, 19
Lucas, John, 238
Luther, Martin, 135, 172

MacDonald, Ramsay, 36, 39, 141
MacNeice, Louis, 5, 14, 18, 45, 59, 63, 64, 65,
      76, 93, 97, 206, 210, 237, 241, 243, 277,
      279, 287, 290, 308, 319, 342, 348, 364
Mademoiselle, 125, 330
Madge, Charles, 205
The Magic Flute, 126, 250, 356
Malaparte, Curzio, 94
Malinowski, Bronislaw, 30
Mann, Erika, 243, 318
Mann, Klaus, 29
Mann, Thomas, 308, 313
Maresca, Giovanni, 59
Marvell, Andrew, 168
Marwick, Arthur, 205
Marx, Karl, 45, 69, 71, 72, 81, 93, 94, 99, 143,
      148, 181, 183, 207, 209, 241, 266, 272, 273,
      308, 314
Mayer, Elizabeth, 31, 107, 308
McClatchy, J. D., 127
McCullers, Carson, 30, 119
Medley, Robert, 79, 92, 95
Melville, Herman, 33
In Memoriam, 92
Mendelson, Edward, 9, 32, 59, 65, 79, 81, 82,
      84, 116, 137, 155, 231, 240, 241, 246, 247,
      249, 250, 281, 287, 292, 293, 298, 303, 340,
      352, 354, 371, 372, 375
Meredith, William, 121
Merrill, James, 60, 122, 126
Merwin, W. S., 124, 355
Michigan (University of), 119, 120, 125
Mid-century, 339
Mirabeau, Comte de, 176
Mitchison, Naomi, 107
Mitford, Nancy, 91
The Modern Scot, 338
Montaigne, Michel de, 356
Moore, Marianne, 186, 188, 189
Mosley, Cynthia, 146

Mosley, Oswald, 36, 38, 39, 40, 141, 142, 144, 145, 146, 147
Mount Holyoke, 119
Muldoon, Paul, 127
Murry, John Middleton, 338, 340, 345
Mussolini, Benito, 44, 48, 123, 141, 144, 146, 224, 242

Nabokov, Nicholas, 59
Nagasaki (bombing of), 87
Nation, 125, 330
National Unemployed Workers' Movement (NUWM), 143
Neddermeyer, Heinz, 95, 319
Negroes, 212, 228, 229, 232, 236
Nenthead, 15, 19
Neue Sachlichkleit, 25, 213, 313
New Country, 341
New Masses, 338
New Republic, 125, 175, 330, 338
New School for Social Research (NYC), 119, 267
New Signatures, 341
New Statesman, 338
New Statesman and Nation, 338
New Verse, 7, 337, 338, 339, 340, 341–2, 343, 344, 345
New Writing, 339
New York, 7, 13, 24, 28–33, 34, 51, 54, 58, 60, 80, 100, 110, 111, 119, 121–2, 124, 128, 129, 150, 151, 152, 201, 246, 248, 267, 274, 311, 320, 321, 322, 323, 325, 330
  Manhattan, 29, 32, 33, 47, 79, 99, 100, 101, 171
New York Review of Books, 125
New York Times, 339
New Yorker, 293, 338
Newton, Esther, 104
Nicoll, Maurice, 161, 167
Niebuhr, Reinhold, 81, 85, 87, 99, 126, 174, 175, 176, 268
Niebuhr, Ursula, 83, 107
Nietzsche, Friedrich, 26, 45, 76, 146, 172, 187–8, 189, 191, 192
Night Mail, 211, 228, 229, 230, 233, 235
Nijinsky, Vaslav, 101
Nixon, Barbara, 223
Norse, Harold, 99, 100, 121
North Pennines, 14, 15, 18, 19, 22, 112, 272
Novalis (pseudonym), 94, 202

The Observer, 220, 339
O'Hara, Frank, 104, 124
Olivet College, 119
Olson, Charles, 56, 123

On Guard for Spain, 225
O'Neill, Michael, 298
Orwell, George, 4, 95, 96, 150, 154, 181, 190, 334
  The Road to Wigan Pier, 95, 237
Overy, Richard, 149
Owen, Wilfred, 150, 283, 377
The Owl and the Nightingale, 261
Oxford, 13, 54, 80, 118
Oxford Poetry, 258
Oxford University, 13, 24, 27, 38, 39, 40, 42, 53, 70, 79, 83, 90, 92, 94, 95, 170, 171, 221, 228, 237, 252, 257, 261, 289, 313, 316, 337, 356

Paris, 80, 160
Partisan Review, 125, 177, 330, 338
Patchen, Kenneth, 123
Patripassianism, 170
Pears, Peter, 30
Pearson, Norman Holmes, 354
Pelagianism, 172
Penguin New Writing, 338, 339, 341
Penn State, 119
Percy, Lord, 146
Petzold, Hedwig, 59
Piers Plowman, 262
Pilcher, Velona, 219, 220
Piper, Myfanwy, 252
Plath, Sylvia, 120–1
Poe, Edgar Allan, 126
Poetry, 338
Poland, 45, 136, 171
Pope, Alexander, 128, 261, 289
Porter, Peter, 297
Portugal, 236, 318
Potter, Beatrix, 14
Pound, Ezra, 123, 288, 317, 339, 347
Prabhavananda, Swami, 321
Pride and Prejudice, 126
Priestley, J. B., 226, 237
  English Journey, 237
Proust, Marcel, 234
Pryce-Jones, Alan, 362
Pudney, John, 94
Pudovkin, Vsevolod, 207, 233, 235
Pulitzer Prize, 33, 123, 157, 247
Purcell, Henry, 247

Query, Patrick, 347

Random House, 118, 319
Rank, Otto, 160
Read, Herbert, 372
Reader's Digest, 125
Reith, Lord James, 338

ReptonSchool, 69
Revelstoke, Lord, 73
Rich, Adrienne, 124, 355
Richardson, Sheilah, 107
Rickword, Edgell, 342
Riding, Laura, 279, 298–9, 301
Riefenstahl, Leni, 207
Rilke, Rainer Maria, 94, 306, 309–12
   DuinoElegies, 310
Rivers, W. H., 25, 30
Roberts, Michael, 338, 341
Roethke, Theodore, 118
Rome, 58, 82, 183
Rookhope, 14, 16, 19–20
Rosenstock-Huessy, Eugen, 174, 181, 185
Rotha, Paul, 205, 211, 212, 231, 232
Rothermere, Lord, 71, 144
Rougemont, Denis de, 181, 184–5
Rowse, A. L., 339
Royal Holloway College, 69
Ruskin, John, 62
Ruttmann, Walter, 212

Saintsbury, George, 369
Saki (H. H. Munro), 91
Salute the Soviet Union, 225
San Antonio(Tx), 54
Saturday Review of Literature, 338
Schiller, Gottfried von, 372
Schuyler, James, 122, 124, 295
Schwartz, Delmore, 118
Scribners, 126
Scrutiny, 36, 39, 337, 340, 341
The Seafarer, 261
Shakespeare, William, 74, 100, 126, 232, 257,
   259, 262, 266–74, 286, 355, 378
   Henry IV, 272, 273
   The Merchant of Venice, 272, 273
   A Midsummer Night's Dream, 274, 376
   The Tempest, 173, 268–9, 272, 365, 378
Shanghai, 24, 28, 320
Shapiro, Karl, 118
Sharpe, Tony, 30, 134, 340
Shaw, George Bernard, 142, 146
Shenandoah, 125
Sidnell, Michael, 350
Simpson, Louis, 121
Simpson, Wallis, 43
Sitwell, Edith, Osbert, Sacheverell, 146, 288
Slump ('Great Depression'), 18, 141, 208, 209
Smith College, 49, 51, 119, 120
Smith, Stan, 29, 243, 244, 276, 282, 294, 337, 338
Southworth, James G., 95
Spanish Civil War, 4, 96, 148, 152, 153, 171, 190,
   207, 264

Spanish Medical Aid Committee, 152
Specimens of early English (Morris and Skeat), 261
Spectator, 322
Spender, Stephen, 4, 93, 96, 97, 144, 154, 206,
   287, 290, 298, 322, 323, 324, 339, 371, 374
Spengler, Oswald, 181
Spice, Evelyn, 229
Spinoza, Baruch, 30
St. Augustine, 87, 177, 334
St. Edmund's School, 70
St. Mark's School, 119
St. Paul, 172
Stalin, Josef, 141, 143, 145, 154, 206, 242
Stanislavsky, Constantin, 224
Stark, Freya, 237
   The Valleys of the Assassins, 237
Stein, Gertrude, 91, 301
Stern, James, 157, 314
Stern, Tania, 107, 314
Stevens, Wallace, 87
Stonewall Riots, 100, 101, 103, 105
Strachey, John, 144, 146–7
Strand Film Company, 230
Strauss, Richard, 246, 249, 251
Stravinsky, Igor, 94, 126, 247–8, 250, 251, 252,
   308, 348, 369
Sunday Times, 226
Sunday Worker, 38
Swaledale, 21, 22
Swift, Jonathan, 258
Symons, Julian, 89, 90, 338

Tandy, Geoffrey, 230
Tate, Allen, 342
Tennant, Stephen, 91
Tennyson, Alfred, Lord, 61, 286, 288, 291
   In Memoriam, 92
Thomas, Dylan, 120
Thomas, Edward, 8, 289, 359
Thoreau, Henry, 79
Thought, 330
Threlkeld, 13
Thucydides, 99
Tillich, Paul, 81, 99
Time, 19
Time and Tide, 338
Tolkien, J. R. R., 116, 261, 263, 332, 334, 350
   The Lord of the Rings, 332, 334
Town and Country, 125
Toynbee, Arnold, 181
Trewin, J. C., 226
Trilling, Lionel, 125, 126, 339, 355
Trotsky, Leon, 94, 345
Twentieth Century, 340, 344, 345
Twentieth Century Verse, 338, 339

U. S. Strategic Bombing Survey, 153, 157
Unity Theatre, 223–5
Upward, Edward, 316, 318

Valéry, Paul, 343, 374
Valois, Ninette de, 219
Van Gogh, Vincent, 372
Vernon, P. E., 251
Vertov, Dziga, 207, 211, 213, 231
Vienna, 63
Viertel, Berthold, 211
Vietnam War, 158
Virginia (University), 120, 286
Vogue, 111, 125, 330, 339, 348

Wagner, Richard, 113, 246
Walcott, Derek, 127
Wall Street Crash, 38, 91, 141, 146
The Wanderer, 261
Warner, Rex, 26
Warrington, 18
Watt, Harry, 211, 229
Waugh, Evelyn, 91–2, 237, 243
  Waugh in Abyssinia, 237
The Way to the Sea, 211, 235
Webb, Beatrice and Sidney, 146
Webster, John, 314, 349
Weil, Kurt, 312, 314
Weil, Simone, 85, 172
Weimar Republic, 24, 25, 26, 27, 28, 35, 89, 101,
  152, 213
Wells, H. G., 146, 210
Wells, Henry, 263
Went the Day Well?, 215

Weston, Jessie, 33
Wetzsteon, Rachel, 127
White, T. H., 89
Whitman, Walt, 31, 33, 48–9, 51, 52
  Leaves of Grass, 48
Who Are the English, 225
Whyte, James Hunnington, 338
Wiechert, Ernst, 339
Wieners, John, 104
Wigan, 18
Wilbur, Richard, 126
Wilde, Oscar, 26, 89, 90–1, 92, 100, 370
Wilkinson, Ellen, 143
Williams, Charles, 79, 80, 86, 171–2, 268,
  334, 354
Williams, William Carlos, 123
Wilson, Edmund, 183, 338
Wolverhampton, 13
Wordsworth, William, 8, 13, 17, 112, 113, 161, 372
Workers Theatre Movement (WTM), 222
Wright, Basil, 211, 228, 231, 233
Wright, James, 124, 355
Wright, Richard, 119

Yale Younger Poets Prize, 124
Yeats, W. B., 4–6, 47, 48, 75, 76, 100, 129, 151,
  162, 195, 203, 269, 276–84, 286, 290, 354,
  365, 373
Yingling, Thomas, 100
York, 13
Yorkshire, 259, 332
Yugoslavia, 142

Zwingli, Ulrich, 308